Understanding Criminal Victimization

An Introduction to Theoretical Victimology

EZZAT A. FATTAH
Simon Fraser University

Prentice-Hall Canada Inc., Scarborough, Ontario

Canadian Cataloguing in Publication Data
Fattah, Ezzat Abdel, 1929-
Understanding Criminal Victimization
Includes bibliographical references and index.

ISBN 0-13-929597-6

1. Victims of crimes. I. Title.
HV6250.25F38 1991362.88C91-093710-9

Prentice Hall, Inc., Englewood Cliffs, New Jersey
Prentice-Hall International, Inc., London
Prentice-Hall of Australia, Pty., Ltd., Sydney
Prentice-Hall of India Pvt., Ltd., New Delhi
Prentice-Hall of Japan, Inc., Tokyo
Prentice-Hall of Southeast Asia (Pte.) Ltd., Singapore
Editora Prentice-Hall do Brasil Ltda., Rio de Janeiro
Prentice-Hall Hispanoamericana, S.A., Mexico

ISBN 0-13-929597-6

Copy Editor: Patricia Buckley
Production Editors: Jamie Bush and Norman Bernard
Production Coordinator: Anna Orodi
Cover and Interior Design: Monica Kompter
Page Layout: Anita Macklin

Printed and bound in the United States of America by R R Donnelley & Sons
1 2 3 4 5 RRD 95 94 93 92 91

To Jenny for her devotion, patience and
invaluable assistance.
To Sonia and Eric for their understanding
of the pressures research imposes on the
life and time of the researcher.

Contents

Foreword x

Preface xiii

Acknowledgments xviii

Part 1
Conceptualization, Measurement, and Patterns

Chapter 1: On Victimization, Criminal and Otherwise 2

The Concept of Victimization 4
The Sources of Victimization 5
Other Classifications and Typologies 12
Victimization in a Broad or a Narrow Sense? 18
Why Criminal Victimization? 19
From the Theoretical to the Applied 21

Chapter 2: Sources of Data on Criminal Victimization 25

Official Crime Statistics as Measures of Victimization 27
Alternative Sources of Data on Criminal Victimization 28
Hidden-Delinquency Studies 28
Victimization Surveys 30
General Problems of Victimization Surveys 35
Why Are So Many Victimizations Unreported? 43

Chapter 3: Extent and Patterns of Criminal Victimization 47

Incidence, Prevalence, and Risks of Criminal Victimization 49
Temporal Patterns of Criminal Victimization 61
Geographical and Spatial Patterns in Criminal Victimization 71
Some Spatial Patterns of Selected Types of Criminal Victimization 73

Part 2
On Victims and Victimizers 79

Chapter 4 Who Are the Victims of Crime?

Why Study the Victim? 83
Defining the Victim 88
Who Is the Victim in Criminal Law? 92
Some Victim Types 95
Cultural Types 96
Structural Types 102
Behavioral Types 103
Criminological Types 106

Chapter 5 The Homogeneity of the Victim/Offender Populations 110

How Many Victims? 112
Sociodemographic Characteristics of Victims of Crime 116
Similarities Between the Victim and Offender Populations 119
How Can the Similarities Between the Two Populations Be Explained? 126

Chapter 6 The Victims and Their Victimizers 131

The Victimizer's Attitude to the Victim 133
The Victimizer's Indifference to the Victim 134

Victimizers' Stereotypes of Probable Victims 135
The Pre-victimization Process 136
The Transformation of the Victim into a Victimizer 147
The Revolving Roles: From Offender to Victim and From Victim to Offender 149
Appropriate and Inappropriate Targets for Victimization 150
Potential Victims' Stereotypes of Probable Victimizers 152

Chapter 7 Victim-Offender Relationships 155

Victim-Offender Relationships 157
Victim-Offender Relationships in Criminal Law 157
Victim-Offender Relationships in Violent Victimization 158
The Need for a Theory of Intrafamily Violence 172
The Psychological Relationships Between the Victim and Victimizer 175
Other Types of Victim-Victimizer Relationships 178
The Intraracial Character of Violent Victimization 179

Chapter 8 The Dynamics of Criminal Victimization 185

Victim-Victimizer Interactions 187
Victim Response to Face-to-Face Victimization 192
Varieties of Victim Response to Face-to-Face Victimization 196
Some Correlates of Victim Response 198
Victim Response and Victimization Outcome 206
Unexpected Outcomes of Victim-Victimizer Interaction 211
The Need for a Theory of Victim Response 213

Part 3
Understanding Criminal Victimization 219

Chapter 9 Victim/Target Selection 220

The Victimizer's Choice of Victim/Target 222
The Process of Selection 225

Methodological Problems of Research on Victim/Target Selection 232
Victim/Target Selection: A Tentative Synthesis 234

Chapter 10 Victims' Personal Characteristics 254

Etiological Explanations of Criminal Victimization 256
Explaining Victimization by Reference to the Personal Characteristics of the Victim 257
Different Types of Proneness 264
Structural Proneness 265
Deviance-Related Proneness 273
Occupational Proneness 277
Situational Vulnerability 283

Chapter 11 Victim Behavior as a Situational Variable 287

Explaining Victimization by Reference to the Behavior of the Victim 289
Victim Behavior as a Situational Variable 290
Other Types of Victim Functional Behavior 296

Chapter 12 Macro Explanations of Variations in Criminal Victimization 311

Repeat and Multiple Victimization 313
Macro Explanations of the Differential Risks of Criminal Victimization 319
Explaining the Differential Risks of Criminal Victimization: A Tentative Integrative Schema 341

Concluding Remarks 347

Integrating the Micro and Macro Level Approaches and Linking Criminological and Victimological Theories 347

Notes 350

References 359

Credits 400

Index 401

Foreword

Criminal justice can be distinguished from criminology by its focus upon society's response to crime; criminology, on the other hand, is more concerned with the social and personal factors that give rise to offending. A similar distinction can be drawn between the two areas of study that comprise victimology. The first of these, infused by humanitarian and reformist ideals, deals with society's response to the plight of victims. This has been the main focus of earlier books by Ezzat Fattah, a pioneer in the field of victimology. In this volume, *Understanding Criminal Victimization: An Introduction to Theoretical Victimology*, he turns to deal in depth with the second major area of study, the social and psychological processes determining criminal victimization.

The modern beginnings of this subject can be traced to attempts by Von Hentig and others in the 1940s to explain the victim's role in the occurrence of crime. These were largely theoretical efforts, sometimes influenced by psychoanalytic thinking, which dealt with concepts such as victim proneness or precipitation. The first empirically derived explanations, dealing with murder and rape, loaned substance to these ideas and, at the same time, they prepared the way for broader "life-style" and "routine activity" theories. These new approaches, grounded not in psychology but in social ecology, were given considerable impetus by the development in the early 1970s of a program of national victimization surveys in the United States and some other countries. These yielded vast amounts of data about the demography of victims and, subsequently, their daily lives. This meant that the empirical base of the new theories was really superior to that of their forerunners and, not surprisingly, these new theories have come to dominate victimological explanation.

Despite the considerable measure of common ground between life-style and routine activity theories, there is also some inevitable confusion of premises and concepts. Identifying redundancy and achieving some integration of theory is the central objective of Ezzat Fattah's timely book. The clarity of the book's organization and the wealth of references make it highly suitable as a text for graduate or upper-level undergraduate courses. The international scope of the literature review, reflecting Dr. Fattah's background of experience in a number of different countries, is especially welcome in a North American publication. Clearly revealed is the way in which different groups of researchers working in various parts of the world came to essentially similar conclusions.

But *Understanding Criminal Victimization* is much more than just a textbook. Like the best of the genre, it performs an important role in defining the field and outlining an agenda for future research and scholarly activity. The scene is set in the first chapter where, having distinguished various meanings of victimization, Dr. Fattah uncompromisingly rejects calls for victimology to cut loose from criminology and to bring within its ambit all sources of "victimization," which include even natural calamities. He is surely correct in his belief that this would render impossible the already difficult task of theory building. The discipline would become hopelessly mired in a swamp of diffuse generalizations and abstractions. Rather, victimology will best achieve its policy goals of reducing the suffering of victims through strengthening its scientific links with criminology. After all, the object of explanation, criminal victimization, is merely one side of a coin, of which the other is criminal action. This recognition provides a clear focus for the book and for its detailed discussion of concepts and findings.

In the final chapter, Dr. Fattah returns to the theme of integrating criminological and victimological explanations. He recognizes that this may be premature at a point when victimological theory has yet to successfully integrate the "macro" lifestyle and routine activity approaches with the earlier "micro" explanations of Von Hentig and others, which focused on the character and behavior of individual victims. Nonetheless, the ultimate goal of integration with criminological theory must not be lost sight of and, in his final few paragraphs, Dr. Fattah gives some hint of how this might be achieved by commending the development of "an interactionist model of criminal behavior, a model that pays equal attention to the victim and the victimizer, their relationships, their reciprocal attitudes, their actions and reactions." Studying target selection processes through further analyses of victimization data would be one route to such a model, though more important in Dr. Fattah's view is the undertaking of detailed qualitative studies of individual offenders. He cites Sutherland's classic study of the professional thief and Lejeune's work on mugging as exemplars of this kind of work.

The development of an interactionist model of criminal behavior would also be well served, in my opinion, by maintaining a crime-specific focus for the necessary research and by locating it within a rational choice perspective. If policy-relevance is the goal, a crime-specific focus is needed, since the kind of preventive action advocated by Dr. Fattah depends upon detailed understanding of the opportunity structure for particular offenses. This opportunity structure consists not merely of the objective conditions of the physical and social environment, but also of the evaluations and perceptions of these conditions by potential offenders. Rational choice theory provides a useful integrating framework for data about these objective and subjective worlds. It may serve the same purpose in helping to understand the victim's choices, which can play as much part in determining crime as those of the offender. Indeed, these choices may prove to be as "rational" and as much constrained by the exigencies of time and effort as those made by the offender. I look forward to Dr. Fattah's future writings and to his further development of the interactionist model of criminal behavior.

Ronald V. Clarke
School of Criminal Justice, Rutgers,
The State University of New Jersey
February, 1991

Preface

This is a book different from the usual criminology texts, dozens of which are published every year. Its point of departure is different and the questions it asks are quite unlike those that have traditionally been the focus of mainstream criminology. Instead of asking why some people commit crime whereas others do not, the main purpose here is to find out why some individuals, households, or businesses become victims while others do not; why some are more frequently victimized than others; and why it is that some are even repeatedly victimized. As I try to show in the chapters that follow, these questions are more important for and more relevant to understanding the phenomenon of crime than the ones that have preoccupied criminologists for more than ten decades. Criminology continues to be obsessed with the search for the causes of crime. Criminology texts, with few exceptions, reflect this obsession and are devoted, for the most part, to a regurgitation of outdated and sterile theories of criminal behavior. This, to say the least, is quite surprising, because criminal behavior is not intrinsically different from other human behavior. Nor is crime qualitatively different from tort, and yet there are only very few theories on the causation of tort. Moreover, if crime is a chosen activity and if a criminal career is a deliberately chosen occupation, then the search for why some commit crime or adopt a criminal career can be no more enlightening than the search for the reasons why some elect to join the police-force or become doctors or lawyers while others choose to become caretakers, bouncers, or car racers.

Becoming a victim of crime is entirely different. In the vast majority of cases, victimization occurs without either the knowledge or consent of those who are victimized and thus needs to be explained. Another reality requiring explanation is the skewed distribution of victimization risks and the fact that crime victims do not constitute an unbiased cross-section of the general population. Several attempts have been made in recent years to offer plausible explanations for the considerable variation in victimization risks and their uneven distribution in time and space. One of the aims of this book is to introduce the reader to these theoretical formulations and to offer a critical assessment of their explanatory value.

The victimological approach to the study of crime is posited upon a basic premise, and it is this premise that guides the present book. Victimization behavior, it is argued, is dynamic behavior, and cannot therefore be explained by the static theories that have dominated the discipline of criminology for over a century. The manifest and generally acknowledged failure of these theories points to the need for a new, dynamic approach that shifts the focus from predisposing factors to environmental, situational, and triggering factors. This is precisely what theoretical victimology offers. In the victimological perspective, violent behavior is viewed not as a unilateral action but as the outcome of dynamic processes of interaction. It is not a one-sided behavior but, rather, a reaction (or an overreaction). That is why victimology pays great attention to the contexts in which violent confrontations occur and analyzes these confrontations as situated transactions. And, in contrast to the traditional criminological perspective, which postulates that the impulses for crime come from within and are manifestations of the psychopathology of the offender, victimology looks upon criminal behavior as a response to environmental stimuli, stimuli that ineluctably include the characteristics and the behavior of the potential victim. Victimology also postulates that the roles of "victim" and "victimizer" are neither fixed nor assigned, but are mutable and interchangeable, with continuous movement between the two roles. Viewed in this light, offenders and victims cannot be totally distinct or mutually exclusive populations. They are bound to be homogeneous and overlapping populations. This position, understandably, will not be welcomed by those who, for a variety of practical or utilitarian reasons, continue to promote the popular stereotypes of victims and victimizers, according to which the two populations are as different as black and white, night and day, wolves and lambs. Like many new disciplines in the social sciences, victimology has its detractors. It is very unfortunate that the ideological criticism of the concept of victim-precipitation (criticism due to an unnecessary confusion of explanatory concepts with exculpatory concepts) has given victimology a bad name by portraying it unfairly as the art of blaming the victim. One of the objectives of this book is to clear up this misunderstanding and to restore academic credibility to this most promising branch of criminology. It is my hope, therefore, that this book will establish the theoretical study of the victim as an integral and indispensable part of criminology.

This book is the culmination of thirty years of research and writing in the field of victimology. I first became interested in the study of crime victims in 1961 while doing graduate work in Austria at the University of Vienna. This interest was fostered by Professor Roland Grassberger who was, at the time, the director of the university's Institute of Criminal Law and Criminology. When I moved to the Department of

Criminology at the University of Montreal in 1964, a department founded a few years earlier by Dr. Denis Szabo, I had the good fortune of studying with Dr. Henri Ellenberger, a psychiatrist and a pioneer in victimology. Under his supervision I completed my Ph.D. dissertation, an empirical study of the factors that contribute to the choice of the victim in cases of murder for robbery. The dissertation, written in French, was later published in book form by the University of Montreal Press. The original ideas expressed in the book continue to generate interest in the scientific community, as evidenced by the recent publication of an English translation of the book's conclusions in *Medicine, Science and the Law* (1990). This was done on the initiative of Chief Psychologist Dr. David Torpy of the Glenside Hospital in Bristol, England, whose collaborators carried out the translation and submitted it for publication. The two decades separating the publication of my doctoral research in 1971 and the present book have witnessed great strides in the young discipline of victimology, and I have tried my best to present in the pages that follow a complete and up-to-date account of the current state of theoretical victimology.

The mounting attention being paid to the plight of crime victims in modern society has led to a fast-growing volume of literature on applied victimology. But, as the title indicates, the present book deals only with theoretical victimology. It is my intention to follow it up at a later date with another one that would cover a wide variety of applied issues, such as the impact of victimization, victim legislation, victim involvement in the criminal justice process, victim-offender reconciliation, and restitution and compensation to the victim. It would have been impossible to include these topics and to do them justice without doubling the size of the book. Due to the large number of books on applied victimology that have appeared in print in the last ten years, the most pressing need at the present time is for texts on theoretical victimology.

The book is divided into three parts. Part 1 is devoted to conceptual and measurement issues and problems, and it also examines the extent, trends, and patterns of criminal victimization. Part 2 deals with victims and victimizers, their reciprocal attitudes, their sociodemographic characteristics, their relationships, and their interactions. Part 3 is a review of micro and macro explanations of criminal victimization. It moves from a discussion of how offenders select their victims to the role victim characteristics and behavior play in victimization, and it ends with a critical review of the models proposed in the past fifteen years to explain the different risks of victimization.

The book consists of twelve chapters. The first chapter discusses the notion of victimization, reviews various classifications/typologies, and explains why victimization by crime was chosen as the focus of the book. Chapter 2 reviews sources of data on criminal victimization, in particular victimization surveys, and the methodological problems encountered when trying to measure the true extent of victimization. The extent and patterns of criminal victimization are the topic of Chapter 3, a chapter that highlights the enormous variations in risks and rates of victimization in time and space. Chapter 4 examines the definitional problems of the term "victim," as well as the difference between legal and criminological conceptions of the victim. It also offers a description and analysis of some cultural, structural, behavioral, and criminological types of crime victims. This is followed in Chapter 5 by an analysis of the sociodemographic characteristics of victims and offenders, which highlights the extraordinary similarities between the two populations and possible explanations for these similarities. Chapter 6 focuses on the victimizer's attitude to the victim and the stereotypes commonly held by offenders and potential victims. This is followed by an analysis of the pre-victimization process in which the techniques of neutralization, legitimation, and desensitization are often used by the victimizer to rationalize the choice of a particular victim/target and to avoid feelings of guilt and post-victimization dissonance. Chapter 7 examines victim-offender relationships and stresses the role and importance of these relationships in violent victimization. A number of hypotheses related to the social laws that govern the phenomenon of criminal homicide and other forms of violence are formulated and discussed. The chapter also examines intrafamily violence and reviews some of the theories that attempt to explain it. All this leads to an analysis of the intraracial character of most violent crime. Chapter 8 moves from the static concept of relationship to the dynamic concept of interaction and examines the problems of communication in conflict situations, the victim's response to face-to-face confrontation, and the impact of the victim's reaction on the final outcome, in particular on offense completion, injury, and death. After reviewing a number of correlates of victim response and some unexpected outcomes (such as the Stockholm Syndrome), the chapter outlines the need to develop a theory of victim response to face-to-face victimization. Part 3, which deals with explanations, starts with a chapter on victim/target selection. The concept of exchangeable/nonexchangeable victim/target is explained and some examples are presented of those who are considered "the right victims" in certain offenses. The main criteria in target selection are examined and the methodological problems of research in this area are outlined. Chapter 9 ends with a tentative synthesis of the selection criteria. The three last chapters successively analyze various approaches to the explanation of differential risks of criminal victimization. Chapter 10 deals with explanations that use victim characteristics as the main explanatory variables for varying risks of victimization and the clustering of criminal victimization in certain groups. Special emphasis is placed on the ideas of proneness-vulnerability. Different types of proneness—spatial, structural, deviance-related, occupational, and situational—are reviewed and are illustrated by various case studies. Chapter 11 moves to explanations that refer to the functional role victim behavior plays in the genesis of victimization. Here, particular attention is paid to the somewhat controversial concept of victim-precipitation, but it is not the only concept examined. Other types of functional behavior by the victim, including facilitation, participation, cooperation, temptation, invitation, and instigation, are also analyzed. The final chapter, Chapter 12, is a critical review of macro explanations of the differential risks of victimization. The interesting phenomenon of multiple and repeat victimization is examined and a summary of its explanations is offered. This is followed by a presentation of the major models, including the life-style model and the routine-activities approach. The limitations of these models revealed by empirical research are presented in detail and in summary form. The book ends by providing a tentative integrative schema of the different explanations.

Acknowledgments

A book like this could not have been written without the help and support of many individuals. Naturally it is impossible to mention everyone by name, but I would like to pay tribute to some whose assistance was vital to the completion of the project. I am particularly and deeply grateful to my wife, Jenny, for the psychological support she has given me over the years and for the long hours of day and night she spent at the word processor without uttering a single complaint. My total involvement in the project over two years has naturally been at the expense of our children, Sonia and Eric, with whom I should have spent much more time than I have been able to do. I ask them for forgiveness and thank them for their understanding. Many of the ideas and thoughts expressed in the book were focused and sharpened through, and as a result of, discussions with my colleagues and students. They deserve special thanks. Special thanks are also due to professor Ronald V. Clarke for kindly agreeing to write the foreward to the book as well as to Professors Goff, Silverman, and Waller for reviewing the text at various stages. My sincere thanks also go to Patrick Ferrier, Managing Editor, College Division, Prentice-Hall Canada Inc., to the copy editor, Patricia Buckley, and to Jean Ferrier and Maryrose O'Neil the project editors, for their helpful suggestions and for ably taking the book through the arduous stages of production. Production editors Jamie Bush and Norman Bernard equally deserve special mention and thanks. I also would like to take this opportunity to pay homage to my former teachers, colleagues, and friends, Dr. Henri Ellenberger and Dr. Denis Szabo. Dr. Szabo's continuing support has always been inspirational and has provided encouragement when it was badly needed.

Last, but not least, I wish to thank the secretarial staff of the School of Criminology, Simon Fraser University, in particular, Sharon Rynders and Mary Sutherland, for their invaluable assistance.

PART 1

Conceptualization, Measurement, and Patterns

ONE

On Victimization, Criminal and Otherwise

The criminal justice system does not protect us against the gravest threats to life, limb, or possessions. Its definitions of crime are not simply a reflection of the objective dangers that threaten us. The workplace, the medical profession, the air we breathe, and the poverty we refuse to rectify lead to far more human suffering, far more death and disability, and take far more dollars from our pockets than the murders, aggravated assaults, and thefts reported annually by the FBI.

Jeffrey H. Reiman (1979, p.86)

The Concept of Victimization

The concept of victimization is a rather complex one. Although frequently encountered in the scientific as well as the nonscientific literature, hardly any attempt is made to define "victimization" or to explain it, as if the term were self-explanatory. The noun "victimization" is conspicuous by its absence from language dictionaries and social science encyclopedias. The *Shorter Oxford English Dictionary* (1980), for example, does not define victimization as a noun. Instead, the dictionary gives the following explanations of the verb "victimize": to make a victim of; to cause to suffer discomfort, inconvenience, and so forth; to cheat, swindle, or defraud; to put to death as, or in the manner of, a sacrificial victim; to slaughter; to spoil or destroy completely. The dictionary gives the year 1830 as the date when the verb "victimize" was first used.

The situation is not much better in the specialized dictionaries. Published long after the term became widely used, *A Dictionary of Criminology* (1983) does not have an entry under "victimization."

The word "victimization" has a negative connotation. The sense it conveys is one of an adverse effect or an undesired and undesirable consequence caused or brought about by some external force or by some individual, group, or organization. It implies the incurring of injury, harm, loss, inconvenience, discomfort, pain, and suffering of one sort or another. Victimization implies an imbalance of strength and a disequilibrium in the positions of power: the strong, powerful victimizer and the weak, helpless victim.

Fattah and Sacco (1989) suggest that the term "victimization," when stripped to its essentials, implies some sort of encounter in which one party preys upon another. They point out that while it might not be too problematic to recognize what is essential to an appropriate conceptualization of victimization, it might be considerably more trouble to recognize the proper conceptual limits of the term. In other words, what sorts of predations are to be included in a definition of victimization, and what sorts of predations are to be excluded?

The concept of victimization is problematic because of the infinite variety of kinds, forms, and types of victimization to which people may be subjected or from which they may suffer. Criminal victimization is just one small category of victimization. People may suffer death, injury, harm, or loss as a result of acts or omissions that have nothing to do with crime or the criminal law. And it is very common to use the word "victim" in a wide variety of areas and contexts totally unrelated to crime. We hear and read about victims of disease, pollution, natural disasters, war, exploitation, oppression, repression, persecution, torture, discrimination, corporate wrongdoing, and so on. Many forms of wrongdoing and many types of negligence, carelessness, or recklessness causing injury, loss, or harm are not criminal. The distinction between crime and tort is quite often an arbitrary one.

As Elias (1986) correctly points out, our definitions of crime exclude many serious harms and, yet, include many other acts whose seriousness or criminality one might seriously question. Thus, while the criminal law recognizes some victimizations, it ignores others, and the decisions about what we label and treat as crime do not necessarily reflect objective harms.

Contrary to popular conception, many forms of violent victimization are not punishable under the criminal law. The physical violence in sports such as boxing, wrestling, football, fencing, and the martial arts comes immediately to mind. Many types of psychological violence are also not criminal in nature. Certain forms of sexual and racial harassment might not qualify as criminal offenses under federal or provincial legislation that protects human rights. The same is true of acts of intimidation, repression, and brutality by government bodies, notably the police. The use of violence by legal authorities, which Bohannan (1969) calls "executive violence" or "legitimate violence" is a sanctioned means of social control. Even the ultimate form of violence and victimization, the deliberate, cold-blooded, paid-for killing of a human being, remains legal in many countries under the euphemism of "capital punishment."

The Sources of Victimization

The infinite variety of deliberate and indeliberate, negligent and nonnegligent actions, behaviors, commissions, and omissions that may be subsumed under the generic heading of "victimization" makes it impractical to examine, analyze, and discuss every conceivable type of victimization or victim. It is necessary, therefore, to attempt some grouping, categorization, or typology. Once this is done, the next step is to narrow the scope of the inquiry by focusing on one or two categories.

As a universal phenomenon, victimization lends itself to endless taxonomies. One may classify victimization according to different criteria such as nature, form, scope, level, degree, effects, and frequency, to mention but a few. For the purpose of this book, that is, understanding criminal victimization, the *source* of victimization seems to be an appropriate criterion. It is appropriate because it allows the separation of victimization by crime from victimization by other sources. There is nothing unusual about choosing a criterion that fits the purpose of a book. Classifications and typologies are, by their very nature, arbitrary groupings subservient to the specific objectives of the researcher.

The sources of victimization, like its forms, are multiple and diverse. They cannot be easily broken down into groups that fit nicely into mutually exclusive categories. Whatever the grouping, it is inevitable that there will be some overlap.[1] Furthermore, as we shall show, some sources interact or interface with one another. It should be made clear, therefore, that the purpose here is not to develop a definitive typology of the sources of victimization. We simply want to show that the same victimization, be it death, injury, harm, loss, or something else, may be caused by several different sources.

The problem is to reduce the endless variety of victimization sources to some orderly arrangement. This can be done through a series of distinctions and subsequent divisions. As a first step it seems logical to distinguish between victimization by nature and victimization by people. In other words, we should separate victimization by such things as natural forces, elements, and agents from victimization by human actions, synthetic substances and products, and conditions created by people. A next logical step is to try to break down this broad group of victimizations by human actions into several smaller groups. Separating victimizations caused by the person who suffers (auto-victimization) from victimizations caused by others appears justified at this point. Victimization by others is still a very broad category that needs to be divided further into smaller groups. A great deal of victimization in modern society is, in reality, a by-product of science and technology rather than the consequence of deliberate, intentional victimization acts. Thus it seems justified to place it in a category apart from victimizations by more concrete human actions. We may further break down this latter and very broad category of victimization into three smaller groups: structural victimization; victimization by crime; and victimization by torts or other acts that are not criminal.

These divisions and resulting categories are shown in Figure 1-1.

This process of consecutive distinctions and divisions yields six master groups, each of which can be further reduced by multiple divisions and subdivisions. These divisions and subdivisions, however, do not concern us here as we are primarily interested in victimization by crime. To better illustrate the difference between criminal victimization and victimization by other sources, we will briefly review each of our six master categories, which are listed below:

1. Natural victimization: Victimization by natural forces, elements, agents, substances, organisms, and so on.
2. Auto-victimization: Victimization by one's own hand or as a result of one's own actions.
3. Industrial/Technological victimization: Victimization by synthetic substances and products and by conditions and changes created in the biophysical environment by people's actions.
4. Structural victimization: Victimization by one's society, culture, government, criminal justice system, and so on.
5. Criminal victimization: Victimization by crime and by acts made punishable by law.
6. Noncriminal victimization: Victimization by torts and other noncriminal acts or omissions.

FIGURE 1-1 **Sources of Victimization**

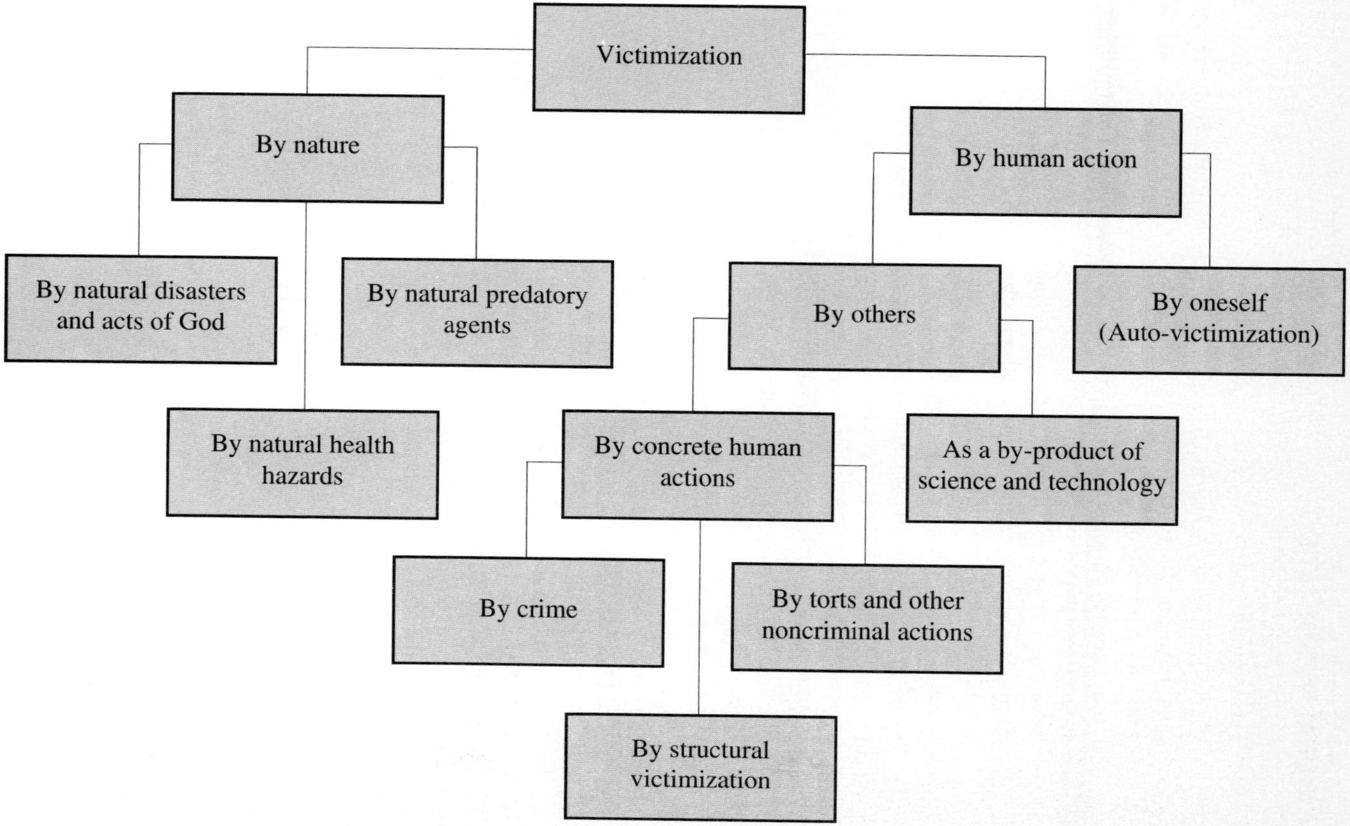

NATURAL VICTIMIZATION

This is victimization by various natural causes.

—Victimization by natural disasters and acts of God: Natural disasters, calamities, and "acts of God" claim hundreds of thousands of victims every year. As a result of disasters, such as earthquakes, volcanic eruptions, hurricanes, typhoons, tidal waves, floods, drought, and famines, whole villages are wiped out and thousands lose their lives, their homes, and their belongings. The large number of victims, the physical destruction, the human displacement, the economic losses, and the ensuing human suffering place natural disasters and catastrophes among the worst kinds of victimization.

—Victimization by natural health hazards: The biophysical environment in which we live contains several natural hazards that cause death, endanger life, or deeply affect health. People die, suffer ill health, and contract diseases caused by natural microorganisms, such as bacteria, germs, viruses, and other natural hazards such as radiation from the sun.

—Victimization by natural predatory agents: Our natural environment also contains predatory agents, such as wild animals, sharks, snakes, insects, and poisonous plants, that claim human victims.

AUTO-VICTIMIZATION

Despite the strong instinct of self-preservation, many individuals seek not only their own victimization but also their own self-destruction. Through their own actions they bring about, sometimes knowingly—other times unknowingly—their injury, ill health, or total demise. Auto-victimization results directly from the acts or the omissions of the person who suffers. It is the "doer-sufferer" phenomenon (Von Hentig, 1948) characteristic of suicide, attempted suicide, self-mutilation, self-inflicted injury, self-caused accidents, self-destroying behavior, and so on.

The abuse of legal and illegal drugs, alcohol, tobacco, and steroids, used with a full knowledge of the harmful effects of these substances to one's health and well-being, are typical forms of auto-victimization.

People can be responsible for their own victimization in many other ways. They can get killed or injured as a result of accidents caused by their own negligence, alcohol consumption, or some other behavior, such as refusing to wear a helmet while driving a motorcycle or not fastening seat belts while in a car. A person may decide to play the daredevil or become a stuntman only to be involved in a deadly or serious accident.

We can thus qualify as auto-victimization all cases where the victimization can be traced directly and solely to the actions, omissions, negligence, carelessness, or recklessness of the person who suffers.

INDUSTRIAL/TECHNOLOGICAL VICTIMIZATION

The hazards to life and health posed by modern technology, which cause actual and potential victimizations, are becoming more and more evident every day. One single technology, nuclear technology, has the potential to wipe out life from the face of the earth. The nuclear explosion in Chernobyl, USSR, vividly showed the horrifying victimizations that can result from nuclear accidents.

Industrial pollution is one of the foremost health hazards in modern life and every year causes countless victimizations in many different forms. Our environment has become unsafe as a result of dangerous substances, such as dioxin, PCB, and pesticides, to mention but a few. Some of the substances produced by the human race are so harmful to the environment that they have caused a hole in the ozone layer surrounding the earth, and this hole represents enormous health hazards to all forms of life on the planet.

There is no way of estimating, accurately or even approximately, the number of people who annually die or suffer ill health as a direct result of dangerous and insufficiently tested drugs, adulterated foods, chemical additions to food and beverages, defective and/or unsafe industrial products, and so on. However, the numbers must be in the millions.

STRUCTURAL VICTIMIZATION

Structural victimization is victimization related to the social and power structures in a given society. It is victimization rooted in society's stratification, values, and institutions. A large part of structural victimization is an outcome of the inequalities of wealth and power.

Structural victimization has no boundaries. In one way or another, we are all victims, to some extent, of one form or another of structural victimization. But some people are victimized more than others, and some suffer more than others. Among the most frequent victims are females in a patriarchal society; members of racial, ethnic, or religious minorities; the have-nots; the underprivileged; and those who suffer from a physical, mental, or social handicap, such as the orphaned, the illiterate, the mentally handicapped, the deformed, the unattractive, the extremely overweight, and so on. Members of deviant minorities are also prime victims of structural victimization.

Structural victimization takes many forms, some visible, some hidden, some subtle, and others not so subtle. One of the most common forms of structural victimization is abuse of power, in particular, the violations of human rights. What sets structural victimization apart from other kinds of victimization is its magnitude and the ubiquitous character of many of its forms, such as war, genocide, tyranny, dictatorship, oppression, repression, persecution, torture, censorship, exploitation, discrimination, racism, sexism, ageism, and classism.

Although some forms of structural victimization may not result in death or physical injuries, they can have dramatic economic, political, social, and psychological effects. Moreover, some forms, such as racism, sexism, or ageism, are actually "processes." In a society plagued by racism like South Africa, where apartheid is government policy, being black is a victimization process that starts from birth and ends only with death.

Reiman (1975) argues that aging in American society is itself a process of victimization because of the negative attitudes society holds toward those who are old. He believes that victimization of the aged cannot be fully understood unless it is seen in a large social context in which aging itself has been rendered a process of victimization. This is because Americans have created and sustain, in a variety of ways, a society in which becoming old is not merely becoming different. Becoming old in America, says Reiman, is becoming less human and more dead.

Structural victimization and cultural victimization, which is caused by customs, traditions, religion, ideology, patriarchy, and so on, often go hand in hand and are sometimes difficult to separate. The extermination or the persecution and oppression of ethnic and religious minorities are both structural and cultural. The same is true of racism, sexism, ageism, and of many other forms of structural victimization. The victimization of blacks in the United States is structural (they are a minority, they are poor, and they are powerless) and cultural (they live in a culture that promotes white superiority). The victimization of blacks in South Africa is equally structural and cultural. Although they are a majority, they are economically deprived and politically powerless (structural) and live in a white supremacist society (cultural). In a patriarchal society, the victimization of women is as structural (weak position in the hierarchy of power, lack of economic independence, and so forth) as it is cultural (living in a culture focused on the notion of male superiority). The victimization of the aged is structural (they are a minority, relatively poor and, like women, occupy a low rank in the power hierarchy) and cultural (they live in a culture in which a great emphasis is placed on work, activity, and productivity, and in which the ideal is to be young and beautiful).

Cultural biases and stereotypes encourage victimization (criminal and otherwise) by creating culturally legitimate victims, worthless victims, and disposable/expendable victims (see Chapters 4 and 6) and by culturally defining certain individuals, groups, or organizations as "appropriate targets for victimization."

CRIMINAL VICTIMIZATION

A simple, workable, and easily operationalized definition of criminal victimization is "victimization caused by, or resulting from, a criminal offense, which is an act committed in violation of the criminal law." This definition uses an objective criterion, a legal one, to determine exactly which types of victimization fall under this specific category. By choosing a legal criterion, the insurmountable problems usually encountered in the search for a sociological definition of crime are avoided. Singling out criminal victimization as a separate group and using an objective definition based on a legal criterion have many advantages. One big advantage is the delineation of a very specific and clearly defined area of study, a precise subject, and a concrete framework. Firm boundaries are set and an easily identifiable (and measurable) category of victimization is isolated for the purpose of scientific inquiry. Another practical advantage of separating criminal victimization from other types of victimization is that data on criminal victimization are readily available whereas data on most other types of victimization are not.

Although criminal victimization constitutes only a small category of all victimization, and although it is limited by our definition to victimization caused by, or resulting from, a criminal offense, this category embraces a huge variety of multifarious and heterogeneous behaviors. The nonexhaustive list prepared by Elias (1986) gives an idea of the heterogeneity of the subtypes of criminal victimization. He points out that criminal victimization may result from violent, personal, property, organized, professional, white-collar, corporate, juvenile, sexual, and family crime, from political crime, such as terrorism and rebellion, or from state crime, such as corruption, structural violence, and repression. Elias adds that violent crime, understandably, creates the strongest public reaction and the most considerable human damage.

NONCRIMINAL VICTIMIZATION

Under this last group fall all victimizations not belonging to any of the first five groups. As mentioned earlier, many harmful and injurious acts are not covered by the criminal law. Some are within the realm of the law of torts, others may come under administrative law, corporate law, labor law, commercial law, international law, and so on, while others may not be covered by any law. Torts constitute a large subcategory of noncriminal victimization. However, people may suffer serious victimization as a result of acts that are not sufficient to claim civil damages or to win a civil suit.

Suffering ill health as a result of the smoking of others is a good and current example of noncriminal victimization. Another example is gossip, which may ruin lives, reputations, marriages, and careers and may even lead to suicide without necessarily coming under the provisions punishing defamation, libel, or slander. The same applies to many other forms of victimization, such as humiliation, agitation, provocation, and so on. Victimization may not even be the result of any specific act or any concrete omission. We hear about people being victims of hate, hostility, anger, envy, and jealousy even when such emotions and attitudes had not been translated into specific harmful or injurious actions. Emotional victimization of women and children is an established and widespread form of abuse. Mental cruelty is a valid cause for divorce. Passivity may constitute victimization. One detrimental form of the emotional victimization of children may not require any actions but the simple withholding of love and affection.

This crude grouping of victimizations according to their source, together with the few examples cited, are only intended to give an idea of how varied the forms and how diverse the sources are. It would have been presumptuous to try to draw an exhaustive list or to come up with a definitive typology. The groupings are meant only to illustrate, not to rigidly classify, the infinite variety of victimizations. Admittedly there is some overlap between the six groups we discussed, but this is inevitable, especially since there is continuous interaction between the sources of victimization and since it is quite difficult at times to trace the victimization to one single source. This overlap, however, should not be a problem since what was presented is not intended as a proper classification but as a convenient grouping.

Other Classifications and Typologies

Although victimization lends itself to various groupings and categorizations, classifications and typologies of victimization have not been as popular as those of victims or those of crime.

PRIMARY, SECONDARY, TERTIARY, MUTUAL, AND NO VICTIMIZATION

One of the earlier classifications was done by Sellin and Wolfgang (1964) as part of their work on the measurement of delinquency. Using the type of victim as a criterion, they identified five mutually exclusive categories of victimization.

Primary Victimization

Primary victimization involves the individual victim who is directly assaulted and injured in a face-to-face offense, who is threatened, or who has property stolen or damaged.

Secondary Victimization

Secondary victimization generally refers to commercial establishments such as department stores, railroads, theaters, chain stores, churches, and the like. The victim is impersonal, commercial, and collective, but not so diffuse as to include the community at large.

Tertiary Victimization

Tertiary victimization excludes both primary and secondary types and refers to a very diffusive victimization that extends to the community at large and includes offenses against the public order, social harmony, or administration of government. Regulatory offenses and violations of city ordinances are typical examples.

Mutual Victimization

Mutual victimization excludes all of the above categories and refers to those cases in which the participants mutually consent to engage in acts that are violations of the law, for example, fornication, adultery, or statutory rape.

No Victimization

No victimization is used as a category for offenses that cannot be committed by an adult and which are now commonly referred to as "juvenile status" offenses, such as running away from home, truancy from school, being declared "incorrigible," and so on.

Refinements and additions to the original Sellin and Wolfgang (1964) classification were made by Silverman (1974), by Wolfgang and Singer (1978), and by Kiefl and Lamnek (1986) among others.

Recently, the term "secondary victimization" had been used in a different sense from that of Sellin and Wolfgang (1964). Secondary victimization (sometimes also called the second victimization) is now being used to refer to crime victims' traumatic experiences with the criminal justice system and to the humiliation and the suffering the victim goes through as a witness or as a justice helper.[2]

SOME OTHER TYPES OF VICTIMIZATION

In the literature on victimization, some types are discussed in their own right, that is, without being part of a general typology. What follows is a brief description of some of the ones most often encountered. They are listed in no particular order.

Corporate Victimization

Corporate victimization is one of the most damaging, most pervasive, and most diffuse types of victimization in modern society. And yet, many victimizations by corporations do not come under the jurisdiction of the criminal law. This has led some researchers to group corporate actions and behaviors causing widespread victimization (whether criminal or otherwise) under the term of "corporate victimization" or "white-collar victimization." In their article "Victim Categories of Crime," Wolfgang and Singer (1978) discuss, what they call, analytical categories for research and theory. In addition to the original five categories used by Sellin and Wolfgang (1964) in their work *The Measurement of Delinquency*, Wolfgang and Singer discuss "corporate victimization." They suggest that secondary and tertiary victimization overlap, to some extent, with the idea implied by corporate victimization. Just as Sutherland (1949) spoke of rates of white-collar corporate crime, Wolfgang and Singer feel it is possible to develop corporate or collective victim rates. Adding that there may bc many subtypes of corporate victimization, they point out that corporate criminality and corporate victimization do not always coincide, although they often do.

Walklate (1989) believes that measuring corporate victimization is not impossible, though it has largely been neglected by both criminologists and victimologists. She also points out that if we are to get some picture of the range and extent of corporate victimization, it is necessary to make a number of inferences from incomplete statistical sources and specialized studies which, for the most part, have not been directly concerned with the victims of such activities.

Collective Victimization

To some extent, corporate victimization is a form of collective victimization since, in many cases, the victims are collectivities. But corporate victimization is just one type of collective victimization, and there are many others. As the word "collective" suggests, collective victimization is victimization directed at, or affecting, not only individuals but also whole groups. In some cases the groups are diffuse, the members have nothing or not much in common, and the group is not targeted as a specific entity. More often, however, the acts of victimization are directed against a special population. Genocide is a typical example of collective victimization aimed at an ethnic or religious group. Here the members of the group are victimized because of their group affiliation. Other examples of collective victimization include victimization of women, the elderly, blacks, consumers, workers, and so on.

In her study of the victimization of slaves in the United States, Galvin (1976) deplores the fact that little attention has been paid to collective victimization. She points out that group victimization relationships are not as simplistic as individual victim-victimizer relationships. They are neither linear nor one-dimensional. Instead there is a continuum of relationship between the victim and the victimizer. Galvin suggests that sometimes the victims of collective victimization (as well as the offenders) may be unaware of, or naive about, their victimization, as well as the extent of their victimization and the role they assume in the victimization process.

Bassiouni (1988) distinguishes between individual and collective victims, and between individual and collective victimization. What he means by "collective victims" is that category in which the individual victims are targeted because they belong to a certain group or collectivity. The criminal conduct, goals, and outcomes are, in this case, predicated on the fact that the victim belongs to an identifiable group or collectivity. Collective victimization, he argues, is victimization directed against groups or groupings of individuals linked by special bonds, considerations, factors, or circumstances that, for these very reasons, make them the target or object of victimization. Among the cognizable groups or groupings under international law, Bassiouni cites the collective victims of the following: international or noninternational war (combatants or civilians); genocide; crimes against humanity; apartheid; slavery and slave-related practices; torture; unlawful human experimentation; piracy; aircraft hijacking; kidnapping of diplomats and other internationally protected persons; hostage-taking of civilians; unlawful use of the mails; and illicit trade and distribution of narcotic drugs.

Bassiouni (1988) points out that since World War II, three noninternational conflicts have produced an estimated total of five million collective victims (one million Biafrans, one million Bengalis/Bangladeshis, three million Cambodians/Kampoucheans). All of these victims belonged to an identifiable group, and their victimization was based on their belonging to that particular group. He also notes that in recent times, intergroup conflicts such as those in Ireland, Cyprus, and Lebanon have generated significant collective victimization. He further cites the practice of apartheid in South Africa as another glaring illustration of collective victimization.

Institutional Victimization

What differentiates this type of victimization from other types is its location. It occurs in institutions, either open (such as schools) or closed (such as penal institutions). In institutional victimization, victim-victimizer relationships may vary from relationships in victimizations occurring outside the institution, though the nature and forms of victimization may not necessarily be very different from those in the open society.

The confinement to a "total institution" (a term popularized by Goffman, 1961) often constitutes in itself a form of structural victimization. Aside from that, certain varieties of victimization, such as abuse, humiliation, degradation, exploitation, experimentation using humans as guinea pigs, mutilation, suicide and attempted suicide, assault and sexual assault, are rampant in total institutions, and their rates could be higher than the general rates for the free population. The high dark figure and the lack of reliable statistics preclude the possibility of comparison.

Unfortunately, institutional victimization has not received a lot of attention from criminological researchers. The literature on the subject remains thin (Bartollas et al., 1975, 1976; Dinitz et al., 1975, 1976; Drapkin, 1976; Fuller and Orsagh, 1977; Bowker, 1980; Porporino and Doherty, 1986). Its hidden nature might have discouraged some from trying to empirically study it. Still, the wide variety of institutions (prisons, penitentiaries, correctional institutions, training schools, mental hospitals, nursing homes, orphanages, boarding schools, and so on) and the total number of people who are in institutions at any given time indicate a great need for more research. Recent revelations about the physical and sexual abuse of boys, which has been going on for many years in an orphanage in Newfoundland, have attracted attention to this insidious form of institutional victimization.

Multiple Victimization

As we will see in the next chapter, victimization surveys conducted in various countries have shown that most respondents do not report any victimization, some report a single victimization, and a small minority report several victimizations of the same kind taking place during the recall period. The repeated victimizations to which these respondents had been subjected have come to be called "multiple victimization" or "series victimization."

The Canadian Urban Victimization Survey (Canada, 1988) differentiates between two subtypes of multiple victimization: repeat victimization and cross-crime victimization. Repeat victimizations describe households that have been subject to several events of the same type of criminal victimization. Cross-crime victimizations, on the other hand, refer to households that experience quite different types of victimization during the reference period.

Repetition is characteristic of certain types of victimization such as the following: family violence, such as wife-beating and child battering; sexual offenses, such as incest and statutory rape; and property offenses, such as shoplifting.

Multiple victimization presents serious methodological problems as it is difficult to count, but may be of great help in understanding certain types of victimization. To do so, it is important to find out whether the victimizations were (1) merely the result of chance or bad luck, (2) related in some way to some structural or behavioral vulnerability on the part of the victim, or (3) due to a specific relationship between the victim and victimizer (see Chapter 12).

Random Victimization

Most conventional types of criminal victimization are not random victimizations. They are directed at a specific target. The concrete target may be chosen for a variety of reasons and according to several criteria. There is strong empirical evidence suggesting that criminals in general do not choose their victims at random (see Chapter 9). In some instances, however, the victimizing act may not be aimed at a specific individual, household, or organization. A great deal of corporate victimization, such as consumer fraud and stock market manipulations, is random victimization. When acts of terror are meant to subjugate and spread fear and panic they are usually perpetrated at random, as, for example, when whole villages are bombed, burned, or demolished. The same also applies to terrorist acts by individuals or groups. When a bomb is placed and explodes in a supermarket, a movie theater, or an airport, usually no one in particular is targeted for the explosion. This can be described as random victimization. The same is true of the sniper who shoots without meaning to kill or injure any specific individual.

Instantaneous Victimization and Continuing Victimization

The stereotypical conception of victimization is one that looks upon victimization as a single event of brief duration, or as Biderman (1981) puts it, as instantaneous events at a point in time, with no attention to their extension on the temporal dimension. But there are states of continuing victimization. Biderman refers to crimes that have extensive duration in time, ones to which the prevalence of people in a victimizing state would be a more appropriate statistic than the incidence of offenses over time. As examples of these kinds of victimization that may be conceived and measured in prevalence rather than in incidence terms, Biderman cites various forms of continuing persecution, terrorization, and extortion. His examples include the worker who is kept in line by union or company goons, the school child who must regularly yield lunch money to tougher children, the merchant subject to a shakedown racket, the prostitute terrorized by her pimp, the spouse or sexual partner kept from separating from a hate relationship by fear of violence, and the person who must ask for an unlisted telephone number because of a series of threatening or obscene calls.

Biderman (1981) also refers to a somewhat different type of continuing victimization suggested by Reiss (1974), who gives as example the cause of a tenant inhabiting a dwelling affected by a building-code violation. The "crime" of the landlord in this instance is similarly a state, rather than incident, form of crime that continues in duration through time, so long as the condition of the structure remains uncorrected.

Direct and Indirect Victimization

Fattah and Sacco (1989) distinguish between direct and indirect victimization. Direct victimization is experienced when an individual in some relatively immediate way becomes the object of criminal harm, as when someone is raped, murdered, or robbed of some property. The individual in question is then personally and directly affected. These direct victimization episodes may be isolated events, or they may be part of a larger pattern of criminal exploitation (as in the case of domestic abuse). Crime also elicits adverse reactions in those who have not been directly victimized, and these may be viewed as indirect victimizations. As a result of crime, some people will increasingly come to fear for their safety and, as they do, the quality of their lives will be lessened. Elderly people, for example, may feel afraid to go shopping by themselves and thus not purchase things that they need. They may be apprehensive about taking a walk in the local park and thus remain at home on warm summer evenings. They may use some portion of their disposable income to purchase extra locks for doors and windows. They may isolate themselves from neighbors and strangers alike. These reactions, and many others among people who have not been directly victimized, represent an "effect of crime," although one that is more vicarious and less immediate than more traditionally understood victim experiences. This effect is indirect victimization and is more abstract and elusive than the more direct forms of victimization that are circumscribed in both time and space. Fattah and Sacco point out that the consequences of indirect victimization are no less real and may be no less damaging than the consequences that result from a more direct encounter with someone who intends criminal harm.

Victimization in a Broad or a Narrow Sense?

There is an ongoing debate in victimology on whether to confine the scope of the discipline to victimization in a narrow sense, that is to criminal victimization, or whether to extend it to victimization in a broad sense, that is to general or global victimization.

A strong proponent of a global victimology (and by no means the only one) is Robert Elias, a political scientist at the University of San Francisco. Elias (1986) believes that victimology's most significant drawback might lie in confining itself almost exclusively to criminological boundaries. Despite its broader origins, according to Elias, the discipline has rarely considered anything but crime victims and criminal victimization. He cites some critics who have challenged the scientific boundaries of victimology by suggesting that it has unnecessarily constrained itself within traditional criminology's boundaries and adopted the same conservative mentality. Elias goes on to criticize victimological research for having accepted, either implicitly or explicitly, a role within criminology, and he sees this as partly due to the fact that most victimologists began in criminology, which still provides them with a convenient framework.

So what does Elias suggest? He pleads for victimology to move beyond criminology. He sees a broader role for victimology, a role which would fulfill not only victimology's now traditional tasks, but also consider broader criminal definitions, the social and governmental sources of victimization, and victim-producing cultures. This, in his view, would allow us to consider other kinds of victims, victimizers, and victimizations. It would promote a wider and more international victimology, that is, a "new" victimology of human rights. As a political scientist, Elias argues against separating science and politics and claims that our politics inevitably give direction to our science, but it need not and should not preordain it. In the final pages of his book, *The Politics of Victimization: Victims, Victimology and Human Rights*, Elias (1986) calls for a "new" victimology embracing a broader definition of victimization that brings all victims, or at least many more victims, within its purview.

Elias's views, though shared by some others, do not represent those of mainstream victimology. The latter views are well represented by Edith Flynn. Flynn (1982) wonders if it would not be more productive for victimology to concentrate on the study of the behavior of victims in crime situations. This approach would study victim behavior during the commission of a crime, the victim's response to crime, and the provision of assistance, treatment, and services designed to overcome the harm done to the victim. She believes that this would not only be more feasible but would also reflect the mainstream of victimological endeavors. As a next step, it will probably be useful, she feels, for the field to conceptually differentiate the tasks of scientific study, research, and analysis of the phenomenon of victimization from professional activities focusing on victims in terms of services, treatment, or programs.

Advocates of a global victimology, a victimology encompassing all types and forms of victimization, are fond of drawing an analogy between this broader victimology and a criminology that does not confine itself to the study of criminal behavior but extends its scope to social deviance. The parallel is attractive but defective. The field of social deviance, though broader than crime, is still a definable, identifiable, and delimitable subject. Social deviance is just a small part of social behavior. As such, it lends itself to scientific inquiry and fits well as a subject for a scientific discipline. Global victimization, on the other hand, has no clear, precise, identifiable, or delimitable boundaries. As Flynn (1982) points out, if all pain and suffering (ranging, for example, from mental illness to neuroses) were to be defined as victimization, who would not be a victim?

Why Criminal Victimization?

As the title suggests, this book is confined to one category of victimization: criminal victimization. The choice of criminal victimization and the decision not to deal with other types of victimization is not meant to suggest that criminal victimization is more serious, more harmful, or more injurious than other types. Nor should the choice be interpreted as suggesting that the material costs of, and the human sufferings resulting from, criminal victimization are more substantial, more traumatic, or longer lasting than those caused by other forms of victimization. Actually, they are not.[3] But for theoretical, as well as practical considerations, it was necessary to circumscribe the subject, to narrow the scope of the book, and to reduce the enormously vast field of general victimization to a single manageable area.

As has been explained, limiting the study to criminal victimization may be faulted by some for being too restrictive and for confining the inquiry within the traditional boundaries of criminology. Some may claim, and rightly so, that the boundaries between injurious and harmful behaviors made punishable by the criminal law and many other uncriminalized ones are artificial and arbitrarily drawn. Others may argue that several types of noncriminal victimization are not any different from criminal ones.[4] Both share similar characteristics and have the same effects and results. These arguments are not without merit. It is felt, however, that the theoretical and practical advantages of limiting the study to criminal victimization far outweigh whatever drawbacks this limitation might have.

In fact, the limitation is not just advantageous; it is essential. As a scientific discipline, victimology has to define, specify, and delineate its subject. It has to delimit the frontiers of its scientific inquiry. And as a branch of criminology, victimology is interested primarily, though not exclusively, in criminal victimization. Victimology has nothing to gain by cutting its ties to criminology and by extending its scope of inquiry to every conceivable kind, type, form, and variety of human victimization. A breakaway from criminology and an extension of boundaries beyond the definable and the quantifiable present real dangers to the young and developing discipline of victimology. Were victimology to broaden its field to victimization in a generic sense, were it to choose such a loose and diffuse subject as general victimization, its specificity would undoubtedly be lost. And by devoting itself to the unmeasurable phenomenon of global victimization, to the undefinable and unquantifiable phenomenon of human suffering, it risks losing its scientific character. It also risks jeopardizing its objectivity, neutrality, and nonnormative character as a branch of social science. The concepts of pain, suffering, victimization, and even harm are normative concepts. Deciding which types of suffering are worthy of study and which forms of victimization warrant denunciation would render victimology a norm-setting exercise. While in the praxis, victimology would be nothing more than a humanist movement. Those who insist on drawing a parallel between a "global victimology" and a sociology of deviance simply ignore the fact that the task of establishing what constitutes a deviation from the norm is not a normative task. Criminology's nonnormative character is due to the fact that it neither prescribes nor proscribes. It does not pass a value judgment on the behavior it studies, whether it is behavior defined by law as criminal or whether it is behavior that simply deviates from the norm.[5]

The plea for theoretical victimology to maintain its scientific character and to circumscribe its subject matter within firm and clearly defined boundaries is in harmony with the goals of applied victimology. The ultimate goal of applied criminology, applied victimology, and of both criminal policy and victim policy is the prevention of criminal victimization as a way of alleviating human suffering and of improving the quality of human life. This goal can only be achieved through a rational, enlightened policy whose roots are anchored not in speculation or political ideology, but in empirical science.

From the Theoretical to the Applied

The task of an "applied victimology" grounded in science is to articulate theory into policy and to translate the policy into action. That is why victimology strives, like other social science disciplines, toward the formulation of theory. This is only feasible if it confines itself to criminal victimization. To try to develop a global or a macro theory of general victimization is not only a futile endeavor, but also a hopeless task. Criminology is a case in point, and there is a good lesson to be learned from its historical development. Despite continuous, strenuous efforts extending over more than a century, criminology has not yet been successful in developing a grand or a macro theory of criminality. This can be attributed to the enormous heterogeneity of criminal behaviors and the elusiveness of the causes of crime. Ultimately, criminologists had to settle for the so-called middle-range theories, and even then without too much success.

Victimology is a much younger discipline than criminology and attempts to speak of a "victimological theory" are premature. We do not yet possess a sufficient knowledge and understanding of the phenomenon of victimization that would enable us to develop a causal or an explanatory theory. In the present state of our knowledge, the best we could do would be to use the available empirical data we have to formulate and test plausible hypotheses, find the answers to some intelligent questions, and try to develop some sound explanatory propositions and models. But these should not be confused with theories, although they do have the potential of being later developed and incorporated in a coherent, integrated theory. To develop these propositions and models we still need a great deal of research, theoretical as well as empirical. Scientific inquiry in victimology has to adhere to the traditional rules of social science and has to follow a logical sequence. In new disciplines, like victimology, this means that research precedes action according to the following formula:

Research→ Theory→ Policy→ Action→ Evaluation.

It also means that effective action to help victims and to control and prevent victimization needs to be grounded in theory, not in politics and ideology. In other words, theoretical victimology is a prerequisite to applied victimology.

There is a two-way relationship between research and theory. Research is essential to the development, formulation, and evaluation of theory. And it is theory that later inspires and guides further research. Whether theoretical or empirical, research has to follow a logical, intellectual process progressing through varying stages. Only by following the logical order of these stages could optimal results be attained, as may be seen from Figure 1-2.

FIGURE 1-2 **Interrelationships between research on criminal victimization and action to help victims of crime**

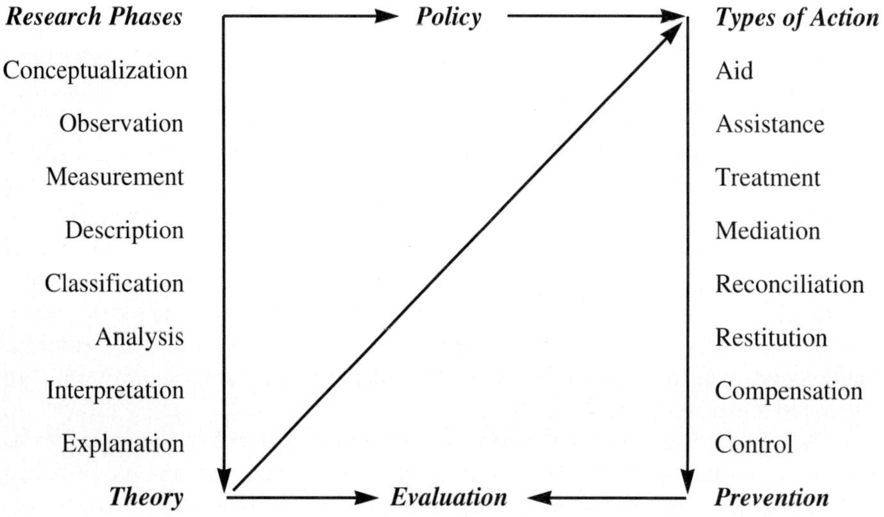

Although Figure 1-2 may give the impression that the research stages are neatly separated in time and that they are carried out consecutively, in practice this is not always the case. Some phases may be carried out simultaneously, and occasionally the order of some may be reversed. Some tasks, such as classification, are difficult to place in the sequence, since they should be, and usually are, performed at varying phases of the research process depending on the nature of the research and the volume of knowledge that had already been accumulated in the field. This, however, is not true of explanations. Explanations are the culmination of the empirical and theoretical research processes, although they are only the first step toward the development of policy and the implementation of that policy.

To summarize then, it may be said that we cannot understand or explain a phenomenon, such as criminal victimization, unless and until we have defined it, observed it, measured it, described it, classified it, analyzed it, and interpreted it. We cannot develop rational policies and undertake effective action aimed at controlling and preventing the phenomenon unless, and until, we have gained some understanding of that phenomenon and have developed some propositions, models, or theories aimed at explaining it. This is the guiding principle of this book, and a principle we will try to follow in each succeeding chapter.

Summary

The concept of victimization is a rather complex one. Despite its frequent use in scientific and nonscientific literature, it has not been adequately defined or explained. The concept is also problematic because of the infinite variety of kinds, forms, and types of victimization to which people may be subjected or from which they may suffer. The infinite variety of deliberate and indeliberate, negligent and nonnegligent actions and behaviors, commissions and omissions that may be subsumed under the generic heading of "victimization" makes it necessary to attempt some grouping, categorization, or typology and to focus on one or two categories.

A convenient grouping that fits the purpose of this book uses the source of victimization as a criterion for distinguishing various types. This leads to six master categories of victimization: natural victimization; auto-victimization; industrial/technological victimization; structural victimization; criminal victimization; and noncriminal victimization. In this book we will be focusing on criminal victimization, which may be defined as victimization caused by, or resulting from, a criminal offense, which is an act committed in violation of the criminal law. This simple, objective definition avoids the insurmountable problems usually encountered in the search for a sociological definition of crime. There are several advantages to singling out criminal victimization as a separate group and to using an objective definition based on a legal criterion. One advantage is to delineate a very specific and clearly defined area of study, a precise subject, and a concrete framework. Another practical advantage is that data on criminal victimization are readily available, whereas data on most other types of victimization are not.

We have also provided a brief overview of other classifications and typologies of victimization. Among these is the earlier classification of Sellin and Wolfgang (1964) that divides victimization into five mutually exclusive categories: primary victimization, secondary victimization, tertiary victimization, mutual victimization, and no victimization. The chapter also discusses other types of victimization that do not form part of any given typology, such as corporate victimization, collective victimization, institutional victimization, multiple victimization, random victimization, instantaneous and continuing victimization, and direct and indirect victimization.

By way of introduction to the book, we have also addressed the ongoing debate in victimology on whether to confine the scope of the discipline to victimization in a narrow sense, that is to criminal victimization, or whether to extend it to victimization in a broad sense, that is to general or global victimization. We made a deliberate decision to limit the study to criminal victimization. We pointed out that this decision does not mean that criminal victimization is more serious, more harmful, or more injurious than other types as it is not. However, for theoretical, as well as practical considerations that were explained, it was necessary to circumscribe the subject matter, to narrow the scope of the book, and to reduce the enormously vast field of general victimization to a single, manageable area. This plea for theoretical victimology to maintain its scientific character, to circumscribe its subject matter within firm and clearly defined boundaries is in harmony with the goals of applied victimology. The task of an applied victimology grounded in science is to articulate theory into policy and to translate the policy into action. Theory is only feasible if the task is confined to criminal victimization. To try to develop a global or a macro theory of general victimization is not only a futile endeavor, but also a hopeless task. It is even premature to talk of a "victimological theory of criminal victimization," as we do not yet possess sufficient knowledge and understanding of the phenomenon of criminal victimization that would enable us to develop a causal or an explanatory theory. However, such knowledge and understanding are essential for achieving the primary goals of applied victimology, namely, to prevent victimization, to help victims, and to alleviate their suffering.

TWO

Sources of Data on Criminal Victimization

Until there is greater sensitivity of data users for the error structures of the National Crime Survey and more information available about error, these data for victimology will be potentially misleading as well as enlightening.

Albert D. Biderman (1981, p.817)

Crime and its control are, rightly or wrongly, important objects of social policy and action in present-day America (and elsewhere); so long as that is so, the quality of our information about crime is important. This means that we must, so far as possible, assess the biases inherent in our measures and sources of information, and we must constantly try to improve their accuracy.

Richard F. Sparks (1982, p.17)

Official Crime Statistics as Measures of Victimization

Although quite useful for many administrative purposes, criminal statistics are not, and will never be, accurate measures of the state of crime. This is because there is always a gap between officially recorded criminality and real criminality, the former being only a sample of the latter. Real or total criminality always remains an unknown quantity. Sellin (1951) is certainly right in criticizing early criminologists and statisticians who drew their conclusions assuming that the sample maintained a constant ratio to the total criminality, no matter what offense or time period was involved. Like other modern criminologists, Sellin knows that this was an error, and he is keenly aware of the problems of official crime statistics. These statistics suffer from several shortcomings due to, in part, problems inherent in the methods used to collect, compile, and process them. The accuracy and, consequently, the utility of these statistics are further lessened by the existence of the *dark figure*. The dark figure (or hidden criminality) is a term used to refer to all those criminal offenses committed that for one reason or another remain undetected, unreported, and/or unrecorded.

The various problems of official crime statistics are by now well known and there is, therefore, little need to discuss them in detail. What follows is just a brief outline of some of the major ones:

— Police statistics are limited to offenses detected, reported, and recorded. Court and correctional statistics are even more limited. Data included in judicial statistics are confined to those arrested, charged, and brought before the courts, while institutional statistics are restricted to offenders who receive a sentence confining them to an institution. For these reasons, court and correctional statistics are of little value in trend studies, as they describe only a small and biased sample of the total of offenders and offenses. However, police statistics, despite their deficiencies, are closer to the real amount of crime than are court or correctional statistics.

— Official statistics on crime and criminals are highly dependent on the diligence and accuracy of the different branches of the criminal justice system. The quality of these statistics is subject to the limitations and biases of each branch.

— Official crime statistics are not a very suitable tool for regional, national, and international comparisons because police practices differ from location to location; variations occur in the methods of collecting, compiling, and processing data; and large differences exist in legal definitions and interpretations of the law. Changes in practices over time also limit the value of official statistics for trend studies, especially statistics extending over a long time period.

— Official criminal statistics are subject to several artificial fluctuations and thus may show upward and downward swings or trends without any actual changes in the offenses concerned. Fluctuations may result from changes in the dark figure, structural modifications (such as the size of police forces or the number of reporting units), or variations in police efficiency and effectiveness. They may also be due to changes in the levels of tolerance of the police and/or the public and changes in the level of enforcement of certain laws, as well as changes in the definition of crime by the police and changes in public attitudes toward crime and the police, and so on.

— Official crime statistics do not link crime figures to etiological variables or to factors that have been identified through empirical research as being positively or negatively associated with high or low crime rates. Furthermore, since official criminal statistics use legal rather than criminological classifications of offenses, they are, at least in their crude form, of limited use to the social scientist unless they are regrouped or reclassified, according to criminological criteria, into more or less homogeneous categories.

Alternative Sources of Data on Criminal Victimization

Three decades ago, criminal statistics published annually by Statistics Canada (and more recently by the Canadian Centre for Justice Statistics) or by the United States Federal Bureau of Investigation in their Uniform Crime Reports were the main source of quantitative data on crime. To solve, at least partially, the problem of the dark figure and to obtain better and more extended information on the real volume of crime, the actual incidence of specific offenses, and the victims of those offenses, criminologists started looking at possible alternative data sources. Two new sources were explored: hidden-delinquency studies and victimization surveys. It was felt that information gathered from these two new sources could be contrasted with the information contained in official statistics in an attempt to have a more realistic picture of the crime situation.

HIDDEN-DELINQUENCY STUDIES

Hidden-delinquency studies, or self-report studies as they are also called, are a supplementary source of data on crime, on delinquency, and, above all, on offenders who have not been detected, arrested, or dealt with by the criminal justice system. Victimization surveys and hidden-delinquency studies may be looked at as two sides of the same coin. In victimization surveys, people selected for a sample (of the general population if it is a national survey) are requested to provide information on whether or not they had been victims of specific offenses, and if they had, they are asked whether they had reported their victimization to the police. In hidden-delinquency studies, the people selected for the sample (usually of young people) are asked whether they had committed specific acts of delinquency or crimes and, if they had, whether they were detected and arrested.

Although hidden-delinquency studies and victimization surveys are usually conducted separately using different samples or different sets of population, they may occasionally be combined. This is what the British Crime Survey Scotland (Chambers and Tombs, 1984) did. While the primary purpose of the survey was to provide information about hidden victimization, it was decided to include some questions about the respondents' own lawbreaking activities. The purpose of these questions, as the authors point out, was not so much to gather systematic data on crime rates as to explore patterns of offending and the relationship of those patterns, if any, to victimization. Respondents, therefore, were asked two questions about their own lawbreaking activities: one related to common law offenses, the other to road traffic contraventions (see Chapter 5).

Hidden-delinquency studies have been conducted in many countries including the United States, Canada, the United Kingdom, and Scandinavia. Despite the relatively small number of studies carried out to date, hidden-delinquency studies have yielded some important findings and have made some significant contributions to the relatively young discipline of criminology. First, these studies have shattered some of the widely held but erroneous beliefs regarding the frequency and distribution of delinquency, and second, they have indirectly helped the development of the labeling perspective. Hidden-delinquency studies have also shown the following:

— Delinquency is by no means exclusive to the lower classes of society as previously thought. It cuts across class boundaries and is more related to age than to social class.

— The great majority of people have, at one time or another, perpetrated acts that qualify as criminal offenses under existing laws.

— Only a tiny minority of those who violate the law are detected, arrested, charged, and convicted.

— Most young people who commit delinquent acts and are not formally processed through the official agencies of the criminal justice system grow up to become "law-abiding" citizens and lead a "normal" life, free of crime.

It is, therefore, fair to say that the major contribution of hidden-delinquency studies has been to demonstrate that delinquency, in one form or another, is a "normal," "developmental," and "transitory" phase in the life of most male teenagers (see Doleschal, 1970).

VICTIMIZATION SURVEYS

The introduction of victimization surveys is without doubt one of the most exciting developments in criminology in the past twenty-five years. When carefully conducted, victimization surveys are apt to yield data on crime that are superior in some respects to official statistics. A comparison of data obtained by means of victimization surveys with official figures allows an approximate estimate of the size of the dark figure for the offenses covered by the survey. In addition to offering a more realistic picture of the state of crime than the picture drawn from official figures, victimization surveys present the following advantages over the traditional sources of data on crime:

— Surveys yield better and more detailed information than that gathered by the official agencies of the criminal justice system, if a good questionnaire is used, and if the interviewers are well trained.

— The picture that surveys provide of a temporal and geographical distribution of criminality is closer to reality than the one provided by official statistics.

— Surveys provide data on several factors usually associated with high or low victimization risks and data on the distribution of risks among various groups within the general population.

— Surveys provide information on the aftermath of victimization, on post-victimization effects suffered by the victims, and on victims' reactions to victimization.

— Victimization surveys make it possible to assess the various agencies of the criminal justice system, their performance, and the quality of services they render to the clients of the system. They also make it possible to measure the effectiveness of programs, such as Operation Identification and Neighborhood Watch programs, that are designed to prevent or to reduce the incidence of certain offenses.

— Surveys provide information on victims' interactions with the criminal justice system or the lack of such interactions, and they make it possible to measure the degree of victims' satisfaction with the system and its performance. In short, surveys make it possible to gauge public attitudes toward the system of justice.

— Surveys make it possible to measure the levels of fear of crime among the general population and among specific groups and to link the levels of fear not only to demographic variables but also to the actual experience of victimization or the risk of being victimized. In this way, surveys make it possible to measure the discrepancy between objective risks of victimization and subjective perceptions of those risks.

— Surveys provide valuable information on the number of victims who do not report their victimization to the police, the characteristics of those victims, and the difference between those who report and those who do not. In addition, they shed light on the reasons for not reporting specific types of victimization.

The complementary functions of police statistics and victimization surveys are best described by a statement made in the British Crime Survey Scotland (Chambers and Tombs, 1984). According to this survey, officially recorded crime statistics provide only limited information about all crime made known to the police, whereas crime surveys provide detailed information about a representative sample of certain kinds of criminal victimization.

HISTORY OF VICTIMIZATION SURVEYS

It is somewhat ironical that victimization surveys, which at present constitute the major source of data on crime victims, were not originally conceived or carried out to gather information on victims. Their original purpose was to count crime, as they seemed to offer a solution to the long-standing problem of the dark figure. They were thus initiated in an effort to better understand the problem, to document the inadequacy of official statistics as a crime indicator, and to estimate the extent of hidden victimization. Before long, however, it became clear that surveys could become an invaluable tool for collecting all kinds of data on criminal victimization and crime victims.

The first victimization surveys were carried out in the United States in 1966 for the President's Commission on Law Enforcement and Administration of Justice. A. Biderman and A. Reiss, Jr. had suggested to the commission that the survey method might provide a better and more accurate alternative to police statistics as a source of data on crime. They were actually reiterating an idea advanced by Anttila in an article published in *Excerpta Criminologica* (1964) on the criminological significance of unregistered criminality. In her article, Anttila explained that by Gallup investigations it should be possible to establish how many of the general public have been made objects of a certain crime and how many of these have reported the crime to the authorities (Sparks, 1981).

Victimization surveys under the title of The National Crime Survey are now being conducted in the United States on an ongoing basis with a sample of approximately 60,000 households. These surveys started with two pilot surveys and a national survey which used a modest sample of some 10,000 households. The first pilot survey was done in Washington, D.C., by the Bureau of Social Science Research under the direction of A. Biderman. Interviews were conducted in April through mid-July, 1966, with a sample of 511 randomly selected adults of age eighteen and over, in three police precincts in the District of Columbia (Sparks, 1981).

The second pilot survey was conducted by the Institute for Social Research of the Survey Research Center, University of Michigan, under the direction of A. Reiss, Jr. It consisted of interviews with the owners or managers of 768 businesses and organizations in Washington, D.C., Boston, and Chicago. A total of 595 persons age eighteen and over were also interviewed in the Boston and Chicago areas using the same questionnaire as that used in the Bureau of Social Science Research pilot survey (Sparks, 1981).

The third survey, and by far the largest, is usually referred to as NORC since it was carried out by the National Opinion Research Center under the direction of Philip H. Ennis. This was a national survey using a probability sample of 9,644 households. The survey revealed some startling information. It showed that the volume of hidden victimization reported by the respondents was far beyond expectations and much higher than previous estimates. The survey revealed, for example, that rates of victimization exceeded those officially reported by 50 percent for robberies, by 100 percent for aggravated assault, and by nearly 300 percent for forcible rape. There were twice as many larcenies and three times as many burglaries as compared to the FBI's Uniform Crime Report.

Although subsequent American surveys used improved methodology and better and much larger samples, the pattern they revealed, which showed a very high volume of unreported victimization, was not substantially different from the one reported in the NORC study. For example, a survey carried out in the first quarter of 1973 in the five largest American cities (Chicago, Detroit, Los Angeles, New York, and Philadelphia) showed that the total number of incidents reported by survey respondents was roughly double the combined number of comparable offenses recorded by law-enforcement authorities in the five cities during 1972. Auto theft came closest, in relative terms, to matching the total reflected in official records. By contrast, the number of larcenies, both personal and household, was nearly four times greater than the number that had come to official attention.

This high amount of unreported victimization is not exclusive to the United States. When findings of the British Crime Survey (Hough and Mayhew, 1983) were compared to officially recorded criminal statistics, they also showed a much higher incidence of victimization. In only one category, thefts of motor vehicles, were the figures similar. But the survey indicated twice as many burglaries as were recorded by the police; nearly five times as many woundings; twelve times as many thefts from the person; and thirteen times as many vandalisms (or criminal damage). When crimes of violence such as sexual offenses, robberies, and woundings were grouped together, the number of estimated incidents, based on the survey findings, was five times that recorded by the police; for incidents involving loss or damage to property, the figure was four times as many. The overall ratio for incidents that had been compared was one in four.

Hough and Mayhew (1983), the authors of the report on the British Crime Survey, caution that the findings should not be interpreted as showing that there is "four times as much crime" as official records suggest. They point out that the survey figures were estimates only and included a high proportion of incidents that were less serious than those recorded by the police. They add that the number of crimes revealed by the survey is likely to be an underestimate because of respondents' forgetfulness, reluctance to admit some incidents, and so on.

The NORC study and its findings created much excitement among researchers inside and outside the United States. Before long, several other victimization surveys, mostly of a smaller scale, were being conducted in several other countries. Surveys were conducted in Scandinavia (Aromaa, 1974, 1984; Hauge and Wolf, 1974; Sirén, 1980); in Germany (Stephan, 1976); in England (Sparks, Genn, and Dodd, 1977); in Holland (Fiselier, 1978; Van Dijk and Steinmetz, 1984); in Switzerland (Clinard, 1978); in France (Levy, Perez-Diaz, Robert, and Zauberman, 1986); and in Australia (Braithwaite and Biles, 1980, 1984).

The above list is by no means an exhaustive one, yet it illustrates the great appeal that victimization surveys had for researchers in the seventies and early eighties. Like the NORC survey and the other American ones that followed it, the surveys in Europe and Australia revealed high percentages of unreported victimizations. The degree of nonreporting varied depending on the nature and the seriousness of victimization.

Victimization Surveys in Canada

Victimization surveys in Canada do not have a long history and are not conducted on as regular a basis as they are in the United States.

In the early months of 1969, Courtis and Dussuyer (1970) interviewed a sample of Torontonians aged eighteen years and over. In total, 967 complete interviews were obtained. The purpose was to analyze individual attitudes toward the phenomenon of crime, criminal offenders, and law enforcement in the city. To do this, the researchers decided to discover, among other things, the extent to which the members of the sample were actually victims of crime.

In 1973, Waller and Okihiro conducted a small-size survey in Toronto that dealt only with the offense of burglary. They published their findings in 1978. In British Columbia, a victimization survey using a mail questionnaire was carried out by sociologist Daniel Koenig (1974). In collaboration with Statistics Canada, the Research division of the Ministry of the Solicitor General conducted two pilot surveys, one in Edmonton in 1977 and the other in Vancouver in 1979. Only partial findings of the latter survey have been published (Corrado et al., 1980). The most extensive Canadian survey was carried out early in 1982 by the Ministry of the Solicitor General, again with the assistance of Statistics Canada (Canada, 1983-1988).[1] The survey, commonly known as the Canadian Urban Victimization Survey, covered seven major urban centers: greater Vancouver, Edmonton, Winnipeg, Toronto, Montreal, Halifax-Dartmouth, and St. John's.[2]

No truly national victimization survey was done in Canada until the General Social Survey was carried out by Statistics Canada in 1988. This General Social Survey gathered information on criminal victimization incidents (as well as accidents) that met certain screening criteria and that occurred during the 1987 calendar year. The results of the survey were made public in the spring of 1990 (Statistics Canada, 1990). Data were collected between January and February 1988 through telephone interviews with respondents fifteen years of age and older in all ten provinces (territories were excluded). The data collection procedure resulted in 9,870 completed interviews (Sacco, 1989). The General Social Survey focused on the investigation of eight specific types of criminal victimization experiences: sexual assault, robbery, assault, theft of personal property, theft of household property, motor vehicle theft, vandalism, and breaking and entering. The first three types are categorized as "violent crimes" and, with the inclusion of theft of personal property, may be categorized as "personal victimization." The remaining types of incidents are categorized as "household victimizations" (Sacco, 1989). On the basis of the information collected, Sacco estimated that 4.8 million Canadians, fifteen years of age or older, were victimized by 5.4 million criminal incidents in 1987. Approximately one-half of these incidents involve personal victimizations (about one-third are violent victimizations and a further 22 percent involve the theft of personal property). The rate of personal victimization was estimated at 143 incidents per 1,000 Canadians over the age of fifteen and the rate for violent victimization at 83 per 1,000.

International Crime Surveys

A recent attempt was made to collect standardized victimization data from a number of countries (including Canada and the United States) using the same questionnaire in each country. The main purpose was to avoid the problems of comparing data collected by means of different instruments using different methodologies. Field data for this international crime survey were gathered in January 1989 and published in 1990 (Van Dijk, Mayhew, and Killias, 1990). The size of each nationally representative sample varied between 1,000 and 2,000, though most participating countries opted for the larger size sample; the Federal Republic of Germany even chose 5,000 interviews. Telephone interviewing was chosen because of its relatively modest costs, and it was decided to use the Computer-assisted telephone interviewing method (CATI method), which allows for much tighter standardization of questionnaire administration. Respondents were asked about their victimization experience with nine types of crimes over the past five years, though victimization in 1988 was highlighted to give up-to-date annual risks. The nine crimes covered were as follows: theft of motor vehicles (cars, motorcycles, and mopeds); theft from motor vehicles; vandalism to motor vehicles; burglary and attempted burglary; robbery and attempted robbery; other thefts of personal property; sexual assault (women only); and assault. Victims were then asked short questions about the nature and material consequences of crime; whether the police were involved (and if not, why not); and their satisfaction with the police response and any victim assistance given.

GENERAL PROBLEMS OF VICTIMIZATION SURVEYS

Although victimization surveys can provide us with a wealth of information unavailable through official crime statistics, they are not without problems. In what follows we will briefly discuss some of these problems, especially the problems of national surveys.

The Sample

Unless the sample used in a national survey is representative of the total population, the reliability of information obtained will be questionable, and it will not be possible to generalize the findings. Experience shows that it is exceedingly difficult to get a truly representative sample. Victimization surveys in the United States, particularly the early ones, suffered from overrepresentation of certain groups and underrepresentation of others in their samples. For example, the NORC study was limited to households, and only household members eighteen years and over were eligible for the interviews. The sample thus excluded businesses as well as citizens under eighteen years. As interviews are usually conducted at home during the day, there is always the possibility that homemakers and pensioners will be overrepresented in the total of those actually interviewed.

Since serious criminal victimizations of the kind usually covered by victimization surveys are relatively rare occurrences, it is necessary to use a large sample. This is done so that the number of actual victimizations within the sample may be sufficient to allow the statistical treatment of whatever variables those conducting the survey are interested in. If the sample is not large enough, and if the number of victimizations revealed is too small, it is not possible to subdivide the victim population into reasonably sized subgroups. The following example illustrates the problem. Although the National Crime Survey in the United States uses a sample of approximately 60,000 households, which are interviewed over six-month intervals, there are too few sample cases of rape victims over sixty-five years old to allow statistically valid examination of this crime (United States, 1981, p. 2).

Even when a well-constructed representative sample is used, it is practically impossible to reach and to interview all members in the sample. If the members are designated in person, there are always some who have moved and cannot be traced. If the sample is constructed on the basis of residences rather than persons, there are always some residences found vacant, demolished, or temporarily closed. Not all members of the sample who are reached can be interviewed. There are always some who refuse to cooperate, to be interviewed, to answer all or some of the questions asked, and so forth. And some of those who agree to be interviewed may not take the survey seriously and thus make no real effort to provide precise information or to answer the questions accurately.

The following example from the American victimization surveys gives a good idea of the attrition in the sample. Among the 73,000 housing units designated for the sample that were to provide information relating to the calendar years 1977 and 1978, interviews were obtained at six-month intervals from the occupants of about 60,000 units. The large majority of the remaining 13,000 units were found to be vacant, demolished, converted to nonresidential use, or ineligible for some reason. However, approximately 2,600 of the 13,000 units were occupied by persons who, although eligible to participate in the survey, were not interviewed, were temporarily absent, or were otherwise unavailable (United States, 1979, p. 25).

The Costs

The costs of large victimization surveys, such as national ones, can be prohibitive. It is not by accident that until now most surveys have been done exclusively in the United States and other wealthy countries of the western world. The excessive costs stem largely from the need for a large sample and because the technique most often used to collect the data is the personal interview, which is a costly method. Economy may be achieved by reducing the size of the sample, and this can compromise, sometimes quite seriously, its representativeness. To reduce costs, researchers have occasionally used one of two alternatives to the personal interview: the mail questionnaire and the telephone interview.

The mail questionnaire. The advantages and disadvantages of the mail questionnaire are summarized well by Garofalo and Hindelang (1977). It minimizes expenses, makes it possible to reach more people than through personal visits (the problem of not finding anyone at home being eliminated), affords more privacy to the respondents, and gives them more time to think about replies to the questions. It also ensures that the presentation of the questions is uniform from respondent to respondent, thus reducing whatever bias may be introduced through variability in interviewer performance. Despite these obvious advantages, the mail questionnaire is by no means an ideal survey technique as it has major disadvantages as well. The disadvantages are that the response rates are generally quite low, and the instrument must be shorter and less complex than for personal interviews, since there is no interviewer to clear up possible misunderstandings and to probe for answers. To these disadvantages might be added the absence of interviewer control over the quality of data, questions left unanswered in the returned questionnaires, and inaccurate replies simply due to lack of comprehension, misunderstanding, or misinterpretation of the question, and so forth.

The telephone interview. This is the technique used in Canada in both the pilot surveys (Edmonton and Vancouver), in the Canadian Urban Victimization Survey, and in the General Social Survey. To avoid the high costs of personal interviews, researchers in the Ministry of the Solicitor General in Ottawa opted for the telephone interview and decided to construct their sample using the technique known as random digit dialing (RDD). Many investigators have avoided RDD for fear that it produces seriously biased results. However, Evans and Leger (1979), who were responsible for the Canadian surveys within the Ministry of the Solicitor General, claim that it is possible to obtain fairly complex victimization data of high quality and free from serious biases over the telephone and through the use of RDD. To support their claim they cite a number of studies, in particular, one conducted by Tuchfarber, Klecka, Bardes, and Oldendick (1976) that used RDD and telephone interviews with encouraging results.

In addition to their relatively low cost, telephone interviews have some other advantages. It is possible to evaluate the performance (and eventually improve this performance) of the interviewers, as they may be observed while conducting the interviews over the telephone. It is also conceivable that some respondents will be more willing to talk and to reveal more personal information over the telephone than in a face-to-face interview. The absence of eye-to-eye contact makes the situation less threatening for both interviewer and interviewee. The stress that interviewers may feel if they happen to find themselves in a hostile environment is avoided when interviews are done by telephone (Garofalo and Hindelang, 1977).

Telephone interviews also have serious limitations. The most serious one is that they exclude from the sample all those who do not have a telephone. Since there is a strong correlation between income, social class, and having a telephone at home, members of the lower classes and the poor will inevitably be underrepresented in the sample, whether it is constructed on the basis of telephone-book listings or through RDD. The seriousness of this bias should not be underestimated because of the possible correlation between income and victimization: the lower the income, the higher the rate of victimization. Moreover, telephone surveys are only feasible in countries where telephones are widespread (such as Canada, the United States, and Switzerland). They are not practical in countries where the percentage of households with a telephone is low.

In addition to excluding those who do not have a telephone, a sample constructed on the basis of telephone-book listings also excludes those whose numbers, for one reason or another, are unlisted. Unlisted numbers include confidential ones and those of new telephones installed after the printing of the guide.

Random digit dialing eliminates this particular bias from the sample, but then it is reasonable to expect that individuals maintaining a confidential, unlisted number would not be very cooperative when called by an unknown interviewer dialing at random.

Unlike person-to-person interviews, telephone interviewing does not allow a lengthy, in-depth interrogation of the subject. Telephone interviewing has to be brief and superficial. The sincerity and the truthfulness of the respondent are more difficult to ascertain, and the quality and accuracy of the information are more difficult to control than in a personal interview.

SOURCES OF ERROR IN VICTIMIZATION SURVEYS

Like other research methods in the social sciences, the survey method has some inherent problems. Thus the information obtained in a victimization survey, whether collected through a personal interview, a telephone interview, or a mail questionnaire, is subject to different sorts of error, some intentional, others unintentional. The two main sources of deliberate error are lying and not telling. Unintentional errors, on the other hand, may result from not knowing, forgetting, misunderstanding the question, misdefining the victimization incidents, or misplacing them in time (telescoping) (Skogan, 1982, 1986).

Deliberate Errors

Victimization surveys, like all other surveys, rely on the respondents' good will and their willingness to cooperate and to provide the information requested. Still, this is not enough. The accuracy of the information depends on the respondents' sincerity, truthfulness, and ability to understand the questions and recall the victimization incidents. In any sample, large or small, there are bound to be some members who will be neither honest nor forthcoming about their victimization. Probing questions about people's victimization experiences are more personal and more intrusive than asking them about their weekly visits to the movies or the number of hours they spend daily in front of their television sets. There are two ways in which the members of the sample can satisfy the interviewer and appear cooperative while hiding the truth about their victimization: lying and not telling.

Lying. Lying means to deliberately misinform and mislead the interviewer. It is a more active way of deceiving than simply withholding information. Respondents may, of course, for different reasons, invent incidents of victimization, exaggerate or distort the facts, or deliberately twist the facts to convert a minor or an ineligible victimization experience into one that qualifies for inclusion in the survey. They may lie about the frequency, the extent or the seriousness of victimization, the date of occurrence, the amount of loss incurred, the particulars of the act, or the attributes of the offender.

Not telling. There are reasons to believe that many participants, while agreeing to take part in the survey, refuse, for various motives, to divulge to the interviewer victimizations they have suffered. Others may report a victimization incident(s) but decline to provide any further information about it. It may be reasonably expected that victimization types that usually have a high dark figure (particularly minor cases of such victimizations as intrafamily violence, violence by nonstrangers, and sex offenses) will also be underreported in victimization surveys. The authors of the British Crime Survey Scotland (Chambers and Tombs, 1984) doubt that victimization surveys are a successful way of uncovering incidents of sexual victimization or of marital and domestic violence against women. They note that, first, women may be reluctant to be quizzed about such matters by unknown interviewers, and second, the circumstances of a household interview make disclosure of incidents of domestic violence highly unlikely.

Unintentional Errors

Not knowing. Not all victims are aware that they have been victimized, and respondents cannot provide information on victimizations of which they are not aware. This is true of individuals as well as businesses. Sometimes it is difficult to tell whether the loss is due to a criminal offense or not. The disappearance of a money purse may be due to misplacement, loss, or theft. Even when a department store is able to establish that some goods are missing, it is not always possible to determine whether this is due to employee pilfering, shoplifting, or "inventory shrinkage." Young children who are victims of sexual offenses may not comprehend the nature of the acts, may not realize that they have been sexually victimized, and may not say anything to their parents. Parents are not going to report the incidents to the interviewer when asked about victimizations against other members of the household in cases where the parents themselves are the physical or sexual abusers. Not knowing is a serious problem in surveys that use proxy for certain groups instead of direct personal interviews.

Forgetting. In addition to those who refuse to be interviewed, those who do not take the survey seriously, those who deliberately provide false information, and those who do not know, there is the important problem of inaccurate information due to memory gaps. Forgetfulness is not restricted to any group. It is universal and affects all categories of respondents, though to varying degrees. It is not surprising, therefore, that many members of the sample will have difficulty remembering victimization events, particularly minor ones, which occurred sometime in the past. Even when the recall period is reduced to only six months, it is conceivable that many incidents will not be mentioned, not because of bad faith, but simply because they were forgotten. The problem is more acute when the respondent is being asked not about his own victimization experiences but about those of other members in the family.

Telescoping. Forgetfulness is not the only memory defect that can affect the accuracy of the information. Another source of error due to memory decay is telescoping. Many victims, especially those who do not report their victimization to the police, do not record the date or the time of the incident. When asked months or weeks later about their victimization, they have to rely on their memory. The recall is subject to distortions, and one of the most frequent errors is to misplace the victimization incident in time. Researchers (Garofalo and Hindelang, 1977) distinguish between backward telescoping and forward telescoping. *Backward telescoping* is the reporting of a victimization incident as having taken place during the reference period, when in fact it occurred after the period or during the days or weeks separating the end of the period from the actual interview. The best way of overcoming this problem is to have the interviews conducted immediately or a very short time after the end of the recall period. *Forward telescoping* refers to a victimization that occurred prior to the beginning of the reference period being "telescoped" forward into that period. Such forward telescoping, Garofalo and Hindelang point out, inflates the estimated number of victimizations reported as occurring in the reference period and serves partially to offset the underestimates which result from forgetting and other biases.

Garofalo and Hindelang (1977) suggest two possible ways to solve, at least partially, the problem of telescoping: the bounding technique and the shortening of the reference period. Bounded interviews are designed to alleviate the problem of forward telescoping. This could be accomplished by providing the interviewer with a summary of the victimizations reported by the respondent in the previous interview. The interviewer could then determine whether the event is or is not the same one that was reported in the earlier period, and, if it is, the event would be excluded from the current interview record. Bounded interviews do not apply to those who are being interviewed for the first time. This type of interview allows the interviewer a great deal of discretion and may thus lead to disparities and judgment errors. Shortening the reference period is another way of reducing the amount of telescoping. The number of victimizations forgotten and those misplaced in time increases with the increasing length of the reference period and decreases with the decreasing length of the period.

Misunderstanding the questions. Accurate information can only be provided by the respondents when the purpose of the research and the questions asked are properly understood. Serious, or even mild, misunderstanding may lead to unintentional errors. As Skogan (1982) correctly points out, some respondents are better than others at comprehending the interview process, understanding the purpose of research, and cooperating with interviewers. He suggests that this may account in part for the suspiciously weak or even positive correlation between education and victimization by violence which has been reported by some surveys.

Misdefining the incident. Victimization incidents reported to the police are subject to scrutiny at various levels to ascertain that they meet the definition of the offense as specified by the law. In victimization surveys it is left to the respondent, with the help of the interviewer, to decide whether the elements required by law are present or not. The problem is particularly acute when it comes to borderline cases that are not clear-cut legal offenses. Acts that may not qualify as crimes in a legal sense may be reported, while others that do qualify may not. Victimization survey data may, therefore, contain incidents that are not really crimes but are simply perceived as such by the respondents. The reverse also happens.

A CONTROL TECHNIQUE: REVERSE RECORD CHECKS

As all these errors became known, researchers tried to devise some techniques aimed at checking the accuracy of information provided by survey respondents. One such technique is reverse record checking. In *reverse record checks*, victims in police files are sampled and subsequently interviewed. Garofalo and Hindelang (1977) point out that to achieve best results, these studies should be conducted without the interviewer or the victim being aware that the respondent has been selected for the study from police files. This condition, however, is very difficult to achieve in practice, and none of the three reverse record checks conducted by the Census Bureau in the United States attained the ideal. Reverse record checks quoted by Garofalo and Hindelang revealed that a number of confirmed victims failed to report their victimization to the interviewer. At least two reasons could account for such failure: first, there was evidence of forgetting; second, there was some indication that in face-to-face personal crimes, especially rape, victimizations committed by persons known to the victim were less likely to be mentioned to survey interviewers than were victimizations committed by strangers.

Reverse record checking, as well as other control techniques using police files, are useful methodological tools, but have no significant practical impact as they do nothing to actually improve the data. Even as a control technique, reverse record checking has its limitations since it is unsuitable for the verification of victimizations that were not reported to the police.

SOME OTHER PROBLEMS OF VICTIMIZATION SURVEYS

The problems outlined above are not the only problems of victimization surveys. There are others. O'Brien (1985) discusses some additional ones. One problem he mentions results from *interviewer effects*. Some interviewers are able to elicit a larger number of reported incidents from respondents than other interviewers. This may be due to a more probing interview style, the creation of just the right amount of rapport with the respondent, or a different interpretation of the aims of the survey by different interviewers.

Another problem outlined by O'Brien (1985) is one referred to as "panel or time in sample bias." The problem is that interviewees who have been interviewed before know that if they answer a screen question positively they will be questioned further about the incident. This leads to a tendency to report fewer victimizations to interviewers the longer the respondent has been in the panel. O'Brien suggests that there is some evidence to this effect, though the effect seems to be relatively small.

O'Brien (1985) also warns that the United States National Crime Survey crime rate estimates often involve sampling errors due to the fact that reports of some victimization types are relatively rare. He points out, for example, that "estimates for rape victimization in Philadelphia were based on only 29 actual interviews with rape victims; and in Detroit only about 150 robbery victims were interviewed in the city surveys. Such low frequencies of events are associated with relatively large confidence intervals" (p.52).

LIMITATIONS OF VICTIMIZATION SURVEYS

Victimization surveys, especially those conducted on a regular basis like the National Crime Survey in the United States, have tried to avoid, as far as possible, some of the problems discussed above. For example, surveys now use larger samples. In the United States, samples as large as sixty thousand households or more and fifteen thousand businesses have been used. While some of the earlier surveys limited inclusion in the sample to those eighteen years and over, shortly after they were conducted, the age of eligibility was lowered to twelve years. Respondents are still asked to provide information on victimization incidents they know of that involve persons under twelve years. And to avoid the problems of recall, members of the panel (the sample) are interviewed twice during the year, at six-month intervals.

Despite these improvements, victimization surveys still have some important limitations:

— They do not provide (and never will do) information on victimizations of which the victim is not aware. This excludes or seriously limits their use in some important areas of victimization such as commercial fraud and employee theft.

— Victimization surveys cannot, and are not, used to gather information on every kind of victimization. High costs and memory problems require that the survey be limited to a small number of serious offenses that can be easily remembered. Restricting the number of offenses is also necessary if the interview is to be kept within reasonable time limits. For example, it would be unthinkable to use national surveys to collect data on minor forms of victimization. Furthermore, certain types of victimization do not lend themselves to this kind of inquiry. The National Crime Survey in the United States probes individuals for only rape, robbery, assault, and personal larceny. For households, the respondents are asked to provide information on burglary, larceny, and motor vehicle theft. The main justification for the choice of these types is a practical one. They are the ones that lend themselves readily to investigation by the survey technique, as they are directed against specific victims who, in most cases, become aware that they have been victimized (which is not always the case in many corporate or white-collar victimizations). However, as Zauberman (1986) points out, it is rather debatable to choose a field of research by virtue of a technique. She suggests that a much sounder procedure is first to determine the object of study on theoretical grounds and then devise a technique appropriate to the object and not the reverse.

— It is difficult and practically impossible to include in the sample every category of victims. Even now that the eligibility age has been lowered from eighteen to twelve years, children under twelve years are not personally interviewed, and no information is obtained from them.

— Victimization survey data, like official statistics, cannot be easily used for transcultural comparisons. Differences in sampling techniques, in the method and instruments used to collect the data, and in variations in cultural and legal definitions of crime make international comparisons fraught with dangers of error.

— Victimization surveys continue to have a person bias. Reiss (1981) points out that most of the theory and much of the research on crime victimization is person-centered, although organizations are also victims.

Why Are So Many Victimizations Unreported?

One of the many advantages of victimization surveys over official crime statistics is the information they provide on the reasons why many victimization incidents, even serious ones, are not reported to the police. The NORC survey asked those people who reported victimization, but did not notify the police, for their reasons. The reasons given fell into four fairly distinct categories (Ennis, 1967a, 1967b):

1. Thirty-four percent of those who did not report their victimization to the police failed to do so due to their belief that the incident was not a police matter. They did not want the offender to suffer or to be harmed by the police, or they simply thought that the incident was a private and not a criminal affair. Typical examples in this category were offenses committed by one family member against another or those between friends.
2. Two percent of the nonreporting victims feared reprisal, either physically from the offender, his family and friends, or both, or economically from cancellation of, or increases in, their insurance premiums.
3. Nine percent of those who failed to report did not want to take the time or the trouble to get involved with the police, did not know whether they should call the police, or were too confused to do so. Here it is worth noting that several studies in the United States have shown that members of certain minority groups are usually unwilling to get involved with the police even as victims or witnesses.
4. More than half of the nonreporting victims failed to notify the authorities because of skepticism as to the effectiveness of police action. Victims in this category believed that the police could do nothing about the incident, would not catch the offender(s), or would not want to be bothered. In short, they failed to report because of a negative attitude toward the police. This finding is of particular importance since it shows that an increase in police efficiency and an improvement in public attitudes toward the police are likely to result in more reporting and in a lower dark figure.

Victims in the British Crime Survey (Hough and Mayhew, 1983) were also asked why the police were not notified. The reasons mentioned most frequently were that the incidents involved no loss or damage, or they were regarded as trivial (particularly true, for example, for thefts from motor vehicles). These reasons were given in 38 percent of personal victimizations and 49 percent of household victimizations. A further important reason for not reporting was the belief (probably realistic) that the police would not have been able to do anything; this applied to many instances of vandalism, for example. This reason was offered by 16 percent of respondents in personal victimizations and 34 percent in household victimizations. The next most frequent reason given was "inappropriate for police; dealt with matter ourselves": 13 percent in personal victimizations and 5 percent in household victimizations. Other reasons (dislike of the police, fear of reprisals, inconvenience) were only rarely mentioned.

The Canadian Urban Victimization Survey (Canada, 1983-1988) found that females had a higher reporting rate than males for sexual assault, robbery, and assault. Generally speaking, those sixty-five and over were also more likely to report incidents than were younger victims. When the reasons for not reporting were checked, the most common was that the incident was "too minor." This reason was given in two-thirds of the incidents in which no report was made. Other major reasons for nonreporting were as follows: the police could do nothing about it anyway (61 percent); it was too inconvenient to make a report, or the victims did not want to take the time (24 percent). The pattern of reasons given by sexual assault victims varied from the average in some respects. The most common reason given by sexual assault victims was the police could not do anything about it (52 percent). This was closely followed by 43 percent who cited concern about the attitude of police or courts toward this type of incident. This reason was given by only 8 percent of all victims. Fear of revenge by the offender was another common reason for nonreporting among victims of sexual assault (33 percent), whereas this reason was given by 4 percent of all victims. For female victims of nonsexual assault, fear of revenge by the offender was mentioned by 21 percent of those who failed to report the incident.

Summary

Though quite useful for many administrative purposes, criminal statistics are not, and will never be, accurate measures of the state of crime. They suffer from several shortcomings due to, in part, problems inherent in the methods used to collect, compile, and process them. Their accuracy, and, consequently, their utility are further lessened by the existence of the *dark figure*. In an attempt to get a better idea of the true state of crime, researchers have devised two new research techniques: hidden-delinquency studies, also called studies of self-reported delinquency, and victimization surveys. When carefully conducted, victimization surveys can yield data on crime that are superior in some respects to official statistics, but they are not problem free. Among the major problems of these surveys are the ones having to do with the sample, the costs, and the interview technique itself. It is difficult to come up with a truly representative sample of a reasonable size, to reach all members of the sample, and to persuade them to cooperate in the survey. The costs of large victimization surveys, particularly national ones, can be prohibitive, and this explains why they have not been conducted on a regular basis except in a few countries such as the United States. Researchers have used three interview methods: the mail questionnaire, the personal interview, and the telephone interview. Canada has opted for the latter method. Each of these methods has its advantages as well as its limitations and shortcomings.

There are several sources of error in victimization surveys. Some of the errors are deliberate, such as lying and not telling. Other errors are not deliberate, such as not knowing, forgetting, and forward and backward telescoping (misplacing the victimization incident in time and thus including or excluding incidents that have taken place outside of the time period covered by the survey). Additional errors may result from misunderstanding the question posed by the interviewer, misdefining the incident, and so forth.

In recent years, researchers have tried to develop various techniques to deal with the most serious and most common problems and sources of error. Despite this, and despite considerable improvements in the techniques, victimization surveys do still have serious limitations. For example, they are not suitable for exploring certain types or certain areas of victimization. They have to be limited to those victimizations that lend themselves well to the survey technique, which leads to the exclusion of several categories of victims. They cannot be easily used for transcultural comparisons, and they continue to have a person bias.

Victimization surveys have revealed that a very large number of victimizations go unreported, and they have shed light on the reasons why many victims do not report their victimizations to the police. Among the most common reasons is the belief that the incident is minor, that it is not a police matter (because of the relationship between the victim and victimizer), and that the police would not be able to do anything to find and arrest the culprit, recover the stolen goods, and so forth. There are added reasons that hinder or prevent victims of sex offenses from reporting them to the police, such as concern about the attitude of police or courts toward this type of incident and fear of revenge by the offender.

THREE

Extent and Patterns of Criminal Victimization

Crime does not occur randomly in time nor evenly during all times of the day and night. Nor does it occur with the same probability during all days of the week. Rather, it has been known for some time that there are times and places when crimes of common theft and assault are unusually frequent. Data from the British Crime Survey reveal this dramatically.

Michael R. Gottfredson (1984, p.4)

Incidence, Prevalence, and Risks of Criminal Victimization

THE INDICATORS

The volume and frequency of criminal victimization may be assessed using different indicators. The two most common indicators are *figures* and *rates*. Figures are indicators of the *incidence* of victimization. Rates are indicators of the *prevalence* of victimization. Figures tell us how many incidents of victimization were reported to the police or to survey interviewers in a given area, city, or region during a given period of time. For example, they indicate how many burglaries, robberies, or motor vehicle thefts were reported for Toronto or Vancouver in 1989. These incident counts do not tell us by themselves how prevalent these victimizations are unless they are related to the size of the population, number of households, registered motor vehicles, or whatever denominator we may decide to choose to calculate the rate. Saying that the rate of robbery is so many per 100,000 inhabitants or that the rate of car theft is so many per 1,000, 10,000, or 100,000 registered motor vehicles tells us more about the frequency of victimization than does the number of incidents. It tells us how prevalent this or that type of victimization is. Despite their usefulness, these two indicators are not perfect, and their imperfections need to be constantly kept in mind when examining the extent and volume of criminal victimization. Two facts should be remembered: first, that the figures produced by victimization surveys are just estimates and thus are subject to error; second, that the rates may be misleading due to the skewness of the distribution of criminal victimization.

1. **Figures are estimates**. Victimization surveys, even national ones, do not measure the incidence of criminal victimization for the whole population. They measure the amount of victimization to which members of the sample were subjected during the reference period. These victimizations are then extrapolated into estimates of the incidence of victimization for the total population. Figures quoted for the country as a whole (or for a given geographical area) are therefore estimates, no more, no less. Like any other estimates they are not error free. The margin of error varies according to a number of factors related to the sample (such as size or representativeness) and to the methodology used. The three following examples illustrate what we mean by "margin of error." The British Crime Survey's "best estimate" of the number of burglaries in 1981 is 726,000, but the figure could fall between 602,000 and 856,000 (Hough and Mayhew, 1983). The 1988 British Crime Survey's best estimate of the number of incidents of burglary in 1987 is 1,180,000; with 95 percent certainty the number falls between 1,334,000 and 1,025,000 (Mayhew, Elliott, and Dowds, 1989). The British Crime Survey

Scotland (Chambers and Tombs, 1984) estimated that during the year 1981, 256,000 households experienced criminal damage. The actual number, however, could vary between 206,000 and 308,000.

2. **Rates can be misleading.** Rates of victimization computed for populations of ten thousand or one hundred thousand are meant to give us an idea about the prevalence of victimization. If, for example, we say that the rate for a given type of victimization is 50 per 10,000 population, what we mean is that in every ten thousand members of the population, fifty will likely suffer this type of victimization. But victimization is not evenly distributed within the general population. On the contrary it is extremely skewed. What this means is that while most people do not suffer any victimization, and while some suffer one or two incidents, a tiny minority is repeatedly victimized. Multiple victimization (see Chapter 12) makes the victimization rate (so many victimizations per 1,000, 10,000 persons or households) highly misleading as an indicator of the *risk* of victimization (Sparks, 1981). As Sparks points out, since all of a multiple victim's incidents are counted in the numerator of such a rate, but he or she is counted only once in the denominator, the resulting rate greatly overstates the risk of victimization for the population; at the same time, of course, it grossly understates the risk confronting the unfortunate minority.

SOME GENERAL RULES GOVERNING THE FREQUENCY AND VISIBILITY OF CRIMINAL VICTIMIZATION

Like other social phenomena, criminal victimization is governed by certain rules that determine its occurrence and its visibility. The following four rules apply to most types of victimization.

1. **The more serious the victimization is, the less frequently it takes place.** The most serious types of victimization occur less frequently than less serious ones. Violent victimization is commonly regarded as more serious than other types and crimes of violence are therefore much smaller in number than such offenses as property offenses and traffic offenses. The incidence of individual offenses also shows that increasing seriousness goes hand in hand with decreasing frequency. Murder is less frequent than manslaughter. The latter is less frequent than aggravated assault. Aggravated assault is less frequent than simple assault. Assault with injury is less frequent than assault without injury, and so on. The same rule applies as well to property crime: robbery is less frequent than burglary, burglary is less frequent than theft, and so forth. Naturally, some victimizations may be rare not because they are too serious, but because the circumstances in which they occur are not common.
2. **The more serious the victimization is, the more likely it will be reported.** Homicides have a higher reporting rate (and consequently a lower dark figure)

than assaults. Robberies resulting in injuries have a greater chance of being reported than the ones not involving injuries. Burglaries (and thefts) resulting in the loss of substantial amounts of money or valuable goods will be reported with a greater frequency than the ones involving petty cash. Except for very special cases (for example, when both victim and victimizer are involved in illegal activities and the victimization is in direct relation to those activities), we can assume that the nonreported incidents of victimization are of a less serious nature than the reported ones. This rule also means that a completed offense is much more likely to be reported than a mere attempt. Burglary is reported more frequently than attempted burglary, rape is reported more frequently than attempted rape, and so forth.

Empirical support for this general rule comes from victimization surveys. The NORC study in the United States revealed that 65 percent of the aggravated assaults in the sample were reported to the police, compared to only 46 percent of the simple assaults. Sixty percent of the grand larcenies were reported to the police compared to only 37 percent of the petty larcenies.

There are, however, exceptions to this general rule. Specific factors, other than the seriousness of the victimization, may be responsible for an underreporting of a serious crime or for a high rate of reporting of an offense not considered too serious. Although rape (aggravated sexual assault) is a very serious victimization, many incidents are, or at least used to be, unreported. The psychological trauma of the act, the interrogation, the trial, and the fear of social stigmatization prevent many victims from reporting to the police. Motor vehicle theft, on the other hand, is less serious than many other offenses in the criminal code, and yet it has one of the lowest dark figures and one of the highest reporting rates. The need to get the police to search for the vehicle and to recover the insurance if it is not found act as strong incentives to reporting.

3. **The larger the social distance between victim and victimizer is, the higher is the likelihood that the victimization will be reported**. Victimization reporting rates rise with increasing social distance and fall the closer the victim and victimizer are to each other personally and socially. The closer the personal relationship between the parties, the lower is the probability that the victimization will be reported to the authorities. It follows that victimizations of equal seriousness have a greater chance of being brought to the attention of the police when caused by strangers than when caused by intimates or friends. Victimization by relatives, friends, and other close associates has, therefore, a lower visibility than victimization by strangers or casual acquaintances.

4. **Criminal victimization declines with advancing age**. After peaking during the teens and late teens, delinquency and crime decline with advancing age. The same is true of criminal victimization. Victimization surveys of the last two decades have amply demonstrated that with one or two exceptions (see Chapter 5) criminal victimization, like criminality, declines with advancing

age. Older individuals are much less likely to commit crimes and much less likely to be criminally victimized than more youthful individuals. This negative age-crime and age-victimization relationship seems to be invariant across sex, race, and culture.

This rule has great significance for the rates of victimization (and crime) in North America and other western countries because of the changing age structure of the population. A decrease in the number of births coupled with increased longevity have led to a disproportionate increase in the size of the upper age groups in the general population, and the trend is continuing. In other words, the population of North America and of most other western societies is aging. With this aging of the population we can expect some reduction or a leveling off in crime and criminal victimization in coming years unless, of course, some other conditions or factors act to push these rates upwards.

SOME GENERAL ASPECTS OF THE PHENOMENON OF CRIMINAL VICTIMIZATION

The Rarity of Criminal Victimization

The biased and sensational reporting by the media may create the impression that crime is rampant and that violent victimization is a very common occurrence and may thus incite people to fear for their lives and safety. The real picture, however, is very different from this portrayal, and empirical evidence from all western countries, including the United States where victimization rates are relatively high, tells us that the opposite is true. Actually, criminal victimization is an extremely rare event, and crimes of interpersonal violence are extremely uncommon (Sparks, 1981). As we will see, the true extent of criminal victimization can be better understood when the risks of this victimization are placed in perspective.

The Uneven Distribution of Criminal Victimization Within the General Population

Even before victimization surveys were conducted, at a stage when our knowledge of the victim population was very rudimentary, some criminologists (Wilkins, 1964) insisted that victims of crime do not constitute an unbiased cross section of the population and that the risks of victimization are not evenly distributed within the general population. Data collected by means of victimization surveys provided empirical support for this intuitive observation. Sparks (1982) points out that there is abundant evidence that criminal victimization is not uniformly or randomly distributed among individuals within the population as a whole, and there is some evidence that it is not randomly distributed among any easily definable subgroup of the population.

The Uneven Distribution of Criminal Victimization in Time and Space

Criminal victimization is not evenly nor randomly distributed in time and space. The frequency of certain types of victimization varies according to season, day of the week, and hour of the day. As we will see, certain times are more dangerous than others. Violent victimization, for example, occurs with greater frequency during the weekend and in the night hours. Unevenness is equally true of the spatial distribution of criminal victimization. Rates of victimization vary greatly between urban and rural areas, between regions, cities, towns, and so forth. The distribution is also skewed within the city itself, with certain areas having higher rates of victimization than others. And while certain types of victimization may occur more frequently within the home, others take place predominantly outside people's residences. Even within the home, certain rooms such as the bedroom or the kitchen may be the scenes of victimization more frequently than others.

Criminal Victimization is Less Injurious Than Other Victimizations

When compared with many other risks to which we are daily exposed in the modern, technological society in which we live, criminal victimization proves to be less injurious than other types of victimization (see Chapter 1).

In the United States, Sparks (1981) observed that "as a cause of *injury*, crimes of violence are much less important than motor vehicle accidents, industrial injuries, falls in the home, and the other natural shocks that flesh is heir to in western industrial societies" (p. 17).

Most Criminal Victimization is Actually Trivial in Consequence

With the exception of very few and rare types (such as murder, rape, or serious injuries) most victimizations, even the ones usually called serious, are actually trivial in nature, as well as consequence. That is why they are easily forgotten. One of the major problems of victimization surveys, which by their very nature rely on the memory of the respondents, is the problem of forgetting. Even when the recall period is shortened to six months, the interviewers have to work hard to get the respondents to remember what victimization they have suffered (see Chapter 2).

It is also the trivial nature of criminal victimization that accounts for the extremely low reporting rates characteristic of most offenses. Even fairly serious personal crimes—such as household burglary and personal robbery—are said in most surveys to be reported to the police less than one time in two (Sparks, 1981). The most common reason given in the British Survey (Hough and Mayhew, 1983) for not notifying the police was that the victimization was too trivial.

While noting that the impact of crime may be less palatable than the impact of other types of victimization, Hough and Mayhew (1983) affirm that in quantitative terms at least, becoming a victim of robbery, wounding, car theft, or burglary is less likely to upset the course of people's lives than the other misfortunes they compared with criminal victimization. They add that although the risks of falling victim to these crimes are small, the chances of suffering a more trivial type of victimization are rather high. Thus, the average person can expect to be the victim of some sort of theft or vandalism once every three years. In other words, "crime," broadly defined, intrudes into very many people's lives each year. However, this intrusion, Hough and Mayhew point out, is best characterized, at least in the vast majority of cases, not as a catastrophe but as a minor upset.

PLACING CRIMINAL VICTIMIZATION RISKS IN PERSPECTIVE

Victimization rates, whether based on official statistics or on the findings of victimization surveys, are meant to convey some idea about the risks we run of being criminally victimized. But the way they are now tabulated tells us little about those risks. The most they can tell us, in their current form, is that the risk of having our motor vehicle stolen is, for example, so many times higher than the risk of being robbed; or that our risk of being killed is so many times lower than the risk of being assaulted, and so on.[1] The annual rates do not place the risks of criminal victimization in perspective since they do not relate them to any variable other than the size of the general population. Computing rates in this simplistic way does not provide an accurate, or even a crude, indication of what the risks of victimization really are. This is because there are marked differences in victimization probabilities. The likelihood of victimization varies greatly by characteristics of persons and by number of available opportunities as it varies in time and space. Risk-related victimization rates are therefore far superior to population-based ones as indicators of the probability of victimization. As Boggs (1965), in her seminal work, correctly points out, a valid rate should form a probability statement and therefore should be based on the risk or target group appropriate for each specific victimization category. For example, rather than calculating residential burglary rates on the basis of population, they should be based on the number of occupied housing units. Skogan (1976) follows the same line when he suggests that the most meaningful crime statistics are those which are related to the number of potential opportunities for victimization in a jurisdiction. Skogan supports his argument by showing the extreme variations in auto-theft rates for New York and Los Angeles when compared on different denominators. He reports that auto thefts per 1,000 population were twelve in New York and twenty in Los Angeles, whereas auto thefts per 1,000 vehicles were fifty-three in New York and only thirty-four in Los Angeles.

Sparks (1981) deplores the fact that the National Crime Survey in the United States collects so little information relevant to the risk of victimization. Sparks (1981) writes:

> *The risk of becoming a victim of crime is, like all risks, conditional; that is, it reflects the probability of being victimized in some time period, given not only demographic attributes such as age and sex but also a particular lifestyle, certain social relations, a certain stock of stealable wealth, particular protective and policing arrangements, and so on. Without data on such risk-determining variables, we cannot make sense of observed victimization rates; we cannot say even if they are in some sense "low" or "high." Nor can we interpret changes in observed victimization rates, unless we know how far other things have changed as well. (p.47)*

ALTERNATIVE WAYS OF CALCULATING AND PRESENTING THE RISKS OF CRIMINAL VICTIMIZATION

A proper calculation and presentation of victimization risks is not only necessary for research and planning, but is also needed for other purposes. Potential victims' perception of risk can be very different when the risk of a particular type of victimization is related not to the general population (as is the practice at present) but to relatively specific populations or to environmental opportunities. In other words, to be meaningful, criminal victimization risks have to be related to at least the fundamental variables that affect them. The situation is the same for any other risk. The risk of being involved in a car accident depends, among other things, on the amount of driving people do. Thus, a realistic assessment of such risk requires that it be related to this particular variable. We may ask, for example, whether the low accident rate for the over-sixty-five age group is due to more careful driving or to a lower mileage. And to be able to compare their accident risks to those of other age groups we have to take into account the difference in the amount of driving.

Calculating meaningful risks of criminal victimization is not very different. Because the number of licensed motor vehicles is far lower than that of the population, rates (and risks) of motor vehicle theft can be very different when calculated on the basis of one or the other. Where the law defines rape as a crime that can only be committed against women, calculating the risks on the basis of the total population, rather than the female population only, automatically cuts those risks in half. Even when the rates are calculated using the number of females as the denominator, the result is misleading because rape victimization is concentrated in the youthful age groups. Women who belong to these age groups run a much higher risk of victimization than very young or very old females. Thus, calculating the differential rates for various age groups (and many variables other than age could be used) would render the risks more realistic and therefore more meaningful for theoretical as well as for practical purposes.

In an attempt to place victimization risks in a proper perspective, researchers in England and the United States have devised some interesting ways of calculating and presenting the risks of some types of criminal victimization. The picture that emerges from these objective estimates is drastically different from the alarming one generally transmitted by the mass media or by law enforcement authorities in their relentless pursuit of higher budgets and more manpower.

Clarke (1981) quotes calculations in Britain indicating that at present levels of risk, the average householder can expect to be burgled once every thirty years (much longer than the average tenancy) and that the average car owner will have his or her car taken only once every fifty years, which is longer than a car owner is likely to be motoring. The risk of a person falling victim to homicide in any one year (one in 100,000) was found to be a small fraction of the risks of being killed on the road or dying of cancer. Only one in 175,000 passenger journeys on the London underground resulted in theft, while one in 8.4 million resulted in robbery. Clarke notes that these risks are not evenly spread and, in fact, the chances of falling victim to crime are quite highly correlated with the chances of being an offender.

In another study, Hough and Mayhew (1983) used the findings of the 1981 British Crime Survey to estimate the various risks of victimization for an average British citizen. They report that, assuming the rates remain at 1981 levels, the survey shows that a "statistically average" person aged sixteen or over can expect the following:

—A robbery (not attempts) once every five centuries.

—An assault resulting in injury (even if slight) once every century.

—The family car to be stolen or taken by joyriders once every sixty years.

—A burglary in the home once every forty years.

Hough and Mayhew (1983) admit that it is somewhat artificial to express the risks in this way since different types of people face very different risks. They argue, however, that nevertheless, the device shows that the risks of these fairly serious crimes are small ones. Thus the "average" person can, for example, expect to be the victim of a burglary or car theft once or twice in his or her adult life, while the chances of being injured in an assault are very much smaller, and the risks of robbery are smaller still.

Hough and Mayhew (1983) compared some risks of victimization to the likelihood of encountering other sorts of mishaps. The chances of burglary were found to be slightly less than the chances (as estimated by questions to British Crime Survey respondents) of a fire in the home. The chances a household runs of car theft turned out to be smaller than the chances (again, as estimated from the British Crime Survey) it runs of having one of its members injured in a traffic accident. The chances of robbery were smaller than those of being admitted to hospital as a psychiatric patient.

In the United States, Sparks (1981) used the 1977 National Crime Survey victimization data to give some indication of how rare violent victimization is and how low the risks of falling victim to violent crime are. The 1977 data revealed that crimes of violence, including robbery, occurred at a rate of 33.9 victimizations per 1,000 persons aged twelve and over. About three-quarters of these incidents involved attempts only and did not result in any physical injury. To take into account the undercounting of such incidents in the National Crime Survey, Sparks arbitrarily doubled the published rate while pointing out at the same time that most of the incidents not mentioned to the interviewers would certainly be of the less serious kind. He concluded that, despite his doubling of the rate, such crimes are still rare. A rate per 1,000 persons per year reflects 365,000 person-days of exposure to risk. Thus, double the published National Crime Survey rate is roughly equivalent to one incident of "violent" victimization per 5,400 such days, with cases involving actual injury probably occurring about once per 25,000 person-days, that is, 68.5 years.

ABSOLUTE AND RELATIVE RISKS OF VICTIMIZATION

Smith (1986) argues that much of the risk of victimization is related to life-style, and that such risk is not only inevitable but also acceptable in so far as it is contingent on generally desirable social processes that work to increase the range and availability of opportunities for social interaction. She suggests that the risks of victimization associated with contemporary trends in urban life-styles be termed *absolute* risks, in that they represent a minimum level of risk incurred when people routinely participate in modern society. To these absolute risks she contrasts what she calls *relative* risks, which are risks of victimization that are above the base level set by life-style. This added vulnerability is also distributed nonrandomly, and it augurs less favorably for the quality of life of those it affects. Smith argues that relative risks tend to be highest in deprived working-class areas and that it is relative exposure to risk that crime-prevention policies ought to target and might realistically seek to reduce. Smith adds that increases in absolute risks reflect the increased opportunities for socializing, which are a valued outcome of contemporary economic and political trends. Relative risks, on the other hand, reflect less desirable processes underlying the unequal distribution of wealth and life chances that produce socioeconomic disadvantage. This leads her to suggest that an equitable distribution of the risks of victimization, rather than a massive reduction of national crime rates, may be the most just and realistic goal for crime-control strategies in Britain.

There is great merit in this innovative way of looking at the risks of victimization, particularly the distinction between acceptable and unacceptable risks.

This is a particularly promising area for research, and, as mentioned earlier, we still have a long way to go before we are able to devise the most meaningful ways of calculating the true risks of criminal victimization.

DIFFERENTIAL RISKS OF VICTIMIZATION

All that we have said above indicates that criminal victimization is not a random occurrence and is not evenly distributed within the general population. Certain sociodemographic variables are associated with high/low victimization rates. As a result, some groups are more frequently victimized, by one type of crime or another, than other groups. Conversely, certain segments of the general population incur much less victimization than others. The risk of becoming a victim of crime, in other words, is not equal for each member of the general public. The differences between the various segments of the population seem to be more pronounced in regard to violent victimization than they are in regard to property offenses.

Murder as a Case Study for Differential Risks

The insurance industry has, for a long time, calculated the differential risks of death for various groups and has relied on these calculations in setting the insurance premiums. Actuarial risk tables used provide estimates of probabilities of death by different causes, such as accidents, suicide, heart attacks, and cancer, for specific population groups. Recently in the United States, an attempt was made to calculate the risks of being murdered using two variables: sex and race. Both the Federal Bureau of Investigation (FBI) and the Bureau of Justice Statistics (BJS) used statistics compiled by the National Center for Health Statistics to estimate the risks of becoming a victim of criminal homicide for a single year as well as for a lifetime. The lifetime risk of homicide was possible to calculate because homicide is unique among violent crimes since, by definition, it can only happen once in a person's lifetime. Estimates of the lifetime risk of rape, robbery, and assault could not be calculated as the necessary information was not available. Calculation of these lifetime risks requires detailed data specifying the age at which the victim was first victimized in his or her lifetime.

Table 3-1 gives the estimates of the lifetime risk of becoming a victim of criminal homicide in the United States as calculated by the Bureau of Justice Statistics and the FBI. The difference in the estimates is probably due to the data used. It seems that the FBI analysis was based on averaged murder victimization data for 1978 to 1980, while the Bureau of Justice Statistics (BJS) used homicide statistics for 1980, the year in which the prevalence of homicide reached its highest level.

TABLE 3-1 **Estimates of Lifetime Risk of Becoming a Victim of Homicide in the United States**

Bureau of Justice Statistics Estimates:	1 out of	Federal Bureau of Investigation Estimates:	1 out of
U.S. total	133	U.S. total	153
Male	84	Male	100
White	131	White	164
Black	21	Black	28
Female	282	Female	323
White	369	White	450
Black	104	Black	117

Source: United States Department of Justice, Bureau of Justice Statistics. *The Risk of Violent Crime—Special Report*, (Washington, D.C.: Superintendent of Documents, May 1985), 2.

Despite slight differences in the estimates of the two agencies, the pattern they reveal is identical. Both show a much higher risk for males of both races than for females and a much lower risk for whites (male and female) than for blacks. The odds for an American black male of being murdered (1:21 or 1:28) are about six times greater than those confronting white men (1:131 or 1:164). Black males run the highest risk of all with the chances being that about one in twenty will become a homicide victim during his lifetime. The same risk for a white female is one in 369! The importance of race as a risk variable can be clearly seen from comparing black females with white males. The probability for one of the former being murdered during her lifetime is one in 104, higher than that for an American white male, which is one in 131.

Other Risk Estimates

One of the rare studies that attempted to quantify, analyze, and compare victimization risks is one conducted in the Netherlands in the late seventies (Steinmetz, 1979). With the help of a log-linear model, the victimization risks of the various Dutch population groups were quantified in a simple way. The findings confirmed that there are enormous differences in the probabilities of becoming a victim. The youngest male respondents from the highest social class living in municipalities of 100,000 or more inhabitants had a victimization risk fifteen times as much as elderly women living in rural areas. A particularly high-risk group consisted of respondents between twenty-seven and forty years old who were living in the three big cities. For the Dutch population as a whole, the average chance of becoming a victim was equal to 1/5.15, meaning that one in six Dutch persons was a victim in 1977.

CRIMINAL VICTIMIZATION TRENDS

Canadian victimization survey data do not allow for a trend analysis. The 1982 Canadian Urban Victimization Survey collected data in seven major urban centers, whereas the 1988 Statistics Canada General Social Survey (GSS) gathered information in all ten provinces and covered both urban and rural areas. In contrast, the United States National Crime Survey and the British Crime Survey, because of their continuity, make it possible to examine and compare victimization rates over a given period of time.

In Britain, victimization figures for 1987, uncovered by the 1988 survey (Mayhew, Elliott, and Dowds, 1989), were higher than the last survey's figures for 1983, though the rate of increase (21 percent) was not quite as rapid as that of recorded crime, which registered a 26 percent increase during the same period. Compared to 1981 figures from the first survey, the British Crime Survey increase in crime (30 percent) was lower than recorded crime (41 percent)—a statistically significant difference (Mayhew et al., 1989). Mayhew et al. point out that this reflects a general increase in reporting to the police. Of British Crime Survey offenses comparable with police statistics coverage, 41 percent were reported in 1987 as against 36 percent in 1981. As may be expected, the rate of increase varied by type of offense. Offenses that have risen more according to British Crime Survey estimates than is shown in police estimates include bicycle theft, motor vehicle theft, and burglary. Violent crime (woundings, robberies, and common assaults), according to the most comprehensive British Crime Survey estimate, showed a relatively modest increase of 8 percent since 1981. Mayhew et al. (1989) suggest that the rise in burglary according to British Crime Survey estimates is due principally to an increase in attempted offenses, which may indicate that better security is making entry harder for burglars. A drop in reporting may partly explain the divergence between British Crime Survey estimates and police statistics. There might also have been some recording change that would account for another part of the difference.

The findings of Mayhew, Elliott, and Dowds (1989) indicate that victimization trends can be very different when measured using victimization survey data as opposed to official crime statistics. Burglaries with loss are a good case in point. For example, the British Crime Survey and a General Household Survey combined indicate an increase in burglaries from 1972 to 1987 of approximately 20 percent, as opposed to the approximately 125 percent in police statistics. It is not easy to explain such a huge difference. When properly conducted, victimization surveys are supposed to reflect only actual changes occurring in the incidence of victimizations they measure. Police statistics, on the other hand, are subject to wide fluctuations in reporting rates resulting from several factors other than a change in the frequency of victimization. It is possible, therefore, that burglaries had been grossly underreported to the police in 1972 and that there has been a greater tendency to report them in recent years.

In the United States in June 1989, the Bureau of Justice Statistics reported that there was no measurable difference between 1987 and 1988 in the percentage of households touched by any of the victimizations measured. The Bureau added that the percentage of all households touched by crime had never shown a year-to-year increase since the inception of the indicator in 1975. The period 1975 to 1985 was one of decreasing victimization. Since 1985 the percentage remained unchanged. The lack of change, however, masks differing trends for urban and rural households and for white and black households. Thus, since 1986, the percentage of urban households victimized has risen from 28 percent to 30 percent, while that for rural households has fallen from 20 percent to 18 percent. White households have become less vulnerable to crime since 1985, while black households have become more vulnerable. The overall difference in the trends for white and black households was caused primarily by differences in the trends for the crime of theft.

Too many factors may be responsible for the fact that victimizations measured by the National Crime Survey decreased from 1975 to 1985. Among the most likely reasons are the demographic changes during that ten-year period, namely the coming of age of the children of the baby boom, which followed World War II.

Temporal Patterns of Criminal Victimization

CRIMINAL VICTIMIZATION AND SEASONALITY

Early criminologists, such as Guerry, Quetelet, Ferri, Aschaffenburg, Parmelee, and many others, firmly believed that the social phenomenon of criminal victimization was subject to the influence of the natural climate and to the seasonal changes in the temperature. Quetelet (1842) for example, discovered that variations in temperature have a well-marked influence in augmenting and diminishing the number of crimes. On the basis of these observations, he formulated what may be viewed as a thermic law of crime. According to this law, crimes against the person reach their peak during the hot months, while those against property reach their maximum in the winter (Quetelet, 1842):

> *The epoch of maximum (June) in respect to the number of crimes against persons, coincides pretty nearly with the epoch of minimum in respect to crimes against property, and this takes place in summer, whilst, on the contrary, the minimum of the number of crimes against persons, and the maximum of the number of crimes against property, takes place in winter. (p.35)*

Quetelet's explanation of these seasonal differences is that in winter, misery and want are more especially felt and cause an increase in the number of crimes against property, whilst the violence of the passions predominating in summer excites people to more frequent personal confrontations. Furthermore, Quetelet observed that crimes against the person are more frequent in warmer regions, that is, southern regions, than they are in the colder regions in the north, while the reverse holds true for crimes against property.

Almost a century later, Parmelee (1926) insisted that excessive heat, and especially a change from a moderate to a hot temperature, stimulates the emotions and tends to increase irritability, thus leading to acts of violence. This fact, he suggests, explains why crimes against the person are almost always more numerous in hot climates than they are in cold climates and more numerous in the warm seasons than they are in the cold seasons. To the heat factor, Parmelee adds an opportunity factor, noting that in warm temperatures more people go outdoors where there are more opportunities for many crimes against the person, such as assault and rape. He goes on to explain that, on the contrary, crimes against property tend to increase as the temperature falls. He attributes this, in part, to the direct effect of the cold in stimulating the activity needed for many of the crimes against property, although he feels that in this case the influence of the temperature probably is more indirect than direct. He adds that with a warmer temperature there is usually a more abundant food supply, less need for clothing and shelter, and sometimes more employment, while the long nights of winter offer more opportunities for certain crimes against property, such as burglary and robbery.

These early explanations of the relationship between the climate and crime rates were perceptive and insightful. And although the later ones stressed the role of opportunity in crime causation, they were still perceived as part of the physical and biological explanations of crime.

Sociological explanations, which dominated modern criminology, were bound to lead to a decline of interest in such relationships. The growing popularity of environmental and ecological criminology renewed the interest in exploring whatever influence the weather, the climate, and the seasons might have on the incidence of various types of offenses.

Some Recent Studies of Seasonality

Wolfgang (1958) reports that the monthly distribution of criminal homicides in Philadelphia for each of the years from 1948 to 1952 shows a considerable amount of capricious oscillation and no consistent pattern. The situation was different when Wolfgang analyzed the data using a seasonal rather than a monthly distribution. Using a winter, spring-autumn, and summer trichotomy for the twelve months, he noted that more homicides occur during the hot months of May, June, July, and August (36 percent); followed closely by the relatively warm spring and autumn months of March, April, September, and October (35 percent); while the lowest frequency is in the winter months of January, February, November, and December (28 percent). He concluded that there is a slight but insignificant association between seasons and the number of criminal homicides.

One of the reasons why Wolfgang failed to observe a significant association may be the heterogeneous nature of criminal homicide. A study of murder for robbery in Austria (Fattah, 1967; Fattah, 1971), suggests that homicides motivated by financial gain likely follow a seasonal pattern similar to property crimes, reaching their peak in the cold rather than the hot season. If this is true, then this might be responsible for the lack of clear seasonal patterns in studies that do not separate robbery homicides from other homicides. Further evidence of seasonality, quoted by Wolfgang (1958), appears in the Uniform Crime Reports for 1950:

> *The effect of the seasons on the volume of crime is clearly indicated in the data presented ... It is apparent that felonious assaults and murder occur with greatest frequency during the summer months and that crimes against property as a group show a tendency to increase in frequency during the winter ... Murders, rapes and assaults during the peak summer months exceeded by approximately one-third the frequency of such crimes during the low months in the cooler seasons. (p. 101)*

McPheters and Stronge (1973) tested for seasonality in reported crime data using FBI index crimes in Miami, Florida, from 1949 to 1970. They concluded that a definite seasonal pattern in Miami crime data does exist, although its importance seems to be declining in recent years. The authors point out that there was a relative absence of seasonality in "crimes of passion," that is murder, rape, and aggravated assault. Economic crimes, on the other hand, appeared to be subject to seasonal variation. Generally, these crimes were higher in the six months of October through March and lower in the months of April through September. The observed seasonal variation, they suggest, is quite large, although it has diminished greatly during the 1960s. Robberies, for example, were usually inflated by about 25 percent in December due to seasonal influences. Moreover, all economic crimes in January were usually over 10 percent above the annual average. On the other hand, these same crimes were usually over 10 percent below the annual average in May. The value of the findings of this particular study and the generalizations that can be made from them are extremely limited, not only because the study used recorded crime data but also, above all, because it was limited to just one area, Miami, which is an area that has been, for many years, a favorite tourist destination. The influx of tourists during a specific period of the year might seriously affect the seasonal distribution of several types of victimization.

In 1980 (United States), the United States Bureau of Justice Statistics published an exploratory study of seasonal patterns for selected crimes included in the National Crime Survey. Contrary to the studies cited above, this one was the first attempt to describe seasonal variations in crime based on data from a large-scale nationwide sample survey. Interestingly, the seasonal patterns revealed by this study are at odds with (and sometimes the opposite of) those that have been accepted for so long in criminology as part of the conventional wisdom. Naturally, there is no reason to believe that seasonal variations in the rates of victimization are universal or that they are static and undergo no change over time. Actually, if the climate exercises its influence on crime not through physiological and mood changes, as earlier believed, but through an increase/decrease in social interaction (crimes of violence) and opportunities (property crime), then we can expect substantial changes over the years due to variations in the opportunity structure and in the volume of social interaction. It is not surprising, therefore, to see that the patterns observed in the 1980 study are different from those observed in nineteenth century Europe or in the United States in the first half of the twentieth century. The principal findings of the Bureau of Justice Statistics study are as follows:

— Seasonal influences were particularly evident in the crimes of household larceny, personal larceny of less than fifty dollars, and unlawful-entry burglary. Other crimes with less pronounced seasonal patterns were personal larceny of fifty dollars or more, forcible-entry burglary, assault, and motor vehicle theft. Personal robbery showed no evidence of seasonality.

— With one exception, these crimes peaked in the summer months and reached their lowest levels in winter. The exception was personal larceny under fifty dollars, which registered its highest point in October and dropped to lows in the summer.

These findings from the National Crime Survey data covering incidents occurring in the years 1973 through 1977 contradict results from early studies, most of which were based on reported and recorded crime. It can be seen that the results of the study cast doubt upon the validity of the climatic principle as originally enunciated because, although violence showed some evidence of a summer orientation, in line with earlier findings, a majority of crimes of theft examined were also most prevalent in the summer and least prevalent in the winter. So, according to the report (United States, 1980):

> *Although the classical theory linking theft with cold weather is now suspect, the association between crime and climate may still be valid. A more appropriate link, however, appears to be environmental opportunity. A high incidence of summertime theft may be associated with changes in living patterns brought about by climate, which in turn enhance criminal opportunity. To illustrate, household security may deteriorate during the warm weather, when doors and windows remain open or unlocked and household possessions, such as lawn furniture, bicycles, toys, etc., are more likely to be left out in the open. Vulnerability to theft may well be reduced in the winter when families spend less time out of doors and easy access to the home is reduced. (p.31)*

The study further suggests a probable link between school vacation and seasonality in personal larceny without contact. School theft is an important component of this type of theft. There is, therefore, reason to believe that the low level of minor personal larceny (less than fifty dollars stolen) in the summer months—a characteristic distinguishing this series from most others—is attributable to school vacation. It is quite possible that the restricting of opportunity resulting from the shutdown of facilities during the summer may account for the 15 percent to 20 percent reduction in petty larceny regularly occurring during the months of June, July, and August (United States, 1980).

Another report on the seasonality of crime victimization was issued by the Bureau of Justice Statistics in May 1988 (United States). The report examines the issue further, this time using National Crime Survey data from 1973 through 1984. The report also compares the seasonal patterns of victimizations reported to the police with those which were not. The most common seasonal pattern revealed by the report is that rates are highest in one or more of the summer months (June, July, and August) and lowest in January, February, and March. This was generally true for both crimes reported to the police and those not reported, and it is particularly evident in crimes against households. The most striking exception to this pattern is for personal larcenies less than fifty dollars, without contact, that are not reported to the police. The highest rates for these larcenies coincide with the first part of the school year, September through January, and the lowest rates occur in the summer, when most schools are not in session. Other departures from the norm among nonreported crimes are robbery and personal larceny with contact, which both peak in December, with the latter having lows in August and September.

The new interest in the seasonal patterns of criminal victimization is to be welcomed, and the tentative findings reported up until now surely indicate the need for further investigation of the issue.[2] Clearly, the emphasis in explaining whatever seasonal patterns may be observed has shifted from the influence of climate on human emotions and the physiological changes resulting from fluctuations in temperature, to the changes in crime opportunities brought about by warm and cold weather. The discrepancies between the findings of recent studies and older ones may be due to the use of victimization survey data that, at least for this type of study, offer better information on the seasonal distribution of crime than do official crime statistics.

CRIMINAL VICTIMIZATION AND THE DAY OF THE WEEK

Criminal victimization is not spread evenly among the days of the week. Violent victimizations, for example, occur with greater frequency during the weekend.

Wolfgang (1958) found a significant association between criminal homicide in Philadelphia and days of the week. Saturday witnessed the highest frequency (32 percent), while Tuesday showed a low frequency of only 7 percent. In other words, nearly five times as many criminal homicides occur on the day of highest frequency as occur on the day of lowest frequency. Friday and Sunday each claimed 17 percent, or almost half that of Saturday. Probing for the sex and race of the victims, Wolfgang discovered that, with the exception of white females who were killed more frequently (and inexplicably) on Thursdays, all the other groups were more frequently killed on Saturday than on any other day of the week.

The significant association Wolfgang found between criminal homicide and the weekend is confirmed in several other studies (Bullock, 1955; Bensing and Schroeder, 1960; Voss and Hepburn, 1968; Wilt, 1974; and Lundsgaarde, 1977). A study of the patterns of homicide in Vancouver from 1980 to 1986 (Coburn, 1988) based on 194 police files concerning 204 victims revealed a slightly different pattern from that of Philadelphia. The highest number of victims were killed not on Saturday (twenty-nine) but on Sunday (forty-one). The lowest frequency was on Wednesday (twenty-three).

The high concentration on the weekend is equally true of other forms of personal violence less serious than homicides. In his study of everyday violence in Sweden, Wikström (1985) observed the same pattern. When the acts of violence were divided according to the contexts in which they occurred, Wikström discovered that relationship conflicts were less concentrated on weekends than other types of circumstance. This he attributes to the concentration of public entertainment on weekends.

The obvious reason for the higher frequency of acts of personal violence on weekends is that more social interaction and drinking take place during the recreational days of the weekend than on work days. In explaining the temporal pattern revealed by the Philadelphia data (and numerous studies preceding it), Wolfgang (1958) notes that drinking is a common accompaniment of crimes of personal violence, and Friday and Saturday nights are traditional periods for social drinking and drinking sprees. Homicide, he points out, is generally committed against persons who are relatively close friends or relatives, and the opportunities for such personal contacts are probably much greater during the leisure hours of evenings and weekends. All this contributes to making the weekend the most dangerous period of a week with regard to homicide.

It is also the most dangerous period for forcible rape. Amir's (1971) study of rape in Philadelphia showed the highest frequency on Saturday (24.4 percent) followed by Sunday (16 percent) and Friday (14 percent), while the lowest frequency was on Monday (8.4 percent). Saturday and Sunday combined accounted for over 40 percent of all the rapes, and, with Friday, witnessed almost 55 percent of the victimizations.

Although robbery is more of a property crime than an act of personal violence, its temporal distribution also shows a greater frequency on Friday and Saturday (Normandeau, 1968; Block, 1977; Pratt, 1980; Roesch and Winterdyk, 1985). Block points out that while most robberies in Chicago occurred during the work week (62 percent), the proportion of those occurring on the weekend (38 percent) was slightly greater than the proportion of weekend hours to hours in the rest of the week (32 percent). He further observed that robberies are most likely to occur on Friday nights and on the street, rather than in the victim's home. This pattern is confirmed in Ottawa by Ciale and Leroux (1984) where 22 percent of armed robberies occurred on Friday and only 1 percent on Sunday. In Vancouver, convenience stores were much more at risk on Friday and Sunday than on other days. The two days accounted for almost 35 percent of the robberies analyzed by Roesch and Winterdyk (1985). In Montreal, Normandeau (1981) found that most armed robberies against banks were committed on Thursday and Friday when the banks were open late. The popularity of Friday as a day for bank robbery is confirmed by Letkemann (1973) who attributes it to the fact that banks usually keep more money in the tills on that day in anticipation of the high number of withdrawals by customers for the weekend. This temporal pattern is not limited to North America. In West Germany, where all banks are closed on Saturdays and Sundays, Büchler and Leineweber (1984, 1986) also found that Thursday and Friday were most often chosen by bank robbers to commit their crime.

CRIMINAL VICTIMIZATION AND THE TIME OF THE DAY

Criminal victimizations are not evenly or randomly distributed over the hours of the day. Violent victimizations show a higher concentration in the night than in the daytime. The National Crime Survey Report for 1987 (United States, 1989, June) indicates that violent crimes occurred more often at night. More than half of all violent victimizations measured by the National Crime Survey took place between 6:00 p.m. and 6:00 a.m., with the largest proportion of nighttime incidents occurring between 6:00 p.m. and midnight. One particularly interesting pattern revealed by the survey shows that the majority of violent crimes involving strangers occurred at night, while the majority of those involving nonstrangers occurred during the day. Contrary to violent victimizations, the largest proportion of incidents of personal theft occurred during the day between 6:00 a.m and 6:00 p.m. On the other hand, the majority of household crimes, where the time of occurrence was known, took place at night. There was, however, a relatively high percentage of personal theft victims (17 percent) and household crime victims (28 percent) who did not know at what time the incident occurred. Armed robberies and armed assaults followed the general trend, occurring more often at night than during the day.

Another National Crime Survey report dealing with household burglary (United States, 1985, January) shows that 35.5 percent occurred during daytime (6:00 a.m. to 6:00 p.m.), 39 percent during nighttime, while in one out of four incidents the time of occurrence was either unknown or not available.

The tendency of violent crimes to occur more frequently at nighttime has been reported over and over again in individual studies examining specific offenses or groups of offenses.

Homicide

Wolfgang (1958) used four six-hour divisions and found the observed distribution of criminal homicides between the periods to be highly significant. His analysis suggests that the most lethal hours are between 8:00 p.m. and 2:00 a.m. Half of all criminal homicides were committed during this six-hour period. The second most dangerous period, 2:00 p.m. to 8:00 p.m., had only half as many homicides as the first period (25 percent). The period between 2:00 a.m. and 8:00 a.m. ranks third with 17 percent, while the least dangerous period, between 8:00 a.m. and 2:00 p.m., had only 9 percent, or less than one-fifth, the number of homicides during the highest period.

Coburn's (1988) study of homicides in Vancouver, previously cited, used the same six-hour periods as Wolfgang (1958). Like Wolfgang, Coburn found that the evening period, 8:00 p.m. to 2:00 a.m., is by far the most dangerous with almost half of all the victimizations (49.5 percent) being perpetrated during that period. The early morning period (2:00 a.m. to 8:00 a.m.) accounted for another quarter of the homicides (24 percent), while 16 percent took place on each of the mid-morning (8:00 a.m. to 2:00 p.m.) and afternoon (2:00 p.m. to 8:00 p.m.) periods. (These percentages, quoted from the original, add up to more than 100 percent.)

Rape

Amir's (1971) study of the hourly distribution of forcible rape in Philadelphia revealed an almost identical pattern to that observed by Wolfgang (1958) for criminal homicide. Almost half of all forcible rapes studied (49 percent) occurred during the 8:00 p.m. to 2:00 a.m. period. The late-night to early-morning period (2:00 a.m. to 8:00 a.m.) followed with 22 percent. The late-afternoon to early-evening period (2:00 p.m. to 8:00 p.m.) had slightly less with 21 percent, while the 8:00 a.m. to 2:00 p.m. period witnessed the lowest proportion of rapes, with only 8 percent occurring during this broad daylight period. Amir summarizes the temporal patterns of forcible rape by stating that it is predominantly a nocturnal crime that tends to be a weekend, midnight, and summer occurrence.

An analysis of National Crime Survey data on rape (United States, 1985, March) confirmed the nighttime concentration pattern. It shows that two-thirds of all rapes and rape attempts occur at night, with the largest proportion (39 percent) occurring between 6:00 p.m. and midnight. The study reveals, however, that the patterns for rape and rape attempts are slightly different. Thus, rape attempts were about twice as likely as rapes to occur during the daytime (6:00 a.m. to 6:00 p.m.) and only half as likely to occur between midnight and 6:00 a.m.

Further evidence that the risk of rape is greatest during the late night hours also comes from England. Smith (1989) studied all rape offenses which were reported to the police in the London boroughs of Islington and Lambeth during the years 1984 to 1986. Information on the time of rape was recorded in 423 reported cases. Although Smith used an uneven hourly distribution, the findings are clear. Over one-third (34 percent) occurred between the hours of 11:00 p.m. and 2:00 a.m.; under one-quarter (23 percent) took place between 6:00 p.m. and 11:00 p.m.; about the same number (22 percent) happened between 2:00 a.m. and 7:00 a.m.; and one-fifth (20 percent) occurred between 7:00 a.m. and 6:00 p.m.

Robbery

The heterogeneity of robbery victimization, such as mugging, residential robbery, and commercial robbery, is likely to influence the hourly distribution and makes it necessary to examine each subtype separately. Thus, while mugging might be predominantly a nocturnal crime, robbery in commercial establishments that are not open twenty-four hours a day will have to take place during the business hours of those establishments. When global robbery is examined without distinction between the different types, the pattern that emerges is also one of a higher frequency during the nighttime.

Using different hourly distributions, Normandeau (1968) found that 38 percent of the robberies in Philadelphia occurred between 8:00 p.m. and 2:00 a.m., while Block (1977) reports that 58 percent of the robberies in Chicago took place at night (6:00 p.m. to 6:00 a.m.). In Cleveland, Pyle (1976) discovered that 57 percent of the incidents were perpetrated between 4:00 p.m. and midnight. As might be expected, the majority of incidents of mugging takes place at night, particularly between 10:00 p.m. and midnight (Pratt, 1980).

Because of their restricted business hours, banks are held up almost exclusively during the daytime period (Letkemann, 1973; Büchler and Leineweber, 1986). Right after opening or just before closing were the favored times for bank robbers in Germany (Büchler and Leineweber, 1986). In Canada, one of the robbers interviewed by Letkemann expressed a preference for the morning opening time when "bank employees and customers are dull and still half asleep" and when it was easier to get the "jump" on them (Letkemann, 1973).

Convenience stores, due to their extended business hours, seem to be victimized more frequently in the evening (Roesch and Winterdyk, 1985). Over 45 percent of the robberies they studied occurred between 8:00 p.m. and midnight, whereas less than 10 percent were committed in the early morning hours (1:00 a.m. to 6:00 a.m.).

Residential robberies seem to follow a different hourly pattern. In Reppetto's (1974) study in Boston, residential robberies clustered in the late afternoon hours when residents would be returning from work or other activities. In his sample, 42.1 percent of the residential robberies occurred between noon and 6:00 p.m.; 29.8 percent between 6:00 p.m. and midnight; 12.5 percent between midnight and 6:00 a.m.; and 15.7 percent between 6:00 a.m. and noon.

Assault

Wikström (1985) paid special attention to the temporal patterns of everyday violence in Sweden. In line with other studies, he observed that the lowest incidence of violent victimizations is in the early morning hours. From then on the incidences steadily increase up to the evening hours when they take a jump upwards and assume a fairly stable level; they are interrupted by peaks in the hours around midnight, and finally decrease and drop significantly between 3:00 a.m. and 4:00 a.m. Wikström further observed that not only the incidence but also the circumstances and characteristics of persons involved in violence show temporal variations. At nighttime there were more marked differences in the scenes of crime (Wikström, 1985):

> *A much higher proportion of the weekday cases occur in apartments. Comparison of the scene of the crime at day and nighttime clearly shows the importance of public entertainment for nighttime crimes and especially at weekends ... as stated in the introduction to this part ... a major proportion of the crimes in streets and on public transport at nighttime, especially at weekends, occur between people out to participate in public entertainment. (p.163)*

Wikström found that temporal and spatial patterns of violence vary according to victim-offender relationships. Thus, in the inner-city areas at all times, but especially at nighttime on Fridays, Saturdays, and Sundays, there is a domination of crimes between strangers. In fact, as many as 42 percent of all crimes of violence between strangers in Stockholm occur in inner-city areas at nighttime during weekends. He also observed that there is a clearly higher proportion of older offenders in daytime than in nighttime violence. Moreover, the proportion of those out of work who are not students was markedly higher at daytime than nighttime. In addition, the proportion of cases in which at least one of the parties had a previous criminal record was higher at nighttime than at daytime and higher in outer-city areas than in inner-city areas. Wikström admits that, at present, there is no good overall explanation for many of these temporal patterns and differences. One thing seems clear: the volume of contacts in the course of public entertainment is important, since many of these contacts do later develop into conflicts and violence.

Although we do not, at the moment, have definitive explanations for these temporal patterns, their relevance and their importance to the understanding of the victimization phenomenon, and the motivational, situational, and causal forces that are at play cannot be overemphasized. They are indispensable to the understanding of explanatory models such as life-style and routine activities (see Chapter 12), and they are also invaluable for the policies and strategies of prevention and control.

Geographical and Spatial Patterns in Criminal Victimization

RURAL/URBAN AND INTRACITY DIFFERENCES

Because the Canadian Urban Victimization Survey was limited to seven major urban centers, its findings do not allow us to compare victimization rates between regions or between rural and urban areas in Canada. The findings of the General Social Survey (Sacco, 1989) show that urban dwellers experience rates of personal victimization (158 per 1,000) almost 40 percent higher than residents of rural areas (114 per 1,000).

The United States National Crime Survey (United States, 1989, June) provides information on the distribution of personal victimizations and household victimizations by region and locality of residence. The National Crime Survey shows the following for 1987 (United States, 1989, June):

— For personal crimes of violence, the rate of victimization was highest among residents in urban areas, but the rate differences were not significant between the residents in suburban and rural areas. The rate among city residents was 40 victimizations per 1,000, which was considerably higher than that of suburbanites (23 per 1,000) or rural residents (25 per 1,000). Household victimizations also showed a higher frequency in large metropolitan areas. In all four size-categories of metropolitan areas, central city householders had higher rates of household crimes than the householders in that city's suburbs. Nonmetropolitan householders had the lowest rate of all. Within the four size-categories of metropolitan areas, the household crime victimization rate was lowest in the suburban portion of the smallest metropolitan areas with populations of 50,000 to 249,999.

— Central city residents had higher rates of violent (and personal theft) victimization, as well as burglary victimization, than others. Within each of the four size-categories of metropolitan areas, the residents of central cities had higher victimization rates than those persons residing in those cities' suburban areas. The same pattern was true for household burglary.

— The motor vehicle theft rate in the rural areas was about one-fourth of that in the central cities of the largest metropolitan areas.

— Overall, the robbery victimization rates were higher in the central cities than their respective suburbs, except in the smallest metropolitan areas where no urban-suburban difference existed.

— Assault victimizations were higher in central cities than their respective suburbs, except in the largest metropolitan areas where no locality difference existed.

— Suburbanites had a higher personal theft victimization rate than rural residents but a lower rate than that for city dwellers. The victimization rate for personal crimes of theft for city dwellers was 80 per 1,000 compared to 70 per 1,000 and 50 per 1,000 for suburbanites and rural residents respectively.

REGIONAL VARIATIONS

Victimization rates vary widely from region to region in the United States. The following differences were observed in 1987 for both personal and household victimizations as measured by the National Crime Survey (United States, 1989, June):

— In both crimes of violence and personal theft, inhabitants of the West had the highest victimization rates, and those residing in the Northeast had the lowest. People in the Midwest had higher rates than those in the South.

— Southerners had lower victimization rates in robbery and personal larceny with contact than those in the Northeast or the West. Assault and noncontact personal larceny in the four regions followed a pattern similar to that of crimes of violence. People in the Midwest had somewhat lower victimization rates in personal larceny with contact than those in the Northeast.

— As is the case with violent victimization, household crime victimization was highest for residents in the West and lowest for those in the Northwest. But the South had a higher household victimization rate than the Midwest.

— Household burglary victimization followed the same pattern as in overall household crime victimization.

— The household larceny victimization rate was the highest in the West and lowest in the Northeast; however, no rate difference existed between the Midwest and the South.

— The West had the highest rate in motor vehicle theft, but there were no differences among the other three regions.

Prior to the General Social Survey there were no Canadian victimization data available to allow comparison and analysis of regional differences. Regional comparisons were based on recorded crime statistics (Fattah, Bissonnet, and Geoffrion, 1972; Fattah, Bissonnet, and Scholtes, 1973; Fattah, Bissonnet, and Scholtes, 1974; Brantingham and Brantingham, 1984). Canada, it should be noted, has a different geographical makeup than that of the United States as the provinces are parallel to one another, and it is impossible to talk about South, Northeast, and

Midwest, as is the case in the United States. Comparisons of Canadian crime rates show a very distinct and consistent regional pattern. Crime rates in Canada, with very few exceptions, increase as one moves from east to west. The most eastern province, Newfoundland, has consistently had the lowest recorded crime rates in the country, while the most western province, British Columbia, has consistently had the highest reported rates of any province. The Canadian General Social Survey data (Sacco and Johnson, 1990) confirm the general east-west pattern and show an increase in the rates of victimization as one moves westward across the country. One exception to this general pattern is the province of Quebec, which has a victimization rate below the national average. Overall victimization rates per 1,000 population were 135 for the Atlantic region, 60 for Quebec, 146 for Ontario, 192 for the Prairies, and 252 for British Columbia. In other words, British Columbia's victimization rate was more than four times that of Quebec and almost twice that of the Atlantic region or of Ontario.

The explanations for such a regional pattern remain tentative, and research is badly and urgently needed to identify the real reasons behind such wide, but consistent, regional differences. One thing is clear: the geographical pattern of increase in recorded crime rates and survey victimization rates from east to west closely follows the migration patterns of the Canadian population, which have always been dominated by an east to west movement.

Some Spatial Patterns of Selected Types of Criminal Victimization

Various types of victimization may be analyzed to establish the frequency with which they occur in various places: outdoors/indoors, at home, on the street, in parks, in places of entertainment, such as restaurants, bars, pubs, and nightclubs, in means of transportation, such as subway, or motor vehicle, and so forth. The spatial analysis may go even further by looking at where exactly the victimization takes place within a particular location. For example, in the home one could determine how frequently or infrequently victimization takes place in the bedroom, the living room, the kitchen, etc. This micro spatial pattern may then be combined with specific characteristics of the victim and victimizer (such as age, sex, or race) and their relationships in an attempt to better understand and explain the different spatial patterns. A meaningful analysis also needs to take into account the amount of time that people (offenders and victims) spend in different places or in the different parts of the home. Until now, however, no studies have linked the frequency of victimization to the time spent in various places.

VIOLENT VICTIMIZATION WITHIN AND OUTSIDE THE HOME

Homicide

Spatial patterns have been examined for violent victimization, notably homicide, rape, and assault. With regard to criminal homicide, Wolfgang's (1958) classic study in Philadelphia offers the most complete and detailed analysis of the micro spatial patterns specific to this type of victimization. Combining sex and place of occurrence, Wolfgang found a significant association between the latter and the former. In terms of total cases, the most dangerous single place is on the highway, defined by Wolfgang as a "public street, alley, or field," where 30 percent of all victims met death. The bedroom emerged as the most dangerous room in the home and the place with the second highest frequency of criminal deaths. Nearly a fifth of all victims were killed in the bedroom, with a significantly higher proportion of women than men. In fact, more women were killed in the bedroom than in any other designated place. Only 14 percent of male victims were killed in the bedroom, while 35 percent—proportionately over twice as many—of females were killed there. More women killed their victims in the bedroom (26 percent) than male killers did (16 percent). Wolfgang notes that the high proportion of bedroom slayings among females is associated with the fact that 87 percent of all female victims were slain by males and 84 percent of all female offenders slew males. The predominant motives inciting these interrelationships were those involving arguments concerned with sex, love, and family. In Wolfgang's study, the kitchen and living room share an equal third ranking (12 percent each) among the places in which homicide occurs. Sex differences were particularly significant in kitchen killings. Among female victims, 15 percent were killed in the kitchen compared to 11 percent among male victims. But most striking is the fact that 29 percent of female offenders slew their victims in the kitchen compared to only 7 percent of male offenders.

A study of crimes of violence in seventeen American cities (Mulvihill, Tumin, and Curtis, 1969) shows that although criminal homicide occurs out-of-doors more than any place else, there is a fairly even distribution among outside (37 percent), home (34 percent), and other inside locations (26 percent). Homicides in inside places other than the home were mainly distributed between miscellaneous indoor locations (14 percent) and bars or taverns (8 percent), while most outside killings occurred on the street (25 percent).

In Vancouver (Coburn, 1988), the percentage of homicide victims who were killed in a residence (64 percent) was considerably higher than the percentage reported by Wolfgang (1958) for Philadelphia (51 percent), and the one reported in the study of seventeen United States cities. One possible explanation is the higher percentage of robbery homicides in the United States. Many of these homicides are committed in outside locations. This suggests that an analysis of spatial distribution for different types of homicide might reveal a different pattern from the one that emerges when homicides are grouped together in a single category. Further locations for homicides reported in the Vancouver study are 26 percent on the street, 4 percent in commercial premises, 3 percent in bars, and 2.5 percent in other locations.

Rape

Spatial patterns for forcible rape victimization reported by the National Crime Survey (United States, 1985, March) show a difference between completed and attempted rapes. A third of the completed rapes occurred in the home, and nearly half the rest occurred on the street or in a park, field, playground, parking lot, or parking garage. Only a fourth of the attempted rapes occurred in the home, and well over half the rest occurred on the street or in a park, field, playground, parking lot, or parking garage. The percentages of completed and attempted rapes occurring in the home and reported by the National Crime Survey are lower than those observed earlier in the study of seventeen American cities (Mulvihill, Tumin, and Curtis, 1969). That survey indicated that about half or more of all forcible interactions occur in the home. Within the home, the bedroom, not surprisingly, emerged as the dominant location (33 percent) while "private transportation vehicles" stood out as the predominant outdoor setting (11 percent). Mulvihill, Tumin, and Curtis indicate that regardless of where and how a man or a group of males may first approach a woman who is subsequently raped, the discernible pattern is toward finding a more intimate, nonpublic place, even if it is only the back seat of an automobile.

Another study of rape victimization in twenty-six American cities (McDermott, 1979) based on National Crime Survey data found that more rapes were reported to have occurred in outdoor public locations than in any other place. Slightly less than one-half (47 percent) of the rapes and attempted rapes took place outside on a street, park, field, playground, school ground, or parking lot. The victim's own home, or close to her home, was the next most frequent location. Eighteen percent of all rape attacks occurred in the victim's own home and an additional 14 percent occurred near her home, that is, in a yard, sidewalk, driveway, carport, or apartment hall. The study further indicates that the attacks that occurred in the victim's home were more serious, that is, more of them were completed. The completion ratio was 1.53 for attacks occurring in the victim's home to .80 for attacks occurring outdoors in a public location. McDermott suggests that the high completion ratio for rape attacks in the victim's home may be due to there being less chance for someone to see the crime, interrupt it, or hear the victim's screams. It may also be due in part to the high percentage of weapon-use in these victimizations.

A word of caution about the spatial distribution of rape is in order. Rape victimization is characterized by a relatively high dark figure. Rapes in which victim and victimizer know each other or are related by some personal relationship tend to be reported less than those involving total strangers. There are also reasons to believe that they might occur more often indoors (in the offender's or the victim's residence) than stranger-to-stranger rapes. As a result, spatial patterns based on officially recorded rapes may tend to underestimate the proportion of those occurring in the home of the offender or victim and to overestimate those occurring on the street. The same is true of minor or simple assaults.

Assault

Spatial patterns based on recorded crime (instead of victimization data) may unduly inflate the percentages of assaults outside the home and deflate those in the home. The fact that intrafamily violence, which occurs mainly in the home, has a high dark figure is likely to distort the patterns even further. Wikström's (1985) study of everyday violence in Sweden was based on police files. This might partially explain the relatively low percentage of assaults taking place in a residence (24 percent). Of the other cases, 29 percent occurred in or around a place of public entertainment, or on streets and squares (21 percent). Of the cases occurring in apartments, 38 percent were in the home of both the victim and the offender, 36 percent in the home of the victim, 13 percent in the offender's home, and the rest in the home of another person. Of cases in and around places of public entertainment, 35 percent occurred in restaurants and 39 percent in entrances to restaurants. Contrasting crimes in apartments with other crimes of violence, Wikström observed some tendency of crimes in apartments to involve people of a similar kind, while outdoor crimes exhibited a tendency to occur between people of different kinds. He hypothesized that it is the social instability of public entertainment that is responsible for a high incidence of violence: a large number of interacting intoxicated strangers of different kinds make it sometimes difficult to anticipate the reactions and behaviors of others. Wikström identified two main types of incidents that occur in the home: (1) relationship conflicts within the family, and (2) heavy drinking parties.

One of the few studies that examined the spatial patterns of aggravated assault is the one done for the United States National Commission on the Causes and Prevention of Violence (Mulvihill, Tumin, and Curtis, 1969). The study shows half of all assault interactions as split between the home and other inside locations; the other half occur outside. The authors point out that more refined aggravated assault breakdowns for locational patterns parallel the results for criminal homicide. This suggests that the two crimes may differ mainly in the seriousness of their outcomes. Like homicide, women (both black and white) were more likely to be assault victims or offenders in the home, while men were more likely to be victims or offenders in outside locations.

Like the temporal patterns of victimization, spatial patterns are relevant and important to both theory and practice. The patterns outlined above are meant to document and illustrate the uneven distribution of the risks and rates of criminal victimization. These patterns unequivocally indicate that certain areas, locations, places, days, and times are more dangerous than others. The relevance of this to the formulation of theory is obvious. It would be impossible to explain the differential risks of victimization, which is the primary task of theoretical victimology, unless and until these differential risks have been clearly established and adequately understood. It would be equally impossible, in practice, to develop effective crime-prevention policies and strategies unless and until we fully understand when and where the danger of victimization lies and why.

Having examined the extent, the trends, and the patterns of criminal victimization, we now proceed to examine who the victims are.

Summary

In the first half of this chapter we examined criminal victimization as a social phenomenon. We began by looking at the incidence, prevalence, and risks of criminal victimization. Figures are indicators of incidence whereas rates are indicators of prevalence. Both indicators are imperfect. Figures produced by victimization surveys are just estimates and thus are subject to error. Rates may be misleading due to the skewness of the distribution of criminal victimization. Like other social phenomena, criminal victimization is subject to certain general rules that govern its frequency and visibility. The more serious the victimization is, the less frequently it occurs and the more likely it will be reported. The more social distance separates the victim and victimizer, the higher are the chances that the victimization will be reported. Criminal victimization, like delinquency, declines with advancing age after reaching a peak in the teens and late teens. Contrary to popular beliefs (undoubtedly influenced by biased and distorted media reporting), criminal victimization is a relatively rare event, and crimes of interpersonal violence are extremely uncommon. Moreover, criminal victimization is not uniformly nor randomly distributed within the population as a whole or within any easily definable subgroup of the population. It is not randomly nor evenly distributed in time and space. Objectively, it is less injurious than other victimizations, and most of it is actually trivial in consequence. When criminal victimization risks are placed in perspective, the picture that emerges is one that is totally different from people's subjective impressions of those risks. Although victimization survey data in Canada do not allow a trend analysis because of lack of continuity, there are data from other countries (Britain and the United States) where surveys have been conducted annually or at regular intervals. The information suggests that the percentages of households touched by crime have remained stable or have even decreased in recent years (United States), or that victimization figures have increased less rapidly than those of recorded crime (Britain).

The second half of this chapter was devoted to patterns in criminal victimization. It examined the seasonal variations that suggest that not all types are susceptible to seasonal influences in the same way. Some exhibit more seasonality than others. Current explanations of seasonal fluctuations stress the link between cold and hot weather and the structure of opportunity to commit certain crimes. This is a marked change from earlier explanations that used to explain these fluctuations by the influence of the temperature on human passions, emotions, and moods. Other temporal patterns, namely the day of the week and the time of day were also examined. There is overwhelming empirical evidence that violent victimizations occur with greater frequency during the weekend and at nighttime. One obvious reason is that more social interaction and drinking take place during the recreational days of the weekend than on work days. Much more violence is associated with public entertainment than with work. Drinking and entertainment are nocturnal and not typical daytime activities. Although we do not have, as yet, definitive explanations for these temporal patterns, their relevance and importance to the understanding and explanation of the victimization phenomenon cannot be overemphasized. They are also essential for developing rational policies and effective strategies of prevention and control.

From the temporal patterns we moved to some geographical and spatial patterns. Urban dwellers, it was found, experience higher rates of personal victimization than residents in rural areas. Central city residents have higher rates of violent personal theft and burglary victimization than others. Victimization rates also vary by region. In Canada, recorded crime rates have shown a consistent tendency to increase from east to west. The distribution in the United States is not as linear as it is in Canada because of the different geographical makeup. Still, in both crimes of violence and personal theft, inhabitants of the West have the highest victimization rates and those residing in the Northeast, the lowest. The frequency with which various types of criminal victimization occur in specific locations varies from one type to the other. The distribution of some violent victimizations (criminal homicide, forcible rape, robbery, assault) has been tentatively examined. However, there is a need for further research before definitive patterns can be established. Still, we have unequivocal evidence indicating that certain areas, locations, and places are more dangerous than others and that even within the home, the risk in certain rooms (bedroom, kitchen) is higher than in others. The analysis of spatial patterns in victimization is as important as that of the temporal patterns for understanding and explaining the differential risks of victimization and for planning intervention and prevention strategies.

Part 2

On Victims and Victimizers

FOUR

Who Are the Victims of Crime?

"The victim" is a social construction. We all deal in a conventional wisdom that influences our perception of the world around us. This wisdom allows us to characterize the victims of crime. Moreover, it defines for us just who is the victim in any situation. What this also means is that alternative victims can be constructed. Why we conceive of some persons as victims and others not as victims is a consequence of our commonsense assumptions.

Richard Quinney (1972, p. 321)

Why Study the Victim?

Since the dawn of scientific criminology, criminologists have tried to find out why some individuals become criminal while others do not. They have conducted countless studies to discover whether criminals are different in any respect from noncriminals. An equally interesting and thought-provoking question is, Why do some individuals become victims of crime while others do not? Is criminal victimization a random occurrence? Is it due simply to chance factors, misfortune, or bad luck? Do victims of crime constitute a representative sample, an unbiased cross section of the general population? Do victims of crime differ in any way from nonvictims? How do offenders select their targets, and how do they pick their victims? But the study of victims of crime is by no means limited to these questions. There are many others for which research is seeking answers. The following are just a few examples:

—Why are certain individuals or groups of individuals more frequently victimized than others? Why are certain targets, such as individuals, households, or businesses, repeatedly victimized? How can the differential risks and rates of victimization be explained?

—Are certain persons or targets more prone and more vulnerable to victimization than others, and, if so, why? What is the nature of this proneness, and what are the elements of this vulnerability?

—Are there born victims, predestinate victims, predisposed victims? Are there recidivist victims? Are there victim stereotypes as there are criminal stereotypes?

—Are there specific characteristics or specific behaviors that enhance the risks and chances of criminal victimization, that are responsible for, or conducive to, becoming a victim? And, if so, what are these characteristics and these behaviors, and what role do they play in the etiology of victimization?

—Is there such a thing as victim-invited, victim-induced, victim-precipitated, victim-facilitated criminality? Do some victims promote, provoke, or trigger their own victimization? Do potential victims emit nonverbal signals, signaling their vulnerability to would-be assailants through gestures, posture, and movements?[1]

These questions and many others raise a number of issues and research topics that are quite different from those that have been the main focus of research in traditional criminology. Although the scientific study of the criminal is more than a century old, the systematic study of the victim is still in its infancy. And yet, it seems axiomatic that to analyze the crime phenomenon in its entirety and in all its complexity, equal attention has to be paid to the criminal and the victim. One can cite several reasons why the study of victims of crime is essential, indeed indispensable, for a better understanding of the phenomenon of crime:

—Motives for criminal behavior do not develop in a vacuum. They come to be through drives and responses, reactions and interactions, attitudes and counter-attitudes. In many cases, the victim is involved consciously or unconsciously in the motivational process, as well as in the process of mental reasoning or rationalization in which the criminal engages prior to the commission of the crime.[2] In some instances the motives for the criminal act develop around a specific victim. An examination of the place a victim occupies or the role the victim plays in these processes is necessary to understand why the crime was committed and why a particular target for victimization was chosen.

—The commission of a crime is the outcome of a process where many factors are at work. In most cases, crime is not an action but a reaction (or an overreaction) to external and environmental stimuli. Some of these stimuli emanate from the victim. The victim is an important element of the environment and of the criminogenic situation that gives rise to the crime.

—Often the criminal act is not an isolated gesture but the denouement of a long or brief interaction with the victim. In such cases it is not possible to fully understand the act without analyzing the chain of interactions that led to its perpetration. It would be futile to examine and analyze the offender's act in isolation from the dynamic forces that have prepared, influenced, conditioned, or determined it, and equally futile to dissociate it from the motivational and situational processes that ended in its commission.

—Current theories of criminal and deviant behavior, whether attempting to explain causation or association, offer only static explanations. Since criminal behavior, like other forms of human behavior, is dynamic, it can be explained only through a dynamic approach where the offender, the act, and the victim are inseparable elements of a total situation that leads to the crime.[3]

—The traits approach, which seeks the genesis of criminal behavior in the characteristics and attributes of the offender, is a simplistic approach. It needs to be replaced by a complex model of total interactions. Theories of offenders' attributes, personalities, or social background and conditions, do not explain why other individuals who have the same traits, same personality type, or same, or similar, upbringing do not commit crime or do not persist in a criminal career. They fail to explain why the offender committed a particular crime in a particular situation at a given moment against a specific victim. The traits approach either ignores or deliberately minimizes the importance of situational factors in actualizing or triggering criminal behavior.[4] The study of victims, their characteristics, their relationships to, and interactions with the victimizers, and the study of their motivational and functional roles in the pre-victimization and victimization phases offers a great promise for transforming etiological criminology from the static, one-sided study of the qualities and attributes of the offender into a dynamic, situational approach that views criminal behavior not as a unilateral action but as the outcome of dynamic processes of interaction.

—As Anttila (1974) points out, the study of the victim has a general informational value. It provides information on the frequency and patterns of victimization and thus allows the measurement of risk probabilities and the establishment of risk categories (high, low, and medium-risk categories). It also provides valuable information on proneness to victimization, fear of victimization, response to victimization, and the consequences and impact of victimization. Such knowledge is essential for the formulation of a rational criminal policy, for the evaluation of crime-prevention strategies, for undertaking a social action aimed at protecting vulnerable targets, for increasing safety, and for improving the quality of life.

—The victim has a strong impact on criminal justice decisions, particularly those of the police and the courts.[5] In most cases it is the victim who decides whether or not to mobilize the criminal justice system by reporting or not reporting the offense. Furthermore, the characteristics, attitudes, and behavior of victims, and their relationship to the offender, have a significant bearing upon the decision of the police to proceed in a formal or an informal way.[6] In the latter case, victim-related factors can largely affect the final outcome. The study of the victim leads not only to a better understanding of the functioning of the criminal justice system but also to improving the decision-making processes within the system. Enhancing victims' involvement in the process and establishing the modalities of such involvement requires a better understanding of the role victims currently play in criminal justice.

—In order to better fulfill society's obligations to the victims of crime, and in order to be able to help, assist, and make the victim whole again, it is necessary to gain a thorough knowledge of the consequences and impact of the crime on those who are victimized. Moreover, an adequate knowledge of the various needs of victims of different types of crime is a prerequisite for setting up efficient victim services such as victim assistance and compensation programs. A better understanding of victims' perceptions of, and attitudes to, the criminal justice system, the reasons for not reporting victimization, and the reasons for their refusal or unwillingness to cooperate with the system are essential to improving attitudes and enhancing cooperation.

— Modern criminology is paying more attention to, and placing more emphasis on, the concept of opportunity.[7] The commission of many crimes is believed to be largely a function of the opportunities to commit those crimes. Opportunities, in turn, are viewed as being greatly influenced by the behavior of potential victims. The collective behavior of potential crime victims may have a strong impact on crime rates, and variations in those rates may be explained, at least partially, through differences or changes in victim behavior (see Chapter 11). For this reason, a better understanding of the attitudes and behaviors of the victims holds great promise for crime prevention. Victim-based prevention strategies have several advantages over the traditional offender-based ones. The former aim at hardening the targets, making the commission of crimes more difficult and less profitable. The role of potential victims in this environmental approach is a primary one.

As useful as the study of crime victims may be, it is not without its dangers. Anttila (1974) points out two potential dangers in victim-centered research:

1. A real danger is the possibility that interest will simply shift from the individual offender to the individual victim. Individual-centered research, in its narrowest sense, takes into account offender and victim independently. More sophisticated research also considers the interaction process and the general situational factors. But even then, if the problems related to society in general and to the volume of criminality are disregarded, the research results tend to be of little importance for decision making.
2. The growing interest in victim-centered research may lead to overemphasis on the types of criminal behavior in which there is an easily identifiable individual victim. This implies a concentration of research efforts on traditional types of crimes, such as assaults, larcenies, and sexual offenses. Some large groups of crimes seem to be neglected altogether, only because there are no easily identifiable victims (Anttila, 1974).

In addition to the problems inherent in, or associated with, general criminological research, the study of the victims of crime has to overcome certain problems of its own.

DEARTH OF DATA ON CRIME VICTIMS

Surveys conducted in the past twenty-five years have yielded a considerable amount of data on criminal victimization and have shed much light on the general sociodemographic characteristics of the victims of the selected offenses they cover. In contrast, we have very little systematic information on victims of those crimes not included in the surveys. Nor are there much data available on the psychological makeup, personality, attitudes, and behavior of the victims of crime in general. As a result, victimology lacks a similar body of knowledge to that which criminology has accumulated over the years on adult offenders and juvenile delinquents. This penury makes it difficult to formulate and test advanced hypotheses, let alone develop theories on the victims of crime.

LACK OF COOPERATION

The most practical way of collecting data on the victims of crime is by means of questionnaires, personal and telephone interviews, and psychological and psychiatric testing. And while superficial interviews like the ones used in victimization surveys may generate little reluctance on the part of the interviewees, in-depth interviews and serious attempts to obtain highly personal information from the victims are likely to be met with strong resistance. A large percentage of those approached would no doubt refuse to cooperate or take part in the interview. There are many cases where the victim's unwillingness to cooperate is to be expected:

— In cases where the victimization was a singularly traumatic experience, as in rape or sexual molestation, the victim might want to forget the whole episode and might, therefore, be unwilling to talk about it or discuss it. This unwillingness is likely to increase when the attempt to interview the victim is made a long time after the victimization has occurred or after the victim has successfully removed the unpleasant memories of the event from his or her mind.

— In cases where victims have demonstrated some naivety, credulity, cupidity, greed, stupidity, or dishonesty, as is common in certain types of con games, fraud, swindling, and so forth, they might be ashamed to reveal an unflattering personality trait to the interviewer.

— Feelings of shame, embarrassment, or fear of the law also prevent many victims of blackmail and extortion from reporting the incidents or from talking about them. The so-called "dirty hands" victims involved in the drug trade, prostitution, illegal gambling, stolen goods, smuggling, and so forth are likely to be among the most uncooperative victims when it comes to research. Fear of retaliation may also be a deterrent for some victims.

— In cases where victims have contributed in one way or another to their own victimization, be it through provocation, precipitation, facilitation, or participation, they are likely to be reluctant to reveal the details of their behavior or the traits of their personality. Typical of this category of victims is the consenting minor in statutory rape.

— Whenever the victim has not reported the victimization to the police it may be assumed that he or she has reasons for not wishing to make the incident known or to reveal all the details of the victimization. The same reasons might prevent the victim from cooperating with an interviewer whose aim is to obtain this information.

THE SITUATION OF THE VICTIM

Collecting data on victims' experiences is often difficult due to the situation of the victim:

— In most instances, for example in nonviolent property crimes, the victims cannot be subjected to medical, psychiatric, or psychological examination without their consent, and it is doubtful that many would be willing to give this consent. Contrary to the offender who, when known, is in the hands of the criminal justice authorities and may be forced, under certain circumstances, to submit to various tests to evaluate his personality, assess his mental condition, measure his intelligence, and so forth, the victim is in a different legal position. In general, victims cannot be coerced or compelled to cooperate as offenders usually are.

— In some cases victims are no longer alive or are difficult to locate. They might have moved out of fear of retaliation or renewed victimization, or for some other reason, and their whereabouts and new location may be unknown.

— While the offender in most cases is an individual or several individuals, the victims of crime are not always natural persons: a victim may be a group, a business, or an organization. Organizations are particularly problematic when it comes to victim-centered research. This is probably why victimization research has always suffered from a person-centered bias (see Chapter 2).

Defining the Victim

Despite the frequency with which the word "victim" is used, it is not that easy to define victims or to answer the question, Who is a victim of crime? Recognizing the difficulty, the United States Bureau of Justice Statistics (United States, 1981) points out that for some crimes, such as rape or murder, it is quite clear who has been victimized. But for other crimes, such as welfare or insurance fraud, embezzlement, public corruption, or vagrancy, the victim is less clearly defined. To show how elusive the concept may be at times the Bureau gives the following examples: (1) Crimes in which corporate funds are taken may ultimately be paid for by shareholders. (2) Welfare fraud is absorbed by the taxpayers. (3) Public corruption may affect the trust of the general public toward officeholders. (4) For crimes of property in general, the economic loss involved may be absorbed by the crime victim or may be covered partially or entirely by insurance.

THE VICTIM IN A LITERARY SENSE

The English word "victim," like its French counterpart "victime," is derived from the Latin word "victima," which was originally used to signify a living being offered in sacrifice to the gods. The modern meaning of the word has undergone considerable changes and is now used in a wide variety of contexts. One of the common usages of the word is to designate a person who suffers from the injurious actions of other people, things, or events. The literary meaning of the word "victim" is intimately linked to the emotional and psychological reactions the word evokes. While the word "criminal" is likely to arouse one's indignation, disapproval, and moral condemnation, the word "victim" inspires pity, sympathy, compassion, and commiseration. The criminal and the victim are usually perceived as opposites: black and white, night and day, evil and good, guilty and innocent, Cain and Abel, Goliath and David.

THE VICTIM IN A LEGAL SENSE

In law, the victim is the injured party, the person who suffers prejudice, damage, or loss as a result of a criminal act. The criminal law uses a purely objective criterion to determine who is the victim and who is the offender. The person who perpetrates the material act or omission is, in the eyes of the law, the offender, while the person who suffers the harmful consequences of the act or omission is the victim. Criticizing this superficial and unsubtle distinction, Hans Von Hentig (1948) wrote:

> *Most crimes are directed against a specific individual, his life or property, his sexual self-determination. For practical reasons, the final open manifestation of human motor force which precedes a socially undesirable result is designated as the criminal act, and the actor as the responsible criminal. The various degrees and levels of stimulation or response, the intricate play of interacting forces, is scarcely taken into consideration in our legal distinctions, which must be simple and workable. (p. 438)*

Von Hentig adds that what the law does is to watch the one who acts and the one who is acted upon. By this external criterion a subject and object, a perpetrator and a victim are distinguished. In sociological and psychological terms the situation may be completely different, and in some cases, affirms Von Hentig, the two distinct categories merge, while in others they may be reversed. In other words, the legal conceptions of "criminal" and "victim" give prominence to material facts, while ignoring the psychological particulars of each case and the subjective attributes of the parties involved. Criminology, on the other hand, takes into account not only the objective but the subjective elements as well. Hence, the criminological conception of the victim does not always correspond to the legal one. Von Hentig (1948) stressed this difference as follows:

> *The law considers certain results and the final moves which lead to them. Here it makes a clear-cut distinction between the one who does and the one who suffers. Looking into the genesis of the situation, in a considerable number of cases, we meet a victim who consents tacitly, cooperates, conspires or provokes. The victim is one of the causative elements ... (p. 436)*

The point Von Hentig makes is that the legal designations of criminal and victim do not always correspond to the actual roles both parties have played. Since criminology and victimology are interested in real and not assumed behavior, in actual and not presumptive roles, we may even go further than Von Hentig to suggest that objective research into the interaction leading to the crime proceed independently of the simplistic and superficial labels and designations of criminal and victim.

THE VICTIM IN A CRIMINOLOGICAL SENSE

Although the word "victim" is one of the staples of the criminological language, and although it was used to coin the term "victimology," its real criminological meaning remains unclear and its utility remains in doubt. Just what does the term, as used in criminology and victimology, mean? Is it a label, a stereotype? Is it a state, a condition? Is it meant to assign a status, a role to the one so described? Is it a self-perception, a social construction, an expression of sympathy, a legal qualification, a juridical designation? And just how useful is the term "victim" to criminology?

If the victim designation is a label, and a debasing one at that, then we may ask whether it should have a place in the scientific language. While the label "criminal" has been widely criticized, the use of the label "victim" seems to generate few, if any, objections or criticism. Labeling theorists have decried the stigma, degradation, and stereotyping attached to the label "criminal" and have pointed to the danger of the person being so labeled identifying with the label. Victimologists, on the other hand, seem all too willing (even anxious) to use the label "victim" in a wide variety of contexts. It might well be that the designation is useful (or necessary) for legal purposes. However, the utility of the label, like that of other labels, for research and policy purposes is rather doubtful. The dichotomized nature of the criminal law requires that acts be divided into crimes or noncrimes or that the participants be assigned the status of criminal or victim (Christie, 1977). More neutral, objective, and value-free terms (such as those used in civil or tort law, for example, litigants) seem more appropriate and more useful for social science research. It is certain, for instance, that the concept of precipitation would have escaped a great deal of the criticism it received had it not had the emotional term "victim" attached to it.

In a paper on critical victimology, Walklate (1990) suggests that the concepts of criminal and victim might not be the most useful ones with which to proceed in the policy arena. We should also question the utility of these concepts for research purposes. One negative consequence of the present indiscriminate use of these labels is to perpetuate the popular stereotypes of the crime protagonists and to reinforce the notion that criminals and victims are as different as night and day. The readiness with which these labels are currently applied ignores the complementarity and the interchangeability of the roles of the victim and offender. Using these labels overlooks the fact that today's victims may be tomorrow's offenders and that today's offenders may be yesterday's victims (see Chapters 5 and 6). There seems to be little, if any, justification to apply these black-and-white labels simply on the basis of one discrete incident of victimization occurring during a brief period of time, be it a year or six months, which is what victimization surveys, national or local, actually do. Yet any call to abandon such labels, whose use is firmly entrenched, is bound to encounter fierce resistance and will even require changing the name of the discipline of "victimology" itself. Still, we hope to have succeeded in showing that these value-laden judgmental labels serve no useful research function and thus can be easily replaced by more neutral designations, such as "participants to the conflict," "parties to the dispute," "protagonists," and so forth.

This neutral terminology has several advantages over the pejorative labels of "criminal" and "victim." First, it represents a much needed return to the notion of crime as a conflict (Christie, 1977; Kennedy, 1990) and the notion of conflict as an interaction. The criminal law is interested in actions; criminology should be more concerned with interactions. As Kennedy (1990) points out:

> *Fundamentally, penal law looks more into acts than into interactions — which removes the negotiated feature of civil disputes from penal or criminal ones. Claiming becomes a process of defining an offender and a victim. But this transformation of the dispute does not deny its origins in conflict or the negotiation over punishment that occurs after the criminality is established. (p. 35)*

Second, the proposed judgment-free terminology reemphasizes the artificial nature and the arbitrariness of the distinction between crime and tort, and between criminal and civil law. A third benefit is to avoid the negative consequences (particularly the stigma) of labeling and to avoid the real danger of the participants' self-identification with their labels. Fourth, as sciences of observation and explanation, criminology and victimology need to use a guilt- and blame-free language and to abstain from using terms or labels that imply a priori value-judgments. The normative designations of "criminal" and "victim" imply such a judgment and therefore preempt a thorough and objective investigation into the real and actual roles each party played in the genesis of the crime.

Who Is the Victim in Criminal Law?

As mentioned above, not every crime has a direct, tangible, easily identifiable victim. Acts that are prohibited and made punishable by penal law may thus be classified, according to the type of "victims" involved, into several categories.

CRIMES AGAINST SPECIFIC VICTIMS

Most conventional crimes are committed against specific, individual victims referred to in law as the wronged, injured, or harmed party. This party can either be a natural person, juridical persons (a corporate body), or an animal.

A *natural person* is a human being, whether alive or dead. Certain offenses, such as homicide, assault causing bodily harm, rape, and so forth, can only be perpetrated against a natural, live person. Dead persons may also be the victims of some offenses, such as in the case of desecrating dead bodies or tombs.

Modern penal law equally recognizes the existence of *juridical persons*, that is, a number of natural persons grouped together in some form of association and having rights and obligations distinct from those of the individual members. The law acknowledges that juridical persons can be the victims of crimes committed against patrimony, honor, and so forth. In general, juridical persons may be public corporations (the State, provinces, towns or cities, public institutions, and so forth), private corporations (businesses, companies, syndicates and unions, societies and associations, and so forth), or international organizations (the United Nations, the World Health Organization, the Red Cross, and others). A large part of the so-called "white-collar crime" is committed by juridical persons. Libel, theft, and embezzlement are a few examples of crimes committed against corporate bodies. The State itself is the victim in crimes of treason, espionage, armed insurrection, and so forth.

The specific victim may also be an *animal* as, for example, in the case of bestiality or cruelty to animals.

CRIMES AGAINST NONSPECIFIC VICTIMS

All criminal offenses, whether against specific individuals or not, are supposed to be harmful to one or several social, political, legal, or religious institutions. Yet, there is a whole category of offenses that, by their very nature, are not directed against a specific person, natural or juridical. In such cases, the victim is merely an abstraction, for it is not a definable, identifiable individual who is wronged or who suffers the injurious or harmful effects of the offense. Public order, public morals, public health, public economy, the courts, and religion are all institutions protected by the criminal law, and, as such, they may be considered the nonspecific victims of certain offenses. Public peace is the abstract victim of offenses such as the acts of propagating false news or rumors likely to cause fear among the people, or acts of inciting people to disobey the law. Public economy and public confidence suffer from the acts of producing counterfeit money, forged public bonds, forged official documents, seals, and so forth. Public authority is collectively victimized in cases of rebellion, escape of prisoners, defilement of public monuments, and the like. The constitution is the abstract victim in cases where the administrative and judicial statutes are violated or in cases of conspiracy by government officials.

CRIMES AGAINST A POTENTIAL VICTIM

Between crimes committed against specific or individual victims and crimes committed against abstract, nonspecific victims there is an intermediate category comprised of offenses against a potential victim. In such cases, the offense is not perpetrated against a specific individual. Nobody is actually harmed, though the dangerous nature of the act implies a threat of potential harm to an, as yet, undetermined victim. Such is the case with illegal possession of offensive weapons, dangerous driving or driving while the faculties are impaired (for example, as a result of alcohol consumption), the manufacturing of noxious products, and the sale of dangerous or harmful substances. In all these cases, the offense is determined by the perpetration of the act, even if no actual harm has resulted from it.

CRIMES WITHOUT VICTIMS

In some cases there is no victim, only *two offenders* who jointly perpetrate the prohibited act. This is the case, for instance, of incest between two consenting adults. In some jurisdictions (and this had been the situation in Canada until the criminal code was amended in 1969), the law prohibits homosexual acts and other sexual "deviations" among adults. The two parties involved may be charged and convicted. If, in any of these incidents, one of the two individuals involved is a consenting or willing minor, the criminal law establishes a legal presumption in his or her favor, thus assigning him or her the designation of victim. This legal presumption of victimization is established by law in favor of the minor, regardless of the facts of the case and the actual roles of the two parties in the commission of the offense (see Chapter 11).

In other cases, the offender and the victim may be united in one person. This is the situation Von Hentig (1948) refers to as the "doer-sufferer": an individual who combines the roles of victim and offender. The wounded party in duels and suicide attempts and individuals who mutilate themselves or get another to mutilate them to escape compulsory military service are all doer-sufferers liable to different sanctions in most jurisdictions.

In recent years, some social scientists, particularly Edwin Schur (1965, 1969), have drawn attention to what they call crimes without victims or *victimless crimes*. It seems paradoxical that acts are made criminal by the law when they have no victim. And it is certainly in contradiction to the popular concept of crime, which in the public mind is always associated with the idea of a criminal and a victim or with an individual who transgresses and another who suffers.

Yet, as mentioned above, an act deemed harmful, dangerous, or threatening need not have a real or specific victim to qualify as a criminal offense. Still, there are certain offenses that cannot be easily classified in any of the previous categories. In such cases, there may be no discernible harm, and if the act involved any harm at all it is primarily harm to the participating individuals themselves. Rather than being harmful, dangerous, or injurious, the behaviors in question are simply immoral or sinful acts.

Rubin (1971) defines victimless crime as "behavior not injurious to others but made criminal by statutes based on moral standards which disapprove of certain forms of behavior while ignoring others that are comparable." And Packer (1968) views victimless crime as "offenses that do not result in anyone's feeling that he has been injured so as to impel him to bring the offense to the attention of the authorities." Schur (1965), who used the term "crime without victims" as a title for one of his books, defines the concept as referring essentially to "the willing exchange, among adults, of strongly demanded but legally proscribed goods or services." Schur feels that the concept should be limited to those situations in which one person obtains from another, in a fairly direct exchange, a commodity or personal service that is socially disapproved of and legally proscribed. He contends that in these situations there is not, in the usual sense, a direct and clear harm inflicted by one person against another. Thus the core of the victimless crime situations lies in "the combination of an exchange transaction and lack of apparent harm to others" (Schur, 1965, p. 171).

Naturally, it can be argued that those so-called "victimless crimes" do cause some harm, of one kind or another, to one or more individuals. Schur (1969) accepts the argument that in each of the situations covered by the concept of victimless crime there may be someone who is, in some way, victimized. Thus the drug addict, the unborn fetus, and the prostitute may be viewed as victims of the drug peddler, the abortionist, the client, or the provider of organized prostitution. But he maintains that "because of the transactional nature of the offense, there is no victim in the conventional sense of a citizen complainant who will seek to initiate prosecution and give needed evidence to law enforcement authorities" (Schur, 1969, p. 195).

We should note that the various categories outlined above are not mutually exclusive. Such a grouping is primarily intended to show how vague and loose the designation "victim" is. It is also meant to demonstrate that the existence of an individual or a specific victim is not the sole criterion that guides the legislator in criminalizing a given behavior.

Some Victim Types

Classic typologies of victims (Von Hentig, 1948; Mendelsohn, 1956; Fattah, 1967) have been repeatedly discussed and critically evaluated in the victimological literature. There is no need to further reexamine these typologies or to explain here what has been said over and over again elsewhere. What we will do in the following pages is to discuss some types of victims, shown in Table 4-1, that either do not appear in the earlier typologies or that were dealt with in a simplistic or fleeting manner. We will examine successively some cultural types, some behavioral types, some structural types, and some criminological types. In addition we will dispel the myth of the so-called "born victim."

TABLE 4-1 **Some Victim Types**

Cultural Types	Structural Types	Behavioral Types	Criminological Types
Ideal victims	Less powerful victims	Provoking, precipitating victims	One-time victims
Culturally legitimate victims	Weak victims	Consenting, willing, inviting, soliciting, and participating victims	Occasional victims
Appropriate victims	Helpless and/or defenseless victims	Negligent, careless, imprudent, and reckless victims	Recidivist victims
. Impersonal victims	Have-not victims		Chronic victims
. Disposable/ Expendable victims	Different victims		
. Worthless victims	Deviant victims		
. Deserving victims			

THE BORN VICTIM

In the early days of criminology, Lombroso claimed that criminals are born. And in the early days of victimology some claimed that there are born victims. In 1941 Von Hentig (1941) suggested that "if there are born criminals, it is evident that there are born victims, self-harming and self-destroying through the medium of a pliable outsider" (p. 303).

Von Hentig was simply reiterating what Aldous Huxley (1928) had already claimed in his famous novel *Point Counter Point*. Huxley (1928) argued that "there are born victims, born to have their throats cut, as the cut-throats are born to be hanged. You can see it in their faces. There's a victim type, as well as a criminal type."

Another pioneer in victimology, Ellenberger (1955), a psychiatrist, believed that born victims do exist. He wrote:

> *In summary, we contend that there are individuals, probably in great numbers, whom one could consider as 'born victims', in the sense that they attract criminals, not so much by external circumstances or fleeting event, but by reason of a permanent and unconscious predisposition to play the role of victim. (p. 277)*

These views might have been acceptable at a time when determinism was still in vogue. At present, however, the concept of the "born victim," in the sense of an individual doomed by birth to become the target of criminal victimization is, like the concept of the born criminal, universally rejected. In contemporary victimology, the fatalistic notion of the "born victim" is replaced by other probabilistic concepts such as predisposition, propensity, proneness, and vulnerability to victimization. It is argued that while few individuals may become victims by pure chance or through chance encounters, others tend by reason of structural or behavioral characteristics (such as life-style) to get themselves in situations or interactions likely to lead to criminal victimization. Still others may invite, induce, provoke, precipitate, or attract victimization (see Chapters 10, 11, and 12).

CULTURAL TYPES

Each culture creates its own popular stereotypes of offenders and victims. Society's attitudes and reaction to actual offenders and actual victims are shaped by the extent to which they fit these images and stereotypes. The "ideal victim" is one such stereotype.

The Ideal Victim (Christie, 1986)

As used by Christie (1986), the term "ideal victim" does not refer to the person (or category) who most perceives himself or herself as a victim. Nor does it describe those who are in the greatest danger of being victimized or most often victimized. By an ideal victim Christie means a person (or category of individuals) who, when hit by crime, are most readily given the complete and legitimate status of being a victim. The ideal victim, writes Christie (1986), is as follows:

> *A sort of public status of the same type and level of abstraction as that for example of a "hero" or a "traitor". It is difficult to count these ideal victims. Just as it is difficult to count heroes. But they can be exemplified ... the little old lady on the way home in the middle of the day after having cared for her sick sister. If she is hit on the head by a big man who thereafter grabs her bag and uses the money for liquor or drugs — in that case, we come, in my country, close to the ideal victim. (pp. 18-19)*

The victimized "old lady" in Christie's (1986) example acquires the status of an "ideal victim" by means of at least five attributes:

(1)The victim is weak. Sick, old or very young people are particularly well suited as ideal victims.

(2)The victim was carrying out a respectable project — caring for her sister.

(3)She was where she could not possibly be blamed for being — in the street during the daytime.

(4)The offender was big and bad.

(5)The offender was unknown and in no personal relationship to her. (p. 19)

Christie (1986) gives a contrasting example of a far-from-ideal victim: a young man hanging around in a bar who gets hit on the head by an acquaintance who then takes his money. He points out that ideal victims need — and create — ideal offenders. The two are interdependent. The more ideal a victim is, the more ideal becomes the offender. The more ideal the offender, the more ideal is the victim. Ideal victims do not necessarily have much to do with the prevalence of *real victims*. Most ideal victims are not most frequently represented as real victims. The real victims are the negation of those who are most frequently represented. In all official counts, notes Christie, the man in the bar is a much more common victim than the "little old lady." However, ideal victims are very much afraid of being victimized. There seems to be a strong relationship between the qualities that qualify a person for becoming an ideal victim and having a particular fear of being the victim of crime, particularly violent crime. Many among the real victims, on the other hand, do not fear, probably because they have more correct information regarding the real risks. They hang around in crime-exposed areas, but they know, by personal observation, that crime is only a minor phenomenon in these areas compared to all other life-activities that go on. The ideal victims, the "little old ladies," get their information through the mass media. They have no personal control of the information conveyed. They get a picture of an area — an existence — where crime is the major activity (Christie, 1986, p. 27).

The Culturally Legitimate Victim

The concept of the culturally legitimate victim was first used by Weis and Borges in 1973 to describe victims of rape. They point out that socialization and especially sex-role learning exploit males and females and produce victims and offenders. The authors suggest that a male-dominated society, where most positions of power and influence are occupied by men, tends to establish and perpetuate the idea of the woman as a legitimate object for victimization. In such a society, social processes prepare the woman for her role as a potential victim and provide the procedures to make her a socially approved or legitimate victim for rape.

The culturally legitimate victim is a broad type, and it is possible to identify several subtypes, that is, groups whose victimization is encouraged, condoned, tolerated, and not condemned by the culture. We will discuss below some types which are culturally regarded as appropriate targets for victimization.

Appropriate Victims

Cultural as well as subcultural norms designate certain individuals or groups as appropriate targets for victimization. In primitive societies, in youth gangs, and in other self-contained groups marked by inner solidarity, violence against members of the out-group is tolerated and sometimes encouraged, while violence against members of the in-group is strongly condemned. The normative system governing these societies or groups designates the out-group members as legitimate targets for victimization. A national survey of attitudes toward violence in the United States found that excluding people from groups to which one feels related can serve as a rationalization that justifies violence toward them or that makes violence inflicted on such people more easily accepted (Blumenthal et al., 1972; Conklin, 1975).

In most jurisdictions, and this had been the case in Canada until the law was changed, forcible sexual intercourse with one's wife is not a criminal offense and is excluded from the code's definition of rape. The wife "raped" by her husband is a culturally legitimate victim. The concept extends to other forms of violence in the family. Despite growing concern over child abuse, children continue to be considered legitimate targets for the use of physical force in the process of training and upbringing. Also, until recently, husband-wife violence was often regarded as legitimate by the police and the courts.

Even now, the unfaithful wife exemplifies the culturally legitimate victim in many cultures, and the husband who kills his adulterous wife is either exempted from punishment or treated with extreme leniency. Writing in 1969, Goode reported that, not long ago, courtroom practice in Texas supported the outraged husband who killed his wife and her lover when he caught them in *flagrante delicto*. And on Sunday, February 21, 1988, the investigative television program "60 Minutes" aired a segment on wife-killing and wife-mutilation in Brazil. The program showed actual cases of Brazilian husbands who slew, burned, or mutilated their wives with impunity. The program made it abundantly clear that female spouses in Brazil are culturally legitimate victims. In other words, they are "fair game" to their husbands.

Impersonal victims. Impersonal, nonspecific, and intangible victims, such as the government, large corporations, and organizations, are considered by many as appropriate targets for victimization. Victimizing them is subject to fewer (if any) moral restraints and arouses less guilt than victimization directed against a personal, identifiable victim. The impersonal and diffuse character of the victim and its intangibility evoke little moral resistance in the person contemplating the victimization. Sykes and Matza (1957) wrote:

> *Insofar as the victim is physically absent, unknown, or a vague abstraction (as is often the case in delinquent acts committed against property), the awareness of the victim's existence is weakened. Internalized norms and anticipations of the reactions of others must somehow be activated, if they are to serve as guides for behavior; and it is possible that a diminished awareness of the victim plays an important part in determining whether or not this process is set in motion. (p. 668)*

The idea of stealing from or cheating the government or a large organization raises fewer moral scruples than the idea of cheating a person or stealing from a family. In his study of crime and customs of the Hungarians in Detroit in the early thirties, Beynon (1935) found that certain coal-stealing gangs received a sort of social approval in the Hungarian colony. The reason for approval had nothing to do with the material act or its perpetrators but with the victim. The coal was stolen, not from some individual, but from the property of an impersonal, unknown railroad company, which translated, in their thinking, to the absentee nobleman in their home country from whose woods their parents used to gather firewood. The conversation between the researcher and the recording steward of a Hungarian church in Detroit illustrates well how impersonal victims are perceived as appropriate targets. In answer to a question Beynon (1935) asked about his fuel for the winter, the steward replied:

> *We buy only stolen coal. It costs us $3.00 a ton which is less than half what we pay the coal dealers. The boys come and take our orders in the afternoon and then steal the coal at night from the cars on the railway tracks. Do you think it*

> *is wrong to steal coal or to buy stolen coal? No, of course not. You see, it is this way, stealing coal is different from other stealing. If I would take five cents of your money, that would be real stealing. You are a man just like me. I know you. I have never in my life stolen like that. No honest man would. Only the gypsies steal from other people that way. But coal stealing isn't like that at all. Why? The coal stands there on that railroad tracks [*sic*], and we never see the man who owns that railroad. It is an estate of some kind just like the estates in Hungary. Why should not the poor people get their coal from it? (pp. 763-764)*

Smigel and Ross (1970), who studied bureaucracies as victims, suggest that the size, wealth, and impersonality of big business and government are attributes that make it seem excusable, according to many people, to steal from these victims. Such popular attitudes are behind a modern preventive technique used by certain American enterprises in an attempt to personalize the victim, thus evoking pity and compassion in the potential offender. Thus, in certain motels in the United States a sign is placed in each room that reads, "If any towels are missing when you leave, the maid cleaning the room will be responsible for them." Smigel and Ross see such a notice as a device to deter theft by evoking sympathy for an individual rather than for a bureaucracy.

Disposable/expendable, worthless, and deserving victims. What characterizes these three subtypes of culturally legitimate victims is society's attitude and reaction to their victimization. Normal public attitude to criminal victimization, in which a fellow citizen and human being suffers tangible injury, harm, or loss, is one of sympathy, compassion, and commiseration. The victimization of individuals belonging to these subtypes, however, does not evoke any of these positive feelings. In other words, nobody feels sorry for the victim. There is no outcry of indignation and little, if anything, is done to pursue those responsible for the victimization or to bring them to justice. When this occasionally happens, the sentence of the court is, more often than not, an acquittal or one of extreme leniency.

Although these three subtypes of cultural victims are similar in many respects, they may still be distinguished from each other. The main difference between them lies in cultural stereotypes and social attitudes and in the way they are perceived and treated by the normative system of society.

Disposable/expendable victims. The attitude to "disposable victims" or "expendable victims" is one of hostility and antagonism bordering on hate, and their victimization is often welcomed with a sigh of relief. This is the lot that, in the past, was reserved for witches. At present, it is reserved for criminals and outlaws. Since they are disposable, they may be readily sacrificed and used as scapegoats to deter others or to show that society really means what it says when it threatens to punish those who commit crime. Whatever victimization they suffer, especially while they are behind bars, causes no uproar or even concern among the general public, who couldn't care less what happens to them. Their complaints, if ever heard, fall on deaf ears, as if they are not entitled to the same kind of protection the rest of society enjoys.

Disposable/expendable victims are, to use a term coined by Spitzer (1975) in another context, "social junk." That is why, whenever they are killed, whether by legal execution or by other inmates, the general reaction is one of "good riddance."

Worthless victims. As a result of deeply anchored prejudices, our culture defines certain groups and the members of those groups as worthless. These are mostly people who are living in society but who are not really part of it. They have chosen their own life-style, which the majority does not approve of, and have decided to live on the margin of society. They have their own subcultures that neatly separate them from the rest of society. Social attitudes to "worthless victims" is one of contempt and their victimization is usually met with tacit approval. They are society's outcasts: homosexuals, prostitutes, pimps, drug addicts, vagrants, skid-row residents, and so on. The slang words used to describe them, such as "faggot," "queer," "whore," "narc," and "hobo," reflect well the disdain society has for them and shape the general reaction to their victimization. Their status as outcasts renders them reluctant to seek the protection of the police or even to report their victimization. They are therefore regarded by potential criminals and juvenile gangs as easy targets who may be victimized with impunity. The general perception of their "worthlessness" also explains the laxity in solving their cases once they are victimized (see Chapter 10).

Deserving victims. These are victims who, through their dishonest, inconsiderate, deceitful, or reckless behavior, are seen as deserving their victimization. The popular judgment, passed when they are victimized, is one of "he only got what he deserved." This epitomizes society's attitude and reaction to this type of victim.

Deserving victims fit both the cultural type and the behavioral type, depending on which criterion one uses for typologizing them: the behavior of the victim or society's attitude. The social attitude to deserving victims is one of indifference coupled sometimes with secret admiration for their victimizer. Their victimization is not met with the proper action but rather with inaction and, occasionally, with inner satisfaction. The perfect example of the deserving victim is the victim of a con game or some other type of swindle who was trying to steal, cheat, or realize some dirty profit but who finally got fleeced.

Deserving victims are characteristically "dirty hands" victims or "guilty" victims. Because of this, their victimization, rather than evoking pity, sometimes elicits this comforting but wicked feeling that the "dirty bastard" finally got what he deserved. In the Oscar-winning movie *The Sting* with Paul Newman and Robert Redford, the elaborate con scheme revolves around a typically "deserving victim," whose manners, arrogance, and dishonesty render him so antipathetic to those watching the movie that his victimization is met not with sympathy for the "sucker" but with applause.

Table 4-2 illustrates the difference between disposable, worthless, and deserving victims.

TABLE 4-2 **Social Attitude and Reaction to Certain Types of Victims**

Type of Victim	Typical Group	Social Attitude	Social Reaction to Victimization
Disposable/ Expendable	Criminals Outlaws	Hostility Antagonism Hate	Outright relief
Worthless	Deviants Outcasts	Contempt Disdain	Tacit approval
Deserving	Dishonest Suckers	Indifference	Inaction Inner satisfaction

STRUCTURAL TYPES

Structural types are groups who, because of some structural variables, are more vulnerable to certain forms of victimization, criminal and otherwise, than others. They are more exposed and less protected than other groups. The hierarchy created by the political and economic systems results in an unequal distribution of wealth and power and casts certain groups and classes in victim roles. Those who are at the bottom of the ladder of the social hierarchy are the ones who suffer the bulk of victimization. Their share of victimization is disproportionate to their numbers.

We can identify several structural types, for example:

- —The less powerful (women in a patriarchal society, unorganized consumers in a consumer society, etc.).
- —The weak (the elderly, the handicapped, etc.).
- —The helpless and/or the defenseless (very young children, institutionalized populations such as inmates in penal institutions, psychiatric patients, the mentally handicapped, children in orphanages, etc.).
- —The have-nots.
- —The different (racial, ethnic, and religious minorities, etc.).
- —The deviant (homosexuals, transsexuals, drug-addicts, alcoholics, prostitutes, gamblers, etc.).

Structural vulnerability may also be related to the exercise of certain occupations that render those who practice them particularly exposed to criminal attacks, such as taxi drivers, bank cashiers, pharmacists, and operators of small grocery stores (see Chapter 10).

As mentioned earlier in Chapter 1, structural and cultural vulnerability often coincide and are difficult to distinguish or to separate. That is why several of the structural types listed above overlap with the cultural ones. But although the victimization of some structural types may be condoned or tolerated by the culture, the victimization of other structural types can be considered a cultural taboo. Young girls, for example, may be considered structural types in incest victimization, although incest is strongly condemned by the culture.

BEHAVIORAL TYPES

Provoking, Precipitating Victims

The existence of a provoking victim type has been acknowledged for a very long time. Modern criminal codes recognize provocation by the victim as an extenuating circumstance that reduces a murder to manslaughter or makes a criminal homicide an excusable one (see Chapter 11).

Victims who fit this type are those whose behavior precipitates, triggers, or acts as a catalyst for the attack against them. Wolfgang (1958) coined the term "victim-precipitated" to refer to those criminal homicides in which the victim is a direct, positive precipitator in the crime. The role of the victim in such cases is characterized by his or her having been the first to show and use a deadly weapon or to strike a blow in an altercation — in short, the first to commence the interplay or resort to physical violence. A couple of cases cited by Wolfgang (1958) and Curtis (1975) will help illustrate this behavioral type. Among the victim-precipitated homicide cases Wolfgang encountered in his research is the case of a husband who accused his wife of giving money to another man. While the wife was making breakfast, the husband attacked her with a milk bottle, then a brick, and finally a piece of concrete block. Having a butcher knife in hand, she stabbed him during the fight. In another case, during a lovers' quarrel, the male (victim) hit his mistress and threw a can of kerosene at her. She retaliated by throwing the liquid at him, and then tossed a lighted match in his direction. He died from the burns.

Curtis (1975) illustrates victim-precipitation with the case of a party in an altercation who hands the other a gun, and, knowing full well the other's hostile mood, accuses him of not having the "guts to shoot." We will have more to say on victim-provocation and victim-precipitation later when we discuss the functional role of the victim (see Chapter 11).

Consenting, Willing, Inviting, Soliciting, and Participating Victims

Contrary to popular conception, criminal victimization does not always take place against the will or without the consent of the victim. Ever since crime came to be regarded as an offense against the Sovereign (and later against the State and society), the nonconsent of the victim is no longer a prerequisite for the constitution of the offense, nor is the consent of the victim necessary to bring charges against the offender and to pursue the case until conviction. As a result, we have in the criminal code offenses that may be committed even when the party who suffers the injury, harm, or loss is a willing, consenting partner. So, why would the law criminalize an act to which the "victim" does not object? Sometimes this is done to protect individuals judged incapable of giving free, enlightened consent or who are unable to protect themselves against victimization and exploitation. The typical example is "statutory rape" where the consenting female is underage. Other examples are violations of laws prohibiting the following: the hiring of children under a certain age to do specific jobs; the use of children in the production of pornographic material; the access of minors to certain places (racetracks, gambling casinos, adult movie theaters, etc.); or the sale of, or serving of, liquor to children. The prohibition may not necessarily have to do with the protection of minors. It is usually extended to other groups judged to be in need of protection, such as the mentally handicapped or even individuals, not mentally handicapped, who are in danger of being exploited, as in the case of loan sharking. At other times, the criminalization of the behavior, in spite of the consent of the victim, is done because the act is judged sufficiently injurious, harmful, or dangerous enough as to warrant its interdiction even when the parties involved are consenting. For example, causing a deliberate injury may qualify as wounding, even when done with the consent or at the request of the victim.

Many of the willing, consenting, participating victims are in reality *legally created victims*. These are persons who are prohibited from doing things under the guise or pretext of protection. Restriction of freedom and outright discrimination are often couched in terms of "protection." A good example is the differential age specified by the law for consent to heterosexual and homosexual relations. It is clear that the higher age of consent required for homosexual acts is not meant to protect those who are homosexually inclined, but to discriminate against them. Even laws that are really meant to protect certain vulnerable or exposed groups often fail to take into account the sexual and emotional needs of the members of these groups. What they do, in fact, is to impose restrictions on the behavior of those judged in need of protection, and thus deprive them of doing things that others are allowed to do. For example, the law that says a minor (under sixteen, eighteen, or twenty-one depending on the jurisdiction) or a mentally handicapped person cannot give free, enlightened consent to have sex amounts in practice to a prohibition for the "protected" person to have sex. All such paternalistic laws are problematic because they raise the question of the extent to which the criminal law should try to protect people against their will and their wishes or restrict the freedoms of those who are under a certain arbitrarily set age.

What these paternalistic laws do is create consenting and conniving victims. Offenses committed against consenting, soliciting, and participating victims have an extremely high dark figure. Not surprisingly, these types of victims are generally uncooperative in their dealings with the criminal justice system and are naturally excluded from compensation programs. However, the consenting, willing, or participating victims should not be confused with victims who cooperate with their victimizer under threat or duress or because of fear, such as victims of blackmail, extortion, or incest.

Negligent, Careless, Imprudent, and Reckless Victims

People do not try to protect themselves or their property against criminal victimization with the same care, zeal, or diligence. Their attitudes and behavior, and the precautions and protective measures they take (or do not take), make it possible to qualify them as prudent or imprudent, careful or careless, circumspect or reckless, cautious or negligent, and so forth. These adjectives or qualities denote extreme points of a continuum, with most people fitting somewhere in-between. Moreover, these are general traits describing the general attitude or behavioral patterns of a given individual; they do not describe the person's attitude or behavior in all situations at all times. One may be prudent in certain situations (being in foreign territory) and imprudent in others (being in familiar territory); circumspect on some occasions (when sober) and reckless on others (when drunk). Still, certain individuals may be designated as being generally of a negligent or careless type, or as a reckless or imprudent type. These attitudinal and behavioral traits are by no means static. It is known, for example, that reckless, imprudent people become prudent and less reckless with marriage or familial responsibilities, advanced age, and so forth. The traits are also dynamic in that they change according to the kind of interaction in which the person is engaged and the kind of person(s) with whom he or she is interacting. A person who may be very prudent and circumspect when dealing with strangers may be totally disarmed and thus lacking in prudence when interacting with members of the family or close friends.

The role these victim types play in property victimization has been empirically demonstrated. But the role is not limited to property offenses as it plays an important part in other victimizations (for example, hitchhike victimization). According to the Opportunity theory, many criminals are opportunists who take advantage of situations and environmental opportunities, many of which are created by the prospective victims' negligent, careless, imprudent, reckless, or facilitating behavior. The popular saying, "The occasion makes the thief," is a vulgarization of the Opportunity theory. While the victim's behavior may be a facilitator of crimes of the opportunists, it is also a target selection criterion in crimes committed by professionals. Except for the few professionals who might be tempted by the challenge a hard target may offer, most will find easier targets more attractive (see Chapter 9).

The distinction between inviting/soliciting victims and careless/negligent ones is not always easy. Opportunities for criminal victimization may be deliberately created by the prospective victims. In her study of shoplifting in Chicago, Cameron (1964) points out that the lavish displays of merchandise that department stores exhibit to encourage impulsive buying are, for the experienced pilferer, there for the taking. Gibbens and Prince (1962) reported that a store in England set out to achieve a certain level of shoplifting to demonstrate the adequate lure of the goods on display. If the shoplifting rate fell below the anticipated level, the store rearranged its shelves and counters on the assumption that they were not offering sufficient temptation for impulse buying — and stealing. Naturally, department stores who act in this way fit the inviting/soliciting type more than the negligent type.

CRIMINOLOGICAL TYPES

One-time, Occasional, Recidivist, and Chronic Victims

The notion of the "born victim" is now generally rejected as a fatalistic and deterministic concept more appropriate to theology than to behavioral science. But there is abundant empirical evidence from victimization surveys indicating that certain individuals may suffer frequent and repeated victimization during the reference period. In other words, they are recidivist or repeat victims.

We may divide victims, according to the frequency of their victimizations, into several categories or types: the one-timer, the occasional, the experienced or recidivist, the chronic, and so on. The one-timer is someone who has suffered only a single victimization. The occasional is someone who has suffered two or three isolated and unrelated victimizations over a lifetime or a very long period of time. The recidivist is someone who is subject to a frequent and persistent pattern of victimization within a relatively short period of time. The chronic victim is someone whose life is a continuing series of victimizations. Categorizing the one-timers does not pose a major operationalization problem. But the lines of demarcation between the other three categories, the occasional, the recidivist, and the chronic, are somewhat arbitrary.

Victimization surveys, without exception, found that while the majority of respondents do not report having been victimized even once, a small top-risk category seemed to be victimized almost incessantly. An earlier victimization survey by Aromaa (1974a, 1974b), in Finland, revealed some striking victimization patterns. The survey found the following:

— One-fourth of all reported violent victimizations were concentrated on 1 percent of the respondents.

— One-third of the acts of violence were concentrated on 2 percent of the respondents.

— More than one-half of the acts of violence reported concerned 5 percent of the respondents.

— Of the respondents, 85 percent did not report any victimization during the two-year period covered by the survey. The figure could have been higher had very mild forms of violence, such as threats, pushing, and shoving, not been included in the questionnaire.

Another study, which examined the attributes of crime victims admitted to the emergency room of a Texas hospital, found that in the population sample of assault victims, recidivist victims comprised 26 percent of the total (Johnson et al., 1973). Ziegenhagen (1976) studied the repeated victimization of some individuals, and his findings suggest that recidivist victims can be distinguished from the general victim population by distinctive individual, social, and attitudinal orientations.

The label "recidivist victim" may be applied to an individual, and also to a business or organization, who has been frequently and repeatedly victimized on separate occasions within a relatively short period of time, either by the same offender or by different ones. When frequent, repeated victimizations of the same kind befall the same person and extend over a very long period or over a lifetime, we may justifiably describe the person as a "chronic victim."

The German psychiatrist Reimer Hinrichs (1987) used the label "chronic victim" as the title for his book. In the book, Hinrichs reports the findings of a comparative research on victimization he conducted in West Berlin and Philadelphia. To define who the chronic victims are, Hinrichs used different categories from the ones suggested above. First, he divided the victims into four categories according to the frequency and the time frame of the violent victimization, which occurred after they were twelve years old. The four categories are as follows:

1. A single victimization.
2. At least two victimizations, but no more than two, within a five-year period.
3. At least two victimizations within a five-year period, but no more than one victimization of the same category within a six-month period.
4. Multiple victimization: at least two victimizations of the same category within a six-month period.

Hinrichs placed the first two groups into a category he calls "occasional victims" and the last two groups in a category he calls "chronic victims." He then set out to compare the characteristics of the two types to find out whether they were different. Hinrichs also talks about "victim careers," an obvious parallel to "criminal careers."

Recidivist and chronic victims are of particular importance to victimological research as they can shed light on the factors and variables associated with certain types of criminal victimization, and they can enhance our understanding of the notions of proneness and vulnerability.

Summary

The first part of this chapter highlighted the importance of studying the victim as well as the problems, the difficulties, and the dangers of such a study. We saw that the study of the victim opens a new, challenging, and extremely promising research area in criminology. It raises a number of issues and questions quite different from those that have been the main focus of research in traditional criminology. And there are many reasons that render the study of victims of crime essential, indeed indispensable, for a better understanding of the phenomenon of crime.

As useful as the study of crime victims may be, it is not without dangers. A real danger is the possibility that interest will simply shift from the individual offender to the individual victim. Another danger is the potential overemphasis on criminal behaviors involving an individual, identifiable victim to the exclusion or neglect of other types, such as corporate victimization.

Victimological research has also to deal with a number of specific problems, such as the dearth of data on crime victims, the lack of cooperation of many victims, and so forth. Even the definition of the term "victim" is a problematic task, and whomever the criminal law considers a victim does not always fit or concur with the criminological concept of a victim. Furthermore, many criminal acts are not committed against specific, tangible victims. There are crimes against nonspecific or abstract victims and others made punishable because of the danger to a potential and, as yet, undetermined victim. And there are crimes that are considered by many as being victimless crimes because they have no victim. All this shows how vague and loose is the designation of "victim." It also demonstrates that the existence of an individual or specific victim is not the sole criterion that guides the legislator in criminalizing those with a given behavior.

In the second part of the chapter some types of victims were discussed which either do not appear in the earlier typologies or, in the early days of victimology, were dealt with in a simplistic or fleeting manner. First, we challenged the concept of the "born victim" and then we examined four major types of victims: cultural types, structural types, behavioral types, and criminological types. Under cultural types we discussed the ideal victim and the culturally legitimate victim, as well as other culturally appropriate victims such as impersonal victims, disposable/expendable victims, worthless victims, and deserving victims. Structural types include those who are powerless or occupy a low position in the hierarchy of power. This includes the weak, the have-nots, the helpless and the defenseless, the different, and the deviant. We also examined some behavioral types, such as the provoking, precipitating, and participating victims and the negligent, imprudent, and reckless victims. We concluded our analysis by dividing victims, according to the frequency of their victimization, into different types: the one-timer, the occasional, the recidivist, and the chronic victims. As the criteria used for typologizing victims are different, the types are not mutually exclusive, and the same victim may thus belong to more than one type. All of these types will be the subject of further discussions in the next chapters, in particular, Chapters 6, 10, 11, and 12.

FIVE

The Homogeneity of the Victim/Offender Populations

Not only does considerable overlap exist between populations of victims and offenders as demonstrated by the substantial proportion of violators having also been victims, but considerable evidence exists that the experience of being victimized increases the propensity for offending and that populations of victims and offenders have homogeneous characteristics ... Clearly any theory that assumes no overlap exists between populations of victims and offenders or that they are distinct types of persons distorts the empirical research.

Albert J. Reiss, Jr. (1981, pp. 710-711)

Empirical research is increasingly gnawing away at the concept of mutually exclusive offender and victim populations, showing it to be a figment of political imagination and a sop to social conscience ... In some instances, therefore, it may be most appropriate to analyze crime as a form of social interaction arising out of specific social contexts in which the distinction between offender and victim is not always conceptually helpful. This is particularly true of direct contact crimes against persons.

Susan J. Smith (1986, p. 98)

How Many Victims?

Having examined, in the previous chapter, various conceptual and definitional issues related to the notion of "victim" and having reviewed and discussed various types of crime victims, we will now proceed to a general description of the victim population using quantitative data collected through victimization surveys. Information on how many victims there are in Canada, the United States, and the United Kingdom will be followed by an examination of their sociodemographic characteristics. This examination will stress the extraordinary similarities between the victim and offender populations.

CANADA

Official crime statistics, such as those published by Statistics Canada or the Federal Bureau of Investigation in the United States give virtually no information on the victims of crime or the incidence of crime not reported to the police. A recent revision of the Uniform Crime Reporting system in Canada will yield incident-based data that will provide information on selected offender, victim, and situational characteristics. Until such time, we have to rely on victimization surveys conducted in various countries in the past twenty-five years. These surveys provide a fair amount of information on the numbers and characteristics of those who are victimized by crime.

In 1982, the Ministry of the Solicitor General, with the assistance of Statistics Canada, conducted the Canadian Urban Victimization Survey in seven major urban centers (Canada, 1983-1988): greater Vancouver, Edmonton, Winnipeg, Toronto, Montreal, Halifax-Dartmouth, and St. Johns (see Chapter 2). The survey (Canada, 1983) provides extensive information on the extent of reported and unreported urban crime during 1981, the risk of criminal victimization, the impact of crime, public perceptions of crime and the criminal justice system, and victims' perceptions of their experiences. Sample sizes for the survey, which was conducted over the telephone, ranged from 6,910 in one city to 9,563 in another, with more than 61,000 interviews completed in all. On the basis of these interviews, statistical estimates were made for the general population of sixteen and over in the seven cities. The eight categories of crimes included in the survey are as follows: sexual assault, robbery, assault, break-and-entry, motor vehicle theft, theft of household property, theft of personal property, and vandalism.[1]

For the year 1981, there were more than 700,000 personal victimizations of people over sixteen (sexual assault, robbery, assault, and theft of personal property), and almost 900,000 household victimizations (break-and-enter, motor vehicle theft, theft of household property, and vandalism) in the seven cities surveyed (see Table 5-1). Table 5-2 shows that 42 percent of these incidents had been reported to the police.

These aggregate numbers cloak great variations in the frequency of the offenses included in the survey. The *Canadian Urban Victimization Survey Bulletin* (Canada, 1983), points out the following:

> *Most of these incidents, it should be noted, did not involve those offences which evoke our greatest fears. There were relatively few sexual assaults or robberies, for example. Far more frequent were thefts of personal property (i.e. without contact), and assaults. Similarly, theft of household property was the most frequent of household offences, followed by break and enter and vandalism, with relatively few motor vehicle thefts. While in the public consciousness crime is generally equated with violence, in the* **experience** *of Canadians, crime is rarely violent. Canadians are far more likely to be victims of crimes against property than crimes against the person. (p. 2)*

TABLE 5-1 **Incident Rates**

Personal Offences	Population aged 16 and older in seven cities			4,975,900
			Males	2,357,000
			Females	2,618,900
Type of Incident	**Estimated Incidents**	**Rates per 1000 Population 16 and older**		
		Total	**Male**	**Female**
- All personal incidents	702,200	141.0	154.0	129.0
- All violent incidents	352,300	70.0	90.0	53.0
- Sexual Assaults	17,200	3.5	0.8	5.8
- Robbery	49,400	10.0	13.0	7.0
- Assault	285,700	57.0	79.0	39.0
- Personal Theft	349,900	70.0	66.0	74.0

Household Offences	Total households in seven cities = 2,424,900	
Type of Incident	**Estimated Incidents**	**Rates per 1000 Households**
All household incidents	898,400	369
Break and Enter	227,400	94
Motor Vehicle Theft	40,600	17
Household Theft	417,300	172
Vandalism	213,100	88

Note: Reprinted by permission, from Table 1, Ministry of the Solicitor General of Canada, *Victims of Crime, Canadian Urban Victimization Survey Bulletin*. (1) (Ottawa: 1983), 3.

TABLE 5-2 **Number of Incidents of Selected Types and Proportion not Reported to Police**

Type of Incident	Estimated Incidents	Percent of Estimated Incidents	Percent Unreported	Percent Reported
Sexual Assault	17,200	1	62	38
Robbery	49,300	3	55	45
Assault	285,700	18	66	34
Break & Enter	227,400	14	36	64
Motor Vehicle Theft	40,600	3	30	70
Household Theft	417,300	26	56	44
Personal Theft	349,900	22	71	29
Vandalism	213,100	13	65	35
TOTAL	1,600,500	100	58	42

Note: Reprinted by permission, from Table 2, Ministry of the Solicitor General of Canada, *Victims of Crime, Canadian Urban Victimization Survey Bulletin*. (1) (Ottawa: 1983), 3.

As we shall see, the aggregate numbers also mask large differences in the rates of victimization by age, gender, area of residence, and other sociodemographic variables.

The Canadian General Social Survey (Sacco and Johnson, 1990) covered the noninstitutional population throughout the ten provinces of Canada. The inclusion age was fifteen rather than sixteen. According to the survey, an estimated 4.8 million Canadians fifteen years of age and over were victimized by 5.4 million criminal incidents in 1987. About one-third of the victimization incidents were of a violent nature, with assault accounting for the vast majority (82 percent). There were actually too few incidents of sexual assault reported by the respondents to produce statistically reliable estimates. Approximately 40 percent of all victimization incidents involved crimes committed against households. Twenty-two percent involved theft of personal property.

THE UNITED STATES

On the basis of data collected by the National Crime Survey, the United States Bureau of Justice Statistics (United States, 1985) estimated that in 1982, 3.2 percent of the nation's population (or about one out of thirty-one Americans aged twelve and older) was the victim of rape, robbery, or assault.[2] This is equivalent to approximately six million Americans. Assault victims were the majority of violent crime victims: 2.5

percent of the population were assaulted (about 1 per 40 people). Robbery victims were the next most numerous: 0.7 percent of Americans were robbed (1 per 143 people). Of the three violent crimes measured, rape was the least prevalent: 0.07 percent of the population were raped (roughly 1 per 1,400 Americans). The proportion of females victimized by rape was about twice as high at 0.14 percent (1 per 700 females), which reflects the fact that nearly all rape victims are females. About two-thirds of those assaulted were victims of simple assault; the balance were victims of aggravated assault. About 1.7 percent of the American population were the victims of simple assault in 1982 (approximately 1 per 59 Americans); and 0.9 percent were the victims of aggravated assault (or 1 per 111 persons).[3]

In 1988, the Bureau of Justice Statistics reported that in the previous year almost 5 percent of the nation's households had a member who was the victim of a violent crime (United States, 1988). Five percent of all households were burglarized at least once during the year, and 17 percent had a completed or attempted theft. Approximately 3 percent of the United States households were victims of both personal crimes (rape, robbery, aggravated assault, simple assault, personal theft) and household crimes (household theft, burglary, motor vehicle theft). About 1 percent of households were touched by both personal theft and violence. These estimates were unchanged from 1986. The percentages revealed by the 1988 survey (United States, 1989) were strikingly similar to those of 1987 and 1986.

THE UNITED KINGDOM

In England, Walmsley (1986) reports that under 5 percent of offenses recorded by the police involve personal violence, and the most serious of these — life-endangering offenses and armed robbery — constitute only one-third of 1 percent of recorded offenses.

Walmsley (1986) points out that while these percentages help put the problem in perspective, crime's seriousness and impact must not be underestimated. Over 150,000 violent offenses were recorded in 1984, over 10,000 of them offenses of the most serious type. In 1984, there were eleven victims of homicide per one million population, a rate less than half of that for Canada.

Walmsley's figures are based on *recorded* offenses and are therefore lower than those estimated from victimization surveys. The British Crime Survey (Hough and Mayhew, 1983) indicated some 6 million incidents involving theft; 2.5 million incidents of vandalism (or criminal damage); half a million incidents involving some form of violence (woundings, sexual offenses, and robberies); and a further 1.5 million incidents of common assault. The survey also indicated around one million incidents involving threatening behavior, while 10 percent of households believed that milk bottles had been stolen from their doorstep at least once in the year covered by the survey (1981), making this the single most common, if least serious, crime in Britain.

The 1988 British Crime Survey (Mayhew, Elliott, and Dowds, 1989) revealed an estimated 13 million incidents in 1987 that fell into the British Crime Survey categories of crimes against individuals and their private property. The vast majority were offenses against property. Wounding, sexual offenses, and common assaults comprised only 17 percent of survey offenses, and when common assaults were excluded, the figure drops to 6 percent. The survey indicates that motor vehicles are a particularly common target for crime. Thus, theft of and from vehicles, and damage to them, accounted for nearly one-third of all crimes uncovered by the survey. One in five owners faced some sort of vehicle offense in 1987.

CANADIAN AND UNITED STATES COMPARISONS

American victimization surveys are national surveys conducted regularly on a yearly basis, and they cover the country as a whole. The Canadian Urban Victimization Survey, on the other hand, covered only seven cities and was conducted once only in 1982. Because of this and because of substantial differences in the methodology used by both surveys, the data are not readily comparable. Comparisons of official crime statistics are fraught with dangers as well (see Chapter 2), and the pitfalls are even greater when it comes to international or cross-cultural comparisons.

Because criminal homicide is not included in victimization surveys and because it has a relatively low dark figure, it is possible to compare the official homicide data in Canada with that in the United States. In 1985, the United States Bureau of Justice Statistics reported that in the previous ten years the highest level of criminal homicides was registered in 1980. One of every ten thousand Americans was murdered that year (United States, 1985). This translates into a rate of 10 per 100,000 population. The same year in Canada, according to Statistics Canada, there was a total of 593 victims of criminal homicide (murder, nonnegligent manslaughter, and infanticide). There were 2.47 victims killed by the three offenses per 100,000 population.[4] In other words, the Canadian criminal homicide rate in 1980 was roughly one-quarter the American rate. The Canadian ten-year average rate for the period 1974 to 1983 was 2.78 per 100,000. The average rate was exactly one-fifth the average rate for suicide during the same period (13.9 per 100,000) and one-eighth the average rate for motor vehicle accident deaths, which stood at 22.1 per 100,000.

Sociodemographic Characteristics of Victims of Crime

Victimization surveys provide empirical support to criminologists' contention that criminality and victimization are clustered within certain groups and certain areas and that there is a much greater affinity between offenders and victims than is commonly believed.[5] The idea that victims of crime share common characteristics with the criminal and delinquent populations runs counter to popular perceptions and to the generally held stereotypes of victims. Singer (1981) points out the following:

> *The idea that victims and offenders are part of the same homogeneous population runs contrary to the public's popular impression that criminals are distinct from their innocent victims. (p. 779)*

Without the information now available from victimization surveys, few would have accepted Anttila's statement, made in 1974, in which she declared that both victims and criminals, particularly in violent crime, appear to be odd people, inclined to unlawfulness, provocative, and easily provoked. She noted that "the same individuals may alternatingly or even simultaneously turn up as offenders and victims, while the majority of society's ordinary citizens are outside."

This is not to say, of course, that *all* victims of crime share the same attributes of their victimizers. It is simply to emphasize that the two populations have several common characteristics. This undeniable reality is based on findings of victimization surveys conducted in the United States, Europe, Canada, and Australia.[6]

The *Canadian Urban Victimization Survey Bulletin* (Canada, 1983) reports that the profile of the victim of a crime against the person is similar to that of the offender:

> *When we examine the categories of people most likely to be victimized, many popular myths are exploded. Using the victimization data we can draw a profile of the victim of crime against the person: young unmarried male, living alone, probably looking for work, or a student, and with an active life outside the home — not very different from the profile we might draw of the offender. (p. 4)*

Criminological studies in Europe, the United States, Canada, and Australia show that offenders involved in the types of crimes covered by victimization surveys share many common characteristics. Victimization surveys reveal that victims disproportionately share these characteristics and that the demographic profiles of crime victims and of convicted criminals are strikingly similar (United States, 1978; Gottfredson, 1984).

Analyzing crimes of violence in Finland, Aromaa (1974) reported that the victims had much in common with the offenders and they were often — especially where the gravest crimes of violence are concerned — closely related to each other. Reporting on the first national victimization survey conducted in Australia, Braithwaite and Biles (1984) declared that the findings provide strong support for the proposition that victims and offenders share many characteristics.

In the United States, the similarities between victims and offenders were stressed by Hindelang, Gottfredson, and Garofalo (1978):

> *To summarize, offenders involved in the types of crimes of interest here are disproportionately male, young, urban residents, black, of lower socio-economic status, unemployed (and not in school), and unmarried. In our brief review of victim characteristics above, and in earlier chapters, it was seen that victims disproportionately share these characteristics. (p. 259)*

The conclusion of Hindelang et al. is the same as that reached by Singer (1981), who found that in crimes of assault victims and offenders were related in their demographic characteristics and in terms of certain shared responses to perceived situations of physical or psychological threat. Their social interaction suggested certain normative constraints where a violent outcome is dependent in part on the victim's reactions. Singer (1981) points out the following:

> *A key question then in explaining personal victimization as a consequence of the victim's exposure to an offender is the extent to which violence reflects a lifestyle that leads victims to alternate as offenders in the same social environment. If victims and offenders share certain understandings and misunderstandings supporting their use of physical force, then both populations are not distinct, but rotate in a web of subcultural relationships. (p. 780)*

It is understandable that the frequency with which some individuals become involved in violence-prone situations will affect both their chances of using violence and of being recipients of violence, of attacking and being attacked, of injuring and being injured, of killing and being killed. Who will end up being the victim and who will be legally qualified as the offender depends quite often on chance factors rather than deliberate action, planning, or intent. Thus victim and offender roles are not necessarily antagonistic or incompatible but are frequently complementary and interchangeable. This is particularly true of brawls, quarrels, disputes, and altercations, which not too infrequently escalate into assault or even homicide situations. Wolfgang (1958), for example, in his study of homicide in Philadelphia observed the following:

> *In many cases the victim has most of the major characteristics of an offender; in some cases two potential offenders come together in a homicide situation and it is probably only chance which results in one becoming a victim and the other an offender. At any rate, connotations of a victim as a weak and passive individual, seeking to withdraw from an assaultive situation, and of an offender as a brutal, strong, and overly aggressive person seeking out his victim, are not always correct. Societal attitudes are generally positive toward the victim and negative toward the offender, who is often feared as a violent and dangerous threat to others. However, data in the present study — especially that of previous arrest record — mitigate, destroy, or reverse these connotations of victim-offender roles in one out of every four criminal homicides. (p. 265)*

In many instances, dangerousness and vulnerability may be regarded as the two sides of the same coin. They often coexist because many of the factors that contribute to dangerousness may create or enhance a state of vulnerability. One such factor is alcohol consumption, which may act simultaneously as a criminogenic and victimogenic factor enhancing the potentiality of violent behavior in one party and of violent victimization in the other (see Chapter 10).[7]

Similarities Between the Victim and Offender Populations

The homogeneity of the victim and offender populations can be easily seen by looking at some of the general sociodemographic characteristics of the two populations.

AGE

When young children, who, according to the law, cannot commit crime, are excluded, it becomes clear that delinquency and victimization rates for the different age groups follow an identical pattern. Those in the younger age groups who commit the largest portion of delinquency and crime are the ones most victimized, while those in the elderly age groups who commit the least crime are also the ones least victimized. Intermediary age groups have intermediary rates of both crime and victimization.

Like other victimization surveys conducted elsewhere, the Canadian Urban Victimization Survey (Canada, 1983) revealed that the risk of victimization is closely tied to age. Contrary to popular belief, elderly people were relatively unlikely to be victimized by crime. Those under twenty-five had the highest rate of victimization in all categories of personal offenses, and these high rates declined rapidly with increasing age after this point. The actual sample counts of sexual assault and robbery incidents for those over sixty were so low that estimated numbers and rates are unreliable.

Findings of the Canadian General Social Survey (Sacco and Johnson, 1990) indicate that the risk of personal victimization decreases with advancing age for all age groups for which estimates could be made. It was found that young Canadians between the ages of fifteen and twenty-four experienced personal victimization nearly two times that of those twenty-five to forty-four years of age and seven times that of those forty-five to sixty-four years of age. The survey reveals that the differences between the youngest Canadians and those aged forty-five to sixty-four are stronger in the case of violent offenses than in the case of theft of personal property. Those in the younger age group were almost eight times as likely as those in the older group to be victims of violence and about six times as likely to be victims of personal theft.

The Canadian findings are consistent with those from other countries. American data show that people over sixty-five years of age (that is the least criminal of all age groups) are the least likely to become crime victims, while young people aged twelve to twenty-four have the highest victimization rates for personal crimes of violence and theft (United States, 1978). Australian data reported by Wilson and Brown (1973), Congalton and Najman (1974), and Braithwaite and Biles (1984) indicate that the twenty to twenty-four year olds have the highest victimization rates on the majority of offenses, and the over-sixties have the lowest.

GENDER

Males commit more crimes and are criminally victimized more frequently than females. This is also a consistent pattern observable in official crime statistics and in the findings of victimization surveys. Sexual offenses are the most glaring exception since they are predominantly committed against women. Regarding property offenses, purse-snatching and some other forms of theft of personal property are more often committed against women than men.

The Canadian Urban Victimization Survey (Canada, 1983) shows that women are about seven times more likely than men to be victims of sexual assault (including rape, attempted rape, sexual molestation, and attempted sexual molestation). They are also more likely than men to have their personal property stolen (theft of personal property). Men, on the other hand, are almost twice as likely as women to be victims of robbery or assault.

In the United States (United States, 1981), it was found that, of the personal crimes measured by the survey, men are more often victimized than women for every crime except rape. In 1979, men were victims of violent crime at the rate of about 45 per 1,000. Women were victimized at the rate of 25 per 1,000. The rates for personal crimes of theft were 99 per 1,000 for men as opposed to 85 per 1,000 for women.

In Australia (Braithwaite and Biles, 1984), a survey was designed in such a way that only women were eligible for victimizations involving rape, peeping, and indecent exposure. Apart from these three, the only offense in which women reported a higher level of victimization was nuisance telephone calls. Men had higher victimization rates for break-and-enter (largely because men were more likely to be nominated as heads of the household), vehicle theft, theft, fraud, forgery, false pretenses, and assault. Other Australian surveys conducted locally by Wilson and Brown (1973) and Congalton and Najman (1974) both confirm that in aggregate, men are more likely than women to be victims of crime.

The lower victimization rates of women in crimes of violence (with the exception of sexual offenses) revealed by both official statistics and victimization surveys is probably part real, part artificial. Certain forms of violence directed predominantely against women, such as intrafamily violence, are reported at a lower rate to the police and to survey interviewers than other forms of violence. The lower rates of victimization for women may also be due to lesser exposure to victimogenic situations. As Stanko (1985) points out, women are specialists in devising ways to minimize their exposure to the possibility of male violence, and they are specialists in survival through avoidance strategies.

MARITAL STATUS

Married people (male and female) commit less crime and are less victimized than single and divorced individuals. These differences are due, among other things, to variations in age and life-style associated with marital status. Skogan (1981) attributes the high victimization rates of divorced, separated, and unmarried women and the lower rates of married women to differences in the daily routines, social activities, and companions of the two groups.

The Canadian Urban Victimization Survey (Canada, 1984b) showed that those who are unmarried (single, separated, or divorced) are at higher risk for personal victimization than those who are married, living common-law, or widowed.

Data from the Canadian General Social Survey (Sacco and Johnson, 1990) indicate that rates of personal victimization for those who are single, separated, or divorced are twice the national average and three times higher than the rates for those who are married. Marital status had a stronger impact on the risk of violent victimization than on the risk of victimization by personal theft.

National victimization surveys in the United States reveal a similar pattern and show that persons who are divorced or who have never been married are more likely to be victims of personal crime than the married or the widowed. In 1979, for example, victimization rates for personal crimes of violence per 1,000 were as follows: divorced—75, never married—62, married—18, and widowed—9. For crimes of personal theft, the rates were: never married—142, divorced—123, married—69, and widowed—33 (United States, 1981).

Australian data (Braithwaite and Biles, 1984) confirm that widowed persons, because of their advanced age, have the lowest victimization rates in most crime categories. However, if they are excluded and only those who have never married or are separated or divorced are considered, the findings are consistent with the Canadian and American survey findings.

RACE AND ETHNICITY

Because crimes of violence are, to a large extent, intraracial (see Chapter 7), races and ethnic groups with high violent crime and delinquency rates, such as the blacks and those who are Hispanic in the United States, also have high violent victimization rates. The American white population, on the other hand, registers lower rates on both counts.

In the United States, a 1979 victimization survey (United States, 1981) shows that blacks were victimized by violent crime at the rate of 42 per 1,000 versus 34 per 1,000 for whites. They were also burglarized at a higher rate (114 per 1,000 households for blacks versus 80 per 1,000 households for whites). For crimes of theft, however, rates for blacks are generally the same or lower than those for whites. In 1979, rates for household larceny for both blacks and whites were 133 per 1,000. Personal larceny rates were 93 per 1,000 for whites versus 87 per 1,000 for blacks. The same survey also indicates that Hispanics generally have higher rates than nonHispanics for household crimes and for most crimes of violence.

In 1988 (United States, 1989) black households were measurably more vulnerable to crime than were white households. Black households suffered, proportionately, a larger amount of violent crime and household theft than did white households, and they had a somewhat higher percentage for assault. The Bureau of Justice Statistics reports that for the first time in the history of the indicator, white households were not more likely than black households to have a member victimized by personal theft.

The higher victimization rate for blacks was again confirmed in a study on black victims (United States, 1990) covering an eight-year period from 1979 to 1986 inclusive. Data from the National Crime Survey showed that black Americans suffer relatively more violent crime than other Americans. The violent crime victimization rate for persons aged twelve and older was 44 per 1,000 blacks and 34 per 1,000 whites. Blacks experienced higher rates of rape, robbery, and aggravated assault, while whites had higher rates of simple assault and personal theft. The study further revealed that violent crimes committed against blacks tended to be more serious and to cause greater injury than similar crimes committed against persons of other races.

UNEMPLOYMENT

Unemployed persons are overrepresented among convicted offenders and among victims. Age and life-style are probably responsible, at least partly, for this pattern.

The Canadian Urban Victimization Survey (Canada, 1984b) shows the highest victimization rates to occur among students and those who were looking for work — a much higher rate than the rates of those who were retired or those who were employed for most of the year in which the survey was held.

Braithwaite and Biles (1984) report that the unemployed in Australia have clearly higher rates of victimization for theft, break-and-enter, peeping, and assault. Most striking is the difference with respect to assault, where the unemployed were more than twice as likely to report victimization than those in full-time jobs and six times as likely to have been assaulted than respondents not in the work force or in part-time jobs.

INCOME

The relationship between income and victimization is not as clear-cut as the relationship between income and crime. Low-income categories are greatly overrepresented among convicted offenders. Concerning victimization, the situation is far more complex. The Canadian Urban Victimization Survey (Canada, 1983), found, as one might expect, that the higher the family income of urban residents the more likely they will experience some form of household victimization or personal theft. However, the differences among income groups in their levels of tolerance for, and awareness of, some types of incidents are likely to affect the level of reporting to the interviewers. The survey found, however, that lower income individuals are as likely or more likely than others to suffer a personal violent victimization — sexual assault, robbery, or assault.

The picture that emerges from American surveys regarding violent victimization by crime is a clear one. According to the Bureau of Justice Statistics (United States, 1985), for both whites and blacks there was a direct relationship between family income and the likelihood of violent victimization in 1982: the lower the income, the greater the victimization. While the pattern was consistent for both races, and the differences between the lowest- and highest-income categories were statistically significant, not all differences between adjacent income categories were statistically significant.

The 1988 survey (United States, 1989) shows that households with higher incomes were more susceptible to crimes involving theft and less susceptible to crimes involving violence than were lower-income households. Interestingly, households earning less than fifteen thousand dollars a year experienced violent crimes and burglary to a greater degree than did households in higher-income categories.

In Australia, both Wilson and Brown (1973) and Congalton and Najman (1974) in their local surveys failed to confirm a negative relationship between socioeconomic status and aggregate victimization rate. Cross-tabulations of National Crime Survey victimization rates by education, occupation, income of respondents, and household income carried out by Braithwaite and Biles (1980) reveal a mixed picture. For example, in some respects, higher socioeconomic status respondents have higher victimization rates. Tertiary educated respondents with little education are more likely to be victims of assault. They did find, however, a consistent positive correlation between the gross weekly income of the household and vehicle theft victimization, possibly because wealthy households own more automobiles.

INVOLVEMENT IN DELINQUENCY

Committing a crime increases the chances of further involvement in delinquency. For example, if someone commits an armed robbery, a burglary, or an act of shoplifting, the chances that the same person will commit a second offense are much higher than for the rest of the population. The same is true for the risks of victimization. Thus, one event of victimization increases the risk of a second victimization, and so on (Sparks, 1981, 1982).

There is evidence suggesting that criminals are more frequently victimized than noncriminals and that victims of violent crime themselves have considerable criminal involvements. In their London, England, victimization study, Sparks, Genn, and Dodd (1977) surveyed for both victim and offender experiences. Their self-report data indicate that a significant association exists for incidents ranging from simple to aggravated assault. This significant association between self-reporting of violent crime and violent victimization held even when controlled for age. In a similar survey quoted by Singer (1981), Savitz, Lalli, and Rosen (1977) contrasted surveyed victimization with juvenile arrest status. They found a significant relationship between assault victims and official delinquent arrest status, but there was no similar arrest status relationship with theft victims.[8]

Thornberry and Figlio (1972) examined victimization and criminal behavior using a 10 percent sample of individuals drawn from a 1945 Philadelphia birth cohort. The sample consisted of 975 members, about 60 percent of whom were found and interviewed. The data revealed that arrest status was strongly and consistently associated with victimization. In *all* twenty-four comparisons those subjects who had been arrested were more likely than those who had not been arrested to be the victim of a crime. Furthermore, eighteen of these twenty-four comparisons were statistically significant.

In the follow-up survey to the Philadelphia birth cohort, a study of self-reported victimization, Singer (1981) examined the extent to which victims are also guilty of serious assault. He reports that cohort members who were shot or stabbed were most often nonwhite, and when they were surveyed they were high school dropouts, unemployed, and single. They were also involved more frequently in official and self-reported criminal activity. Victims of serious assault had the highest probability of having a friend arrested, belonging to a gang, using a weapon, committing a serious assault, and being officially arrested. Singer concluded that his findings, along with those of other studies examining the victim-offender interaction, indicate support for the homogeneity of victim-offender populations involved in serious assaultive conduct.

Johnson et al. (1973) followed up all victims of gunshot and stab wounds admitted to the City of Austin Hospital in Texas during 1968 and 1969. They found that 75 percent of the male victims had a criminal record, and 54 percent had a jail record. Savitz, Lalli, and Rosen (1977), using a Philadelphia cohort, also observed an association between official records of having committed assault and assault victimization. And in their London, England, survey, Sparks, Genn, and Dodd (1977) found victims of violent crime to be significantly more likely than nonvictims to self-report the commission of violent crimes.

The positive association observed between violent offending and violent victimization apparently extends to property offenses as well. In two studies of Dutch juveniles, Van Dijk and Steinmetz (1983) discovered a substantial overlap between being a victim of various theft offenses and admitting to having committed them. One of the explanations they offer for the observed overlap is the possibility that theft might result from normative curbs being weakened by victimization or because it is a convenient way of recouping losses.

The British Crime Survey Scotland (Chambers and Tombs, 1984), which included questions about the respondents own criminal activities, revealed that 40 percent of respondents admitting an assault had themselves been the victim of an assault during the survey period: only 1 percent of those who did not admit an assault were themselves assault victims during that period.

Gottfredson (1984) analyzed the 1982 British Crime Survey data and was struck by the relatively strong interrelationship between offending and victimization. For persons with at least one self-reported violence offense, the likelihood of victimization was 42 percent, or seven times the likelihood of personal victimization for persons reporting no self-reported violence offenses. Suspecting that the source of the relationship between offending and victimization might be the common association between age and delinquency, Gottfredson controlled for age. The relationship between self-reported delinquencies and self-reported violence and personal victimization persisted despite the controls. And the relationships between self-reported offending and both personal and household victimization also seemed to hold regardless of place of residence. Gottfredson suggests that there is probably a life-style that, for some, includes high probabilities of misfortune, victimization, and offending, due perhaps to where they live, where they go, and with whom they associate. In other words, the social processes that produce high rates of offending in some segments of the population may also be productive to high rates of victimization. Gottfredson went on to test various hypotheses about these interrelationships using the British Crime Survey data. The data strongly suggested that life-styles conducive to victimization of all forms are also conducive to offending.

Self-reporting questions related to offending were improved in the 1984 British Crime Survey in an attempt to get better admission rates. The data were analyzed by Mayhew and Elliott (1990). The notion that victims of crime are also more likely to be offenders gained only partial support. Being a victim had a significant, independent relationship to higher levels of offending only among elderly victims. However, the weaker effect of victimization in other age groups, as the authors point out, is not necessarily at odds with Gottfredson's analysis of the 1982 British Crime Survey data. This is because, in the Mayhew and Elliott study, all forms of victimization were aggregated, which may well have concealed finer relationships between offending and different forms of victimization. Mayhew and Elliott, (1990) conclude the following:

> *In the broadest terms, the self-report evidence from the BCS, especially Gottfredson's (1984) analysis, bears on thinking about victims insofar as it highlights the inappropriateness of seeing victims and offenders as distinct groups ... The fact that men and the young face higher risks of personal crime, especially violence, has been one of the most significant findings of victimization surveys, countering the idea that it is the weakest and most vulnerable who are uniformly sought out by offenders. (p. 20)*

Despite the obvious difficulties of getting information about the previous criminality of victims of violent crimes, several Swedish studies have done just that.

One of them concerned patients in casualty departments in Stockholm (Lenke, 1973). Another, also conducted in Stockholm, examined people admitted to casualty departments for treatment of knife wounds (Blomquist et al., 1980). Both these studies show that a rather large proportion of the victims of violent crimes are known for previous criminality. In his study of everyday violence in contemporary Sweden, based on official records, Wikström (1985) found that during the six years he covered (1968-1970, 1973-1975), 12 percent of the offenders also appeared as victims of violent crimes in the municipality of Gävle. Of the offenders victimized, as many as 38 percent were reported, more than once, for committing a violent crime during these six years. Wikström suggests that there is clearly a group among the offenders that seems to be active in crimes of violence both as offenders and victims. He also observed that most of the offenders and many of the victims were to be regarded as "socially loaded persons" (alcoholics, criminals, addicts). Another finding was that most of the crimes occurred either between two socially loaded persons or between a socially loaded and a "conventional" person, while crimes involving two "conventional" persons were comparatively rare.

All these findings are in line with another reality that has been observed for a long time, namely, that marginal groups arc more involved in crime and more often victimized than nonmarginal groups. Typical examples of those prone to victimization are persons implicated in illicit activities or those who have opted for a deviant life-style such as drug pushers, drug addicts, prostitutes, and persons involved in illegal gambling, loan sharking, fencing stolen goods, and organized crime. (See Chapter 10.)

How Can the Similarities Between the Two Populations Be Explained?

Although most victimization surveys that have probed for offending report a significant association between self-reporting of violent crime and violent victimization, the direction of the relationship and the chronological order in which the two behaviors occur remain unclear. Thus, it is not possible yet to tell whether offending precedes or succeeds victimization. It is quite possible that becoming a victim of violence creates the motivation for offending (revenge or retaliation) and provides the necessary means of neutralization (getting even). Van Dijk and Steinmetz (1983) seem to lean toward this explanation for property victimization/offending. But the reverse chronological order is also plausible: violent offending may increase the chances of becoming a victim of retaliatory violence. It could be that involvement in delinquency and adoption of a delinquent life-style do enhance, in other ways, the likelihood of violent victimization. There seems to be little doubt, however, on the basis of the data we have reviewed, that offender and victim populations, particularly in violent crime, are homogeneous populations that have similar characteristics. The affinity between the victim and offender populations should not come as a surprise. Crimes of violence, particularly those not motivated by sex or financial gain, are known to be interpersonal crimes or crimes of relationships. Since the motives for violence do not develop in a vacuum, it is understandable that these crimes are frequently committed between people who know each other, and who interact with each other and between those who are bound by family, friendship, or business ties. The typical contexts in which criminal homicide, attempted murder, or assault occur are those of a domestic fight, a family dispute, a quarrel between nonstrangers, or other altercations where insult, abuse, or jealousy are present. The interpersonal character of crimes of violence, particularly criminal homicide, is well documented in several studies carried out in different cultures (see Chapter 7).

The similarities between the victim and offender populations may, therefore, be attributed to the social and geographical proximity between victims and victimizers. Geographical proximity is particularly evident in certain types of property offenses. There is a well-established distance-decay pattern in human spatial behavior. Brantingham and Brantingham (1984) point out that people interact more with people and things that are close to their home location than with people or things that are far away. Interactions decrease as distance increases (distance-decay). Some of this decrease in activity as distance increases is the result of the "costs" of overcoming distance. They further note that the bias of greater density of interaction close to home is also the result of biased spatial knowledge. People have more experience of and are more aware of what exists around them. Brantingham and Brantingham (1984) write:

> *Searching behavior starts from home and first covers likely areas that are "known". Criminals probably follow a similar searching pattern. Although specific studies have not been done on the spatial searching patterns of criminals, the results of other studies show strong traces of such patterns. Crimes generally occur close to the home of the criminal. The operational definition of* ***close*** *varies by offense, but the distance-decay gradient is evident in all offenses ... Generally, violent offenses have a high concentration close to home, with many assaults and murders actually occurring in the home. The search pattern is a little broader for property offenses, but these are still clustered close to home. (p. 345)*

Braithwaite and Biles (1984) advance three broad types of interpretations for the striking similarities between victims and offenders. First, they offer the provocative explanation that victims are often themselves criminals. Differential association with criminals might lead to "an excess of definitions favorable to violation of law over definitions unfavorable to violations of law" (Sutherland and

Cressey, 1970, p. 75). Perhaps, in addition, that differential association might produce "an excess of exposures to violation of law." In other words, if you mix with criminals, they can teach you their tricks, or use them on you — or both. This could be why victims and criminals appear similar. They also suggest that victimizations and offenses might be, in some measure, part of the same social process. With respect to violence, Singer has expressed one of the many possible versions of how victimizations and offenses could be part of the same social process (Braithwaite and Biles, 1984):

> *If violence is learned as a legitimate form of conduct, it appears not only in the role of an offender as a winner, but in the important position of a loser as well. The school yard fight may leave only one of its combatants with a loss — awaiting the chance to turn the experience into a win and the victimization to another (p. 7)*

A second explanation offered by Braithwaite and Biles (1984) is that people with victim/offender characteristics (young, male, unemployed, unmarried, etc.) are more likely to spend their time in public space — in trains and buses rather than private automobiles, streets and parks rather than offices and homes, public bars rather than private clubs. Most crucially, they are more likely to spend their time in public space in the evening, when crimes disproportionately occur. Braithwaite and Biles add another element borrowed from the life-style model (Hindelang, Gottfredson, and Garofalo, 1978), namely, the fact that people with victim/offender characteristics are people who spend a large proportion of their time with nonfamily members. They also refer to Cohen and Felson's (1979) success in explaining variations in crime rates between 1947 and 1974 by indicators of the proportion of time spent outside the home in different periods (see Chapter 12).

The third and final type of interpretation offered by Braithwaite and Biles (1984) is that common victim/offender characteristics are associated with certain behavior patterns and attitude sets that produce both offenses and victimization. Braithwaite and Biles point to three specific characteristics that might be associated with youth, maleness, being unemployed, and being unmarried. The three characteristics are propensity to risk taking, to violence, and to alcohol.

These three explanations, Braithwaite and Biles (1984) suggest, deserve systematic investigation and hold great promise for criminology:

> *It is possible that moving from separate studies of criminals and victims to studies of the victim/offender nexus could be the kind of paradigm shift that criminology needs. Victimization surveys in the future will be of particular value if they incorporate self-reports of participation in crime as well as a range of items on the use of leisure time spent in public space and interpersonal relationships. (p. 8)*

Summary

This chapter informs the reader about the numbers of victims and their sociodemographic characteristics and compares these characteristics with those of the offender population. This is done to show that the two populations are not different but homogeneous, not distinct but overlapping.

Thanks to victimization surveys that have been conducted in some countries in the past twenty-five years, we now have information on the numbers and characteristics of those who are victimized by crime. Surveys conducted in Canada and in Britain show that, while large numbers of minor and trivial victimizations were reported to the interviewers, relatively few sexual assaults or robberies were reported. The United States, on the other hand, seems to have much higher rates of violent, serious victimization. For example, a comparison of the criminal homicide rate in Canada and the United States shows that the United States has a rate approximately four times that of Canada. Victimization surveys provide empirical support to criminologists' contention that criminality and victimization are clustered within certain groups and certain areas, and they indicate that there is a much greater affinity between offenders and victims than is commonly believed.

The idea that victims of crime share several common characteristics with the criminal and delinquent populations runs counter to popular perceptions and to the generally held stereotypes of victims. Pointing to the similarities of the two populations is not to say that *all* victims share the same attributes of their victimizers. It is simply to emphasize that the two populations have several common characteristics and that the profile of the victim of crime against the person is similar to that of the offender. The homogeneity of the victim and offender populations can be easily seen by looking at some of the general sociodemographic characteristics of the two populations, such as age, gender, marital status, race and ethnicity, unemployment, income, and involvement in delinquency. Victimization surveys show that delinquency and victimization rates for the different age groups, with the exception of young children, follow an identical pattern. Younger age groups who commit the largest portion of delinquency and crime are the ones most victimized, while elderly groups who commit the least crime are also the ones least victimized. Intermediary age groups have intermediary rates of both crime and victimization. With the exception of sex offenses, which are committed predominantly against females, males are criminally victimized more frequently than women and commit many more crimes than women. Married people commit less crime and are less victimized than single and divorced individuals. These differences are due, among other things, to variations in age and the life-style associated with marital status.

Because crimes of violence are, to a large extent, intraracial, races and ethnic groups with high violent crime and delinquency rates, such as the blacks and those who are Hispanics in the United States, also have high violent victimization rates. Unemployed persons are overrepresented among convicted offenders and among victims. Here again, age and life-style are probably responsible, at least partially, for this pattern. There also seems to be a direct inverse relationship between income and violent victimization as the lower the income, the greater the victimization.

Committing a crime increases the chances of further involvement in delinquency and the same is true for the risks of victimization. Thus, being victimized once increases the risk of a second victimization, and so on. There is evidence suggesting that criminals are more frequently victimized than noncriminals and that victims of violent crime themselves have considerable criminal involvement. There is also evidence suggesting that marginal groups are more involved in crime and more often victimized than nonmarginal groups. The similarities between the victim and offender populations may, therefore, be due to the social and geographic proximity between victims and victimizers.

SIX

The Victims and Their Victimizers

The shakedown (extortion from homosexuals and certain other violators of law) is safe because the victims, being themselves violators of the law, cannot complain to the police. The confidence game is safe for the same reason, for the victims have entered into collusion with the thieves to defraud someone else and were themselves defrauded in the attempt. Stealing from stores is relatively safe because the stores are reluctant to make accusations of theft against persons who appear to be legitimate customers.

E. Sutherland (1937, p. 217)

The Victimizer's Attitude to the Victim

The victimizer's attitude to the victim is a neglected but extremely important area of study in both criminology and victimology. This attitude often plays a crucial role in the motivational process leading to the victimization and a decisive role in the process of selecting a victim. This is because the choice of a particular victim is not infrequently a function of the offender's perception of, and attitude to, that victim. When victim and offender interact, as in the case of rape, the offender's interpretation of the victim's words, gestures, and behavior depends largely on the opinion and image he has of that victim. Sparks (1982) argues that some of the ways in which victims can be involved in the causation of crime are functions, not so much of the victim's behavior or attributes, as of the offender's perception of that behavior or those attributes.

Attributes such as attractiveness, vulnerability, suitability, and appropriateness are neither objective nor absolute. Their importance as factors influencing the choice of a specific victim depends on the personal perceptions of the potential victimizer as to who is attractive, vulnerable, or appropriate. The offender's reaction to the victim's behavior is determined to a certain extent by the offender's relationship with, and attitude to, that victim. Furthermore, the views the offender has of the victim enable him or her to redefine and rationalize the victimizing behavior, to overcome any inner restraints, to avoid hurting his or her self-image, and to escape post-victimization feelings of culpability.

Despite the importance of the offender's attitude toward the victim to the understanding of motives, behavior, and choice of target, and as vital as this attitude is to current programs of victim-offender reconciliation, it has received only scant attention from researchers. One has to meticulously scan the criminological and victimological literature to come across some passing remarks or comments on this important aspect of the victimization process. This situation is starting to change due to the growing attention being paid by feminist writers to the rapist's attitude to his victim.

RAPISTS

The rapist's attitude to his victim is often a reflection of a more general attitude to the female sex. This general attitude is molded by two things: first, personal experiences, that is, the rapist's own life experiences and relationships with women, particularly his mother (Kanin, 1970; Cohen, Garofalo, Bouscher, and Seghorn, 1971), and second, cultural experiences shaped by the dominant views of a patriarchal society. Viewing the female victim as a sexual object to be used simply as a tool for male sexual satisfaction, believing that women have a subconscious desire to be raped, so that a woman's "no" is taken for a "yes," and so forth, are all views that have their origins in the cultural norms and popular beliefs of a patriarchal society, which degrades and denigrates the female sex.

The growing literature on rape suggests that rapists have a devalued image of the female. One particular stereotype of probable rape victims is the one male drivers have of young female hitchhikers. Young women who continue to solicit rides despite the persistent warnings about the dangers of hitchhiking are often perceived as women who do not mind being raped or, at the very least, are taking a chance on being raped. This stereotype and the attitude accompanying it naturally influence a driver's interactions with a young woman to whom he gives a ride and distorts his personal perception of any rape that takes place. In his mind, it was not rape, it was sex requested or offered by the female hitchhiker.

One of the few empirical studies of rapists' attitudes to their victims was done in Israel. In the study, Ben-David (1982) interviewed an unspecified number of imprisoned sex offenders while working in the Mental Health Center of the Israeli Prison Service. Only a few expressed emotional feelings toward the victim. More feelings were exhibited by those whose act remained at the stage of attempt than by those whose act was completed.

PROFESSIONAL THIEVES

Next to rape, the area that has attracted some comments about the offender's attitude to the victim is that of professional theft. Sutherland (1937) suggests that, in general, the professional thief does not have any attitude toward the victims. The victims are perceived simply as a means to an end, the possessors of wealth that the thief desires. Thus, professional thieves do not have any consideration for their victims whose wealth they attempt to steal. They think of their victims like fishermen think of a place to fish or hunters of a place to hunt.

Regarding the attitudes of professional criminals to their victims, Inciardi (1974) notes that the victim becomes defined as no more than a means to an end, and as a vehicle to be used without consideration. The victim, he adds, is also a symbol, a representative of a culture that the thief does not understand and has rejected, and "in this capacity, the victim is hated by some, disliked by many, and disenfranchised by all" (Inciardi, 1974, p. 338). It is for this reason, suggests Inciardi, that professional thieves, feeling superior to their victims, react in a negative and hostile manner to being robbed, as it places them, too, in the status and role of the sucker.

The Victimizer's Indifference to the Victim

In very rare instances, the animating force behind the act of victimization may be love, compassion, or even pity. Such positive feelings for the victim are encountered in cases of euthanasia (mercy killing), in cases of extended suicide, such as the parent suffering from depression who kills his or her young children out of concern for their future before committing suicide, and in some cases of passionate crimes perpetrated against the beloved person in a moment of sudden loss of control.

However, in many more cases, the offender's attitude to the victim is dominated by negative emotions such as hate, rejection, anger, hostility, animosity, antagonism, contempt, and disdain. The most common attitude, however, seems to be one of indifference, a "don't care" or "couldn't care less" attitude. In an attempt to explore offenders' attitudes to their victims, Göppinger (1976), a German psychiatrist/criminologist, interviewed fifty-four prisoners. The sample included offenders convicted of serious crimes and sentenced to life imprisonment. The most prevailing attitudes were "affective indifference" and "emotional detachment." Fifty percent of the subjects were indifferent to their victims. An additional 25 percent did not express any emotional feelings toward their victims. Only nine out of the fifty-four criminals (16.6 percent) expressed feelings of pity for the victims or their families. The remainder did not relate to the victim, instead, they stressed their own suffering as a result of the crime or tried to portray themselves as victims.

Victimizers' Stereotypes of Probable Victims

Sutherland's (1937) biographical account, *The Professional Thief*, and Cressey's (1953) study, *Other People's Money*, provide evidence that delinquents' stereotypic definitions and consensually validated images of victims do exist. In their experimental study of noninstitutionalized delinquents' and nondelinquents' verbal responses to a set of conditions, Schwendinger and Schwendinger (1967) noted that there was a tacit agreement among the delinquents that the victim was a worthless human being. Their data reinforced the assumption that delinquents tacitly hold a common attitude toward the victim. The emergence and development of the stereotypic images are described by the Schwendingers (1967) as follows:

> *As they engage in initial forms of deviant activity, youngsters legitimate their behavior by developing consensually validated images of victims. At this stage, some youth focus on the moral issues involved and fashion the images of the victim out of the conventional moral rhetoric. After this stage, however, the stereotypic images become standardized in the form of metaphors which catalogue persons by typical kinds of victim terms; words like Punk, Chump, Box, Pigeon, and Fag emerge and represent the standardization of the typical moral relations with the victim as perceived from the standpoint of the victimizers' ideology. (p. 98)*

Sutherland's (1937) *The Professional Thief* offers a good description of the stereotype that con-men have of their probable victims. They are "suckers who are gloating over their prospective gain ... with larceny in their souls ... and with little sympathy for those they are hoping to beat." Swindlers and con-game artists have a well-known saying that "you cannot cheat an honest man." The words used in the argot of professional criminals to refer to their victims betray the stereotypes they hold of those victims. The victim is a "sucker," and an easy victim is a "mark." (According to Inciardi [1974], the word "mark" has maintained its current meaning since the mid-1700s.)

The Pre-victimization Process

Prior to the act of victimization, the victimizer goes through a mental process of varying duration. It may take seconds or may last for years. When the process extends over a reasonable period of time it is called by the legal name of "premeditation." The mental process preceding victimization consists of a chain of interactive and complementary intellectual operations. Whether these operations have to do with the victimizer, the contemplated act, or the prospective victim, they are taking place simultaneously and, for the victimizer, they are neither separable nor distinguishable.

These thought processes become more understandable if distinctions, which must inevitably be artificial, are made between them. The processes can be split into three processes: neutralization, redefinition/auto-legitimation, and desensitization. The three processes, their foci, and their aims are summarized in Table 6-1. The first process, neutralization, has the victimizer as its focus, and its main purpose is to enable the victimizer to overcome the moral and cultural barriers that stand in the way of the victimization act. The process neutralizes the mechanisms of formal and informal social control and makes it possible to overcome the moral inhibitions and inner restraints that have been built in through the process of socialization.

The second process, redefinition/auto-legitimation, has the victimization act as its focus. Its main purpose is to redefine, rationalize, and justify the act. Through the redefinition, the act is stripped of its delinquent, illegal, and immoral character. The rationalization and justification make it possible to commit the act while avoiding self-condemnation and the condemnation of others and without tarnishing the victimizer's self-image.

The third process, desensitization, has the prospective victim as its focus. Its aim is to desensitize the victimizer to the pain and suffering inflicted upon the victim, thus making it possible to commit the act without suffering from guilt feelings or post-victimization dissonance.

The first process makes the commission of the act possible, as it paves the way and removes the moral obstacles. The second makes it possible to commit the act while the self-image of the victimizer remains intact. The third makes it possible to hurt, injure, or harm the victim without feeling bad about it.

TABLE 6-1 **The Pre-victimization Process**

The Process	The Focus	The Aims
Neutralization	The victimizer	—Neutralizing the mechanisms of formal and informal social control. —Overcoming moral inhibitions and inner restraints.
Redefinition/Auto-legitimation	The victimization act	—Redefining the act to strip it of its delinquent, illegal, or immoral character. —Avoiding damage to self-image as well as condemnation by self and others.
Desensitization	The prospective victim	—Desensitizing the victimizer to the pain and suffering caused to the victim. —Avoiding post-victimization dissonance and guilt feelings.

THE NEUTRALIZATION PROCESS

The neutralization process operates to render the mechanisms of social control ineffective. Building on Sutherland's theory of differential association, Sykes and Matza (1957) developed a theory of delinquency that has as its central focus the techniques of neutralization delinquents use to lessen the effectiveness of social controls. They argue that much delinquency is based on what is essentially an unrecognized extension of defenses to crimes in the form of justifications for deviance that are seen as valid by the delinquent, but not by the legal system or society at large.

Sykes and Matza discuss five major techniques of neutralization: (1) the denial of responsibility; (2) the denial of injury; (3) the denial of the victim; (4) the condemnation of the condemners; (5) the appeal to higher loyalties.

If we examine these five techniques in the light of the distinction between neutralization and desensitization, we find that two of the techniques discussed by Sykes and Matza, the denial of injury and the denial of the victim, also fit the techniques of desensitization, as they are directly related to the victim.

While Sykes and Matza (1957) call the justification techniques used by the delinquent "techniques of neutralization," Redl and Wineman (1951), both psychologists, speak of techniques of "tax evasion from guilt feelings." They also refer to the special tricks or "alibi tricks" that the delinquent ego uses to allow delinquent behavior without feeling much concern and to keep all phases of delinquent behavior "tax exempt" from feelings of guilt. Redl and Wineman cite the following rationalizations commonly uttered by delinquents: "He did it first"; "He had it coming to him"; "But somebody else did the same thing to me before"; "He is a no-good so-and-so himself"; "They are all against me, nobody likes me, they are always picking on me." All these rationalizations either refer to the victim or to the delinquent's perception of himself or herself as a victim.

THE REDEFINITION/AUTO-LEGITIMATION PROCESS

Beynon (1935) cites an example of a Hungarian church steward who sent boys out to steal coal at night from the cars on the Detroit railway tracks (see Chapter 4). This was not perceived by the steward as theft as, for him, it was not censurable behavior or hurtful, harmful victimization. Instead, it was seen as a way for the poor church to get its coal supply for the harsh winter in a way similar to the poor peasants who got their heating wood from the large rich estates in Hungary. What made this form of theft (property victimization) acceptable to the steward was the redefinition process through which the act was legitimized and the victim (or the injury) denied. Thus, the redefinition process makes the criminal behavior acceptable even though it is condemned by society and made punishable by law. Once the behavior is redefined, it loses its delinquent character in the eyes of the victimizer who is then able to engage in the victimizing behavior while avoiding guilt, damage to self-image, self-indignation, and the condemnation of all those who share the same redefinitions.

The techniques used in the redefinition process are learned. It is either the global culture or the delinquent's subculture that provide the rationalizations and justifications necessary for the redefinition. Goode (1969), for example, points out that as part of the socialization *toward* degrees of violence, we acquire a range of rationalizations that justify our own lapses into physical aggressiveness. He notes that few people are so deprived intellectually as to be unable to create a moral or ethical justification for their assault on another, and he adds that most of these rationalizations are neither cynical nor morally obtuse.

This is not to suggest that the redefinition process takes the form of an explicit dialectic between the delinquent and his or her self or conscience. Yet, it is surprising how often the rationalizations and justifications, upon which the redefinition is based, are mentioned whenever delinquents and criminals are asked about their victimizing behavior. What should be emphasized is that the process of redefinition, or justification and rationalization, is not simply a purely manipulative effort to reduce one's culpability in the eyes of the law and the criminal justice system. Nor is the process just an *ex post facto* maneuver by the delinquent to reduce the feelings of guilt and shame. Rather, it is an intellectual process that takes place *before* the victimization behavior occurs and makes the victimization possible in the first place.

THE DESENSITIZATION PROCESS

Criminal victimizations, whether directed at the victim's person or property, are harmful actions. They cause physical injury, material loss, psychological trauma, or a combination of all three. Feelings of guilt associated with intentional victimizations are stronger than those evoked by negligent victimization. Most intentional victimizations involve the deliberate infliction of pain and suffering upon a fellow human being. While a small minority of victimizers may fit the psychiatric label of the heartless, callous, unfeeling "psychopath," the majority are not completely insensitive, apathetic, or impassive and are not totally devoid of the human feelings of pity and empathy. Thus, unless the victimizer becomes desensitized in advance, the victimization is bound to create moral tension and to elicit feelings of guilt, shame, remorse, and reproach in the perpetrator. Since the source of these negative feelings is the pain and suffering the victimization will cause to the victim, negating this pain and suffering can be an effective means of desensitization. To do so, the victimizer can use one or more of several techniques of desensitization. These include the denial of the victim, the reification, deindividuation, and depersonalization of the victim, the denial of injury to the victim, the blaming of the victim, and the devaluation, denigration, and derogation of the victim. These techniques and their results are shown in Table 6-2.

The desensitization process in which the victimizer engages prior to the commission of the act explains better than do the terms "psychopathy," "moral perversion," or "emotional indifference" why certain offenders show no sense of guilt, remorse, or repentance after having committed brutal and cruel acts. It explains why certain killers, while exhibiting extreme cruelty, brutality, and callousness toward their victims, show tender love and compassion for others and even for animals. In one case (Fattah, 1971) a murderer, after savagely killing his victim and robbing the victim's house, took utmost care to feed the victim's dog and cat; he even left them enough food for several days for fear that nobody would come to the scene of the crime for some time.

TABLE 6-2 **The Desensitization Process**

Techniques of Desensitization	Victimizer's Attitude to the Victim	Redefinition of the Act
Denial of the victim.	The victim does not exist.	The act is victimless. It is simply a norm violation.
Reification, deindividuation, depersonalization of the victim.	The victim is only an object, a nonperson, and a tool.	The act is victimless. It is simply a norm violation.
Denial of injury to the victim.	The victim will not be hurt. The victim will enjoy the act (sexual victimization).	The act is harmless. The act is enjoyable (sexual victimization).
Blaming the victim.	The victim is guilty. The victim is the true aggressor.	The act is an act of justice, of retaliation, of self-defense, and a means of getting even.
Devaluing, denigrating, derogating the victim.	The victim is deserving. The victim is worthless. The victim is blameworthy.	The act is necessary and warranted (moral obligation). The act is blameless (morally right).

THE TECHNIQUES OF DESENSITIZATION

The Denial, Reification, Deindividuation, and Depersonalization of the Victim

One of the common techniques of desensitization is to deny the existence of the victim, to turn him or her into an object, or to try to depersonalize and to deindividuate him or her. Some victimizers, for example, adolescent gangs, are adept at using this particular technique. In delinquent acts committed by the members of a gang, the victim is not only ignored but is also reduced to a state of "nonbeing." In a similar way, a car stolen does not really have an "owner," it is *res nullius*. In rape, a woman is negated as an equal human being and becomes just a sex object. The way in which a collective rape is legitimated by a gang is described by Robert et al. (1974):

> *In sum, in every delinquent act, the victim, member of the external environment, of the out-group, is at the same time denied, reified, used, and then rejected for the maximum profit of the gang. Enemy and object, the victim of the collective*

rape is a particularly good example ... She incarnates, in a typical way, the segregation that makes it possible to attack the female victim: she is wrong, and more exactly, she has to suffer for being wrong ... But one can also see in this crime the depersonalization of the victim. Not only is she an enemy, she is wrong and has to pay. Furthermore, she is an object, an experimental object, at the mercy of the group. (my translation, p. 15)

In murder for robbery, committed generally by young people against old, sick, and helpless victims, young offenders use the victim's old age as a justification to deny the victim's existence and right to live. The killer reasons that the victim has lived long enough. If the victim is sick and suffering from a serious, incurable disease, it is rationalized that it is better to put an end to the suffering. The murderous act is thus perceived and carried out, not as an act of aggression, but as a merciful gesture and an expression of pity and charity.

The Denial of Injury to the Victim

The denial of injury to the victim is another common technique of desensitization used by victimizers in an attempt to shield themselves against the victim's plight, to ease their conscience, and to free themselves of any feeling of guilt. It is a common technique among rapists before and during the act. Despite the cries and pleas of the victim and despite the obvious physical and psychological injury being inflicted on her, the rapist is able to convince himself that he is not actually doing the victim any harm. Having been raised in a patriarchal society, rapists have internalized the erroneous but popular claim that women subconsciously want to be taken by force. This belief distorts the rapist's perception of what is really happening. Through the denial of injury he no longer sees the act of rape for the serious sexual victimization that it is, but as a favor done for the victim. Hence the rapist's misperception that the victim is "enjoying" it. So effective can the denial of injury be that even the moaning of the victim is not taken as a deeply hurt human being's cry of pain, but as the expression of pleasure.

The denial of injury is a very popular technique in the rape of prostitutes and women perceived by the rapist as having loose morality. Here, devaluation and derogation of the victim are combined with the denial of injury. Rape is viewed by the victimizer as an act that does not cause any injury or tort to the victim.

The denial of injury is also common in property victimizations. In his study of trust violations, Cressey (1953) quotes a rationalization he often heard from the embezzlers he interviewed: "Well, at least I didn't hurt anybody." Easing the conscience is much easier when the delinquent act is portrayed in the delinquent's mind as not causing harm or injury to the victim.

In theft, fraud, cheating, and vandalism against the government or a large organization or corporation, the common reasoning is that the victim is too rich and therefore will not suffer. "The insurance will pay" is another popular way of minimizing guilt by denying that the victim will suffer as a result of the victimizing act. By redefining automobile theft as "borrowing" or as a "joy-ride," the injury to the victim is denied. The same is true in embezzlement. The delinquent and injurious aspects of the act are denied as the potential embezzler succeeds in becoming convinced that the victimization is not stealing or embezzling but merely "borrowing" the money. As Cressey (1953) points out:

> *In most instances, the rationalization that the conversion of deposits would merely amount to "borrowing" the deposits for a short time was an easy and logical step to make, since the ordinary practice of the businessman interviewed was similar to such borrowing. (p. 103)*

The Blaming of the Victim

Once victimizers are able to convince themselves that the victim has done them wrong and that he or she is guilty of some injustice, they can rid themselves entirely of any compassion for that victim and of any sense of personal culpability. By blaming the victim and transforming him or her into a person deserving to suffer, victimizers are able to go ahead with the victimization without conceiving of themselves as criminals and while shielding themselves against post-victimization dissonance. The establishment of the victim's guilt beforehand, whether the guilt is real or imagined, acts as an anesthetic on the conscience of potential victimizers, enabling them to destroy or injure their victim without pity or empathy.

As Sykes and Matza (1957) put it:

> *The injury, it may be claimed, is not really an injury; rather, it is a form of rightful retaliation or punishment. By a subtle Alchemy, the delinquent moves himself into the position of an avenger, and the victim is transformed into a wrongdoer. (p. 253)*

Although blaming the victim is a common and often-used technique of auto-legitimation, neutralization, and desensitization, it is not a process of intentional distortion. In most cases, victimizers are actually convinced of their victim's guilt. Nowhere is this more evident than in crimes of passion, in political crimes, and in the crimes of paranoiacs.

Crimes of passion are characterized almost invariably by a justiciary attitude on the part of the offender. This attitude, in which offenders feel they are doing themselves justice, as Hesnard (1963) points out, is one of the conscious and justifying motivations of the crime:

> *The homicidal act is committed as a justiciary act. The criminal perceives himself as having been injured in his love, particularly the male in his virile "honor," and he considers the wrong done to him as an undeniable injustice. The homicidal act is the outcome of a process which we have called auto-legitimation. It is triggered by a situation that has amplified, more or less unexpectedly, the perceived wrong. (my translation, p. 165)*

The late psychiatrist, De Greeff (1950), devoted a great deal of attention to the justiciary aspect of the crimes of passion. He affirms that the killer in these crimes proceeds only toward the criminal act insofar as the act seems to be justified and even needed. This excessive justiciary attitude of the victimizer toward the victim can only be maintained by resorting to subterfuges and by nurturing a negative image of the victim prior to the killing. This negative image reduces the prospective victim to "nothing," or even less than nothing, and the death of the victim, therefore, becomes insignificant.

Blaming the victim is also the dominant feature of crimes motivated by revenge, the typical example of which is the vendetta. Here the victimization is seen as a legitimate reprisal, a rightful form of retaliation. The chain reactions resulting from the use of this type of legitimation is the development or perpetuation of a subculture of violence. As Wolfgang and Ferracuti (1967) write:

> *When the attacked see their assaulters as agents of the same kind of aggression they themselves represent, violent retaliation is readily legitimized by a situationally specific rationale, as well as by the generally normative supports for violence. (p. 161)*

The technique of blaming the victim plays an equally important part in acts of "vigilantism" as well as in certain violent victimizations perpetrated by blood-thirsty, uncontrollable crowds, such as lynching. Lynching is a perfect example of spontaneous victimization legitimized and made possible through the behavior of the victim.

The justiciary aspect is also evident in many types of political and ideological crimes. Many political assassinations are committed by intellectuals or members of the elite who perceive themselves as saviors and consider it a moral duty to kill a despot, a cruel dictator, or a disliked tyrant. In some cases, assassins act out of a personal sense of victimization, while, in other cases, they set for themselves the task of avenging a group, a political party, or even a whole nation or race. Examples of this latter attitude are the violent acts by Armenian nationalists against Turkish targets. The Armenian violence is an act of retaliation motivated by the Turkish massacres of the Armenian people. The same is true of members of other violent political groups who have integrated a political ideology opposed to existing political values. By viewing the existing social order as illegitimate, unjust, and oppressive, the use of violence to change that order seems to them perfectly legitimate and justified.

Blaming the victim is a technique used by oppressed and oppressors alike. Terrorist acts by those in power are legitimized using this technique. Killings, disappearances, torture, and violations of human rights are held to be warranted because those against whom these acts are committed are seen as deserving of punishment since they pose a threat to the established order. Even genocide, the ultimate form of power abuse, may be legitimized by blaming the victim and may be seen as an act that is not just necessary but absolutely indispensable. Prior to the actual perpetration of genocide, the targeted minority group is blamed for various social and economic ills so that any compassion for the group is eliminated, and its annihilation is seen as a perfectly legitimate and justified act of self-defense.

The widespread use of blaming the victim as a technique of desensitization may be finally illustrated by three concrete examples: patricide, the crimes of the paranoiacs, and the choice of a white victim by a black victimizer in the United States.

Patricides and matricides require, more than any other form of killing, a great deal of pre-victimization desensitization. The killing of the family tyrant by one of his sons needs to be perceived by the killer not as an act of aggression, but as an act of vengeful justice. The cruelty of the father to the mother, together with the son's hostility and aggressiveness toward the father, serve as the starting point for the process of desensitization. In most cases, the patricide is the culmination of a justiciary revolt animated by the father's aggression toward the mother. This aggression, in the eyes of the son, makes the father guilty and justifies the crime that is being prepared (Hesnard, 1963). Hesnard points out that many of the cases of patricide could be easily understood by the natural aggressiveness the son, seeing himself as a protector of the mother, feels for his father. This aggressiveness, believes Hesnard, stems directly from the Oedipus complex and is liberated through the legitimation of the act, which is genuinely perceived by the hostile son as a necessary protective gesture toward a mistreated or seriously threatened mother.

While in patricide and tyrannicide the homicidal act is directed against the tormentor, in killings committed by individuals suffering from paranoia or paranoid schizophrenia, the murder victim is usually the "persecutor." A number of those who suffer from systematized delusions of persecution, after having made so many efforts to get "justice," reach a point where they become convinced that their only salvation is to kill their "persecutor." And it is their invincible conviction in the reality of the prospective victim's crime that quite naturally legitimates the homicidal act (Hesnard, 1963) and also explains the great sense of relief the paranoiac feels after having killed the "guilty" victim.

Blaming the victim is also characteristic of interracial crimes in the United States where the victimizer is black and the victim is white. Often the choice of a white victim is legitimated by blaming the victim. The victimization is rationalized as a justiciary act against the white race for all the exploitation and injustices it had inflicted over the years on the black race. An illustration of this attitude is given by Richard Wright (1945) in his book *Black Boy*:

> *I gave him a pledge of my honesty, feeling absolutely no qualms about what I intended to do. He was white, and I could never do to him what he and his kind had done to me. Therefore, I reasoned, stealing was not a violation of my ethics, but of his; I felt that things were rigged in his favor, and any action I took to circumvent his scheme of life was justified. (p. 178)*

This reasoning is quite similar to what Eldridge Cleaver (1968) felt and did when raping a white victim:

Rape was an insurrectionary act. It delighted me that I was defying and trampling upon the white man's law, upon his system of values, and that I was defiling his women — and this point, I believe, was the most satisfying to me, because I was very resentful over the historical fact of how the white man has used the black woman. I felt I was getting revenge. (p. 26)

The Devaluation of the Victim

In an attempt to desensitize themselves to the victim's plight, victimizers often attribute inferior qualities to the victim. They may devalue, denigrate, and derogate the victim's worth, so that the victim appears blameworthy and deserving of the victimization fate as a person (he or she is a bad person) or because of a behavior (he or she did something very bad). This psychological process of devaluing the victim is not worked out in a logical, rational, or conscious way (Ryan, 1971).

Redl and Wineman (1951) claim that even where the delinquent act itself has to be admitted as being guilt provoking, the possibility of being able to devalue the victim involved eases the guilt:

This type of "logic" which the delinquent ego displays sometimes assumes fantastic proportions. This is especially the case where the very value issue which makes the perpetrator's behavior so obnoxious is used to depreciate the victim himself. Thus, some of our thieves would consider it quite a good excuse for their act, that the person they stole from was "only a goddamn thief" himself ... (stealing) seems to them justified simply on the basis that the people from whom they steal "are such lowdown, despicable bums" themselves. (pp. 180-181)

The preparation of the criminal act at the moral level is done, almost always, with reference to the attributes, personality, attitude, behavior, and conduct of the victim. In the case of crimes of passion, Hesnard (1963) describes the mental process of auto-legitimation through the devaluation of the victim as follows:

The potential criminal judges his victim more and more unfavorably, depreciates him in his mind, and ends up by making a bad, harmful and dangerous being out of the victim. As a result of this mental process of justification, the homicidal act appears to the potential murderer as a necessity, a legitimate intervention, sometimes even as a moral duty. The act is no longer conceived as a betrayal, but as an act of moral salubrity and of human justice. (my translation, pp. 181-182)

In studying collective rape, Hijazi (1966) noticed that the majority of the delinquents studied have a devalued image of the female. She can only consent, submit, and suffer. There is never any sentimental or emotional attachment to her. She has to be possessed. Even thefts from the victim, which sometimes accompany collective rape (such as taking the money out of the victim's purse), seemed to be motivated more by contempt than by greed (Hijazi, 1966).

Certain attributes or qualities of the potential victim may be used to discredit and devalue him or her in an effort to present the victim as a legitimate and deserving target and to justify the delinquent act. Attacks on homosexuals and on prostitutes are often so legitimized. Redl and Wineman (1951) found that for certain adolescents, stealing from homosexuals is a perfectly justifiable and legitimate act. Property crimes committed against prostitutes are rationalized in a similar manner. Furthermore, the forcible rape of a prostitute is also conceived of as a legitimate and guiltless act. Her style of life is interpreted as denying her the right to dispose of her own body as she pleases, as if, because she sells her body to whomever pays the price, she no longer has the right to protest when someone tries to possess her by force. In such cases, the attitude toward the potential victim and the possibility of justifying the act are undoubtedly important factors in the choice of the victim.

In cases of property crime, the dishonesty of the victim seems to be seen in the same way as the life-style of the prostitute. The businessman is defined as a "monopolistic miser," or as a "dishonest merchant" who cheats his customers and therefore deserves to be victimized, and the illegal act is defined as an act of moral indignation (Schwendinger and Schwendinger, 1967). The repugnance toward the victim overcomes any thought of the victim's rights. This is concordant with Cressey's (1953) findings of embezzlers. He discovered that in their justifications the victim is defined as a deviant in order to maintain a typically moral self-definition. In this sense, the criminal defines his criminal act as an act of a morally indignant man.

In *The Professional Thief*, Sutherland (1937) makes it clear that "the con mob generally has a good deal of contempt for their suckers. They believe that if a person is going to steal, let him steal from the same point of view that the thief does: do not profess honesty and steal at the same time" (p. 178). Elsewhere Sutherland (1937) stresses that "in the confidence games, the principle is the same — beat a man who is trying to do something dishonest. It is impossible to beat an honest man in a confidence game" (p. 69).

DESENSITIZATION IN SOCIAL PSYCHOLOGY RESEARCH

The reification, deindividuation, derogation, and blame models find a great deal of empirical support in research done in social psychology (Brock and Buss, 1964; Bercheid and Walster, 1969; Godfrey and Lowe, 1975; Diener, 1976; Diener and Fraser, 1976; Cialdini et al., 1976; Katz et al., 1977). Experimental studies by social psychologists reveal that when the victim is not seen as an individual a state of deindividuation may result, which will lower inner restraints. The case of the Hungarian boys stealing coal from the cars on the railway tracks in Detroit (Beynon, 1935) is a perfect real-life illustration of how the deindividuation of the victim makes the delinquent behavior possible and acceptable. Psychological research also shows that victim derogation and victim denigration lead to reduced feelings of responsibility and a lessened post-aggression dissonance. In the words of Lerner (1974): "If the subjects can attribute to the victim characteristics that deserve to be punished, then the harm can be seen as appropriate and just."

Psychologists' explanations of the derogation/denigration process are mostly inspired by Lerner's (1974) "just world hypothesis" and revolve around people's need to believe in a just world. The process, however, seems to be an indication of the delinquent's attempt to become desensitized and to justify and rationalize his harmful, injurious actions. Support for this comes from studies by Cialdini et al. (1976) who found evidence suggesting that the mediation of the victim-derogation phenomenon in the Lerner situation is not a tendency to believe in a just world, but a tendency to justify one's complicity in the harm done. Further research on the desensitization process and the mechanisms used to achieve this end is needed. It seems that only through an analysis of this process will we be able to understand how a socialized, seemingly normal individual could be transformed into an uninhibited, ruthless aggressor capable of committing acts of extreme cruelty and savagery with no trace of empathy or compassion for the victim and with no sign of guilt or remorse.

The Transformation of the Victim into a Victimizer

Feelings of injustice and the sense of having been victimized are important mechanisms in the processes of neutralization, redefinition/auto-legitimation, and desensitization. It is not surprising, therefore, to find that a large number of delinquents and criminals perceive themselves more or less as victims. The real or vicarious experience of having been victimized, as well as the adoption of the role and the identity of a victim, provide strong motivations and justifications for offending that are capable of transforming the victim into a ruthless victimizer. Examples of this transformation are many, and they have acquired a vocabulary of their own in everyday language such as self-defense, auto-justice, popular justice, vigilantism, and getting even. Cases of store or house owners who, once victimized, sit waiting with a firearm in hand for the next robber, burglar, or thief, in order to welcome the victimizer with a hail of bullets have occurred with increasing frequency in the past few years. But these are just the extreme examples of this transformation. In schools, it is a common experience to find children whose books, articles, or supplies have been stolen by other children taking revenge by stealing the same or similar things from their school mates. Some youthful and adult car owners who have had some piece or part, such as a hubcap or mirror, stolen, do not report their victimization to the police, but instead, "help themselves" to the same parts from a similar car. In doing so they feel they are only righting the wrong done to them.

As important as this process of transformation from a victim into a victimizer is to the explanation of many forms of delinquency and crime, it has hardly been investigated by criminologists or victimologists. Occasional mention of this transformation can be found in the writings of some clinical psychologists who have had direct contact with offenders.

Redl and Wineman (1951) cite among the "alibi tricks," or the techniques the delinquent ego uses to appease feelings of guilt and to legitimize the act, the argument that "somebody else did that same thing to me before." They cite several examples of delinquents who really tried to prove that their stealing was all right because "somebody swiped my own wallet two weeks ago."

Debuyst and Joos (1971) relate the story of a seventeen-year-old boy, Raoul, who had a collection of firearms, one of which was stolen from him. Sometime later, he broke into a firearms shop and stole some firearms. His mother, breaking down in tears over her son's conduct, could not understand how such an honest boy, who was from a well-to-do family, working, and well considered by everyone, could do such a thing.

In addition to concrete feelings of victimization resulting from a specific incident or incidents in which the person was actually victimized, individuals or groups may have sentiments of injustice and a vague sense of victimization unrelated to any specific event(s).

In many offenses against property, resentment over economic exploitation and social injustices serves as a means of auto-legitimation. Many thieves, professional and occasional, tend to justify their delinquent behavior by citing social injustices and by contrasting the scandalous wealth of the upper social-classes with their own misery and poverty. White-collar tax evaders convince themselves that the tax system is unfair as it victimizes and penalizes the hard-working, like themselves, while allowing many others to pay less or no taxes. Cressey (1953) discovered that perceived injustice and the sense of being victimized play an important role in the cases of embezzlement and trust violations. This may take the form of feeling underpaid or overworked, or of feeling unfairly treated in some other way involving finances. Cressey points out that it is not the fact of being maltreated that is important, if such a fact can be established. Rather, it is the fact that the individual feels maltreated, while, at the same time, for some reason, feeling obligated to continue in the service of the organization.

Feelings of injustice and of victimization play a crucial role in the acts of political terrorists and of other minority groups who have been historically the targets of violence, maltreatment, and exploitation.

A study in the United States of how black males view crime and criminal law (Davis, 1974) found that the historical injustices inflicted on blacks under the United States law have produced a black consciousness that views the law as simply another instrument for upholding white supremacy. They do not regard the law as an instrument for justice and little, if any, stigma is attached to violating it. Davis observed what appeared to be a generalized set of motives among black males that justify and explain their illegal acts. The core of explanations that emerged, and that was unique to the black experience, has as a central theme the feelings of injustice held by black males. Most of the respondents to the questionnaire gave explanations such as the unequal access to institutional participation between blacks and whites, the injustices of that situation, the historical weight of four hundred years of unjust treatment, the initial involuntary servitude of blacks, the lack of rights and privileges for blacks under the law and citizenship, and the statement that black people are a conquered people.

Commenting on his findings, Davis (1974) suggests that the demonstration of a generalized attitude of injustice among American black males is rather startling. He adds:

> *The essential point is that if a black male finds himself drifting into a life of crime, he will have experienced a network of justifications in his environment which he can use to explain his criminal motives due to the generalized attitude within the community that blacks suffer under the law. (p. 82)*

What Davis observed among American black males is similar to what Hijazi (1966) observed among young delinquents in Europe. Their feelings of injustice, of being rejected, and of perceiving themselves as innocent victims significantly lowered the degree to which they felt themselves bound to the moral and legal codes of society. Hijazi reports that young delinquents nurture a feeling of injustice, which legitimates their attitudes. Considering that the justice of society is hypocritical, they want to implement their own justice. Perceiving themselves as victims of a social system whose legitimacy they are challenging, the young delinquents consider as justified any act of vengeance. According to Hijazi (1966) a young delinquent

> *blames the responsibility for his acts on society, on others, on the circumstances. Considering that the justice of men is unjust, he denies the legitimacy of the rules of that justice. He feels exempted from respecting those rules in his conduct. The delinquent act, then, does not constitute a violation of his own moral rule, but of the moral code of society whose validity he is questioning. (my translation, p. 221)*

The Revolving Roles: From Offender to Victim and From Victim to Offender

Despite the proliferation of victim assistance and victim-offender reconciliation programs, no attempt has been made to collect systematic data on the social history of representative samples of victims of specific offenses. The only exceptions are the cohort studies such as the one in Philadelphia (Thornberry and Singer, 1979; Singer, 1981). Victimization surveys do not provide the needed data for two reasons: (1) they are limited to a small number of personal and household victimizations; and (2) the information they provide on victims is largely sociodemographic. Thus, they do not inform us about those individuals who successively assume the roles of offenders and victims so that it is not known how many offenders become victims, how many victims had been offenders or committed criminal acts following their victimization, and so on.

In their study of the Philadelphia cohort, Thornberry and Singer (1979) discovered that 64 percent of the young victims became offenders in their adult age, whereas only 22 percent of the ones who were not victimized as children became adult law violators.

There is some indication, however, that there is a constant movement between the victim and offender roles and that the victims of today might be the victimizers of tomorrow. Research on child abuse, for example, has shown that most of the abusers were themselves abused as young children. Studies of rapists and child molesters also reveal that a high percentage of them were victims of sexual abuse. Through a process of learning, rationalization, justification, and legitimation, the transformation of the victim into victimizer is achieved.

That a large number of criminals and delinquents suffer from feelings of injustice and a sense of victimization is too well documented in the literature to need further confirmation. In addition, De Greeff (1950) claims that the number of events that criminals consider as "injustices" is much higher than among nondelinquents and that delinquents' reactions to such unjust events are usually longer, more frequent, or more violent. Based on his extensive clinical knowledge of criminals, he affirms that this perception of injustice is neither an excuse nor a pretext, but is a real sense of injustice deeply felt by the delinquents and with which they identify. It is an attitude that characterizes their personality.

To summarize, we may say that the passage from the state of victim to the state of offender, from the state of aggressed to the state of aggressor, from the state of oppressed to the state of oppressor, is an easy passage. The actual or perceived injustice, the concrete or vague sense of victimization, the retaliatory feelings, which are not necessarily directed toward the victimizer, and the ensuing legitimation of the act, which is seen as a rightful reprisal, are all mechanisms that facilitate this passage. The feelings of injustice neutralize the inhibitory forces and act as a palliative for the person's conscience.

Appropriate and Inappropriate Targets for Victimization

Beynon's (1935) study of the Hungarians in Detroit (see Chapter 4) is a perfect illustration of the distinctions delinquents and criminals make between appropriate and inappropriate targets for victimization. The railway tracks from which the boys steal the coal upon the orders of the church are perceived as perfectly legitimate targets. They are owned by an impersonal, unknown company. According to the steward of the Hungarian church interviewed by Beynon, this makes stealing from it different from other stealing, such as the stealing from a person like himself.

That delinquents and criminals make subtle distinctions between who is to be victimized and who is not finds overwhelming confirmation in numerous empirical studies. Drawing upon such evidence, Sykes and Matza (1957) insist that juvenile delinquents in particular often draw a sharp line between those who can be victimized and those who cannot. Thus, certain social groups are not viewed as "fair game" in the performance of supposedly approved delinquent acts, while others warrant a variety of attacks.

In his study of adolescent gangs in France, Robert (1966) discovered that the gangs make a careful choice of their victims and that the personal qualities of the victim play an important role in this choice. For instance, the gangs make a clear-cut distinction between "serious girls" and "fast girls." With a serious girl, the member of the gang may entertain only a platonic relationship. A fast girl, on the other hand, has to submit to the sexual demands of the group, and, if she refuses, she will be the object of a collective rape. Robert also found a clear distinction between the girls of the in-group and the girls of the out-group. The latter are reduced to an abstraction, and the acts committed against them are not seen as delinquent, but as rightful and just acts.

These subcultural definitions and distinctions in France are very similar to the ones that exist in the United States. Gagnon (1974) refers to society-wide sexual attitudes exacerbated in those subcultures where a basic distinction is made between good girls and bad girls. The latter are often the victims of sexual assault because of local codes about the sexual accessibility of such females. The appellation "bad," denotes that they have given up the protections normally given to young women who are marriageable. In these situations, adds Gagnon, such girls are vulnerable to group rape situations, which grow out of masculine values of the male youth culture in certain ethnic areas.

In another French study carried out by the Vaucresson Center (1962), it was found that certain gangs attack only a category of people, such as homosexuals, who are unlikely to complain or to report the victimization to the police. Members of the gang are able to easily legitimize their actions by reversing the situation. For example, a boy member of the gang was a victim of a corrupting homosexual adult. The group reacted in moral indignation and exploited the situation by victimizing that corrupt adult.

In his fascinating biography, *The Professional Thief*, Sutherland (1937) shows time and time again that professional thieves have their own "code of ethics." In their choice of victims, they scrupulously follow the dictates of this moral code. Sutherland (1937) gives the following example:

> *Thieves make some distinctions among suckers, and also make some attempt to justify the distinctions. Persons who are personal or business associates are*

safe from thieves of all professional types ... Cannons do not approve or have any part in slave grift, feeling that, if the money of a poor man is taken, his family will be distressed. They do not like the cannon grift, because you may be robbing a poor man who really needs the money for his family ... Catholic cannons will rarely beat a Catholic priest. Jewish cannons will beat a Jewish rabbi whenever possible, as well as Catholic priests and Protestant ministers. There is a generally accepted rule among cannons not to beat cripples. It is believed that this rule is due to a feeling that the cripples are less capable of getting money, and also there is a certain amount of superstition involved in it. (pp. 174-175)[1]

What the professional thief told Sutherland was echoed by the delinquent subjects in the experimental study (1967) carried out by Schwendinger and Schwendinger. In this study it was found that most delinquents stereotype persons in the context of delimited situations and that certain codes of honor specify the conditions under which persons are considered legitimate objects of victimization.

Potential Victims' Stereotypes of Probable Victimizers

Potential victims' opinions and mental images of criminals are not based on direct personal experiences but on secondary sources of information. Most of us are exposed daily to atypical cases sensationalized by the mass media, to widespread misinformation about criminals, and to widely shared cultural prejudices against those who commit crime. All this is responsible for the development of stereotypes and the formation of distorted opinions and images of who the probable victimizers are. As a result of these stereotypes, many people mistakenly believe that they can recognize criminals as well as bad and dangerous people on sight. Young female hitchhikers, to give only one example, may naively think they can judge the driver in seconds and ascertain whether he is potentially dangerous or not. The existence of shared mental images of criminals and dangerous people is confirmed when subjects are shown photos of persons with no history of criminal behavior. The subjects seem to agree on who looks dangerous or harmless and who looks like a criminal and who does not. As they are not based on scientifically based information, these popular mental images and stereotypes of probable victimizers are not only misleading, but also outright false. For example, the general stereotype of the rapist is that of a raging, oversexed, ruthless brute. Yet, as Menninger (1966) points out, most sex crimes are committed by undersexed rather than oversexed individuals, often undersized rather than oversized, and impelled less by lust than by a need for reassurance regarding an impaired masculinity. The popular stereotype of the killer is that of a violent, tough, and sadistic monster. Yet, most killings are committed within the family or a circle of friends and work associates by frustrated individuals suffering, not from an uncontrollable urge to kill, but from a sense of helplessness, hopelessness, or both.

Summary

In this chapter we explored the victimizer's attitude to the victim. This is an important area that has received only scant attention from researchers. The situation is changing due to studies by feminist researchers on the rapist's attitude to his victim. In many cases, the offender's attitude to the victim is characterized by apathy and indifference. Victimizers also seem to hold to stereotypic images of probable victims. These attitudes, images, and stereotypes play an important role in the offender's mental reasoning preceding victimization.

The pre-victimization process may be artificially split into three processes: neutralization, redefinition/auto-legitimation, and desensitization. Neutralization has the victimizer as its focus, and its main purpose is to enable the victimizer to overcome the moral and cultural barriers that stand in the way to the victimization act. Redefinition/auto-legitimation has the victimization act as its focus, and its main purpose is to redefine, rationalize, and justify the act. The third process, desensitization, has the prospective victim as its focus. Its main aim is to desensitize the victimizer to the pain and suffering inflicted on the victim. The neutralization process operates to render the mechanisms of social control ineffective. The redefinition process operates to strip the act of its delinquent, illegal, or immoral character. The desensitization process makes it possible to hurt, injure, or harm the victim without feeling bad or guilty about it and without suffering post-victimization dissonance.

The victimizer can use various techniques of desensitization. These techniques are the denial, reification, and depersonalization of the victim; the denial of injury to the victim; the blaming of the victim; and the devaluation of the victim. An extremely popular technique is blaming the victim. In this technique, the victimizer is able to convince himself or herself that the victim has done him or her wrong and that the victim is guilty of some injustice. Once the guilt of the victim is established any compassion for that victim and any sense of personal culpability can be discarded. Although blaming the victim is a common and often used technique of desensitization, it is not a process of intentional distortion. In most cases, the victimizer is actually convinced of the victim's guilt. These techniques of desensitization have received a great deal of empirical support in research done in social psychology.

Feelings of injustice and the sense of having been victimized are also important mechanisms in the processes of neutralization, redefinition/auto-legitimation, and desensitization. It is not surprising, therefore, that a large number of delinquents and criminals perceive themselves more or less as victims. There also seems to be a constant movement between victim and offender roles so that the victims of today might be the victimizers of tomorrow. Studies of child abusers, molesters, and rapists reveal that a high percentage of them were themselves victimized as children. All this suggests that the passage from the state of victim to the state of offender is an easy one.

Empirical studies suggest that delinquents and criminals make subtle distinctions between appropriate and inappropriate targets and between who is to be victimized and who is not. Certain groups such as professional thieves seem to follow a specific "code of ethics" in their choice of victims. Potential victims also appear to have mental images and stereotypes of probable victimizers. These, however, are based not on direct personal experience but on secondary sources of information. This might explain why these images are often distorted and do not correspond to the reality of victimizers.

SEVEN

Victim-Offender Relationships

I maintain that many criminal deeds are more indicative of a subject-object relation than of the perpetrator alone. There is a definite mutuality of some sort. The mechanical outcome may be profit to one party, harm to another, yet the psychological interaction, carefully observed, will not submit to this kindergarten label. In the long process leading gradually to the unlawful result, credit and debit are not infrequently indistinguishable.

Hans Von Hentig (1948, p. 384)

Publicly, at least, we think of the family as a loving, tranquil, peaceful social institution to which one flees ***"from"*** *stress and danger. Privately, the family is perhaps society's most violent social institution.*

Richard J. Gelles (1983, p. 157)

Victim-Offender Relationships

The study of victim-offender relationships constitutes one of the most important elements of victimology. The dynamics of the specific relationship can often reveal the motives behind the crime as well as the reasons for committing the act against a particular victim. The relationship can also shed light on victim-offender interactions that preceded the criminal act and may offer valuable clues as to the extent of the victim's contribution, if any, to the genesis of the crime. The victim-offender relationship is also of great importance to police investigators. One reason why criminal homicide has a relatively high clearance rate is that killer and killed are often related, and it is this relationship that often betrays to the investigators the identity of the perpetrator. What makes most cases of sexual murders particularly difficult to solve is the absence of a specific relationship between the killer and the victim.

Victim-Offender Relationships in Criminal Law

Criminal law, in general, pays little or no attention to whatever relationship may exist between the criminal and the victim. There are, however, a few exceptions. In some instances the relationship may be considered an aggravating or an extenuating circumstance. This is the case, for example, in incest and infanticide. Infanticide, according to Section 216 of the Canadian Criminal Code, is the offense of a mother who causes the death of her newly born child by a willful act or omission if, at the time, she is not fully recovered from the effects of giving birth to that child. Infanticide is an indictable offense liable to imprisonment for five years (Section 220 of the Canadian Criminal Code). Section 150 of the Canadian Criminal Code stipulates that incest is committed when a person who, knowing that another person is by blood relationship his or her parent, child, brother, sister, grandparent, or grandchild, as the case may be, has sexual intercourse with that person. In Canada, incest is an indictable offense liable to imprisonment for fourteen years.

Some criminal codes consider the crimes of patricide (the deliberate killing of one's father) or matricide (the deliberate killing of one's mother) as more serious forms of killing than murder, and, where the death penalty is retained, they qualify as capital crimes.[1] In certain jurisdictions specific offender-victim relationships may be cause for exemption from punishment. For example, the expropriation of money, jewelry, or other goods between parents and children may be excluded from the provisions of theft and treated as a civil matter.[2]

Victim-Offender Relationships in Violent Victimization

Although victim-offender relationships are more prevalent in violent crimes than in other types, they are not totally absent in property offenses. A victim-offender relationship often exists in embezzlement, breach of trust, and blackmail, to mention but a few. Our focus here will, however, be victim-offender relationships in violent victimization.

A substantial portion of violent victimization, in particular criminal homicide, attempted murder, and aggravated assault, are interpersonal crimes. In German they have acquired the name "Beziehungsverbrechen" — crimes of relationships. They are the outcomes of various types of personal relationships and interactions between the aggressor and those who suffer from the aggression. A large number of these violent victimizations take place within or near the home of the victim or the offender and occur between persons well known to each other, between individuals bound by interpersonal bonds, and, mostly, between family, friends, or those bound by affective ties. While instrumental violence, such as violence employed to overcome the resistance of the victim in robbery or rape, may be frequently employed against strangers, expressive violence is predominantly used between people who know each other. One of the typical contexts in which criminal homicide, attempted murder, or aggravated assault occur is that of a domestic fight or a family dispute where alcohol is present and insulting, abusive, and jealous behavior arises (Wolfgang, 1958).

THE FAMILY AS A NUCLEUS OF VIOLENCE

The current attention being paid to violence in the home, such as wife beating, child battering, and elder abuse, has highlighted the family as a nucleus of violence. It is sad but true that those whom we love and with whom we live and those who care for us and for whom we care are precisely the ones most likely to harm us or be harmed by us. Why do intimates commit violence against one another? Goode (1969) suggests that the most powerful, if crudest, answer is that they are there. It is not surprising, he adds, that more violence is directed against those with whom we are in more intimate contact, as we are all within easy striking distance of our friends and spouses for a majority of the time. Goode also points out that we are violent toward our intimates — friends, lovers, and spouses — because few others can anger us so much. Just as they are a main source of our pleasure, they are equally a main source of our frustration and hurt. What they do affects us more directly and painfully than what most strangers do.

Sebastian (1983) offers more elaborate explanations for intrafamily violence. He suggests, first, that family violence is more common than other forms of violence because family members have especially great instigational potential for one another and because restraints against aggression are weaker in the family than they are in other social settings. He points out that while inhibitions against aggression outside the home are quite strong, they are weak in the home. Thus the legal consequences of assault against a family member are minimal in comparison to what would follow if a similar attack was made against a nonfamily member. The second reason suggested is that there is an absence of strong disapproval from outsiders in the home, which minimizes or eliminates altogether any influence they might have and makes physical aggression in the family, or any other private setting, more probable. A third reason Sebastian gives for the weakness of inhibition against aggression in the home is that family members have intimate knowledge of one another. Therefore, they will have a rough idea of how much inappropriate aggressive behavior or abuse their victims will tolerate. They know what they can "get away with." Family members will also "put up with" more inappropriate behavior from another family member than others would. Thus, as long as these limits are recognized and as long as the aggression stays within them, or exceeds them only minimally, the potential for aggression is more probable than under conditions where little or no tolerance for aggressive behavior can be expected. The fourth reason Sebastian offers to explain the weaker inhibitions against violence in the home is the interdependence between family members. The greater dependency of some members on others "forces" them to put up with even serious attacks from those others. The final factor in Sebastian's explanation, a factor that affects inhibitions governing aggression in several forms of family violence, is the inability of the victim, such as a child, wife, or elderly relative, to retaliate or defend himself or herself successfully because of differences in size, strength, or both. Sebastian (1983) summarizes his explanations as follows:

> *In summary, inhibitions against physical aggression in the family are hypothesized to be much weaker than they are in other settings because (1) adverse legal consequences are much less probable; (2) social disapproval from non-family members is less likely; (3) aggressors have a fairly accurate sense of how much inappropriate behavior family members will tolerate; (4) victims of physical aggression are often highly and involuntarily dependent on their assailants; and (5) some of the most victimized family members are weaker and smaller than their attackers. All other things being equal, the weaker the individual's inhibitions, the more probable and the more intense the person's aggressive behavior will be. (p. 186)*

The concept of instigational potential requires some further elaboration. It is certainly true that the more indifferent we are toward a certain individual the less likely it will be that we have a motive for using expressive violence against that person, for killing him, or for deliberately injuring him. Attraction, love, affection, compassion, and emotional attachment, as well as repulsion, hate, jealousy, envy, and emotional detachment are subject to, and conditional upon, social proximity and social distance and upon the volume and intensity of social interaction. In the light of this we can hypothesize that socially distant individuals and groups will be more popular targets for victimization in rational crime (property offenses), while socially close individuals and groups will be more popular targets in expressive violence and crimes of passion.

This hypothesis has a fair amount of empirical support. Robbery, for example, which belongs more to property offenses than to offenses against the person, does have a higher percentage of victims who are strangers to the victimizer than do homicide or assault offenses (Mulvihill, Tumin, and Curtis, 1969). It is also reasonable to hypothesize that the intensity of violence incrcases with the closeness of the relationship. This means that a higher percentage of assaults than of criminal homicides will be committed against strangers. This hypothesis also has empirical support (Mulvihill, Tumin, and Curtis, 1969). It should be noted, however, that many assaults, especially minor ones, between nonstrangers are never reported to the police or in victimization surveys. As a result, the frequency of personal relationships between victim and offender in assault is an underestimate.

To illustrate the interpersonal character of most crimes of violence we will now examine the victim-victimizer relationship in criminal homicide as well as in some other violent offenses.

CRIMINAL HOMICIDE

Studies of criminal homicide in different societies and different cultures leave no doubt as to the role personal relationships play in this form of aggression. The striking similarity in the frequencies of the various types of personal relationships between killer and victim reported by the studies suggests the existence of social laws governing this phenomenon of lethal victimization.

A cross-cultural study by Palmer (1970, 1975) indicates that in the vast majority of nonliterate societies analyzed (forty-one out of forty-four), homicidal victims and offenders are rarely, if ever, strangers. In a study of murders committed in England and Wales between March 1957 and December 1960, Morris and Cooper (1964) found that 81 percent of the killers were either related to, or acquainted with, their victims, while only 19 percent of the killers murdered strangers. In a study of Danish murders committed between 1934 and 1939, and between 1946 and 1951, Svalastoga (1956) discovered a family relationship or some type of acquaintanceship in 87.8 percent of the cases. Only 12.2 percent of the murders were committed against strangers. This highly interpersonal character of criminal homicide is limited neither to nonliterate societies nor to West European culture. In India, Driver (1961) found some kind of personal relationship between the offender and the victim in 91 percent of all homicide cases studied, compared to only 9 percent of the cases where the killer and victim were total strangers. In his study of criminal homicide in Philadelphia, Wolfgang (1958) reports that only in 14.4 percent of the cases were the killer and the victim neither related nor acquainted. This situation is by no means unique to Philadelphia. Another study of criminal homicide in seventeen American cities (Mulvihill, Tumin, and Curtis, 1969) revealed that only 15.6 percent of the cases were between strangers.

A recent study of homicide in Canada covering a ten-year period from 1976 to 1985 (Statistics Canada, 1987) found, as in previous years, that more than three-quarters of all solved homicides (76.9 percent) involved victims and suspects who were known to each other. These relationship cases were almost equally divided between domestic (38.4 percent) and social or business relationships (38.5 percent).

A study of police homicide files over a fourteen-year period from 1968 to 1981 in New South Wales, Australia, reports that 80 percent of homicides occur within the family or among friends and acquaintances (Wallace, 1986).

Family Relationships in Criminal Homicides

The most frequent type of victim-offender relationship observed in criminal homicide is a family relationship. This pattern is more pronounced for female victims than it is for male victims.

A study of murder in England undertaken by the British Home Office Research Unit (Gibson and Klein, 1961) over a period of six years from 1955 to 1960, reveals that more than two-thirds of all female victims are killed by their husbands, lovers, or close relatives. Only a few are murdered by strangers. Children under sixteen years of age are slain by their parents or by members of their family in 70 percent of the cases. Men, on the other hand, are killed by strangers in approximately 50 percent of the cases during either a brawl or a robbery and, more frequently, by their acquaintances rather than by members of their family. They are rarely killed by their wives or lovers.

A ten-year study of murder in Canada, covering the period from 1961 to 1970 and published by Statistics Canada (1976), shows that 41.7 percent of the murder victims were related to their assailants by some kind of family relationship. Female victims were much more likely to be killed by a member of their family than their male counterparts. Out of a total of 2,674 victims, 417 (15.6 percent) were killed by their male or female spouse. An updating of the study, covering the fourteen-year period from 1961 to 1974, revealed that of all female victims, 60 percent were killed in the context of a domestic relationship. This is more than double the proportion (26.8 percent) of male victims. The same study shows that over three-quarters of all child victims under the age of eleven years are killed by immediate relatives in family homicides, with no difference in proportion between male and female child victims.

Silverman and Kennedy (1987) used twenty-two years, from 1961 to 1983, of national homicide data to examine the relational distance in Canadian homicides. The study confirms that female victims are most often killed by spouses or lovers. Men, it was found, are only about one-third as likely as women to be victims of homicide in intimate relationships, but are three times more likely to be murdered by a stranger than women and almost five times as likely to be killed by a friend or acquaintance. In general, the authors report, the more distant social relationships in which murder was committed involve higher proportions of males as both offenders and victims. Silverman and Kennedy further found that while female victims are most often killed by spouses or lovers, there is a marked downward trend in this pattern over the years, from a high of approximately 70 percent in 1961, to a low of approximately 45 percent in the early 1980s. Homicide by strangers involving female victims increased fourfold in twenty-five years, from a low of about only 5 percent to over 20 percent in 1981. Without further research it does not seem possible to offer a valid explanation for these trends.

A more recent study of homicide in Canada spanning the years from 1976 to 1985 (Statistics Canada, 1987) shows that, as in the past, females represented the greatest proportion of all domestic homicides in each of the ten years covered by the study. Over this period, females accounted for an average of 55.5 percent of all domestic homicide victims, while males represented 44.5 percent. Homicides involving immediate family relationships represented 64.5 percent of all domestic homicides. The second largest category within the domestic group involves those persons living in a common-law family arrangement (21.3 percent). They include not only partners of the union itself but also children and siblings in common-law unions. The smallest proportion is occupied by other kinship relationships (14.2 percent). This category includes members of the extended family, such as grandparents, uncles, and aunts. Statistics Canada (1987) reports that the largest concentration of immediate family relationships involved spousal homicides (47 percent). The overwhelming majority in this group involved female victims (81.2 percent). Parents who killed their children accounted for the second highest category within immediate family relationships (27.7 percent). However, unlike spousal homicides, which are dominated by female victims, the victims of parent-child killings are more evenly divided between the two genders (53.7 percent males and 46 percent females). Children who killed their parents accounted for 13.6 percent of all immediate family homicides during the period from 1976 to 1985. A greater proportion of fathers (58.1 percent) than mothers (41.9 percent) were killed by their offspring. Sibling homicides were the rarest type of immediate family relationship homicides (11.8 percent), and the overwhelming majority of victims in this group were male (77 percent).

One distressing aspect of family homicides in Canada is the disproportionate involvement of native people. The social isolation and relative segregation of native people, a majority of whom live on reserves, means that violence will be predominantely an intraracial and intragroup phenomenon. Statistics released in 1989 by Statistics Canada and reported by Canadian Press provide a vivid illustration of this social tragedy. According to Statistics Canada, nearly one in four family-related slayings in Canada from 1974 to 1987 involved native people, even though natives make up just 3 percent of the Canadian population. The report reveals that of the country's 7,582 solved homicides from 1974 to 1987, 39 percent involved people related to one another through marriage, common-law union, or kinship. However, among native people, almost half of solved slayings (49 percent) were family-related. About 23 percent of offenders and 22 percent of victims in all family homicides in Canada were native, accounting for nearly seven hundred slayings.

In Australia a New South Wales study (Wallace, 1986) found that by far the largest category of criminal homicide consisted of those classed as domestic. Five hundred and forty-one (42.5 percent) of the homicide victims were killed by members of their own family. Homicides committed by friends and acquaintances accounted for one in five homicides (20 percent). Analysis of the sex of offenders and victims in particular relationships reveals that both male and female victims were most at risk from family members. However, a much larger proportion of female than male victims were killed in domestic situations. Females were almost 2.5 times as likely as males to be killed by relatives: 310 (67.4 percent) females died at the hands of family members compared with only 231 (28.4 percent) of the males. Both as a proportion of their sex and in absolute numbers, females were far more likely than males to die in domestic homicides. Similar differences emerged when the sex of the offender was examined. The overwhelming majority of homicides committed by women (81.2 percent) occurred within their own family. Women were very rarely involved in the deaths of friends and acquaintances or of neighbors or roommates. Even rarer were incidences where women were involved in killing strangers, lovers, or sexual rivals. When men killed, they were far more likely than women to kill outside the family. Thus, females were most likely to kill and be killed within the family. Males, on the other hand, while also most likely to kill and be killed within a domestic context, were considerably more involved in homicide outside the family.

Homicide and the Size of the Social Group

It is again distressing but true that, if any of us is going to be killed, the chances are far greater that the murderer will be a member of our families or a friend than a stranger.

Family and other interpersonal relationships are an essential part of any social life. For each of us, society can be roughly divided, according to the type and intensity of the relationships we maintain with others, into three groups of unequal size. The first, and by far the smallest, is the primary group of the family, that is, individuals to whom we are related by kinship or marriage. The second is an intermediate group, and, though it may be somewhat larger than the family, it is still quite small. This second group embraces each person's social circle, which consists of members of society with whom the person maintains an interpersonal relationship of one kind or another, such as friends, neighbors, workmates, club members, team members, and business partners or associates. The third group, which is by far the largest, is comprised of the thousands or millions of persons unknown to us and with whom we have no personal contact nor any relationship whatsoever. To us they are total strangers. Crimes of personal violence committed within relationships are committed largely between members of the first and second groups. There seems to be a social law governing these crimes of personal violence, which is that there is an inverse relationship between the size of the social group and the probability that criminal homicide, if it occurs, will be committed by a member of that social group; the smaller the group, the higher the probability; the larger the group, the lower the probability.

The family group is the smallest group, yet the likelihood that the killer will be a member of the family is greatest. On the other hand, the largest group is that of strangers whom the person does not know and with whom he or she does not interact. Yet, the probability that a person will be killed by a stranger is much lower than that of being killed by a family member. The middle group occupies an intermediate position on both counts: the size of the group as well as the probability that the attack will come from within that group. The probability is somewhat lower than that of being killed by a family member, but higher than being slain by a complete stranger.

Support for this social law of criminal homicide comes from countless studies carried out in many different countries. One example from these studies will help illustrate the validity of this law. After analyzing the patterns of criminal homicide in Denmark, Svalastoga (1956) remarked that for every Dane who commits homicide there is approximately a 60 percent chance that the offender will select the victim from among members of his or her family, while there is approximately a 30 percent chance that the offender will choose a victim from his or her acquaintances and approximately a 10 percent chance that the offender will kill a complete stranger. Having made an approximate estimate of the size and importance of each group and the degree of risk facing members of each group, Svalastoga concludes that the closer the group, the greater is the chance that the murderer will choose the victim from its members.

Sessar (1975) offers an explanation for the difference between criminal homicides committed within the context of a primary or a secondary relationship. Primary group relationships, he suggests, are total in that they embrace both partners in most segments of their existence. Because most of these relationships are legally protected and socially controlled, they possess a kind of inescapability. Both partners do not or cannot always separate without difficulty when their relations are becoming worse or are about to break down. Sessar points out that the situation in a secondary relationship is different. These relationships are never very close and can be dissolved at any time. The offender and the victim *come* together, whereas in the primary group, they *are* together; a secondary relationship does not have the aspect of inescapability that a primary one does. Sessar (1975) explains the implications of this distinction in criminal homicide:

> *In the primary group the crime emerges from the offender-victim relationship itself which is a kind of* ***conditio sine qua non*** *for the deed. Consequently, this victim is meant. In the secondary group the relations are not close enough to be so decisive, which means that the particular personality of the victim is of minor*

importance; the crime is linked much more to a particular situation. This distinction means further that in secondary groups, the victim is interchangeable because the actual situation moulds the act more so than a particular person; in primary groups the crime is mostly unthinkable without the specific victim involved. (pp. 38-39)

The Age of the Victim and the Relationship to the Victimizer in Criminal Homicide

Kennedy and Silverman (1990) used the Canadian national homicide data from 1961 to 1983 to examine victim-offender relationships for various age groups. Their findings are reproduced in Table 7-1. The "other" victim-offender relationship is defined by Kennedy and Silverman as "friends and acquaintances." Under this heading they grouped "business relationships, friendships, casual acquaintances, or other nonkinship relationships."

TABLE 7-1 **Victim/Offender Relationship In Homicide by Age of the Victim (Canada, 1961-1983)[a]**

	Age				
Relationship	<18	18-25	26-45	46-64	≥65
Spouse/	36	450	1218	441	74
Lover	(3.9)	(28.3)	(40.0)	(28.0)	(12.5)
Other	507	176	311	259	114
Family	(55.0)	(11.1)	(10.2)	(16.5)	(19.3)
Other	174	636	993	494	139
Relationship	(18.9)	(40.0)	(32.6)	(31.4)	(23.5)
Stranger	204	329	520	379	264
	(22.1)	(20.6)	(17.1)	(24.1)	(44.7)
Total N	921	1591	3042	1573	591
Row Percentages	(12.0)	(20.6)	(39.4)	(20.4)	(7.7)

Notes: N = 7718.
Unk = 1387.
[a] Column percentages in parentheses unless otherwise noted.

Source: Reprinted by permission, from Table 2, Kennedy, L.W., and Silverman, R.A. (1990). The Elderly Victim of Homicide: An Application of the Routine Activities Approach. *The Sociological Quarterly*, 31(2), 312.

As may be seen from Table 7-1, there is considerable variation in the frequency of the victim-offender relationship according to the age of the victim. Over half those who were under eighteen (55 percent) were killed by a family member other than a spouse or a lover. For victims over sixty-five, this relationship was present in only 19.3 percent of the cases. Four out of ten victims aged twenty-six to forty-five were killed by a spouse or lover. The corresponding percentage for victims over sixty-five was 12.5 percent, and, understandably, for those under eighteen, it was merely 3.9 percent. Elderly victims of sixty-five and over were the least likely of all age groups to be killed by someone they knew and the most likely to be killed by strangers, either during the course of another crime or not. Forty-five percent of the elderly victims fell into that group, which is almost twice as high as it is for any other age group. Kennedy and Silverman found that those in the elderly group were more than twice as likely to be victims of theft-based homicide than those in any other age group. Forty-one percent of all homicides with elderly victims were theft precipitated and another 4 percent involved sex-related crime. In light of these findings, the elderly's fear of strangers seems to be justified. The finding that the elderly are preferred targets for theft-based homicide is not unique to Canada: a similar pattern was revealed in research conducted in Austria (Fattah, 1971) on murder for robbery.

AGGRAVATED ASSAULT

Aggravated assault is an offense difficult to classify, as the lines between aggravated assault and attempted murder, on one hand, and between aggravated assault and common assault, on the other hand, are somewhat arbitrary. And although, in many cases, the clear absence of an intention to kill coupled with the seriousness of the injury may render it easy to classify the act under the category of aggravated assault, in other cases, particularly borderline ones, the classification is merely a matter left to the discretion of the police or the prosecutor.[3]

We can reasonably hypothesize that the probability of being violently victimized by a given person, as well as the intensity of violence employed, increase with the volume of interaction the victim has with that person. If someone is to become a victim of a violent act of expressive violence, then the greater the volume of interaction he or she has with a particular individual, the greater are the chances that this individual will be the victimizer. The higher the intensity of violence, the greater is the likelihood that the two parties are personally related.

Mulvihill, Tumin, and Curtis (1969) report, on the basis of violent crime data in seventeen American cities, that the proportion of interactions involving strangers is relatively low in homicide (16 percent), rises in aggravated assault (21 percent), becomes a majority in forcible rape (53 percent), and dominates in armed (79 percent) and unarmed robbery (86 percent). They point out that generally the percentage of involvement of nonprimary group relationships steadily rises from homicide to robbery, while the percentage of involvement of family and other primary group relationships uniformly declines.

If the hypothesis that there is a positive relationship between the intensity of violence and the closeness of the victim-offender relationship is true, then we would expect the frequency of family relationships and other close relationships to be lower in aggravated assault than in criminal homicide, and lower in assault than in aggravated assault. We would also expect the frequency of stranger-to-stranger violence, where no relationship exists, to be higher in assault than it is in aggravated assault and higher in aggravated assault than it is in criminal homicide. Although studies on aggravated assault and common assault are extremely rare, in sharp contrast to the abundant literature on criminal homicide, the available data do lend credence to the forementioned hypothesis.

The study of crimes of violence in seventeen American cities (Mulvihill, Tumin, and Curtis, 1969) shows that 14 percent of all aggravated assaults were between family members, 7 percent involved other primary group contacts, and 55 percent occurred in nonprimary group relationships. In comparison to criminal homicide, primary group involvement in aggravated assault was lower and nonprimary group involvement somewhat higher. While friends and intimates appeared to play an important role in aggravated assault, the extent to which strangers and other nonprimary group relationships are involved was higher than in criminal homicide. Husband-wife assaults dominated the general family-relationship category, with 7 percent of all interactions.

ASSAULT

Studies of common assault or nonaggravated assault are extremely rare. None seems to have been undertaken either in Canada or in the United States. One reason might be that assaults have a significantly higher dark figure than other more serious forms of violence. This dark figure is also substantially higher for assault involving a close personal relationship, such as with family members or friends, than for assaults occurring between strangers. This might produce artificially high percentages in the "no relationship" category and artificially low percentages in primary group relationships. In other words, the frequency of the different types of relationships is much less reliable for common assault than it is for criminal homicide.

In his study of what he calls "everyday violence"[4] in contemporary Sweden, Wikström (1985) found that a little less than half of the cases he examined occurred between strangers, while, in the remainder, the victim and the offender had some sort of acquaintance. As might be expected, a markedly higher proportion of cases in urban areas involved strangers. There was also a domination of crimes between strangers in the inner-city areas at all time, but especially at nighttime on Fridays, Saturdays, and Sundays.

SPOUSAL VIOLENCE

Although spousal violence is as old as the institution of marriage itself, it is only recently that the phenomenon has become the focus of research and social policy. This is due to the work of women's movements and feminist writers whose exclusive focus has been on wife assault, wife beating, and wife battering, as well as marital rape. Violence by the female spouse against her male partner was thought to be extremely rare. Women's concerns about the high incidence of male violence in marital relationships have empirical support. We have seen above the extent to which wives are killed by their husbands in contrast to the very small number of husbands murdered by their spouses. While the killing of the male spouse by the female partner is an extremely rare phenomenon, minor forms of violence against males in marriage do not seem to be as uncommon as is generally believed.

Straus and Gelles (1986) warn that violence by women against their husbands is not something to be dismissed as uncommon or overlooked because of the even greater violence used on wives by their husbands. Surveys on family violence conducted by Straus and Gelles (1986) for the Family Research Laboratory of the University of New Hampshire in 1975 and in 1985 reveal a high incidence of wife-to-husband violence. The surveys suggest that while women rarely commit violence outside the family, within the family, women are about as violent as men. This highly controversial finding from the 1975 study was again confirmed by the 1985 study. Straus and Gelles also cite a dozen other studies that reached similar conclusions, thus confirming the pattern shown by both the 1975 and 1985 surveys and leaving little doubt about the high frequency of wife-to-husband violence. The authors admit that the context and consequences of female-to-male spouse violence are different from those of male-to-female violence. The greater average size and strength of men and their greater aggressiveness mean that the same act, for example, a punch, is likely to be very different in the amount of pain or injury inflicted when directed by a male against a female than that inflicted by a female on a male. An important point, Straus and Gelles explain, is that a great deal of violence by women against their husbands is in retaliation or self-defense. They also add that one of the fundamental reasons as to why women are violent within the family, but not outside the family, is that her own home is where there is the greatest risk of assault for a typical American woman.

FORCIBLE RAPE

As mentioned, interpersonal relationships between offenders and victims are more pronounced in acts of expressive violence than in acts of instrumental violence. If that is the case, then we can expect a high percentage of close relationships in offenses where the primary objective is to kill, hurt, injure, or harm the victim. We may expect, as well, a high percentage of stranger-to-stranger interactions in offenses where hurting or harming the victim is a by-product or is simply a means of achieving another end, such as when violence is employed to overcome the resistance of the victim in robbery or sexual assault.

Sexual offenses in general have a relatively high dark figure, and those committed between individuals well known to each other have a lower rate of reporting than those involving complete strangers. We can therefore assume that the real frequency of relationships between rapist and rape victim is somewhat higher than what appears in police statistics or victimization survey findings.

Certain types of rape, such as "date rape," tend to occur between persons who have known each other for a brief or a long period of time. Other types, such as "hitchhike rape," are predominantly committed between people with no previous relationships. Some authors (Burgess and Holmstrom, 1974; Schwendinger and Schwendinger, 1983) distinguish between, what they call, "the blitz or sudden-attack rape" and "the confidence rape." The "blitz rape" occurs without warning and without prior interaction between assailant and victim (Burgess and Holmstrom, 1974, p. 4). The majority of blitz rapists are strangers to their victims. One variety of the blitz rape is the "felony rape" where the sexual assault is, in the majority of cases, not a planned act but, rather, a by-product of the burglary (Schwendinger and Schwendinger, 1983, p. 46). In this variety, the rapist and his victim are most likely to be strangers. This is the opposite of the "confidence rape," where the victim and the offender generally know each other and a relationship exists between the two.

While police statistics tend to underestimate the frequency of personal relationships between victim and victimizer in rape cases, these statistics do suggest that approximately one in two reported rapes occur between strangers. In Amir's (1971) study of forcible rape in Philadelphia, 51.9 percent of the rapists were strangers to their victims. The study by Mulvihill, Tumin, and Curtis (1969) of crimes of violence in seventeen American cities found an almost identical percentage of forcible rape cases involving strangers (52.8 percent). Percentages reported in European studies are similar to the American ones. In Denmark, Svalastoga (1962) reports that in 54 percent of the cases of rape there was no previous personal relationship between the rapist and the victim. Such a relationship was present in 43 percent of the cases, and no information was available in 4 percent. National Police statistics for the Federal Republic of Germany (Federal Republic of Germany, 1988) reveal the following relationships in rape cases (completed and attempted) reported to the police in 1987: relative, 4.1 percent; friend or acquaintance, 31.1 percent; landlord, 1.4 percent; brief encounter prior to the attack, 17.4 percent. The remainder of the cases were between strangers.

A British Home Office study, (Smith, 1989) analyzed all cases of rape and attempted rape reported to the police in two London boroughs (Islington and Lambeth) from the year 1984 to 1986. In all, 507 victims reported a total of 591 offenses. One of the objectives of the study was to contrast how far the popular images of rape match the "reality." The study, like several others, challenges the popular stereotype of rape as an offense committed by strangers in alleys, parks, cars, or on the street. Rape, the study found, was committed primarily by men known to the victim, and in only one out of three rapes was the rapist a stranger. Moreover, women were most likely to be raped in their own homes or in the offender's home. Information on the relationship between victim and offender was available in 421 of the reported cases. Of these, almost two-fifths (39 percent) involved men well known to the victim, and almost four out of ten rapes in this category involved current or former boyfriends, cohabitants, or husbands. A further three-tenths of the cases (29 percent) involved men with whom the victim was briefly acquainted. Just under one-third (32 percent) involved strangers.

SEXUAL VICTIMIZATION OF CHILDREN

Despite the dearth of data, there are reasons to believe that victim-offender relationships are more frequent in cases of sexual molestation of children than they are in forcible rape. The victim-offender relationship is an important element in the crime of incest. In other sexual assaults on children a personal relationship of one kind or another seems to characterize a significant number of cases. A study by Dr. Charles R. Hayman (1968) of 451 female child victims of sexual assault in the District of Columbia reports that one-fifth of the assaults were committed by strangers, while in four out of five cases the assaulters were older friends, relatives, or family acquaintances. As may be expected, assaults in the latter category occurred most frequently in the home of the victim or the aggressor, whereas about 50 percent of the sexual assaults committed by strangers against children took place in parks or playgrounds.

In another study of sex offenses against children, done in West Germany (Weiss, 1963), the victim-offender relationship was examined. The study was based on cases that had occurred in the state of Rhineland-Palatinate and reached the criminal court of Ludwigshafen. Out of a total of 385 victims there was a family relationship in 34 (8.8 percent), an "other type relationship" in 159 (41.3 percent), and a stranger-to-stranger relationship in 192 (49.9 percent). "Other type relationships" included relationships developed through friendship, the neighborhood, cohabitation, school personnel, and business. It also included acquaintances who did not have a close relationship to the child. Sex offenses by strangers were more frequent in cases of male child victims (67.2 percent) than in cases of female child victims (46.4 percent). Weiss noted that the percentage of strangers in his data is considerably higher (50 percent) than in other studies, which are usually 30 to 40 percent, and suggests that this may be due to the inclusion of twenty cases of exhibitionists. Acts of exhibitionism, usually committed at a distance, involve a higher percentage of strangers than acts involving physical contact. We should also add that sexual assaults involving family or other relationships have a higher dark figure than those involving strangers. This means the real frequency of these relationships is usually higher than what the studies report. Due to the extremely high dark figure in sexual victimization of children, some researchers have resorted to the survey technique. This does not entirely solve the problem of the dark figure. However, if it is true that the closer the victim-offender relationship the less likely it is that the experience will be reported, then we can expect the frequencies of victim-offender relationships to be higher in studies based on survey data than in studies relying entirely on police or court files. Finkelhor's (1979) study of sexually victimized children provides support for this hypothesis.

Finkelhor (1979) administered an anonymous questionnaire to students at six New England colleges and universities. The sample used for the data analysis consisted of 796 students: 530 females and 266 males. The sample had the expected college-age distribution with 75 percent being twenty-one years of age or under. Almost half of the girls' experiences (N=119) were with family members (43 percent) including fathers, stepfathers, brothers, uncles, cousins, and grandfathers. An experience with at least one of each of these relatives is represented in the sample. Acquaintances account for another 33 percent of the relationships in the cases of female victims, while one in four of the sexual experiences was with a stranger (24 percent). The number of sexually victimized boys was relatively small (N=23). Of these experiences 17 percent were by a family member, 53 percent by an acquaintance, and 30 percent by strangers. Thus, the percentage of victimizers who were strangers was slightly higher in the case of boys than in the case of girls, but in 76 percent of female victims and 70 percent of male victims, victims and victimizers were either related or acquainted. These findings, suggests Finkelhor, provide additional confirmation of the now well-established fact that sexual victimization occurs to a large extent within a child's intimate social network.

The existence and closeness of the relationship have a strong impact on the traumatic effects of sexual victimization. According to Finkelhor (1979), almost all researchers agree that experiences with close family members are potentially more traumatic than those with acquaintances or strangers. This belief, he suggests, seems to be based on a number of assumptions: (1) the closer the relationship, the greater the violation of the child's trust and security; (2) the closer the relationship, the more complicated the family dynamics triggered by the sexual relationship; and (3) the closer the relationship, the more serious the taboo violated and, hence, the greater possibility for guilt. In addition, he reports, family members, police, and agency personnel all seem to unite in support of a child who is victimized by a stranger, whereas when the victimizer is closer to home, the child always faces divided loyalties and suspicion. Finkelhor believes that the starkest contrast is between a child victimized by a parent and one victimized by a stranger. His findings support the belief that father-daughter incest is the most traumatic kind of sexual experience that can occur.

The Need for a Theory of Intrafamily Violence

Like hidden delinquency studies, epidemiological research on intrafamily violence has shown that its incidence is much more widespread than previously believed and is not limited to any ethnic group or any particular social class. The prevalence and pervasiveness of intrafamily violence cast serious doubt on the validity of theories that seek to explain the etiology of such violence with reference to the psychopathology of the perpetrators or to some static traits of the participants. They highlight the importance of the situational and triggering factors and indicate that no explanatory theory can afford to overlook the contexts, the situations, and the circumstances in which intrafamily violence occurs. Nor can the dynamic interactions that precede the use of violence among family members be ignored. Unfortunately, despite the great attention that family violence receives and the voluminous research the problem has generated, there has been relatively little theorizing and very few solid theoretical explanations.

Finkelhor et al. (1983) reviewed the research on family violence and reached the conclusion that very little has been achieved in the way of theory and theory building. They deplore the fact that many researchers tend to work in a kind of theoretical vacuum. Another expert on family violence, Richard Gelles (1983), contends that the current state of the art in theory construction consists of profiles of abusers and abused, and simplistic, unicausal models. He suggests that the family-violence knowledge base suffers from the inadequate operationalization of the dependent variable and nonrepresentative sampling of subjects. Gelles's reasons for the present lack of sophisticated theoretical models in the study of intrafamily violence are as follows (Gelles, 1983, pp. 154-156):

— Most investigations concentrate on one aspect of family violence — either child abuse, wife abuse, or even husband or parent abuse. Little effort is made to develop a general model of family violence.

— One important difficulty is the problem of nominally defining violence and abuse and the ensuing variations in the way they have been defined and operationalized in the different studies. Because of the wide variation in nominal definitions of violence, there is a resulting lack of comparability among various investigations of types of domestic violence.

— One of the most difficult methodological problems facing researchers in this field has been to select an adequate sample of abusive and violent families to study. Most tend to choose individuals and families who have been publicly labeled as abusers or violent. There is, therefore, considerable information on which families are vulnerable to being labeled "abusers" and very little knowledge about which factors actually cause abuse.

A PROPOSITIONAL THEORY OF FAMILY VIOLENCE (STRAUS, 1973)

The victimization of women in patriarchal societies is due, in part, to the differing social roles of men and women and the unequal power relationships that these roles imply. It is generally acknowledged that violence is an expression and manifestation of power by the dominant partner (the husband) over the less powerful partner (the wife). However, it may also be a mode of compensation for the husband's shortcomings and his frustrations in not being able to fulfill his culturally assigned social role as the dominant figure in the family (see Chapter 10). Straus (1973) observed that the level of violence in the family is greatest when the wife is dominant in making decisions. He explains that this is because such a power structure violates the norms of the American family, which require that the husband be the "head" of the household. Straus believes that wife-dominated family structures tend to emerge when the husband lacks the economic, intellectual, interpersonal, or other resources to fulfill the leadership role assigned to the position of husband-father in American society. When this happens, certain processes occur. First, there is tension and dissatisfaction with the marriage that reduces barriers to actions, such as physical force, which might threaten the unity of the couple. Second, the husband, lacking other resources, is more likely to use physical force in attempts to maintain his power. Third, rather than altering the basic power structure of the family, such acts on the part of the husband tend to produce counter-violence on the part of the wife and role-segregation by both husband and wife to minimize the possibility of further violence.

Straus (1973) goes on to offer what he calls a "propositional theory of family violence." The theory is predicated on the assumption that violence between members of a family is a "systemic product" rather than a chance aberration, a product of inadequate socialization, or the result of a warped or psychotic personality. Straus's theory (1973, pp. 113-116) consists of eight propositions:

1. Violence between family members arises from diverse causes including normative expectations and personality traits such as aggressiveness, frustrations due to role-blockages, and conflicts.
2. Relative to the rate of publicly known or treated violence between family members, the actual occurrence is extremely high.
3. Most violence is either denied or not labeled as deviance.
4. Stereotyped imagery of family violence is learned in early childhood from parents, siblings, and other children.
5. The stereotypes of family violence are continually reaffirmed for adults and children in the mass media and through ordinary social interaction where, for example, high value is placed on a tough male.

6. Violent persons may be rewarded for violent acts if these acts produce the desired results. This reinforcement serves to increase the probability that violence will be used again.
7. Use of violence, when it is contrary to family norms, creates a conflict over the use of violence to settle the original conflict. This "secondary conflict," in turn, tends to produce further violence.
8. Persons labeled as violent may be encouraged to play out the role through the development of a "violent" or "tough" self-concept and through the expectations of others.

What these propositions add up to is the idea that violence is, in part, a system product. Straus (1973) writes:

> *In brief, the strain of everyday interaction, which constitutes the operation of the family as a social system, generates accommodations and conflicts, including violence. Violence as a mode of operation of the system tends to increase when there is "positive feedback" through such processes as (a) labeling, (b) creation of secondary conflict over the use of violence, (c) reinforcement of the actor using violence through successful use of such violence, (d) the development of role expectations and self-concepts as tough or violent. Under any of these circumstances, violence becomes an element in a deviation amplifying system (which may then stabilize at a higher level through negative feedback or dampening processes). (p. 116)*

AN EXCHANGE/SOCIAL CONTROL THEORY OF FAMILY VIOLENCE (GELLES, 1983)

Taking as his starting point the proposition that human interaction is guided by the pursuit of rewards and the avoidance of punishment and costs, Gelles (1983) proceeds to formulate what he calls an "exchange/social control model of family violence." A central, though greatly oversimplified, proposition of this theory is that people hit and abuse other family members because they can. It follows that people will use violence in the family if the costs of being violent do not outweigh the rewards. Another proposition Gelles derives from social control theory is that family violence occurs in the absence of social controls that would bond people to the social order and negatively sanction acts of violence for family members. Gelles adds that certain social and family structures serve to reduce social control in family relations and, therefore, reduce the cost and/or increase the rewards of being violent. He indicates that the private nature of the modern family serves to reduce the degree of social control exercised over family relations. For example, inequality in the home can reduce both social control and the costs of being violent. The image of the "real" man in society also reduces social control in the home and increases the rewards of being violent.

It is easy to see the similarities between the model offered by Gelles and the explanations for intrafamily violence suggested by Sebastian (1983). Yet the tentative nature of the theoretical formulations offered by Straus, Gelles, and Sebastian is clear. Their main advantage is to provide an impetus for further theory building. They also indicate to researchers that more attention should be paid to theory by sensitizing them to the gaps that currently exist in this important area of criminology and victimology. Another merit of these models is that they emphasize the importance of system and cultural factors. This is a commendable departure from the earlier attempts to blame family violence on the psychopathology of the participants, and it is a healthy shift from traditional theories, which viewed those who perpetrate the violence as sick, mad, or bad.

The Psychological Relationships Between the Victim and Victimizer

Except for a few clinical studies that examine one or a small number of cases, most criminological and victimological studies of victim-victimizer relationships content themselves with developing a typology of possible relationships and then providing a frequency distribution of each given type. While the type of relationship might give some rough indication of the degree of the intimacy or the social closeness or distance of the victim and victimizer at the time of the attack, and while it may give a crude idea of the volume and intensity of their personal contact, it often says nothing about the psychology and the quality of the relationship. It does not tell us how harmonious or discordant the relationship was. For example, Wolfgang's study (1958) of criminal homicide in Philadelphia provides the following classification of the victim's relationship to the victimizer and the frequencies of those relationships: close friend (28.2 percent); family relation (24.7 percent); acquaintance (13.5 percent); stranger (12.2 percent); paramour, mistress, prostitute (9.8 percent); sex rival (4 percent); enemy (2.9 percent); paramour of offender's mate (2 percent); felon or police officer (1.1 percent); innocent bystander (1.1 percent); homosexual partner (0.6 percent). Some of these types, such as enemy, sex rival, paramour of offender's mate, and police officer, imply an antagonistic relationship. But the nature of the other types does not betray the degree of their discord or harmony. These types do not indicate by themselves whether the relationship was characterized by amiability or hostility, love or hate, attraction or repulsion, like or dislike, sympathy or antipathy.

Several reasons might be responsible for the scarcity of empirical studies dealing with the psychological relationship between victim and victimizer. This kind of study requires a micro analysis of individual cases, and information about the quality of the relationship, except, perhaps, in homicide cases, is usually absent in police files. There is also the difficulty for an outsider (the researcher) to pass an accurate judgment and to qualify the psychological character of the relationship. Another difficulty is the fact that human relationships, whether family, friendship, or other relationships, are almost never perfectly harmonious or completely discordant. They usually have their ups and downs, go through smooth and rocky periods, and oscillate between conflict and reconciliation, sourness and sweetness. We often hear about couples who are locked together in a love/hate relationship which may continue for several decades and only ends when one of the two partners dies.

One of the very few theoretical studies of the psychological relationship between the offender and the victim was published in 1955 by Henri Ellenberger, a Swiss-Canadian psychiatrist. In this study, Ellenberger took three concepts originally put forward by Hans Von Hentig and elaborated on them much further. The three concepts are the "doer-sufferer," the "latent or potential victim," and the "victim-offender relationship." The "docr-sufferer" is a term used to designate cases in which the person can either be the offender or the victim depending on the circumstances and the situation. In some cases, the individual can be successively the victim and the victimizer, such as a mistreated child turning delinquent, or be simultaneously the offender and the victim, such as an aggressor killed or injured in self-defense. The term "potential/latent victim" is used by Ellenberger to refer to individuals who display, or suffer from, an unconscious wish or proneness to become victims and who, as a result, attract the criminal in the same way a lamb attracts the wolf. Among the types cited by Ellenberger are individuals dominated by masochistic and self-punitive tendencies, those who display a certain fatalism and those who suffer from Abel Syndrome (a syndrome in which "an individual who feels vaguely guilty because fortune has favored him, is envied, and lacks resistance and self-assertion" [p.287]). The third concept elaborated on by Ellenberger is the "victim-offender relationship." In developing this concept, Von Hentig (1948) dealt with the symbiotic relationship that sometimes exists between the victim and the victimizer.

For his part, Ellenberger distinguishes three different types of psychological relationships. Though distinct, the three types are nevertheless compatible and may exist simultaneously:

1. The purely "neurotic relationship," which may be observed notably in certain cases of parricide.
2. The "psychobiological relationship" characterized by mutual attraction between two constitutionally opposed types who complement each other. In

this type of relationship one party is a negative complement of the other, such as the sadist/masochist relationship, the alcoholic tormentor/sufferer relationship, or the prostitute/pimp relationship.

3. The "genetic-biological relationship" characterized by mutual attraction based on a common heredity.

THE PSYCHOLOGICAL RELATIONSHIPS BETWEEN THE VICTIM AND VICTIMIZER: THE SADOMASOCHISTIC RELATIONSHIP AS A CASE STUDY

Feminist writers categorically reject the idea that an abusive relationship can be a symbiotic relationship and are critical of the concept of the sadomasochistic couple. Psychiatrists use the concept of sadomasochism to refer to a relationship where violence, abuse, and mistreatment are not only a common occurrence but also where they seem to be the ingredient that attracts the two partners to each other or that holds them together. Since, in most abusive relationships, it is women who are the recipients rather than the perpetrators of violence, the concept of the sadomasochistic relationship has been criticized for implying that females who remain in a violent relationship, despite the beating and abuse they take, are masochistic and want or enjoy being hurt. New fuel was added to the controversy with the publication in 1981 of an article in *New Society*, by Erin Pizzey and Jeff Shapiro, under the provocative title "Choosing a Violent Relationship" and the subsequent publication of their book *Prone to Violence* (1982).

Pizzey and Shapiro (1981) use the term "violence-prone" to define women who experience gross physical and mental abuse, but who choose, despite other viable and attractive alternatives, to remain within the confines of their abusive relationship. The authors distinguish between a woman who accidentally becomes involved with a violent partner and who now wishes to leave and never return again and a woman who, for deep psychological reasons of her own, seeks out a violent relationship or a series of violent relationships with no intention of leaving. This latter type led Pizzey to believe that violence was a form of addiction. Such is the case of many women who have presented themselves to many agencies asking for refuge but who had no intention of using the refuge as anything other than another move in their warring relationships.

Despite her significant contribution to the women's cause, Pizzey did not endear herself to other feminists by suggesting that both husbands and wives in domestic assaults are violence-prone nor by asserting that some female victims of domestic violence become addicted to violence and feel that they need to be hurt. It is this addiction that explains, according to Pizzey, why, when the violent relationship ends, these violence-prone women quickly find other abusive partners.

One of Pizzey's many critics, Elisabeth Stanko (1985), believes that the assumption that some women only establish relationships with violent men because they are addicted to violence is one that betrays a blindness to the social context within which women experience sexual and/or physical assault. Stanko feels that it is easier to explain violence against women using an individually based, chemically rooted theory of violence as Pizzey does than it is to address the entrenched, male-dominated conditions in which many women have no recourse but to be part of a couple and no recourse to change patterns of behavior that fit neatly in grooves carved not by their own hands. Stanko explains that some women return to violent men or become locked in violent relationships simply because there is no escape from male violence outside or inside the home. Being with a man, however violent, seems to be better than being without a man.

Other Types of Victim-Victimizer Relationships

PRIMARY AND SECONDARY GROUP RELATIONSHIPS

In his study of victim-offender relationships in criminal homicide, Sessar (1975) cites Coser's (1964) distinction between primary and secondary groups:

> *Like Simmel, Freud derives ambivalence of feelings from the intimacy of the relationship within which it occurs. He traces the simultaneity of feelings of love and hate to the numerous occasions for conflict to which intimate relations give rise. This would mean that there is more occasion for the rise of hostile feelings in primary than in secondary groups, for the more the relationship is based upon the participation of the total personality — as distinct from segmental participation — the more it is likely to generate both love and hate. (p. 62)*

Sessar actually found the distinction between primary and secondary groups to be "one between intricate links of positive and negative sentiments on one side and a dominance of negative sentiments on the other side." When there were "cases other than those determined by conflict, the sentiment of indifference prevails. In such cases the offender regards the victim only as an obstacle to be removed" (p. 38).

SPECIFIC, NONSPECIFIC, AND SEMISPECIFIC RELATIONSHIPS

In an attempt to group together the criminological, psychological, and dynamic aspects and to provide a frame of reference encompassing the total situation of the crime, that is, the doer, the deed, and the victim, Cormier (1975) defined three types of relationships in which homicide acts occur: specific, nonspecific, and semispecific. Cormier defines a homicide committed in a "specific relationship" as one in which the relationship between the killer and the victim was such that the cause, the motivation, and the dynamics of the crime are to be found in the conflictual nature of the relationship. A specific relationship thus implies that the doer and victim know one another. What is more important, suggests Cormier, is the fact that the crime is understandable only within the conflicts between these persons. Marital murders and those committed within the family are classic examples of such homicides. The second type described by Cormier is the homicide committed in a "nonspecific relationship." It occurs in a setting in which the doer either does not know the victim, or, if he or she does, the psychological relationship or other bonds that exist between them are not the determining factors. Homicide in this type of relationship often is not intended but may occur in the commission of another crime, or it may be incidental. The victim has no special psychological meaning for the doer, such as in an armed robbery where killing is neither intended nor desired, but the risk is tacitly accepted by the offender since he or she is carrying a lethal weapon. Homicide committed in a "semispecific relationship" is, at one and the same time, the most complex and most difficult to define. Cormier suggests that in such homicides the doer kills because of motivation and psychodynamics that are to be found in the doer's own psychopathology. The doer may or may not know the victim, usually the latter, and because the meaning of the victim is found within the doer's own psychopathology, one or many victims are killed indiscriminately or because they happen to belong to a particular group with certain characteristics. Cormier cites the sadistic killer of children who kills them for his own perverted gratification as an example of the type of homicide occurring in a semispecific relationship.

The Intraracial Character of Violent Victimization

The interpersonal nature of violent victimization, with the exception of robbery, means that violence is frequently employed between individuals related or known to each other and who interact with one another. It is not surprising, therefore, to find that most of these violent victimizations are intraracial, that is, they occur between members of the same race and the same ethnic group. We may assume that the more a given society is racially or ethnically segregated, the higher are the chances that nonpolitical violent victimization will be an intragroup phenomenon.

Where, for example, there is strong racial segregation, the percentage of intraracial homicide, assault, and rape will be much higher than where there is less segregation or no segregation. Growing desegregation is likely to lead to an increase in the proportion of interracial violence.

Studies conducted in the United States, where there are two major racially distinct groups, blacks and whites, show unequivocally that assaultive violence, such as criminal homicide, aggravated assault, and forcible rape, is overwhelmingly intraracial. The majority of these violent victimizations involve blacks killing, assaulting, or raping black victims while the majority of the remainder involve whites victimizing other whites. Robbery, on the other hand, has a high interracial component mainly composed of younger black males robbing older white males (Mulvihill, Tumin, and Curtis, 1969). Studies undertaken for the United States National Commission on the Causes and Prevention of Violence further suggest that criminal homicides, as well as aggravated assaults, are predominantly intrasexual in nature, that is, committed largely between members of the same sex. The intrasex pattern is, however, much less pronounced than the intraracial one. Most criminal codes continue to define rape as the act of a male perpetrator on a female victim. So defined, rape becomes an exclusively intersex crime. Recently, some criminal codes have broadened the definition to include homosexual rapes. It will be of interest to see whether homosexual rapes do follow the same intraracial pattern that characterizes heterosexual rapes. Armed robbery and, to a lesser degree, unarmed robbery seem to be strongly intrasex crimes.

CRIMINAL HOMICIDE

In his now classic study of criminal homicide in Philadelphia (1958), Wolfgang discovered that the ratio of intraracial to interracial homicides is 15.2 to 1. The ratio of homicides involving members of the same sex (intrasex) to homicides involving members of the opposite sex (intersex), is only 1.8 to 1. Wolfgang points out that the very personal nature of homicide accounts for its racially in-group character, since the quasi-caste barrier apparently prohibits the kinds of personal contacts between the races that ordinarily lead to homicide and, hence, operates to reduce interracial homicides. He further suggests that intimate and personal contacts, often with high emotional content, do take place between the sexes within each race, so that a higher proportion of homicides involve victims and offenders of the opposite sex.

Of the 550 identified relationships in Wolfgang's study, no less than 94 percent involved victims and offenders of the same race: 72 percent of the total were homicides involving blacks killing blacks and 22 percent were of whites killing whites. In another study of criminal homicide, this time in Chicago (Block, 1977), the percentage of intraracial homicides was somewhat lower than in Philadelphia. Block reports that in 1965, 90 percent of homicides in Chicago, where the race of the offender was known, were intraracial. In 1974, the corresponding percentage was 88 percent. The study by Mulvihill, Tumin, and Curtis (1969) of violence in seventeen American cities reveals very similar percentages: 89.7 percent intraracial homicides (65.7 percent blacks killing blacks and 24 percent whites killing whites) and only 10.3 percent interracial killings (6.5 percent blacks killing whites and 3.8 percent whites killing blacks). Sex patterns were less pronounced. However, two-thirds of all criminal homicides in the seventeen cities were intrasex ones (62.3 percent males killing males and 3.8 percent females killing females). Intersex homicides constituted one-third (17.5 percent males killing females and 16.4 percent females killing males).

AGGRAVATED ASSAULT

The race and sex patterns of aggravated assault are almost identical to those of criminal homicide. The study of crimes of violence in seventeen American cities (Mulvihill, Tumin, and Curtis, 1969) shows that nine out of ten aggravated assaults were intraracial: 23.9 percent whites assaulting whites and 65.9 percent blacks assaulting blacks. Little less than two-thirds of the aggravated assaults, that is 63.7 percent, were intrasex ones: 56.6 percent males assaulting males and 7.1 percent females assaulting females. Slightly over one-third, or 36.3 percent, were intersex assaults: 27 percent males assaulting females and 9.3 percent females assaulting males.

FORCIBLE RAPE

Forcible rape exhibits the same intraracial character as criminal homicide and aggravated assault. Only 7 percent of all the rapes studied by Amir in Philadelphia (1971) were interracial: 4.3 percent blacks raping whites and 2.7 percent whites raping blacks. The overwhelming majority, 93 percent, of the rapes reported to the police were intraracial: 76.9 percent blacks raping blacks and 16.1 percent whites raping whites. The study of the seventeen American cities conducted by Mulvihill, Tumin, and Curtis (1969) reveals similar percentages. Thus, intraracial rapes accounted for nine-tenths, or 89.2 percent, of the total: blacks raping blacks, 59.6 percent, and whites raping whites, 29.6 percent. In only one out of every ten rapes, or 10.8 percent, did the rapist cross the racial line: blacks raping whites, 10.5 percent, and whites raping blacks, 0.3 percent.

The intraracial pattern of violent victimization seems to be less pronounced on the West Coast of the United States than it is in other parts of the country. Since cities on the West Coast are less segregated along racial lines than Eastern, Midwestern, or Southern cities, this pattern lends credence to the hypothesis associating the degree of segregation/desegregation and the level of intraracial/interracial violence. A study of forcible rape in Oakland, California, during 1971 (Agopain, Chappell, and Geis, 1972) indicates that only two-thirds, or 66 percent, were intraracial: 40 percent, blacks raping blacks; 19 percent, whites raping whites; 7 percent, Indian-Mexicans raping Indian-Mexicans. The other third, 35 percent, was interracial: 33 percent, blacks raping whites; 2 percent, whites raping blacks.

Violent crimes, other than rape, seem to follow a similar pattern to West Coast rape statistics. Percentages of intraracial violence in San Francisco in the year 1973, quoted by Curtis (1974), are much lower than those observed for other cities, such as Philadelphia, Chicago, or New Orleans.

ROBBERY

Robbery, being mainly a property crime, is not as intraracial as criminal homicide, aggravated assault, or rape. Despite this, Normandeau (1972) reports that over three-quarters, 76 percent, of the robbery cases he studied in Philadelphia were intraracial: 63 percent, blacks robbing blacks, and 13 percent, whites robbing whites.

In the study of 17 American cities by Mulvihill, Tumin, and Curtis (1969), robbery exhibited an almost even division between intraracial and interracial incidents. Intraracial incidents accounted for 51.6 percent, with blacks robbing blacks in 38.4 percent of the cases and whites robbing whites for the remaining 13.2 percent. Interracial incidents accounted for 48.4 percent of the total, with whites far outnumbering blacks as victims: blacks robbing whites, 46.7 percent, and whites robbing blacks, 1.7 percent.

Curtis (1974) quotes the following percentages of intraracial robberies in some American cities, based on 1973 figures: Philadelphia, 56.9 percent; Washington, D.C., 63.2 percent; and San Francisco, 29.9 percent. For New Orleans in 1967, Curtis quotes a percentage of 64.6 percent. Thus the percentage of intraracial robberies in San Francisco was less than half the corresponding percentage in either Washington or New Orleans.

While robbery is less of an intraracial offense than criminal homicide or aggravated assault, its intrasex character is more pronounced than that of both offenses. The Mulvihill, Tumin, and Curtis (1969) study of seventeen American cities makes a distinction between armed robbery and unarmed robbery. Of all armed robberies, 85 percent were committed between members of the same gender: 84 percent, males against males, and 1 percent, females against females. In 10 percent of the cases, males robbed females and in 4 percent, females robbed males. The percentage of intrasex incidents, 72 percent, was somewhat lower in unarmed robberies: males robbing males, 69 percent; females robbing females, 3 percent. Slightly more than one in four robberies occurred between members of different gender: males robbing females, 26 percent, and females robbing males, 2 percent.

Summary

Although the criminal code does not pay attention to victim-offender relationships except in a few very specific instances, these relationships are of fundamental importance to victimology. As we have seen, crimes of violence, particularly those in which the violence is expressive rather than instrumental, are to a large extent interpersonal crimes. Thus, they cannot be fully understood unless examined and analyzed in the context of victim-offender relationships and interactions. The analysis of victim-offender relationships in serious forms of violence, such as criminal homicide, in various societies reveals striking similarities. Their analysis in the same society over time reveals surprising stability, consistency, and regularity. All this suggests the existence of social laws governing the phenomena under study.

In an attempt to draw attention to the need to develop a theory of victim-offender relationships, we have proposed a number of hypotheses that seem to have a fair amount of empirical support. One hypothesis suggests the presence of an inverse relationship between the size of the social group and the likelihood that violence, if violence is employed, will originate from that group. Another hypothesis suggests the presence of a positive link between the intensity of violence and the closeness of the victim-offender relationship. A third hypothesis suggests that the more segregated a group is, the stronger is the likelihood that violence will be predominantly an intragroup and an intrafamily phenomenon. The characteristics of criminal homicide among natives in Canada lend credence to this hypothesis.

Research on intrafamily violence suggests that it is more prevalent and more widespread than previously thought. Several studies in the United States indicate that, while women rarely commit violence outside the family, within the family, they are about as violent as men. The amount of pain and suffering women endure as a result of male violence is, however, greater than that suffered by men. A great deal of violence by women against their husbands is retaliation or self-defense. The prevalence of family violence casts doubts on theories that seek its etiology in the psychopathology of the participants and highlights the need for a situational dynamic theory explaining the different varieties, such as child abuse, wife abuse, and elder abuse. Unfortunately, there has been much research but little theorizing. Some of the theoretical explanations, such as those of Goode, Sebastian, Straus, and Gelles, were examined.

Victim-offender relationships further explain the predominantly intraracial character of violent victimization. Since expressive violence, in general, is the outcome of interpersonal interaction, the intraracial nature of this type of violence is understandable. It is to be expected, therefore, that nonpolitical violence in biracial or multiracial societies practicing strict racial segregation will exhibit an extremely pronounced intraracial character. This intraracial character is likely to weaken with increasing desegregation. Comparisons between cities in the United States provide some empirical support for this hypothesis. Although all of these hypotheses require further testing, the interest of researchers seems to have shifted in recent years from the somewhat static concept of victim-offender relationship to the more dynamic concept of victim-offender interaction. This is the topic we will examine in the next chapter.

EIGHT

The Dynamics of Criminal Victimization

The manner in which the victim responds depends on two conditions. First, the victim considers the offender's capacity to inflict death or serious injury. The offender is considered capable when he/she appears to possess lethal resources and to be in a position to use them, and when the victim cannot mobilize resources for opposition. Second, the victim evaluates the offender's intent regarding the use of force — whether the offender intends to inflict punishment only for opposition or regardless of opposition. If the offender appears capable of inflicting severe punishment and the use of force seems contingent on opposition, the victim complies.

David F. Luckenbill (1981, p. 34)

Outcomes of an aggressive interaction are not predetermined by either the characteristics or the initial goals of participants; rather, they are at least partly a function of events that occur during the incident. In other words, violence is, in part, situationally determined — the result of events and circumstances that cause a conflict to escalate.

Richard B. Felson and Henry J. Steadman (1983, pp. 59-60)

Victim-Victimizer Interactions

THE SITUATIONAL APPROACH TO THE UNDERSTANDING OF CRIME

The study of victim-offender relationships, which received much attention from researchers in the early stages of victimology, is currently giving way to the study of victim-offender interactions. One reason may be the quasi-uniformity in the frequency of various types of relationships reported by different studies and the fact that these frequencies do not seem to change substantially over time. This of course does not exclude the possibility of fluctuations due to social and cultural changes. While confirming the interpersonal character of most violent crimes, victim-offender relationships tell us little about the causes of criminal victimization. An analysis of victim-offender interaction is, on the other hand, indispensable for understanding the dynamics of violent victimization and might facilitate the development of a dynamic theory of criminal behavior. Many crimes of personal violence, particularly spontaneous, impulsive, unplanned, and unpremeditated ones, are outcomes of long or brief interactions between two or more individuals. As such, these crimes cannot be adequately explained by static theories of criminal behavior that focus on offender characteristics but give no consideration to the dynamic forces unique to each situation.

It is these dynamic forces that determine, condition, shape, or influence the victimizer's behavior in that particular situation. Criminal behavior is a response to stimuli originating in the environment. It would be impossible, therefore, to understand or to explain it while ignoring these stimuli. The victim's attitude and behavior, as well as the victim's response to the victimizer's initial gestures, are no doubt among the most important of all environmental stimuli. Theories attempting to explain criminal behavior by referring to the biological or psychological characteristics or social background of the offender ignore the crucial role played by situational and triggering factors in the etiology of crime. In contrast to the biological, psychological, and sociological approaches, which are, by their very nature, static approaches, the situational approach is a dynamic one. One of the underlying premises of this approach is that character attributes and personality traits, such as aggressiveness, callousness, and dishonesty, are neither constant nor absolute and, thus, alone have very little explanatory value. Some individuals become aggressive only when they have consumed alcohol or when they are provoked. Others may use violence only when their vanity is hurt. Some men become violent in situations where they feel the need to assert their maleness. Some people may be shy and withdrawn without peer support only to become extremely mean when in the presence of, and under pressure from, their peer group. People may be scrupulously honest in one situation and shamelessly dishonest in another. Many "honest" people, whose moral scruples would never allow them to cheat or steal from a friend, a neighbor, or, in general, another human being, become totally unscrupulous when it is a matter of cheating the government, a large corporation, or the general public. These people are totally without inhibitions when it comes to committing a white-collar crime, such as tax evasion, insurance fraud, or price fixing.

An individual's attitudes to others are not indiscriminate. Clifford Olson, the man who was found guilty of killing eleven children in British Columbia, and whom the police suspect of having slain even more, was proven to be a loving husband and affectionate father. Yet he had no sympathy or empathy for the several young victims he brutally killed to satisfy his deviant sexual desires.

The popularity of the traits/attributes approach lies in its central premise that criminals and delinquents are different from the rest of us. Propagating the view that some individuals are inherently bad or in some way abnormal allows the average citizen to perceive offenders as different beings capable of committing the terrible crimes of which he or she is incapable. It is a self-assuring approach.

The situational approach highlights the inherent weaknesses of current theories of criminal behavior by showing that each one of us is capable of committing a crime in certain situations, when under certain pressures, in the presence of certain triggering factors. The experiments of Milgram (1969) and Zimbardo (1972) prove this, as does Nils Christie's (1952) study of Norwegian guards in concentration camps during the Nazi occupation of Norway, the Mai Lai massacre in Vietnam, and the looting by the masses in the aftermath of natural disasters.

VICTIMIZATION AS A SITUATED TRANSACTION

The need for a dynamic approach to criminal behavior might appear self-evident. Yet, as axiomatic as this may seem, it has not gained much recognition among criminologists. One of the few who have acknowledged the need to search for dynamic explanations that go beyond the current static ones, is Hepburn (1973). Hepburn notes that in cultures where a proclivity toward violence seems to exist, its specific occurrences are not random and are thus susceptible to scientific examination and explanation. This, he suggests, requires the examination of the transaction that occurs between the participants prior to the perpetration of violence. Thus, a search for the "cause" of violence in interpersonal situations must include both the structured factors and the processual development that occur within enduring dyadic relationships, since it is their complementarity that allows for an examination of violent behavior in interpersonal situations. Hepburn adds that violent behavior is constructed within a situation between two or more persons through a process of interaction. This process consists of different stages. Excluding violence in gang fights and brawls, violence having a motive extraneous to the interaction, such as robbery, and violence involving premeditation, Hepburn focused on nonpremeditated violence occurring in the context of dynamic relationships. The first stage in the process leading to such violence is a perception of a threat to situated identities such that identities must be negotiated and the interaction becomes identity directed. He identifies reciprocal accountability and claiming behavior as factors facilitating the transition to identity-directed interaction. Once the threat is perceived, Hepburn explains, "encapsulation" may occur, and the individual must then decide upon a tactic of reducing the threat.[1] Avoidance and acceptance are not likely to escalate the hostility. Retaliation, on the other hand, may lead to violence. Hepburn identifies several factors that facilitate a violent response. These are a pervasive norm of violence, referred to as the subculture of violence; the person's prior experience with violence in similar situations; the presence of intoxicants, such as alcohol; the overt and/or covert support of the audience to the interaction; and the perceived cost of failure.

Despite the dynamic and interactionist nature of violent crimes, criminological research, with only a few exceptions, has focused on the perpetrator's characteristics and behavior and thus ignored the verbal exchanges between victim and victimizer prior to the use of physical force. Studies that paid attention to the dynamics of victimization indicate that the majority of acts of expressive violence usually begin with an altercation over relatively trivial matters. For example, in a study of the situational aspects of everyday violence in contemporary Sweden, Wikström (1985) found that most crimes of violence develop out of a conflict between the parties involved, although a nonnegligible proportion are preceded by molestation or constitute what may be termed as a "sudden attack." Molestation and sudden-attack violence generally occur between strangers, while verbal arguments ending in violence are characteristic of social and economic relationship conflicts.

THE PROBLEMS OF COMMUNICATION IN CONFLICT SITUATIONS

The situational, interactionist approach analyzes various types of criminal victimization not as unilateral, one-sided behaviors, but as situated transactions (Luckenbill, 1977, 1981). This is the case of face-to-face victimization where a brief or prolonged interaction between victim and victimizer takes place. In such encounters, nothing is objective. Everything is determined by the subjective perceptions each party has of the other's attitude and behavior. These subjective perceptions guide each party's actions, reactions, and the responses to those reactions. The totally different stories that may later be told by victim and victimizer about what "really" happened represent their own varying perceptions of what occurred in a very tense and highly emotional situation.

THE RAPE SITUATION

One such situation is the rape situation. The rapist and victim often offer two radically different versions of the event that ended in the assault. This is hardly surprising since what may be viewed by the rapist as consent, encouragement, precipitation, or resistance is not an objective reality but a subjective interpretation. A subjective interpretation could very well be, and often is, a misinterpretation. Still, it is crucial to the understanding of the rapist's behavior. In their criticism of Amir's (1967, 1971) use of the concept of "victim-precipitation" in rape, Clark and Lewis (1977) claim that Amir confuses "the victim's behavior with the offender's interpretation of that behavior" (p. 154). They also blame him for never reaching the logical conclusion "that it is the offender's mistaken interpretation which 'precipitates' rape." Though Amir's methodology and working definition of victim precipitation are in many ways deficient, Clark and Lewis's critique fails to recognize the importance of the participants' *subjective* definitions and interpretations of the situation in which they find themselves to the understanding and explanation of their actions and responses. Viewed in a social and behavioral science perspective, the victimizer's perception or misperception of the victim's attitude and his subjective, even if erroneous, interpretation of her gestures, actions, and behavior are important clues to his personality, motives, and conduct.

From a legal point of view, these subjective interpretations or misinterpretations may or may not constitute sufficient grounds to excuse the victimizer, to reduce the charges against him, or to mitigate his punishment. Whether his definitions and interpretations were correct or incorrect, or whether he was justified in inferring what he had inferred and in acting the way he did, are all important questions for establishing guilt, assessing responsibility, and measuring punishment. Social and behavioral scientists, on the other hand, are interested in explanations, not justification; in etiology, not guilt; in the interpersonal dynamics leading to the crime, not in legal presumptions, excuses, or extenuating circumstances. Establishing the rapist's guilt and responsibility is a legal matter that uses abstract notions such as the average reasonable man, the *pater familias* of the Roman law. Explaining the rapist's behavior, on the other hand, is a criminological research issue, which requires the examination, analysis, and understanding of the victimizer's attitude to the victim, his interaction with that victim, as well as his subjective perceptions and interpretations of the victim's attitude, words, gestures, and actions.

The rape situation is, after all, a conflict situation. In a conflict situation, as Weis and Weis (1975) point out, the participants often struggle to interpret the verbal and nonverbal gestures of the other and to assign them social meaning, which allows a definition of the situation. Weis and Weis (1975) add:

> *Conflict situations are characterized by misperceptions and misunderstandings resulting in discrepant definitions, and the negotiation and renegotiation of the definition of certain behaviors and of the situation. These attempts and the rigid adherence to different definitions hinge upon the need of the actors to morally justify their behavior. (p. 11)*

Violence in essence is a language, a mode of expression employed when other means are lacking or have failed. If this is true, then the analysis of the verbal utterances of both parties in their brief, or prolonged, encounter before, during, and after violence is used is an essential dimension of the situational analysis. In conflict situations where physical force and coercion are used, by one party or by both parties, it is fair to assume that a communication problem existed or that there was total lack of meaningful communication. In such encounters, the parties have to rely on their cultural norms and rules and their cultural role expectations to define, interpret, and assign meanings to the other's intentions, threats, and actions in order to try to predict the other's subsequent moves. The problem is as acute in rape situations where the assailant and victim are known to each other or have been dating for some time, as it is in cases of brief acquaintanceship or of an encounter between total strangers.

In an attempt to explain the dynamics of date rape, Goode (1969) suggests that dating in America is governed by a set of understandings, which is at least widespread in lower class areas. One of these understandings is that if anyone has a duty to control the situation, it is the female's alone. The male is permitted to go as far as she will permit. If her permission extends very far, then the consequences are her responsibility. There is a further understanding that women are to be exploited, if possible. The third understanding in lower class male society, and increasingly at all levels of American society, is that sexual intercourse is expected if dating continues. With each successive date, the male will try to go as far as he can, and he will judge the dating to be a failure if there is no progression toward full sexual intercourse. Goode notes that this set of values and treatise positions is supported by male friends in their gossip and philosophic exchanges about girls, and these values and positions are also present in a setting in which violence is common. Thus, if a young man enters a dating situation or even visits a close friend at her house with such a set of understandings, it is likely that he will interpret almost any acquiescence as a signal to proceed. Moreover, he is also likely to become angry when he is blocked as he feels he is being "cheated." Goode (1969) adds:

> *Still more important, in his experience, force is an almost legitimate technique for getting his way, and not least with women. Few would wish to admit that they could obtain sex only through force, but men at all class levels, from fraternity boys and college football players to ghetto dwellers, can brag from time to time that they used a bit of forcible persuasion on a date, especially when they could do so safely. (p. 972)*

Goode insists that a reciprocal failure to communicate is common in such situations. This failure to communicate, coupled with the lack of adequate techniques for deflecting the aggression, may well lead to still more violence and even brutality along with the rape itself.

What is said above means that as long as these sexist attitudes persist, no female can be safe in a dating relationship, because the scales are heavily tipped against her. It shows the social handicap from which women have to suffer, as well as the risks and dangers to which they are exposed whenever they interact with a male brought up and socialized in our sexist culture.

Victim Response to Face-to-Face Victimization

Becoming a victim is not a matter of choice. Most victims do not voluntarily assume this role but are forced into it through the offender's behavior. As a result, the victim's response to the unwanted and usually unexpected victimization is, to a large extent, unpremeditated and unplanned. The spontaneity of the reaction is no doubt partially responsible for the extreme variations in victim responses to identical situations and to very similar victimization experiences. The same offensive behavior, be it assault, rape, or robbery, does not elicit identical reactions from different victims.

Recently a few attempts have been made to examine and analyze those different reactions and to establish the typical and atypical responses to the most common types of face-to-face victimization (Block, 1977, 1989). Rare are the studies that have tried to link differential responses to the personal attributes of the victims, to the behavioral norms of the victim's culture, and to the final outcome of the victimization incidents. The variables most frequently examined in the context of victim response are victim-offender relationship, type of weapon, and the victim's resistance, which we will expand upon in this chapter.

In face-to-face victimization, victims often find themselves in situations where quick and sometimes irreversible decisions have to be made. Once the victim becomes aware of the victimizer's intention he or she is faced with several dilemmas such as to comply or not to comply with the offender's demands, to struggle or not to struggle, to resist or to give in, to scream or not to scream, to remain motionless or to try to escape, to argue with the offender or to keep silent. The personal characteristics of both victim and victimizer, their relationship, if a relationship exists, the situational characteristics, as well as the nature of the threatened victimization will determine the victim's response, the victimizer's reactions to that response, and the final outcome. The victimization process, the actual or potential use of physical violence, the presence or absence of a weapon and the nature of the weapon, the potential danger inherent in the situation, and the range of options and alternative courses of action available evoke specific psychological and behavioral responses in the victim. Very little research has been done to determine what type of person is likely to react in a specific manner when placed in a victimogenic situation, and past research has not explained why, in identical or similar situations, some victims are more likely to be subjected to physical violence of varying degrees than are others. And yet, we know that not all victims give in when finding themselves face-to-face with a victimizer such as a mugger, robber, rapist, burglar, kidnapper, or extortionist. Some will attempt to defend themselves or to protect their property with quite exceptional vigor. Such self-protective behavior may trigger a violent attempt to subdue or to silence the victim on the part of an aggressor who is tense, fearful, or panicky. The violence of such a panic reaction may well result in serious injury or even in the death of the victim. Obviously, there is a need to assess the probabilities of physical injury or homicide in the course of the commission of crimes such as robbery, rape, burglary, and kidnapping and to relate these probabilities to several variables, most notably, the reaction of the victim. One serious methodological difficulty when using official crime statistics or victimization survey data is to establish the time sequence of resistance, use of force, and injury so that it can be determined whether the victim's resistance was to counter the offender's use of force or whether the victimizer's use of force was to overcome the victim's resistance. Nevertheless, a scientific assessment of such probabilities and of the effect of the victim's reaction on the final outcome is essential if we are to inform potential victims of the nature and levels of risk associated with specific responses in situations of face-to-face victimization.

VICTIM-OFFENDER CONFRONTATIONS AND THEIR OUTCOMES

The frequency of injury to the victim varies by type of offense and by a large number of other determinants. Information on victim injury comes from a special study conducted by the United States Bureau of Justice Statistics (United States, 1989) using National Crime Survey data from the years 1979 to 1986. The study carried out by Caroline Wolf Harlow estimated that 8 percent of all victims of attempted or completed violent crimes were injured. Frequency of injury varied by type of crime. Thirty-nine percent of rape victims reported having been injured compared to 33 percent of robbery victims, 32 percent of the victims of aggravated assault, and 25 percent of simple assault victims. The study further shows that although rape victims were the most likely to report an injury, they were only half as likely as victims of aggravated assault to have sustained a serious injury.[2] Victims of aggravated assault were also more likely than other victims of violence to have received treatment in a hospital or emergency room and to have stayed in a hospital at least one night.

Sociodemographic variables were strongly associated with the probability of sustaining injury. Those most likely to sustain injury as a result of criminal victimization were males, blacks, those aged nineteen to twenty-four, persons who attended at least a year of high school but less than a year of college, separated or divorced persons, those with family incomes of less than $10,000, and residents of central cities. The least likely victims to sustain an injury were the following groups: females, whites, widows, those fifty years of age or older, persons with incomes of $30,000 or more, those who had attended college for a year or more, and those who lived outside central cities.

Another finding reported in the same study is that the risk of sustaining injury and the seriousness of injury, at least for survey respondents, are greater for males than females. Not only were male victims more likely to be injured than female victims, but also, when injured, a higher percentage of males than females sustained serious injuries and spent at least one night in a hospital or emergency room. Race was another important factor as the findings show that blacks had higher injury rates and a larger proportion of serious injuries than did whites. A third significant factor was marital status, with separated and divorced persons reporting an injury rate 2.5 times higher than the national rate, 6.5 times that of married persons, nearly 9 times that of widowed persons, and 1.5 times the rate of persons who had never been married.

Understandably then, the risks of sustaining injury follow an identical pattern to that of the risks of criminal victimization in general.

Burglary: The Frequency of Confrontation and Injury

Confrontation between the victim and the burglar seems to be the exception rather than the rule. In 92 percent of the 1,910 police-reported cases studied by Reppetto (1974), the premises were unoccupied when the burglary occurred. On the other hand, when Waller and Okihiro (1978) asked their Torontonian sample whether anyone was at home at the time of the incident, a surprisingly large proportion (44 percent) responded affirmatively. Of these, just under half indicated that there was a confrontation between burglar and person in the household. When the nature of the confrontation was probed, three out of twenty-five respondents said they left the scene before an actual confrontation with the burglar took place. Over half of those who confronted the burglar said the most serious thing that happened was a verbal exchange. Three of those confronted reported that the burglars were armed, two with knives, while eighteen said they were unarmed and four did not know. No offender was seen with a firearm. With regard to injuries, two persons reported that someone in the household received minor bruises or injuries, while one respondent reported that an injury occurred that required hospitalization and days off work.[3]

Robbery: The Frequency of Injury and Death

According to the National Crime Survey in the United States, there were approximately 14,681,100 robbery victimizations in the United States from 1973 to 1984 (United States, 1987b). Victims were injured in 33 percent of all robberies: 15 percent of the victims received medical care; 10 percent required emergency room or other hospital treatment; and 2 percent were hospitalized for at least an overnight period. About one in twelve robbery victims experienced serious injuries such as rape, knife or gunshot wounds, broken bones, or being knocked unconscious. Offenders displayed weapons in almost half of all robberies; they had guns in about one in five robberies. Offenders with weapons were more likely to threaten than attack their victims. Victims who were attacked were likely to be injured if they were female, if the incident occurred at night, if there was more than one offender, or if a weapon was present. The National Crime Survey report on criminal victimization in the United States in 1987 (United States, 1989) indicated a slightly higher frequency of physical injury in robbery (36.2 percent).

Since robberies ending in the death of the victims are classified as homicides, it is difficult to tell what percentage of all robberies culminate in the killing of the victim. There are, however, some figures available on the so-called "robbery homicide" in some American cities. Zimring (1979) studied robbery killings in Detroit during the thirteen-year period from 1962 to 1974. During that period, the number of robberies increased from about 4,200 to slightly over 20,000; the number of robbery killings increased from 15 to 155. In other words, robberies increased approximately fivefold while robbery homicides increased tenfold. The 1974 figures indicate that approximately 1 in every 130 reported robberies ends with the death of the victim.

Block (1977) reports that the number of robbery homicides in Chicago increased from 33 in 1965 to 212 in 1974. Robbery homicides increased from a total of 8 percent of all homicides to 22 percent of all homicides. The rate of robbery homicide in Chicago increased from 1.1 per 100,000 in 1965 to 6.4 per 100,000 in 1974.

Rape: The Frequency of Physical Injury

Because rape incidents culminating in the death of the victim are usually classified as murders or homicides, there are no available statistics indicating the percentage of rapes in which the victim is killed. Statistics are available, on the other hand, on the frequency of physical injuries sustained in addition to the rape itself. The frequencies differ, however, from study to study due to, among other things, the variety of methods and samples used, the data (police data, victimization survey data, medical data) and to the ways in which "injury" is defined.

The British Home Office study of rape in two London boroughs during the years 1984 to 1986 (Smith, 1989) reports that about two-fifths (41 percent) of the victims suffered additional injuries. The most frequently mentioned injuries were bruises (19 percent), and multiple injuries were sustained in over one in ten reported cases (11 percent). Cuts or stabs — despite the use of knives as weapons — were infrequent (3 percent) suggesting that knives were more commonly used to threaten than to inflict injury. The remainder were either incurred through the rape itself or were of a minor nature, for example, scratches.

Fisher (1980) investigated 814 rape and attempted rape cases occurring in Newark, New Jersey, during a thirty-month period. He found that 30.6 percent of all victims suffered some physical injury, which he defined as physical harm in addition to the sexual assault itself. Of those victims who were injured, 73.9 percent suffered mild injury such as scrapes, bruises, and minor lacerations; 17.7 percent suffered moderate injury such as lacerations sutured, prolonged or extensive beating, and fractures; 8.4 percent were seriously injured — injuries for which the victim was admitted to the hospital.

Massey et al. (1971) report that 10.6 percent of the rape victims they examined had external evidence of trauma, ranging from small cuts to severe contusions and facial fractures (5.2 percent had gynecological injuries). And Selkin (1975) found that less than 9 percent of the Denver victims sustained anything more serious than a cut or bruise.

Katz and Mazur (1979) quote a study by Peters et al. (1976) that indicates that of external injuries, the most frequent trauma recorded was facial (17.4 percent). A pelvic examination showed that of internal trauma, the most frequent injury was vulval (19.5 percent); this occurred frequently in children. One in four of the total sample suffered some genital trauma, although most injuries were not medically serious.

Varieties of Victim Response to Face-to-Face Victimization

THE NEED FOR A TYPOLOGY OF RESPONSES

How do victims respond to face-to-face victimization? How do they react when confronted with one or more offenders? Why do victims respond differently to identical or similar threats? What individual and situational variables are associated with different responses? What impact does the victim's reaction have on the final outcome of the victimization event? Answers to these questions are essential for developing a theory of victim response to confrontational victimization. But first, we need to develop a typology of responses. Resistance takes different forms, and there are various levels of struggle. The victim may attack the attacker and may attempt to hurt, injure, blind, or even kill. Some victims may simply attempt to defend themselves and protect their body from injury or penetration. Others may try to call for help or assistance and scare the attacker by yelling and screaming. Some victims may try to escape or run away; others may decide that the best course of action is to reason with their attackers and talk them out of the attack. In so doing, these victims might use varying techniques of persuasion or dissuasion to make their victimizers stop. How frequent is each of these response types? Are certain responses more effective than others in thwarting attacks? What is meant by "effective" and how can effectiveness be measured? Answers to these questions are not yet available.

THE NEED TO MEASURE THE RESISTANCE LEVEL

In addition to a typology of responses, we need to develop a scale for measuring the different degrees of victim resistance. We may distinguish between varying degrees of resistance such as vigorous, fierce, strong, or moderate and between such actions as avoidance, submission, compliance, and consent. The response of the victim in each case may thus be ranked along a continuum ranging from active resistance to passive compliance. Research on this topic requires an operationalization of the concept of resistance and the development of objective indicators to measure its level. Very little research has been done in this area, and some of it has not even separated the measurement of the degree of struggle from the final outcome. Some researchers have even used the effectiveness of the resistance as the criterion for judging its degree. Block (1977), for example, defined victim resistance using a three-point scale: (1) resistance that physically threatens the robber; (2) resistance that poses no physical threat but results in a robbery attempt failing; and (3) no resistance.

Once the type of response has been determined and the level of resistance, if resistance there was, has been measured, it would be possible to link the type of response to the characteristics of the victim, the offender, and the situation, to link the presence or absence of struggle to varying outcomes, and also, to link the different degrees of resistance to these outcomes.

Despite the recent proliferation of criminological literature on rape, there have been few research attempts to determine how women can best extract themselves from a potential rape situation or to measure the differential effectiveness of various available responses when threatened by a man. Curtis (1976) reviewed the literature and noted that the matter remains largely controversial. Feminists and some authors, he points out, assert that physical resistance is the best response a woman can make in a rape situation. Such resistance, it is believed, reduces the chances that the rape will be committed and results in a milder psychological trauma should the rape take place. Police, on the other hand, usually advise women not to resist for fear of bodily harm or of being killed. Curtis suggests that research should examine three basic classes of independent variables: the victim, the offender, and the situational dynamics between the victim and the offender. He believes that any comparison of attempted and completed rape and degree of injury would do well to systematically search for combinations of victim characteristics and behavior, offender characteristics and behavior, and situational contexts that serve to differentiate these outcomes.

HOW OFTEN DO VICTIMS RESIST?

Using National Crime Survey data, Block (1989) analyzed patterns of response in stranger-to-stranger robbery and rape. He concludes that most targets of robbery (55.5 percent) and rape (83.2 percent) resist. The frequency of resistance is much higher in rape than it is in robbery. Block distinguished two forms of resistance: nonforcible resistance, which includes reasoning or verbally threatening the offender, yelling for help, or running away and forcible resistance, which includes physical attack with or without a weapon. Block found that robbery targets were only slightly more likely to use nonforcible than forcible resistance (30 percent versus 25 percent). Among rape targets, nonforcible resistance is much more common (51 percent) than forcible resistance (32 percent).

United States National Crime Survey data for 1987 (United States, 1989a) confirm the higher frequency of resistance among rape victims. Victims of rape were more likely to defend themselves (83.1 percent) than the victims of other violent crimes. Assault victims tried more often (70.2 percent) to defend themselves than robbery victims (61.2 percent). For all violent victimizations combined, the percentage of victims who took a self-protective measure was 68.9 percent. These self-protective measures included the following: reasoning with the offender; fleeing from the offender; screaming or yelling for help; hitting, kicking, or scratching the offender; and using or brandishing a weapon.

The scarcity of research on this topic makes generalizations and definitive conclusions impossible. Although compliance with the demands of robbers, muggers, and holdup men is frequent, it is neither universal nor uniform. Many robbery victims refuse to remain passive or to hand over their money or belongings voluntarily. The degree of resistance, however, varies. There are certain categories of victims who generally offer little or no resistance. Cashiers and bank tellers are usually instructed by their employers to comply with the demands of the robber in case of a holdup. They are often told not to resist, though they are encouraged to try to alert other bank employees discrectly to what is taking place. Airline pilots also do not resist in the crime of skyjacking. In the overwhelming majority of cases, the pilots have meticulously obeyed the orders of the hijackers. In a few incidents, resistance resulted in bringing the hijacking episode to a nonviolent end, while in a couple of cases, attempts to overcome the hijackers resulted in injuries to, or death of, the passengers or members of the crew. The particular helplessness of the victims of skyjacking and the tight space within the aircraft are probably responsible for the lack of struggle in most cases. The helplessness of the victims is a direct result of their total isolation while the aircraft is in the air. As long as the plane is in flight, the victims cannot rely on help from the protection agencies such as the police or the army. When the skyjacker is armed with explosives or a deadly weapon, such as a handgun or a machine gun, as is usually the case, the whole aircraft, its passengers and crew, are totally at the mercy of the hijacker. The situation is rendered more dangerous by the fact that what happens to the pilot or copilot endangers the life and safety of all passengers.

Some Correlates of Victim Response

Victims do not react in the same manner when they find themselves face-to-face with a mugger, rapist, or burglar. What are the determinants of individual responses? What are the personal and situational variables associated with different types of reaction? As research in this area is still in its infancy we do not have conclusive answers to these questions. There is some tentative evidence that victim response varies according to sociodemographic variables such as age, sex, and race. Though empirical data are lacking, it is also conceivable that the reaction will differ along many other individual variables, such as the victim's occupation, social class, sociocultural background, and psychological variables, such as personality, self-esteem, attitudes toward victimization, perceptions of effectiveness, attitude toward fear (risk-taker, risk-avoider, impulsive-reflective, courageous-cowardly), and sense of vulnerability or invulnerability. It is also likely that victim response will depend on the relationship to the offender and will vary if the attacker is a complete stranger, a member of the victim's family, or someone well known to the victim. There are also a host of situational variables likely to determine, condition, or influence the response of the victim. The following is a brief discussion of what seem to be the most important variables.

AGE, SEX, AND RACE OF THE VICTIM

In his study of 1,027 robbery offenses from the Philadelphia birth cohort, Wolfgang (1982) found that age is an important factor in resistance. Greatest resistance by victims (52 percent) came from those from eighteen to twenty-nine years old, while the least resistance came from juveniles of eighteen and under (29 percent). He reports that even among the elderly, aged sixty-five and over, slightly more than 40 percent resisted the robbery threat.

Using United States National Crime Survey data on stranger-to-stranger robbery and rape, Block (1989) reports that the decision to resist a robber is related to the victim's age, sex, and race. From the twenties to old age, the percentage of victims who do not resist increases linearly from 37 percent to 64 percent. Of those who do resist, the percentage who forcibly resist declines with age from 51 percent among victims in their twenties to 29 percent of those who are older than seventy. Block points out that blacks were less likely to resist a robber (58 percent) than whites (41 percent). One possible reason for the difference is that blacks were more likely to be robbed with a gun than whites. However, if the offender's weapon threat remains as a constant, blacks still remained less likely to resist than whites. Thus, 36 percent of white victims and 28 percent of black victims of gun robberies resisted. Block found that the victim's age was less strongly related to resistance to rape than to robbery. He noticed again that black women were less likely to resist a rapist (30 percent) than were white women (14 percent). Part, but not all, of this difference might be related to the far greater likelihood that a black woman will be attacked with a gun. However, regardless of the offender's choice of weapon, black women were less likely to resist than white women.

The United States Bureau of Justice Statistics (United States, 1987a) reports that National Crime Survey data indicate that elderly violent crime victims of sixty-five and over were less likely to take self-protective measures than were younger victims (52 percent versus 72 percent). The Bureau suggests a number of factors likely to influence a victim's decision to take self-protective measures, including the victim's physical strength, the ability to fend off or evade a potential offender, and the perception that protective actions will prevent injury or loss. The Bureau adds that crime victims in general may be reluctant to try to defend themselves when offenders are armed with a potentially dangerous weapon, such as a gun or a knife. Thus, the lower proportion of elderly violent-crime victims who took self-protective measures is consistent with the greater likelihood that they will face offenders armed with guns. The same report indicates that among violent crime victims who took self-protective measures, the elderly were less likely than younger victims to use, or try to use, physical force against the offenders. They were more likely than younger victims to try to get help or to argue or reason with the offender, and they were about as likely to resist without force or to take evasive action. These findings confirm those reported in an earlier study of crime against the elderly in twenty-six cities (Hochstedler, 1981).

PRESENCE OR ABSENCE OF A WEAPON

Spontaneous and panic reactions cannot be expected to be rational. Still, it is reasonable to assume that the decision to resist is, in general, negatively related to the victim's perception and assessment of the potential danger inherent in the situation. This assessment will be based on many elements, including the victim-offender relationship or lack of it, the number of attackers, the level of force actually employed or threatened, the presence or absence of a weapon, and the type of weapon if one is present. The presence of a weapon, particularly if it is a deadly one such as a firearm, is a strong intimidating factor capable of reducing the probability of resistance and, thus, forcing the victim into compliance and enhancing the likelihood that the crime will be completed. There is, in fact, evidence suggesting that the presence of a weapon is inversely related to the offender's use of force, as well as to victim resistance. Conklin (1972), in his study of robberies in Boston, found a strong negative relationship between the use of guns in robbery and the use of force. In Chicago, Block (1977) discovered that robbers who use a gun are also less likely to use force (gamma=-.62). Twenty-six percent of the offenders with guns used force, as compared to 65 percent of those who threatened the victim without a gun. The reason why robbers who use guns are less likely to use force than other robbers is clear, Block suggests: the threat of a gun is usually enough to convince a potential victim not to resist. Few victims resisted the threat of a gun attack (18 percent), while victims of attacks with other weapons and no weapons were more likely to resist (32 percent). In neither case did a majority of victims resist. Block adds that the negative relationship between weapon and resistance is matched by a positive relationship between resistance and use of force. Force is much more likely to be used against victims who resist than against victims who do not.

Wolfgang's study of the Philadelphia birth cohort robbery offenses (1982) presents a different picture of victim response to the threat of a gun versus that of other weapons. According to Wolfgang, knives appeared to be the most feared threat, for in seven out of ten times, when a knife was part of the drama of intimidation, the victim displayed no resistance. There was even more resistance to a gun threat (40 percent) and the most resistance was shown when a blunt instrument was used (53 percent).

At this stage of our knowledge it is not possible to draw any definitive conclusions or to try to explain the difference between the findings of Block and Wolfgang. Any explanation would be speculative.

The presence or absence of a weapon varies by type of offense, age, sex, and race of the victim, as well as by victim-offender relationship. According to the United States Bureau of Justice Statistics (United States, 1989), approximately one-third of violent crimes involved the presence or use of a weapon: 30 percent of rapes, 31 percent of assaults, and 46 percent of robberies. Weapons were present more frequently in stranger-to-stranger violent confrontations than in incidents involving nonstrangers.[4] Of violent incidents committed by an armed offender, 25 percent involved a knife, 37 percent a firearm, and 37 percent a weapon other than a firearm or a knife.

Another Bureau of Justice Statistics study, this time of robbery (United States, 1987b) shows that victims under the age of sixteen and those sixty-five and over were less likely to be robbed by offenders with weapons than victims with ages falling between these two extremes. The same study indicates that male victims were more likely to face a weapon than females. Males who were attacked were slightly less likely to be injured (62 percent) than females (65 percent). Victims of both sexes experienced the same proportion of serious injuries (males, 17 percent and females 14 percent), but females suffered a higher proportion of minor injuries (51 percent) than did males (45 percent).

A study of violent crime based on police reports in Chicago suggests that whites are less likely than blacks to be attacked with a gun in either a robbery or an aggravated assault (Block, 1977). For example, 55 percent of blacks robbing blacks were gun attacks, as compared to 39 percent of blacks robbing whites. Homicides involving blacks killing whites, on the other hand, were more likely to involve gun use than intraracial crimes. The high percentage of gun use in these homicides, suggests Block, may be the result of the relatively high percentage of robbery homicides involving blacks robbing whites.

VICTIM-OFFENDER RELATIONSHIP

One important factor likely to influence victim response to the attack is the victim's prior knowledge of the victimizer. It seems natural to expect that victims will react differently depending on who is attacking, threatening, or coercing them. Their reactions are influenced by whether the offender is a family member, a close friend, someone they know well, a mere acquaintance, or a complete stranger. The victimization situation is a highly dynamic one in which the offender, through words, gestures, and actions, generates specific responses from the victim. We can assume, therefore, that the offender's characteristics, the victim's perception of the offender's attitude and behavior, and the victim's assessment of the victimizer's intentions, potential for danger, and the seriousness of his threats, will greatly influence the victim's response. The depth of these perceptions and these assessments, together with the victim's belief that he or she can predict the offender's next move(s), depends on how well the victim knows the attacker. In view of this it might not be too surprising to find out that victims in general are more intimidated by strangers than by victimizers they intimately know and that the frequency and the degree of resistance are higher when victim and offender are personally related than when they are total strangers. And since forcible resistance from the victim is positively and strongly related to injury to the victim (McDermott, 1979; Fisher, 1980; Gibson, Linden, and Johnson, 1980; Wright, 1980; Swift, 1985), we can expect a lower rate of injury in stranger-to-stranger attacks. There is empirical support for this hypothesis. Hindelang, Gottfredson, and Garofalo (1978) found that of those who were victimized by strangers, 23 percent received some physical injury, whereas among those who were victimized by nonstrangers, 35 percent received some injury. The authors note that one of the reasons victims of nonstrangers suffer higher rates of injury than victims of strangers is that the former are more likely than the latter to take self-protective measures, especially physical force self-protective measures. Hindelang et al. (1978) write:

> *The greater tendency to take self-protective measures when the offender is a non-stranger may be due to the victim's belief that he or she can predict the offender's probable reaction if a self-protective measure is taken, something that persons who are victimized by strangers may be less likely to believe. Further, it is possible that when the victim and the offender are known to each other, victim-precipitation, which in retrospect may become defined as a self-protective measure, disproportionately occurs. (p. 60)*

A study of violent crime by strangers and nonstrangers by the United States Bureau of Justice Statistics (United States, 1987a) confirms the findings of Hindelang et al. The study reports that among crimes committed by nonstrangers, those committed by relatives involved an attack more often than those committed by acquaintances. Violent crimes by relatives also involved injury more often than crimes by either acquaintances or strangers. Close to half of all victimizations involving a relative resulted in injury, compared to about one-third of the crimes committed by acquaintances and about one-fourth of those committed by strangers. The Bureau of Justice Statistics offers an alternative explanation for the difference. It is suggested that the definition of a crime may vary in the mind of the victim, depending on the victim's relationship to the offender. For example, victims who were threatened or attacked by relatives, but not injured, may not perceive the incident as serious or as a crime at all, and they may not report it to a survey interviewer. On the other hand, threats or attempted attacks by strangers may be perceived as serious and, therefore, are reported to an interviewer more frequently. The same study reveals that, although victims of relatives were injured more often, the injuries resulting from crimes by strangers and acquaintances required medical attention or hospital care more often than those resulting from crimes by relatives. Most injuries, however, were minor, regardless of the victim-offender relationship.

A third study (United States, 1980) of violence among friends and relatives, based on the data collected through victimization surveys from 1973 to 1976, reports that "the likelihood of sustaining injury appeared to increase the more intimate the victim-offender relationship" (p. 13).

SOME OTHER VARIABLES LIKELY TO INFLUENCE VICTIM RESPONSE

In addition to the variables of age, sex, and race of the victim, presence or absence of a weapon, and victim-offender relationships, there are several other situational variables likely to determine, condition, or influence the response of the victim. The following is a brief discussion of some of these variables.

Time and Location of the Attack

Victim response is likely to vary depending on the time and location of the attack: whether it takes place during the day, in the evening, or late at night; indoors or outdoors; in open, closed, or tight space such as a car, van, elevator, stairway, or residential garage; or in a place such as a street, alley, park, car park, or vacant lot. Attempts to link the victim's reaction to the time and location of the attack are extremely rare. Block (1989), for example, found in his study of stranger-to-stranger rape that the woman's decision to resist the attack is related to the environment in which the victimization occurs. Contrary to what one might have expected, women who were confronted at home were less likely to resist than women attacked outside their homes.

The Element of Surprise

Whether the victim is caught off guard or not will inevitably influence the response to the attacker, as will the procedure employed by the latter. In many cases, victimizers try to neutralize victims' defense mechanisms by approaching them in a normal, nonthreatening, and unsuspicious manner. Luckenbill (1981) found that 65 percent of the robbers he studied established their presence near the victim by appearing normal and attempting to behave as someone the victim would see as an ordinary, legitimate part of the setting. In a grocery store, for example, the offender enters under the guise of a customer intent on purchasing goods. On a street late in the evening, the offender stops a passerby by making what appears to be a legitimate request for information or matches. Luckenbill points out that when the offender fails to establish a presence without alarming the victim and provoking strong opposition, the robbery is jeopardized. In this case, the robbery plans might break down if the intended victim flees before the robber moves into striking range, or if the victim becomes alarmed and prepares to counterattack.

The Number of Victims and Victimizers

In most cases of face-to-face victimization, the numbers are irrelevant, as the situation involves a single victim facing a lone attacker. United States National Crime Survey findings (United States, 1980) indicate that irrespective of victim-offender relationship, violent crimes involving more than one victim are uncommon. Only about one-tenth of intimate or nonintimate crimes were characterized by the victimization of more than a single person, with the vast majority of these acts having only two victims. Roughly 87 percent of acts of intimate violence were committed by a single offender and about 6 percent each by either two offenders or by three or more. In crimes between nonintimates, involvement by multiple offenders was more common, even though the one victim/one offender was still the model pattern. In about one-third of these crimes, two or more offenders confronted a single victim. In 6 percent, two or more victims were encountered by a single offender, and there was a comparable number of cases characterized by multiple victims and offenders. In about 11 percent of the intimate crimes, two or more offenders confronted one victim. Thus, it seems that the one-on-one model is by far the dominant pattern of face-to-face victimization.

In the minority of cases where there are multiple victims, multiple offenders or both, such as gang rapes, hijacking, hostage taking, and holdups, the number of attackers is likely to have an impact on the response of the victim(s). In their study of rape in Winnipeg, Gibson, Linden, and Johnson (1980) found that the presence of more than one male lessens any resistance offered by the rape victim. Rape events involving more than one perpetrator accounted for 20 percent of the total. The role of confederates in these cases was to keep the victim subdued and compliant.

In the case of robbery, Block (1977) reports, on the basis of his Chicago study, that the greater the number of offenders, the less likely is resistance. As may be expected, those "multiple-offender robberies with guns and just the threat of force were those least likely to result in victim resistance" (p. 81). In his study of the Philadelphia birth cohort robberies, Wolfgang (1982), on the other hand, found that the single/multiple offender dichotomy showed no relationship to attempted versus completed acts. Robberies were successfully completed in 72 percent of single offender cases and 75 percent of multiple offender cases, hence, no significant difference. Here, again, further research is evidently needed.

Racial and Gender Homogeneity/Heterogeneity

Does the reaction of the victim differ when the attacker is one of the other sex or of another ethnic group from when there is a gender or racial similarity? The empirical data necessary to answer this question are not available. In the case of heterosexual rape, as has been shown, a high percentage of victims do resist. In the Winnipeg study, Gibson, Linden, and Johnson (1980) report that while most women are physically weaker than most men, efforts to resist the threat proved to be effective in a large number of cases.

The Age Difference Between Attacker and Victim

What role does age difference play in determining, shaping, or influencing the response of the victim? Do victims react differently when the attacker appears younger or older than the victim, or of a similar age? Empirical data on these questions are not available. Yet, we might assume that an age difference which gives the advantage to the attacker would have an intimidating effect on the victim and, thus, reduce the probability of resistance and enhance the probability of consent or compliance. However, the hypothesis needs to be tested. We also need research to know whether age difference is particularly influential for specific age groups, such as the extremely young or the extremely old.

The Presence of Alcohol and/or Drugs

Because of their effect on the mind and on behavior, alcohol or other drugs used by the victim, the offender, or both, may influence, sometimes quite considerably, the victim's reaction to the attacker. On one hand, alcohol consumption by the victimizer may increase the potential danger to the victim. On the other hand, it can also impair or cloud the victim's judgment, thus eliciting irrational or reckless responses. Active resistance may be excluded altogether if the victim is in a state of total sedation or numbness (Fattah and Raic, 1970).

The Presence of Others

The presence of third parties such as passersby can reduce the victim's feelings of helplessness, insecurity, and vulnerability. It may, therefore, increase the probability of active resistance on the part of the victim. This is likely to be true in cases where the victim feels that he or she can rely on the intervention of those others and on their help in thwarting the attack.

Felson and Steadman (1983) suggest that "third parties, as well as antagonists, may affect the outcome of violent incidents" through three types of actions:

> *First, they may engage in physical or verbal attacks themselves, and in such a case they act as an ally of one of the antagonists. Second, they may instigate the*

conflict if they encourage an antagonist to fight on their behalf, or if they define the situation as one in which violence is appropriate. Finally, they may attempt to mediate the conflict. Mediators may constrain the antagonists and allow the conflict to deescalate with neither side appearing to back down. (p. 61)

Victim Response and Victimization Outcome

The successful completion of confrontational crimes often depends on the cooperation of the victim. The victimizer's use of force or threats is meant to secure the victim's submission and compliance. That is why the response of the victim during the event can have a dramatic impact on the final outcome. What the victim does or does not do during the actual encounter with the victimizer often determines how the victimization will evolve and how it will end. It is true that in some cases the outcome will be affected by factors other than the victim's behavior. These include unsolicited intervention by third parties and the victimizer's change of heart or plans independent of the victim's actions. Still, the victim's reaction is, without a doubt, crucial to determining whether the crime will be successfully completed or will simply remain an attempt. It also determines whether the victim will endure physical injury or not and influences such factors as the extent of injury, and the intensity of post-victimization guilt.

VICTIM RESISTANCE AND SUCCESSFUL COMPLETION

Victim resistance seems to be the variable most strongly correlated with the completion or noncompletion of the offense. In his study of violent crime in Chicago, Block (1977) discovered that victim resistance is a primary determinant both of a robbery's success or failure and the probability of death or injury to the victim. Wolfgang, in his study of the Philadelphia birth cohort robbery offenses (1982), found that nonresistance by the victim significantly results in a completed robbery. Only 14 percent of nonresistant robberies were incompleted; however, 42 percent of resisted ones were incompleted. Wolfgang points out that lack of completion where there was no resistance was most likely due to fortuitous factors external to the interaction, such as other persons approaching or a police car passing by. Whatever the reason, he notes that among attempted robberies, two-thirds were resisted by the intended victims, whereas among completed acts, over two-thirds of the victims offered no resistance. The United States Bureau of Justice Statistics *Special Report on Robbery Victims* (United States, 1987b) reveals the same pattern observed on the basis of national victimization data from 1973 to 1984. Thus, victims of attempted robberies, with or without injury, were most likely to have taken self-protective measures. Victims who lost property but were not injured were least likely to have tried to protect themselves. The percentage of victims who used at least one self-protective measure was much higher in attempted robberies (84 percent) than in completed robberies (59 percent), thus indicating the important role victim resistance plays in hindering the completion of the robbery.

This is also true of rape victimization (Quinsey and Upfold, 1985; Block and Skogan, 1986; Lizotte, 1986; Kleck and Sayles, 1990). In the Winnipeg rape study, Gibson, Linden, and Johnson (1980) found support for the hypothesis that there is an increased chance of sexual assault resulting in an attempted rape where greater efforts were made by the victim to resist the attack.

Studies of the effect of varying victim responses on the completion of rape do not reveal a uniform pattern. Brodsky (1976) observed that, while crying and signs of personal weakness on the part of the victim might deter the dominant, aggressive rapist, such behavior was likely to increase the sexual excitement of the rapist who is more tentative in his approach.

In her study of twelve convict rapists, Marques (1981) reports that the most striking result was the dramatically higher levels of sexual arousal produced by the plea for sympathy condition compared to the assertive refusal, establishing a relationship, or nonresistance control conditions. All twelve subjects were most aroused by the pleading victim, and only one failed to show a mean prepost increase in penile circumference for the plea for sympathy condition. By contrast, the assertive refusal condition produced arousal decrements in ten of the twelve subjects, while the other two conditions tested had highly variable effects. The finding confirmed Marques's hypothesis that resistance strategies would differ in their effects on rapists' levels of sexual arousal.

Chappell and James's (1986) interviews with fifty convicted rapists at Atascadero State Hospital indicated the following: (1) passivity or compliance was the victim reaction most rapists preferred; (2) physical resistance, including screaming, was more likely to provoke harm to the victim than was verbal resistance; and (3) convincing the offender of the victim's altered state of health (such as pregnancy or sickness) or eliciting his sympathy "might terminate the attack or minimize injury" (p. 77).

It seems obvious that different victim behaviors can and do elicit varying responses from different types of rapists. This is the primary conclusion of a study of 108 convicted, incarcerated rapists and their 389 victims (Prentky, Burgess, and Carter, 1986). The authors identified four clinical prototypes of rapists: (1) the *compensatory* rapist, for whom the assault is primarily an expression of his rape fantasies; (2) the *exploitative* rapist, whose sexual behavior is expressed as an impulsive predatory act; (3) the *displaced anger* rapist, whose sexual behavior is an expression of anger and rage; and (4) the *sadistic* rapist, whose sexual behavior is an expression of sexual aggressive (sadistic) fantasies.

In general, the authors found that for all rapist types there was a higher incidence of brutal aggression associated with combative resistance than with noncombative resistance. However, the degree of association and its significance was not identical for all four types. For exploitative rapists, the difference in the use of brutal aggression did not reach statistical significance. Brutal force was associated with 30 percent of victims who combatively resisted compensatory rapists and 5.4 percent of those victims who did not. In the cases of displaced anger rapists, brutal force was associated with 84.7 percent of those victims who resisted combatively and 18.2 percent of those victims who did not. Among sadistic rapists, brutal force was associated with 80 percent of those victims who resisted combatively and 20 percent of those victims who did not. These percentages, and the conclusions to be drawn from them, need to be viewed with caution since they depend largely on the accuracy with which the rapists were typologized. Moreover, the terms "brutal aggression" and "brutal force" are vague, and the distinction between brutal and nonbrutal aggression is necessarily arbitrary. The study also suffers from certain methodological problems, some of which are acknowledged by the authors themselves.

VICTIM RESISTANCE AND PROBABILITY OF PHYSICAL INJURY

Among the variety of victim responses, active physical resistance is the one most likely to elicit a violent reaction from the victimizer. Thus, while a victim's resistance is apt, in many instances, to stop the completion of the offense, it is also likely to physically endanger the victim and to increase the chances of physical injury or even death. All available empirical evidence seems to suggest that resistance of the victim does increase the level of force employed by the offender. Hindelang, Gottfredson, and Garofalo (1978) found the victim's use of a physical self-protective measure to be the variable most strongly associated with injury. The injury rate for those who used a self-protective measure (56 percent) was nearly three times greater than for victims who did not use such self-protective measures (20 percent). Other researchers have examined the relationship between victim resistance and the probability of injury in two offenses: rape and robbery.

Rape

The study of rape victimization in twenty-six American cities (McDermott, 1979) reports that additional injury, that is, injury not directly related to the act of rape, was much greater among victims who tried to protect themselves in some way.

Among the victims of rape, additional injury was reported by 34 percent of the victims who didn't use self-protective measures, compared to 66 percent of the victims who used self-protective measures. The comparable figures in attempted rape victimization were 29 percent and 49 percent respectively. McDermott's interpretation of the finding is that by trying to protect herself the victim increases the likelihood that the rape will not be completed, but she also increases the likelihood that she will receive some physical injury not classified as rape or attempted rape injury.

Fisher (1980) used 814 rape and attempted rape cases occurring in Newark, New Jersey, during a thirty-month period to develop a path model that predicts injury to rape victims. The model reveals the central role victim resistance plays as all indirect paths in the model pass through the variable of victim resistance. The magnitudes of the direct paths from victim resistance (.278) and presence of a knife (.288) are the highest in the model. Fisher makes a distinction between "instrumental injuries" and "noninstrumental injuries." The former are the ones inflicted prior to the point of intimidation, that is, the point at which the victim assents or becomes submissive to the will of the rapist. They are directed toward the accomplishment of the rape objective. "Noninstrumental injuries," on the other hand, are injuries inflicted subsequent to the point of victim intimidation, whether before, during, or after the actual rape. They are inflicted as ends or goals in themselves rather than as measures directed toward the attainment of the rape. Of the cases in which a knife was present, 65.9 percent of the victims did not resist. Of that group, 27.8 percent were injured of which over half, 54.1 percent, were the victims of noninstrumental injury. On the other hand, of the victims who physically resisted when a knife was present, 78.9 percent were injured, with 90.8 percent of those injuries being of the instrumental type.

Corroborating evidence for the positive relationship between victim resistance and injury in rape comes also from Canadian and British studies. In Winnipeg, Gibson, Linden, and Johnson (1980) found moderately strong associations between the degree of resistance offered by the victim and the severity of injury sustained by her, both for completed and attempted rape cases. And in England, Wright (1980) reports that victims putting up a severe struggle were more likely to receive a severe beating, though they were also more likely to avoid being raped.

Further evidence for the positive correlation between resistance and injury comes from the rapists themselves. Chappell and James (1986) gathered information from fifty rapists through the use of an elaborate questionnaire in a face-to-face interview situation. Rapists' responses indicate that "struggling, screaming and otherwise refusing to co-operate seems likely to increase the chances that the rapists in the group interviewed would harm their victim" (Chappell and James, 1986, pp. 73-74). The responses also suggest that physical resistance is a much more dangerous form of behavior on the part of victims than verbal resistance.

Even Swift (1985), who claims to have put to rest the conventional wisdom according to which resistance will exacerbate the attack and increase the probability of the victim's mutilation or death, says that resistance is positively correlated with increased injury, but adds that such injuries are of a nonserious nature and are preferred to the trauma of a completed sexual assault.

Robbery

As in rape, resistance of the victim in robbery situations seems to enhance the likelihood of injury and even death. In his study of violent crime in Chicago, Block (1977) found victim resistance to be strongly related to the probability of a robbery being completed and to the probability of death or injury of the victim. Resistance decreased the probability of success and increased the probability of death or injury. Block further found that most of the variation in probability of death or injury between different robbery settings is also explained by the victim's decision to resist. In a subsequent study, Block (1989) reports that nonforcible resistance has little effect on the probability that a victim will be attacked or injured during a robbery. Forcible resistance, on the other hand, is strongly related to the probability that the victim will be attacked and injured, and it is also related to the probability that the injury will be serious enough to require hospitalization.

Block's findings are confirmed by Cook (1986) who analyzed United States National Crime Survey data for the period from 1973 to 1979. He found the probability of no attack is about twice as high when the victim does not resist forcefully as when the victim does resist.[5] This result holds for all three of Cook's weapon categories and seems to suggest that a victim who is not initially assaulted should not resist forcefully, since forceful resistance in these circumstances appears to provoke violent reprisals. Cook adds that for each weapon category, the forceful resisters have the highest chance of being attacked and of being seriously injured. Nonforceful resisters, on the other hand, are slightly less likely to be attacked and seriously injured than those who do not resist. Cook offers two possible interpretations for this pattern:

1. Forceful resistance provokes a violent response, whereas nonforceful resistance actually discourages violence. Hence, victims should not attempt to use force, but may be well advised to scream or run away.
2. Forceful resistance usually occurs only when the victim is physically attacked. Nonforceful resistance is usually attempted only when the robber does not initially attack the victim. Hence, there are no lessons about prudent victim behavior to be learned from the data (p. 411).

In a study of robbery in Chicago, Zimring and Zuehl (1986) classified victim response into three categories: (1) no resistance noted; (2) passive noncooperation in which the victim usually says he or she has no money; and (3) active noncooperation which includes refusal, flight, and physical force. They found loss of life in robbery to be strongly associated with active victim resistance. Active noncooperation was associated with a death risk from robbery approximately fourteen times as great as cooperation or passive noncooperation. Passive noncooperation was about twice as likely to produce a lethal outcome as no resistance. The pattern held when the cases were separately analyzed by robbery location. The authors point out that finding active resistance to be associated with a much higher death risk is not the equivalent of proving a causal relationship between the victim's resistance and increased risk of death. In some cases, the lethal intentions of the robber may provoke an otherwise passive victim rather than the victim's active resistance transforming the robber's intent. The inability to make confident assessments of the sequence of resistance in the killing cases, such as whether resistance altered or resulted from the offender's intention to injure, limit the ability to estimate with precision how many additional deaths are generated by victim resistance. Zimring and Zuehl (1986) add:

> *But our current data suggest the independent role of resistance is substantial. Even if half of all robbery killings associated with active resistance would have occurred in any event, active resistance would still escalate the risk of death by a factor of between three and four. Under such circumstances, prudent victims should avoid most noncooperation when involved in armed robbery. And the strong relationship between the victim's gender and the death risk from robbery is further circumstantial evidence that resistance provokes higher death risks in armed robbery. (p. 19)*[6]

The advice that robbery victims should not resist in order to minimize the risk of serious injury is not one that all researchers offer. Ziegenhagen and Brosnan (1985) believe that encouraging victims to resist robbery is as misleading as encouraging them not to resist. According to them, victims and the robbery situations in which they find themselves vary far too widely to be controlled by prescriptions of public policy. The authors analyzed the National Crime Panel data for thirteen cities, which gave information on 3,679 incidents for the year 1974. The analysis, they point out, discloses that victim resistance to execution of robbery is not often associated with serious injury but is linked to preventing the successful execution of the crime. In other words, victims may play a critical role in the control of robbery outcomes. They thus conclude that policy prescriptions that entail limiting the range of responses open to victims may be harmful to both the victim and the interest of society in controlling crime.

Unexpected Outcomes of Victim-Victimizer Interaction

Research on the dynamics of victim-offender interactions in face-to-face victimization is still in the embryonic stage. Too many questions remain unanswered. We know that most of these interactions are marked by anger, hostility, and antagonism. It has been observed, however, that in some incidents of kidnapping, hostage taking, and aircraft hijacking, particularly when they lasted days or weeks, the victim reacts with a positive rather than a negative emotional response to the victimizer(s). In certain cases, this positive response may even develop into a deep emotional attachment or a strong affective bond. Various explanations have been offered for this curious and unexpected phenomenon. Some researchers (Ochberg, 1978) believe these positive affective ties between victims and victimizers result from the state of dependency that develops between hostage and keeper, kidnapped and captor. Others try to explain it by using the Freudian concept of "identification with the aggressor": (*Time*, 1976). A third group of researchers (*Time*, 1976) point to the strong feeling of gratitude a survivor feels toward the captor for sparing his or her life. Cooper (1976) explains:

> *Most experiences, particularly those of a prolonged character, reliably suggest the development of an empathy between the terrorist and the hostage victim. It is suggested by some that, in prolonged cases, a state of dependency develops between the hostage and his keeper, to the extent even of giving rise to serious ethical and identity problems on the part of the victim. (p. 236)*

While it is not clear what leads to the affective ties between victims and their victimizers in kidnapping or hostage-taking situations, two syndromes have been observed that describe the situation. These are the Stockholm Syndrome and the Hijackee Syndrome.

THE STOCKHOLM SYNDROME

The Stockholm Syndrome is used to describe the dramatic and unexpected realignment of affections, the positive bond between hostage and captor, and the feelings of distrust or hostility on the part of the victim toward authorities (Ochberg, 1978).

The term was coined after a Swedish incident in 1973. Following a bank hold up in Stockholm, two robbers held bank employees hostage in the bank's vault from August 23 to August 28. It was reported that an affective tie developed between one of the female hostages and one of the offenders. Following their release, the victims asked that mercy be shown toward the offenders. Although the Stockholm Syndrome does not always occur, it does not seem to be too infrequent. Similar affective reactions have been described in various kidnappings and hostage takings.

Ochberg (1978) suggests that the positive bonds do not form immediately, but are usually established by the third day. He pinpoints four factors which promote the Stockholm Syndrome: (1) intensity of the experience, (2) duration, (3) dependence of the hostage on the captor for survival and (4) distance of the hostage psychologically from authority.

THE HIJACKEE SYNDROME

The Hijackee Syndrome is a similar phenomenon. It is the experience of passengers on a hijacked plane, train, or bus who emerge from the experience with warm praise for the hijackers instead of reactions of rage, anger, and outrage. Dr. Hubbard, author of *The Skyjacker: His Flights of Fantasy*, said in an interview with *Time* magazine (*Time*, 1976) that hijackers cash in on widespread hostility to authority. Once air passengers believe they will not be killed, they can view their captors as dashing desperadoes lashing out against the establishment. Hubbard adds that sometimes victims also see the hijacking as a free ticket to adventure and personal publicity. Moreover, because the hijacker does not use all the force available to him, the passengers are grateful.

A similar opinion was expressed by psycholinguist Murray Miron (*Time*, 1976), who noted that a hijacker builds admiration through sheer menace. "Someone who holds your life in his hands rewards you every time he doesn't kill you." Even so little a reward as permitting the passengers to light up a cigarette or go to the bathroom forges a subtle link to the captors.

Psychiatrist Lawrence Freedman (*Time*, 1976) explains that the coalescing of the aggressors and hostages into a united group deploring the intransigence of outside authorities who refuse to meet the hijackers' demands is a manifestation of what Freudians call "identification with the aggressor," which refers to children's identification with a punitive parent-figure and their incorporation of his or her aggressive qualities.

Such an explanation, however, as Ochberg (1978) points out, ignores the fact that the hijackers' victims do not necessarily incorporate the violence of the hijackers. Ochberg leans more toward a hypothesis of gratitude:

> *It seems rather that hostages successfully deny the danger engineered by the terrorists. Having separated this from awareness, they are overwhelmingly grateful to the terrorists for giving them life. They focus on the captor's kindnesses, and not his acts of brutality. Intellectual appreciation of the terrorists' cause may be related to this irrational affection, but the relationship is not complete. That is, one can love a captor and not his or her cause, and vice versa. (pp. 161-162)*

The Need for a Theory of Victim Response

Most violent crimes involve a face-to-face confrontation between the victim and the offender. There is a brief, and much less frequently a prolonged, interaction, exchange, or verbal or nonverbal communication between the victim and offender.

The demands made by the victimizer and the actual violence or threats employed elicit specific responses from the victim. These responses vary enormously from victim to victim and from situation to situation depending on a host of individual and situational variables.

Despite the vital importance of the victim's response to the final outcome, only a few researchers have addressed the issue. Fewer still are those who have tried to establish the optimal response in offenses such as rape and robbery. And yet, a theory of victim response is essential if we are to be able to give potential victims sound advice as to how they can best extract themselves from a situation of confrontational victimization. For example, as Cook (1986) points out, one policy option for reducing robbery violence is to educate potential victims about how they should respond if confronted or assaulted by a robber. Cook adds that it is plausible that some of the serious injuries and deaths in robbery could be avoided if the victim behaved differently during the course of the crime.

To develop a theory of victim response, extensive empirical research is needed to find conclusive answers to the following six questions:

1. How do victims respond to specific types of face-to-face victimization? How do they react when confronted with one or more offenders?
2. Why do victims respond differently to identical or very similar types of attacks? What individual or situational variables are responsible for, or associated with, different types of response?
3. In what way does the victim's immediate reaction determine, shape, or influence the final outcome of the victimization event?
4. What types of response are most effective in thwarting the attack and in stopping the offense from being completed?
5. What types of response are most effective in avoiding physical injury and death?
6. What types of response result in the most and least psychological trauma to the victim?

Another research task is to develop a typology of responses and to establish the frequency, the determinants, and the correlates of each response.

A third research issue is to establish the criteria according to which the effectiveness of the response may be measured. How exactly can effectiveness be defined? If the person being mugged succeeds in keeping his or her money but suffers bodily harm, if the truck driver being held up manages to get away with the truck but is shot by the offender in the process, or if the female victim of rape is able to prevent penetration but sustains serious injury, then could these responses be classified as effective or successful?

Lorna Smith (1989), for example, is critical of the way "rape avoidance" was defined and operationalized in some studies. She notes, for example, that in the Bart and O'Brien study (1985) some of the women who defined themselves as "avoiders" had for brief moments, the assailant's penis in their vagina. Others were digitally penetrated or forced into oral sex. It seems that women forced into fellatio did consider themselves raped whilst those who were subject to cunnilingus regarded themselves as avoiders. Smith believes not all women would agree with such definitions as "avoidance of rape."

To define and measure the success or the effectiveness of the victim's reaction (particularly resistance) solely in terms of completion or noncompletion of the crime seems too restrictive. It overlooks other important dimensions of the victimization ordeal, for example, the duration of the episode. In general, the shorter the episode, the less suffering the victim goes through. The effectiveness of victim response may therefore be assessed not only in terms of its impact on completion or noncompletion, or on the avoidance or sustenance of injury, but also in relation to the duration of the ordeal. Certain responses are apt to prolong the duration of the victimization experience, while others can hasten its termination.

Success and effectiveness of the victim's response should also be measured in relation to the psychological impact of the ordeal. Every victimization, and this is particularly true of confrontational ones, leaves the victim with short-term, persistent, or even permanent emotional scars (Shapland, Willmore, and Duff, 1985; Mezey, 1988; Waller, 1989). Victims suffer psychological trauma manifested by anger, depression, fear, worry, anxiety, stress and distress, feelings of shame, embarrassment, guilt, humiliation, abandonment, enhanced sense of vulnerability, and so on. The traumatic effects depend, among other things, on the nature of the victimization, as well as a large number of individual, situational, and social variables. It is not unreasonable to expect that the way the victim responded to the attack would have an effect on the psychological outcome of the incident.[7] Feminist writers on rape (Swift, 1985) insist that victims who struggle, even when they do not succeed in stopping the rape from taking place, suffer less psychological trauma than those who offer no resistance to the attacker. This means that while victim resistance enhances the probability of physical injury, it may have beneficial psychological effects. This makes it extremely difficult to advise potential victims of sexual assaults as to what course of action they should take when finding themselves in a rape situation. In property victimization, on the other hand, sound advice based on empirical research findings is not to resist. As Wolfgang (1982) puts it, "So long as avoidance of physical injury has a higher value than protection of property, the victim should offer no resistance, whatever the form of intimidation." This advice is identical to the one offered by Hindelang, Gottfredson, and Garofalo (1978):

> *For the victim who is most concerned with reducing his or her risk of injury in theft related victimizations, the optimal strategy is clear: give up the property and refrain from attacking the offender. (p. 62)*

This advice, needless to say, does not imply any moral judgment on the desirability or appropriateness of resistance, struggle, or self-defense. It simply informs the potential victim of the dangers of resistance. The ultimate decision to resist or not to resist, to struggle or not to struggle, will always be one that the victim has to make.[8]

Summary

The study of victim-offender relationships, which received much attention from researchers in the early stages of victimology, is currently giving way to the study of victim-offender interactions. An analysis of these interactions is indispensable for understanding the dynamics of violent victimization and might facilitate the development of a dynamic theory of criminal behavior. This situational, interactionist approach analyzes various types of criminal victimization not as unilateral, one-sided behaviors, but as situational transactions. This is the case of face-to-face victimization where a brief or prolonged interaction between the victim and victimizer takes place. In such situations, the victim's response to the unwanted and usually unexpected victimization is, to a large extent, unpremeditated and unplanned. The spontaneity of the reaction is no doubt partially responsible for the extreme variations in victim responses to identical situations and to very similar victimization experiences. And the variety of victim responses is, in turn, responsible for the different outcomes of these confrontational victimizations. The outcome is also determined or conditioned by a large number of variables. The victim's sociodemographic characteristics are, for example, strongly associated with the probability of sustaining injury. Injury also varies by type of offense and is somewhat higher in rape than in robbery, aggravated assault, or simple assault.

Research on victim response to face-to-face victimization is still in an embryonic stage and has yet to solve a number of conceptual and methodological problems. It needs, among other things, to develop a typology of responses and adequate measures of the resistance level. One important data problem is the time sequence of resistance and response: the inability to establish on the basis of available data whether the use of force preceded the victim's resistance or was employed to overcome that resistance.

In an attempt to shed light on the dynamics of the victimization experience, we examined various correlates of victim response to face-to-face confrontation, namely age, sex, and race of the victim; presence or absence of a weapon; victim-offender relationship; time and location of the attack; the element of surprise; number of victims and victimizers; racial and gender homogeneity/heterogeneity; age difference between attacker and victim; the presence of alcohol and/or drugs; and the presence of others in the victimization situation. This was followed by a discussion of the impact victim resistance has on the completion of the crime. Several studies were reviewed, and they showed that victim resistance is the variable most strongly associated with the completion or noncompletion of the offense. There is also empirical evidence indicating a positive association between resistance and the frequency and seriousness of injury sustained by the victim.

While most victim-offender interactions are marked by anger, hostility, and antagonism, it has been observed in some incidents of kidnapping, hostage-taking, and aircraft hijacking that some victims react with a positive rather than a negative emotional response to the victimizer(s). It is not yet clear what leads to the development of these affective ties but two syndromes have been observed: the Stockholm Syndrome and the Hijackee Syndrome. All this highlights the need for a theory of victim response.

Part 3

Understanding Criminal Victimization

NINE

Victim/Target Selection

When asked how they choose their victims almost all respondents indicate two common sense principles which govern their selection. The victim of choice is one perceived by the mugger as unlikely to resist and likely to yield an acceptable payoff ... Most respondents also take some pride in their ability to spot such victims ... The mugger is influenced by two other kinds of factors while selecting his victim. The first, and most important, is the ***set of opportunities****—the particular range or array of potential victims likely to be encountered "on the stroll." The second is the* ***set of predispositions****—the attitudes which make a particular type of victim more or less emotionally acceptable as a target.*

Robert Lejeune (1977, pp. 134-135)

The Victimizer's Choice of Victim/Target

If victims of crime were chosen at random we would reasonably expect them to constitute an unbiased cross section of the entire population. It would also be reasonable to expect the risks as well as the rates of criminal victimization to be evenly divided within the general population. This, evidently, is not the case. The clustering of victimization in certain geographical areas and within certain groups suggests the presence of some crude or sophisticated selection processes. It seems reasonable to assume that criminals in general do not pick their victims or targets in a totally random, blind, or haphazard fashion. On the contrary, we have reasons to believe that many criminals, particularly those who commit property crime, white-collar crime, and similar types of profit-oriented offenses, are more or less rational operators who, most of the time, would go about selecting their victims/targets in a carefully considered, circumspect manner approaching rationality. In other words, they are reasoning criminals. A reasoning criminal would not pick a target totally at random and would not attack the first available victim. Professional criminals, for example, are known to carefully select their victims/targets. Selection, however, is not exclusive or limited to professional or semiprofessional criminals. To illustrate this point, Wilkins (1964) gives a simple example in his book *Social Deviance*:

> *Let any (non-criminal) reader try to imagine himself in the position of being required to commit a crime—say one of the most common crimes like larceny or breaking and entering—within the next twelve hours. Few readers would select the victim completely at random, unskilled at victim selection though they might be. There will be something approaching rationality in the selection of the victim. (p. 75)*

So what attracts a given offender to a specific victim? What exactly do criminals look for and consider when searching for a suitable target? How and why does an offender select a particular target from the wide array of available ones? What general or specific criteria are used in the selection process? These are important questions not only for understanding the offender's behavior but also for explaining the differential risks of victimization and for developing effective strategies and techniques of crime control and prevention. Despite their importance, these questions did not arouse, in the past, the interest of criminological researchers.[1] Today, the situation is somewhat better. The rational-choice perspective (Cornish and Clarke, 1986) has become a respectable approach in criminology, and there is a growing interest in conducting empirical investigations on how criminals choose their victims/targets in specific offenses, particularly rape (Chappell and James, 1986), burglary (Bennett and Wright, 1984; Maguire and Bennett, 1982), and robbery (Blazicek, 1985; Feeney, 1986; Wilson, 1987).

One pioneering study of victim selection in cases of murder for robbery was undertaken in the 1960s (Fattah, 1971). The study examined not only how the victims in this particular crime are chosen and the criteria used in the process, but also the specific moment at which the choice is made in the chronology of events leading to the crime. The analysis revealed two distinct categories of victims. The first are those specific, determined victims for whom there was no substitute. The murder could only have been committed against these "nonexchangeable victims." The second category comprised those truly selected or "exchangeable victims" whom the killer chose from many other potential targets, any of whom could have been victimized. The central idea underlying the study was rather simple: if the majority of crime victims are not chosen at random, then it is necessary to understand the criteria various types of criminals use in selecting their victims and to carefully analyze the selection process. Such knowledge is invaluable for both theory and practice. From a theoretical perspective, victim/target selection is an important aspect of the victimization phenomenon. It can tell us a great deal about why certain individuals or targets are more prone to victimization than others and why some are more popular as victims than others. It can shed light on why certain targets are more frequently victimized than others and why some are repeatedly victimized. In other words, it can make a significant contribution not only to the understanding of the differential risks of victimization, but also to phenomena such as recidivist victims or multiple victimization. In addition, insights gleaned from such knowledge, and analysis of the selection process and selection criteria, can be extremely useful in developing policies, strategies, and techniques of protection and prevention and for providing potential victims and vulnerable targets with helpful strategies as to how to avoid criminal victimization. To summarize, we may say that the way in which offenders perceive and select their victims/targets is of utmost importance to situational prevention and to the development of an explanatory theory of criminal victimization.

EXCHANGEABLE AND NONEXCHANGEABLE VICTIMS

A meaningful discussion of victim selection has to begin with a distinction between victims who are selected from among many others and those who are, in some way or another, fixed, determined, or pre-designated. In acts of expressive violence against the person as well as in some sexual offenses, such as incest, or violent crimes, such as infanticide, there is no real selection of the victim. The victim is "determined" and "specific," in the sense that the crime can only be committed against that particular person. No one else can constitute an adequate substitute. In such cases, the victim is not exchangeable. The so-called "crime of passion" exemplifies the concept of the "nonexchangeable victim." Here, the criminal's existential malaise is centered upon just one person who lives at a short distance and whom the criminal regards as symbolizing negative and malevolent values (Hesnard, 1963). In the potential killer's mind, only the death of this particular individual can provide a solution to the conflict and a way out of his or her predicament. It is easy to see that in such cases the assailant does not have a choice between different persons against whom to direct the pent-up aggression. The victim is designated beforehand. It is only this specific person at the center of the conflict and on whom the criminogenic situation revolves who can be victimized. In most cases of criminal homicide motivated by a strong passion, such as hatred, jealousy, envy, anger, or even pity, it is not a question of killing just anybody, but of killing a nonexchangeable person. Similarly, in murder for revenge, it is only the person, or a very close relative of that person, responsible for the injustices or injuries against which the killer is retaliating who can become the object of the vengeful reprisal. The same is true of homicides in the family, such as infanticide, filicide, patricide, and matricide. It is also true of many other types of killing, for example, killing the insured person to collect the money, disposing of a child to avoid the payment of alimony, shooting the policeman who is trying to arrest the fleeing robber, and killing an attacker in self-defense. All these examples illustrate well what we mean by nonexchangeable victims. They are cases in which there is *no* true victim selection.

"Exchangeable victims/targets" are different. Here the potential offender, such as a robber, mugger, burglar, rapist, car thief, or shoplifter, has a choice between a wide range of exchangeable victims/targets. When considered by the person planning the offense, some will appear more attractive, more suitable, and more accessible than others. The one to be chosen in preference, or to the exclusion of others is the one who, in the offender's point of view, is the most appropriate.

When the decision to commit the offense is made independently of a specific victim/target, the selected victim/target may be qualified as exchangeable. On the other hand, when the decision to perpetrate the crime is inextricably tied to a specific victim/target, the latter may be qualified as nonexchangeable.

Göppinger (1974) views the concept of victim exchangeability or nonexchangeability as one of great significance. He points out that the nonexchangeable victim is generally bound by a specific relationship to the offender, and it is this relationship that may cause, support, or shape the offense. He notes that the situation in such cases is very different from that more often encountered, namely, the criminal who wants to "do something" and who seeks or waits for a good opportunity. In the latter situations, the victim is generally exchangeable even if known to the delinquent. Göppinger, a psychiatrist, was interested in the implications of this distinction to clinical criminology.

As a general rule, we may say that acts of expressive violence are committed predominantly against nonexchangeable victims, while acts of instrumental violence are often committed against exchangeable victims. And whereas the majority of crimes against the person are directed toward nonexchangeable targets, most property offenses are directed toward exchangeable ones. However, the distinction between exchangeable and nonexchangeable victims/targets is not absolute. In some property crimes, such as burglary or robbery, committed on the spur of the moment to take advantage of a specific opportunity that presented itself, where there has been no prior planning nor search for a target, the target may be qualified as "nonexchangeable" in the sense that this particular offense was inspired by, and will be committed against, this specific target and none other. In other words, the target in the same type of crime may be exchangeable in some situations and nonexchangeable in others.

A good example of this is the case of victims in hitchhike rape. The rapist who deliberately searches for a female hitchhiker to attack is looking for an exchangeable victim. But the driver who picks up a hitchhiker without thoughts of rape and later decides to have sex with her, with or without her consent, is actually committing the crime against a nonexchangeable victim. The victim in this case is a nonexchangeable one because the idea of rape emerged in connection with this particular victim and because the act of rape in this specific situation could only be committed against her. In general, however, the concept of opportunity, as an explanatory concept, applies more, at least when used at a macro level, to crimes where the victims are usually exchangeable rather than to crimes where the victims are predominantly nonexchangeable. Concepts such as victim-provocation and victim-precipitation apply exclusively to nonexchangeable victims, whereas characteristics, such as attractiveness, vulnerability, proneness, accessibility, negligence, and carelessness, may apply to both exchangeable and nonexchangeable victims. These characteristics apply more often to the former than to the latter.

It should also be noted that the importance of the distinction between exchangeable and nonexchangeable victims/targets is not purely theoretical. The distinction has practical relevance. The likelihood of recidivism is much lower for those who offend against specific, nonexchangeable victims/targets than it is for those who commit their crimes against exchangeable victims/targets. The phenomenon of displacement applies mostly to crimes generally committed against exchangeable victims/targets. It hardly applies to offenses whose victims/targets are predominantly nonexchangeable.

The Process of Selection

It should be clear from the discussion on exchangeable and nonexchangeable victims/targets that when we talk about victim/target selection we are referring to exchangeable victims/targets and to crimes in which the offender makes a conscious, deliberate choice between different possible or potential victims/targets.

Offenders, even those who commit the same type of crime, such as rape, residential burglary, car theft, bank robbery, and mugging, exhibit wide variations in their *modus operandi*. One dimension of their manner of operating is victim/target selection. It would be stating the obvious to maintain that offenders differ in how they choose their victims, the types of targets they select, and the reasons for their personal preference for particular victims/targets over others. This, of course, does not mean that they can pick and choose as they please. Most of the time, their choice is severely constrained by a large number of factors, such as availability, accessibility, manageability, and urgency. Also, some offenders are more choosy than others, and certain situations offer more possibilities for selection than others. In other words, victim/target selection varies greatly according to the type of offender, offense, and situation. The degree of sophistication used in selecting the victim/target, the duration of the selection process, and the chronological order of the selection phase in the planning episode are also likely to vary from crime to crime, offender to offender, and situation to situation.

Some attempts have been recently made to identify the criteria some offenders use in choosing a particular victim/target and to develop theoretical models of victim/target selection. Most of these models focus on those attributes of the victim/target that might be of particular significance to certain groups of offenders (robbers, burglars, rapists) when making their choice.

One of the authors, Blazicek (1979) treats victim/target selection as a cognitive decision-making process and proposes a social psychological model of victim/target selection based upon interpersonal perception and risk taking. The perpetrator in this model is viewed as a rational operator who cognitively assesses and evaluates the crime opportunity situation. The perceptual model developed by Blazicek involves three major dimensions: (1) an evaluative dimension, (2) a potency dimension, and (3) a dynamism dimension. The evaluative dimension represents a general good/bad continuum of the "common sense psychology" of the perpetrator's perception and cognitive assessment of whether a particular individual is a likely victim/target risk. The potency dimension involves the cognitive evaluation by the perpetrator of any potential resistance a selected victim may offer and any action, by either the victim or bystander, that may prevent, prohibit, or impede the completion of the criminal act. The dynamism dimension, again based on a high/low continuum, includes the perceived likelihood that any assessed potency factor will indeed be carried out or implemented. Blazicek admits that his attempt to develop a theoretical model of victim/target selection is exploratory in nature and is only a first step toward the development of a more elaborate and more sophisticated model. The measurement of risk, assessed largely in terms of the likelihood of victim resistance, is the central focus of Blazicek's model. Future models will have to incorporate various additional dimensions and factors, other than risk, that determine or influence the selection of a specific victim or a given target.

While not attempting to develop a theoretical model of victim/target selection, some authors have identified and differentiated between various types of search for a suitable victim/target.

Bennett and Wright (1984) point out that opportunistic burglars whose offenses are precipitated might be inflexible in terms of target choice, whereas those who typically search for targets are probably the most flexible group in terms of target selection. However, few of the burglars they interviewed mentioned committing opportunistic crimes. This may have something to do with the composition of their sample, which represented the more experienced burglars both in terms of the number of offenses committed and their involvement in the criminal justice system. Most searched for a suitable target prior to committing a burglary. The nature of the search varied. The most discerning form of search revealed to Bennett and Wright involved traveling to a particular area containing the kind of target that the burglar found suitable. This usually meant traveling to "well-off" or "rich" areas in order to select from more lucrative targets. The second type of search revealed is a slightly less discriminating type than the first. It involved seeking out a suitable target from wherever the burglar happened to be when the decision to commit the crime was made. Bennett and Wright note that although the offenders in this group were less discriminating in terms of the area selected, they made a thorough assessment of potential targets. The least discriminating type of search Bennett and Wright encountered was conducted by offenders who cared little about either the type of area or the choice of target. Bennett and Wright also report that there are two main types of planned burglary. In the first, there is no time gap between the decision to offend and the selection of a target. In the second, there is a time gap between the decision to offend and the selection of a target. Offenses of this type occur when the decision to offend is made independently of the discovery of a target. It differs from the "search" type of burglary in that the offense is not committed immediately upon locating a suitable place to burgle.

A Swedish study of burglary, based on interviews with arrested offenders (Knutsson, 1984), reports that the crimes were generally unplanned. The perpetrators were in acute need of money—usually due to drug addiction—and decided to commit the crime. They then selected an area in which to operate. There they decided upon their target, a house or an apartment, which, after checking the situation, they broke into. Some of the burglars preferred detached houses, others went solely for apartments.

Like Bennett and Wright's research, the pattern revealed by this Swedish study (and probably by others) may have to do with the particular makeup of the sample used. Arrest rates are undoubtedly lower for well-planned and carefully executed burglaries than they are for those hastily decided upon and carried out right away. There is also little doubt that targets in the former category are more carefully chosen than those in the latter one. It is to be expected, therefore, that studies using samples of arrested or convicted offenders would yield a high percentage of unplanned burglaries and would reveal less sophisticated patterns of target selection than those meticulously planned. Or to put it differently, samples of arrested and convicted offenders are likely to contain a high number of unskilled burglars, and would, therefore, reveal different and less discriminating methods of target selection than samples composed largely of skilled burglars. Skilled burglars presumably invest considerable effort in locating profitable targets—sometimes traveling considerable distances. The less skilled, in contrast, are more likely to tackle available targets indiscriminately (Hough, 1987).

One predatory offense usually committed without long or elaborate planning is mugging. Unlike bank robbery, some burglaries, and other more skilled utilitarian crimes (crimes committed for profit or financial gain), mugging is usually planned immediately prior to its occurrence (Lejeune, 1977). According to Lejeune, in some cases, conception, execution, and completion occur in a matter of seconds. At another extreme the likely victim is observed over a period of weeks, and the actual confrontation follows a plan of action based on observation of the behavior and schedule of the prospective victim. Lejeune points out, however, that most typically a mugging, from conception to completion, occurs within the time span of a few minutes. Lejeune's analysis of the different phases of mugging is fascinating and enlightening. In the preparatory phase, the pre-confrontational phase, the mugger mobilizes for the confrontation with the victim. This is accomplished by managing his or her own fear and by selecting an appropriate victim. The mugger manages the fear in two ways: (1) by changing the *definition* of the situation from one of high risk to one of low risk, and (2) by attempting to *control* the elements in the mugging situation in ways that are judged to reduce risks. Lejeune (1977) describes this as follows:

> *In the first instance he reduces his fear largely by lowering his subjective estimate of the risks and by raising his estimate of his ability to handle the situation. In the second, he seeks out ways to minimize his risk, e.g., by the selection of the most vulnerable victims. (p. 130)*

Lejeune suggests that of all the possible sources of danger and causes of fear, such as police, witnesses, and the victim, uniformly it is the victim that is perceived as potentially the least predictable and least controllable threat. Thus, when the mugger walks casually in search of prey, much of his or her attention and concern is directed toward the selection of the "right" victim.

WHO IS THE "RIGHT" VICTIM?

Mugging

When Lejeune (1977) asked the muggers how they choose their victims, almost all indicated two common sense principles that governed their selection. The victim of choice is one perceived by the mugger as unlikely to resist and likely to yield an acceptable payoff. Lejeune (1977) writes:

> *Most respondents also take some pride in their ability to spot such victims; those who are weak (the lames) and those who foolishly flash their money in public (the chumps). There is, however, limited consensus on the specific characteristics of such targets; respondents do not share any clearly formulated set of rules or indicators for implementing the selection of the "right" victim.*

For example, some will see women or old people as ideal "lames"; others will disagree and prefer middle-aged or young men. In each case it is claimed that the preferred type of victim is less likely to resist. (p. 134)

Lejeune adds that while almost all respondents justify their victims in terms of the anticipated vulnerability and/or lucrativeness of the victim, such statements may only represent rationalizations for actions determined mostly by impulse and circumstances.

Rape

In a clinical study of rapists, Selkin (1975) discovered a fairly consistent pattern of victim selection. Two factors seemed to guide the choice of victims: availability and vulnerability. Chappell and James (1986) conducted extensive interviews with fifty convicted and incarcerated rapists who were indeterminately committed to Atascadero State Hospital, a maximum security mental institution in California for the treatment of mentally disordered sex offenders. Although the respondents showed a marked preference for attacking women who were total strangers to them, they did not in the main, select their victims at random. It was obvious that most of the rapists in the group had some notion of the "type of woman" they wished to rape, as well as a reasonably firm idea about the most suitable location at which to identify and apprehend such a person. When subjects were asked if they selected a victim who reminded them of someone else, the majority (58 percent) said no; 20 percent said they looked for someone who reminded them of their girlfriend; 18 percent, their wife, and 4 percent, their mother. When questioned in more detail about their victim preferences, the composite of the description they provided resembles the "American dream woman"—a nice, friendly, young, pretty, middle-class white female. The age of the victim preferred by the rapists ranged from fourteen to forty-five and the preferred height ranged from five feet two inches to six feet. Not unexpectedly, the respondents gave a profile of their actual victim that was in accord with their desired victim preference.

Blackmail

Hepworth's study of blackmailers in England (1975) was based not on interviews with blackmailers but on an analysis of judicial files. He found that blackmailers are, above all, selective—primarily in terms of their everyday social relations with those who become defined as victims. He adds that secondhand insight into the processes making for the selectivity of their actions can be gleaned by taking into account the social assumptions permeating various justificatory statements put forward over time. Some blackmailers, for instance, chose their victims from socially stigmatized groups, such as homosexuals. In one particular case, the blackmailer drew his victims entirely from what he called "the homosexual trade." He got homosexual men into compromising situations with a number of goodlooking youths he had on his payroll. Then, posing as their irate father or guardian he demanded money to send the boy away at great expense "to start a new life."

Professional Confidence Games

Sutherland's (1937) account of a professional thief in his biography, *The Professional Thief*, provides an excellent profile of the right victim in con games—a dishonest sucker who is preferably away from his hometown. Sutherland's thief insists that the central principle in all true con rackets is to show suckers how they can make some money by dishonest methods and then beat them in their attempted dishonesty. Sutherland (1937) points out:

> *In the confidence games the principle is the same—beat a man who is trying to do something dishonest. It is impossible to beat an honest man in a confidence game. (p. 69)*

Sutherland quotes another professional confidence man who, upon reading the manuscript of *The Professional Thief* heartily concurred with the statement that if there was no larceny in a man and if he was not trying to get something for nothing and rob a fellow man, it would be impossible to beat him at any real con-racket. A third confidence man cited by Sutherland confirmed that a confidence game will fail absolutely unless the sucker has got larceny in his soul. He adds (Sutherland, 1937):

> *One of the first questions asked of a prospective sucker after the buildup is developed is "Have you larceny in your soul?" This question is asked outright and a "yes" or "no" answer is necessary. If he answers "no" and the mob believes he is telling the truth he is dropped immediately. If he answers "yes" they can go on with him. (p. 69)*

Sutherland provides additional victim characteristics that professional confidence men look for in their prospects. Bankers, for example, are considered very good prospects. The reason is that they engage in a lot of speculative business and anyone who speculates is viewed as a good prospect. One confidence man declared the following (Sutherland, 1937):

> *Of course, we select our prospects ... We try to find someone who is living beyond his means, who has social ambitions, or whose wife has social ambitions which are beyond their income. The banker who is speculating is probably short in his accounts already, and a chance at a big profit will generally appeal to him as a way out of his difficulties. (p. 70)*

Choosing a dishonest victim provides additional safety to the con-rackets. As the victim has attempted to do something dishonest and been beaten at it, he is not usually in a position to make a complaint (Sutherland, 1937, p. 73).

Stock Fraud

Doctors are considered "prime suckers" by high-scheming swindlers and stock-fraud artists. According to an article in the *Wall Street Journal* (Bilking, 1970), sometimes all it takes is a single phone call to obtain sizable sums of money from a doctor. After relating several actual cases in which doctors were easily swindled by means of one or two telephone calls, the article offers some explanations for doctors' easy gullibility. The article suggests that doctors are high-income earners with plenty of cash on their hands but with little time to devote to studying investment opportunities. Many regularly work twelve- to fourteen-hour days. Furthermore, many doctors aren't psychologically disposed to seek competent investment advice. They are used to giving advice—not taking it—and become convinced of their omnipotence early in practice, because they are constantly called upon to play God with patients in life-and-death situations. All this renders them ideal victims for unscrupulous manipulators and swindlers of all kinds. It is not surprising that they are besieged by promoters with all types of investment schemes—many of dubious value. An S.E.C. official (Bilking, 1970) observed:

> *Doctors are sitting ducks. After all, they are the most identifiable high-income group around, and they are all listed right in the Yellow Pages of the phone book.*

Another S.E.C. official insisted that doctors are invariably among the victims in most stock fraud cases. However, doctors, like many other embarrassed investors, usually take their loss quietly and refrain from reporting it to the authorities. Occasionally, some cases come out in the open. Such is the case reported by Associated Press (the *Montreal Star*, 1973) of three Toronto men jailed in the United States on federal charges of mail fraud in an alleged scheme to sell $10 million worth of AT & T stock to Detroit doctors at cut-rate prices.

Doctors are also prime targets for other types of offenses, as they are likely to have money or narcotics in their homes or offices. An article in the *Montreal Star* newspaper (Kitchen, 1973) reports on a spot check of 227 family physicians and internists by *Medical Times*, a leading medical journal, which turned up seven who had been personally assaulted or were the victims of armed robbery. Sixty-four had been burglar victims 173 times in the preceding two or three years, while one doctor reported more than six burglaries over the previous five years.

Many con-artists specialize in bilking the affluent investor. One such artist is Tony Foster, who, the police estimate, took close to $4 million from businessmen in London, Ontario, during a five-year period. An article in *Weekend Magazine*

(Alderman, 1979) provides details of some of Foster's scams. The article relates how pillars of the business community thrust money at him, in cash and without a receipt, begging Foster—whom half an hour ago they'd never heard of—to invest for them in hot diamonds from Amsterdam, municipal bonds purchased from the Mafia, jet fighter planes for the Pakistanis, and, Tony's favorite, gold bullion to be smuggled out of Brazil and sold to the Arabs. According to Tom Alderman, the author of the article, Tony Foster always asked his victims what they could afford to lose, and he wouldn't let them get in any deeper than that. One of the benefits of such a policy was that it reduced the outrage of those who could absorb their losses as they tended to be more philosophical.

All these examples, covering a wide range of offenses, provide ample evidence confirming that (1) many criminals carefully choose their victims, and (2) some victims/targets are more vulnerable, more attractive, and easier to victimize than others.

Methodological Problems of Research on Victim/Target Selection

While there are problems and limitations in the few existing studies of victim/target selection we will now cautiously proceed to examine the factors that seem to play an important role in the process and influence the offender's decision to attack a given victim/target. It must be reiterated, however, that research in this relatively new area of victim/target selection is still in a very early developmental stage. One can only speculate on the reasons for the underresearching of such a relevant and fascinating topic.

One reason is that, as interesting and as exciting as the study of the offenders' choices of victims/targets may be, it is not easy to conduct. It is not surprising, therefore, that the few studies, which tried to explore this new territory, suffer from methodological problems of varying seriousness, which limit the ability to generalize and, hence, utilize the findings. The major problems have to do with the samples and the techniques used to gather the information. The nature of the information sought generally dictates the best way of obtaining it. Since the purpose of victim/target selection research is to explore offenders' thought and decision-making processes, there seems to be little else to do except to ask them about these processes. This is precisely what most researchers did (Bennett and Wright, 1984; Blazicek, 1985; Wilson, 1987; Wright and Logie, 1988). The distinct preference of researchers for the interview method does not mean that it is the only possible technique. We may learn quite a lot about offenders' preferences, choices, and decisions by studying, analyzing, and comparing actual victims and targets. We may compare houses that are burgled to houses that are not, banks that are held up to banks never victimized, and we may gain insight into what burglars or robbers look for or prefer in a target. We can gain some understanding of how offenders select their targets/victims by analyzing the characteristics of stolen cars, of houses and apartments broken into, of individuals mugged, raped, swindled, and so on.

Severe limitations of the traditional interview method led some researchers to add some innovative experimental techniques. Bennett and Wright (1984), for example, used three different methods, each designed to explore a different aspect of offenders' victim/target selections. The first method involved showing a video recording of houses to a sample of convicted burglars. The subjects were asked to assess each house as a potential target and to state whether they would break into it if they were looking for a house to burgle. The other two experiments involved showing photographs of various aspects of houses to samples of burglars in an attempt to identify the wide range of factors that seemed to affect their choice of targets and to assess the relative importance of these factors.

Despite the variety of techniques used, research on victim and target selection suffers from a host of practical and methodological problems. The first series of problems have to do with sampling. Whether researchers decide to use as subjects incarcerated offenders or offenders at large, their decisions inevitably result in unrepresentative and biased samples. The covert nature of criminal activities, the confidentiality of agency files, and the difficulty of penetrating criminal networks all make the task of identifying and contacting criminals and ex-criminals a hard one (Cornish and Clarke, 1986). Due to the formidable problems of identifying and contacting those offenders who have not been arrested and convicted, as well as those who have been released, the studies are usually limited to those who are serving prison sentences in penal institutions. The representativeness of the samples, even when selected at random from all inmates fitting the criteria of the study, is thus highly questionable. The lack of representativeness is compounded by the attrition in the sample: those released or transferred before being interviewed, those unwilling to cooperate, those who are kept in total segregation, and so on. In Wilson's study of convicted robbers in Canadian penitentiaries (1987) the attrition reduced the original sample of 224 robbers to only one-third (74 robbers) with no less than 81 robbers (36 percent) declining to be interviewed. This manifest lack of cooperation on the part of many is quite understandable. What would motivate convicted or nonconvicted robbers, burglars, or rapists to agree to be interviewed? Why would they be willing to divulge their inner thoughts, secrets, and *modus operandi* to a researcher or an interviewer? What do they stand to gain by collaborating in the study? Nothing! On the contrary, it is the motives of those who willingly agree to participate that may be suspect. And whenever the motives are suspect, the accuracy and veracity of the information provided are questionable. How much confidence one can have in information gathered by means of interviews with incarcerated offenders is difficult to tell, since it is extremely difficult to check the accuracy of such information. Even when the subjects are truthful and sincere, they might not be able to articulate their thoughts.

Walsh (1986) decided to use captive offenders rather than those at liberty because of the twin difficulties with the latter of obtaining sufficient numbers and sufficient privacy for realistic interviews free of audience effect. Walsh lists a number of problems attached to using either group: (1) potential unrepresentativeness of the subjects; (2) subject response difficulties such as that of coherently summarizing complex, and possibly emotional, events, and the possibility of substantially different accounts being given to different interviewers; (3) recall problems in discussion of past events such as condensing, distorting, and rationalizing; (4) reticence concerning disclosure of trade secrets; (5) deliberate use of deceit; and (6) problems of analyzing the nature of patterns perceived in such data.

Hough's (1987) summary of the research problems common to this type of research echos many of the problems mentioned above. He too stresses the researchers' difficulties in obtaining adequate samples of offenders. Most of the samples are likely to overrepresent high-rate offenders or unskilled offenders and to yield cohorts at specific stages in their progression through the hierarchy of penalties. He adds that many of the subjects are unlikely to be especially introspective, articulate, or even accurate about decisions they took sometimes on impulse, sometimes when under the influence of alcohol or other drugs, sometimes in the distant past, and always in circumstances very different from those of the interview. As a final point Hough adds that an unknown proportion of respondents will be disingenuous or downright dishonest by amplifying their professionalism and skills and minimizing the hurt they caused. As an alternative source of information on victim/target selection, Hough suggests interviewing the victims themselves. He believes that victimization surveys can tell us a lot about the sorts of people chosen by offenders as victims. Using the findings on burglary of the British Crime Survey, Hough offers a conceptual framework for examining victim/target selection. The suggested framework focuses on three key elements: proximity to offenders, potential yield, and accessibility.

Victim/Target Selection: A Tentative Synthesis

The number of studies devoted to victim/target selection in predatory crime is quite small, consisting of only about a dozen. Although the offenses studied, the variables examined, and the models that emerged vary, and although the findings reported are by no means uniform, we will try to use these disparate findings to develop a tentative synthesis of the factors that seem to influence the choice of a particular victim or target. Factors identified by the different researchers may be grouped under five broad categories: proximity, accessibility, attractiveness, manageability, and the degree of risk the victim/target represents for the offender. The classification of some variables under one category or another is arbitrary, as they could easily fit under more than a single category. Proximity has to do with the offender's awareness of, and familiarity with, the victim or target. Accessibility has to do with the feasibility of the criminal plan. Attractiveness refers to, in crimes committed for financial gain, the lucrativeness of the target and the potential reward the offender can expect. In sexual crimes, attractiveness can refer to the physical characteristics of the victim. Attractiveness, however, as will be explained, can also refer to other aspects of the victim/target. Manageability has to do with the offender's ability to control and overcome the potential resistance of the victim/target. The final category refers to the offender's perception and assessment of the potential risks associated with victimizing the particular victim/target. The relative importance of each category, of the variables within the different categories, and of the weight assigned to each variable or category in the choice of a particular victim/target, vary from offense to offense, from offender to offender, and from incident to incident.

PROXIMITY

Territoriality is a key concept in people's normal and deviant behavior. It is, therefore, only natural to expect it to be an important influence in target or victim selection. Angel (1968) insists that offenders and potential offenders cling to areas in which they can function inconspicuously and feel secure and in which they have enough knowledge to make a fast and efficient escape. The inclusion of the factors of territoriality, proximity, and mobility in any explanatory model of victim/target selection is necessary because there is substantial evidence available confirming that patterns of criminal activity are related to the distances that separate offenders from victim/target opportunities (Costanzo et al., 1986).

Physical proximity to the victim is a necessary ingredient in many crimes. Sexual offenses, with few exceptions, such as exhibitionism, peeping, and obscene phone calls, require physical contact with the victim. Offenses against the person, such as homicide or assault, cannot be committed at a distance unless a firearm, an explosive, an incendiary device, or a poison is used. But how important is geographical proximity as a target selection variable in offenses involving a spatial decision and an optional choice of location, such as burglary or robbery? We have already touched upon proximity in the explanations of the homogeneity of the victim and offender populations (see Chapter 5). Here it will be discussed as a factor in victim/target selection.

Offenders' spatial behavior and their criminal mobility have been subjected to empirical investigations in recent years. Several of these studies have been reviewed by McIver (1981). Other reviews include those by Phillips (1980) and by Rhodes and Conly (1981). More recent studies include those done by Costanzo et al. (1986) and LeBeau (1987). These studies have focused on such factors as the criminals' cognition of their environments, "mental maps" and cognitive representation, criminal action-space, journey to commit a crime, and distance-decay pattern in the length of the journey to commit a crime. On the basis of these studies it seems well established that most criminals do not travel long distances to commit their crimes. Another consistent finding is that offenders travel longer distances to commit crimes against property when compared to the distances traversed by those who commit crimes against people (LeBeau, 1987). The journey to commit a crime may even vary for different types of the same offense. Curtis (1974) found that armed robbers traveled proportionately longer distances to their targets than unarmed robbers. Muggers, on the other hand, seem to pick their victims in their immediate environments. Lejeune (1977) suggests that muggers, unlike professional robbers, are usually either too young or down-and-out to own cars. They may use public transportation to seek out victims, both in transit and in distant neighborhoods. Yet, according to Lejeune, the mugging typically takes place within walking distance of the "hangout," where alleyways, rooftops, parks, and other escape routes and hiding places are well known.

Proximity also seems to be a key factor determining the choice of target for most burglars. Based on the geographical distribution of the offenses covered by the British Crime Survey, Hough (1987) discovered that the explanatory power of area variables, such as proximity, outstrips that of others, such as potential yield or accessibility, for crimes such as burglary.

Why does proximity play a preponderant role in target selection? The answer seems to lie in three interrelated factors: awareness, familiarity, and confidence.

Awareness

To choose a target, a criminal has to be aware of its existence. Burglars, for example, cannot commit their crime unless they are aware of a location that provides an opportunity for burglary. This location is contained within the criminal's "awareness space" (Rengert and Wasilchick, 1985). Rengert and Wasilchick define this awareness space as "the set of all places about which the criminal has some knowledge ... it is a subset of the total regional environment" (p. 55). They point out that the awareness space of a burglar contains places of varying usefulness for criminal exploitation. The potential burglar does not consider all places within this awareness space; only the ones that are above a threshold or "breakeven" level of expectation for profitability and probability of success are considered. The awareness space is then reduced to a "search space," and this is further reduced to the "criminal activity space." The process is explained by Rengert and Wasilchick (1985) as follows:

> *The places that are above the threshold of profitability and safety form the criminal's "search space." The search space is a further subset of the criminal's awareness space. At each step, the field of potential areas for burglary become fewer. Finally, within the criminal's search space is an area considered best or most comfortable for criminal activity. This chosen area is termed "criminal activity space." It is the area actually exploited by the criminal. (p. 55)*

Familiarity

Proximity in most cases means greater familiarity with the area and with the victim/target. In Wilson's (1987) study, some robbers stated that their choice of one target over another in the same category, such as financial institutions or jewelry stores, was influenced by their familiarity with the area in which the target was located. This knowledge, they felt, enhanced their chances of making a successful escape from the scene of the robbery. Many robbers also cited their familiarity with the specific target they robbed as an important selection criterion. Such familiarity, they observed, reduced the likelihood of surprises during the robbery.

Feelings of Safety and Security

Familiarity is generally associated with feelings of safety and security. People are likely to feel safer in areas they know well than in areas with which they are not familiar. And offenders are likely to feel more confident attacking a target that is familiar to them than one that is totally unfamiliar. A Vancouver city detective told Wilson (1987): "Criminals are funny people, they really like to be on their own turf. Unfamiliar turf turns them off." Another detective added, "There is one thing about robbers. They like areas they know. They feel comfortable there because they know every possible escape route and hiding place" (p. 252). Maguire and Bennett (1982) report that even when traveling by car to other towns, many burglars were reluctant to venture into totally unknown territory. They cite one burglar who said the following (Maguire and Bennett, 1982):

> *I stay within my own area. I never go more than about 20 miles from home. It makes me feel secure because I know all the little roads to get back home if I'm in trouble. (p. 82)*

ATTRACTIVENESS

Victim/target attractiveness is a very relative and subjective selection criterion. The extremely diverse nature of crimes committed against victims and targets means that the appealing features will vary from one type of offense to another. Assessment of victim/target attractiveness is also a subjective exercise in that what may be a highly attractive victim/target for one offender may be totally unappealing to another. In general, however, victim/target attractiveness for any given offender is determined by weighing the positive versus the negative features of that particular victim/target and the potential rewards against the perceived risks.

Profitability and lucrativeness are, no doubt, primary considerations in judging target attractiveness in crimes motivated by financial gain. While for sex offenders, physical attractiveness and other personal characteristics of the victim might be important factors in determining the person's appeal. The personal characteristics of the victim can also be important decision-making criteria in certain predatory offenses, such as mugging, blackmailing, or extortion. For these offenses, and many others, certain potential victims may be judged unattractive because they possess certain traits that render them "inappropriate" for victimization. Whereas others, due to certain negative qualities that may facilitate the neutralization process, are considered legitimate and, hence, attractive victims (see Chapter 6).

Lucrativeness/Profitability

Wilson's study of convicted robbers incarcerated in the West Coast region of Canada (1987) revealed definite opinions as to which targets are the most attractive and which ones are the least appealing. It was clear from the subjects' statements that not all commercial establishments are perceived as equally attractive. Among those who had a general preference for commercial targets over other target types, a majority (61.7 percent) expressed a predilection for financial institutions. Supermarkets and armored cars camc second and third respectively, while liquor stores, hotels or motels, and small retail stores ranked seventh, eighth, and ninth on the preference list. The attraction of financial institutions was related not only to the potentially high payoff, but also to the fact that the money is liquid and handy. Recent precautions requiring bank tellers to keep only small amounts of cash in their tills were deplored by some of the robbers interviewed. Department stores were considered less attractive as targets than financial institutions because most customers pay for their purchases with checks or credit cards. That the money is not centrally located was mentioned as another drawback. Collecting the money from different cashiers dispersed throughout the department store was held to be time consuming and, therefore, too risky.

Potential yield seems to be a selection consideration in burglary as well. Burglars in Bennett and Wright's study (1984) made assumptions, on the basis of cues relating to the house, garden, and immediate area, about the wealth of the occupants and the likelihood of cash and goods being in the house. Houses that looked as if little attention had been paid to them were generally disliked. Another factor cited was whether the house was owned by the local council. For many of the burglars interviewed, council houses represented poverty and, hence, were unattractive.[2]

As most of the empirical investigations done till now have used unrepresentative samples of robbers and burglars, it is not yet possible to assess the real importance of lucrativeness and potential payoff in target selection. The distinct preference expressed by burglars in the Bennett and Wright study (1984) is somewhat incongruent with what most victimization surveys reveal. Hough (1987), for example, suggests that data from the British Crime Survey show that burglars select poor homes no less often than homes owned by those with average income, though affluent households did seem to be more at risk than others.

Affluence, profitability, and potential yield are also selection criteria in property offenses other than robbery and burglary. Inciardi (1974) affirms that professional pickpockets seek only those victims who appear to have money enough to make the theft worthwhile. The ability to select the proper victim is, for them, an occupational intuition and is based upon many years of experience.

Personal Characteristics of Victims of Robbery and Mugging

Reported findings on the importance of the victim's personal attributes to being chosen as a robbery victim are also somewhat inconsistent. In an attempt to assess the relative importance of different criteria to the offender's choice of victim, Blazicek (1985) conducted structured interviews with sixty-four robbers at a United States maximum security prison. He examined four dimensions of the robbery situation: (1) personal characteristics of the victim; (2) the place of the offense; (3) the environment of the offense; and (4) the planning of the offense. The information provided by the robbers suggested that the various personal attributes of the victim, such as age, race, gender, body build, and physical condition, are of little importance to victim selection. This conclusion is corroborated by Wilson (1987) who also discovered that the personal traits of the victim do not play a crucial role in the selection process. He reported that even though certain groups are disproportionately victimized by robbery, personal attributes are not terribly important from the offender's point of view.

In contrast to these findings, Lejeune's (1977) study of mugging attributes more significance to the victim's personal characteristics. The contrast might be due to the difference in the composition of the samples, as there were few muggers in Wilson's (1987) group. Muggers, according to Lejeune, hold certain attitudes that make a particular victim more or less emotionally acceptable as a victim. This set of predispositions, which guide the selection of the victim, includes a variety of personal inclinations, prejudices, and antipathies, as well as group-held values and attitudes. Lejeune (1977) suggests:

> *In practice such predispositions are not unimportant, but they appear to play only a secondary role in the selection process when compared to the more vital concerns of reducing personal risks and of locating a victim within the usually limited temporal and spatial scope of the stroll. Thus, for example, while the predisposition to mug men rather than women is verbalized by most respondents, this preference is easily eroded in the attempt to select the most accessible or vulnerable target. (p. 135)*

Lejeune (1977) adds that any visible or imagined characteristic of potential victims toward which the mugger is predisposed to feel contempt or hostility is likely to create a situation of opportunity as well as to facilitate the mugger's neutralization through denial (see Chapter 6):

> *Thus, for example, homosexuals and drunks, either sought out or happened upon by chance, are both favorite and frequent targets, and most likely to be seen as deserving of victimization. The fact that they are also accessible where those who may mug hang out, can easily be "set up," and are perceived as less likely to resist or report their victimization to the police, further increases their vulnerability. (p. 136)*

ACCESSIBILITY

Another seemingly important criterion in victim/target selection is accessibility. A victim/target attractive in some respects may be available but is, for one reason or another, inaccessible or difficult to reach. Hence, it is reasonable to assume that the ease with which the potential offender can have access to the victim/target will contribute to the overall assessment of the victim/target as a "good" or a "bad" one. Accessibility may thus be considered an attractiveness feature, since readily accessible victims/targets are obviously more attractive, other things being equal, than those to which access is limited, difficult, or too problematic.

Accessibility is a recurring theme in studies on victim/target selection. It is one of the concepts Angel (1968) uses to explain high-crime environments. One of the behavioral characteristics of offenders and potential offenders cited by Angel is that they cling to areas that are easily accessed from areas of criminal habitation. Rengert (1972), quoted by Brantingham and Brantingham (1984), found that opportunities, risks (relative to police efficiency), familiarity, and the accessibility of various areas in Philadelphia could explain or describe 73 percent of the variance in the distribution of the crimes studied.

Many crimes, such as violent offenses, sex offenses, and property offenses, can largely be explained in terms of accessibility of the victim/target. Goode (1969) offered accessibility as an explanation for domestic violence and it is an important variable in incest as well as in hitchhike rape. Taxi drivers are readily accessible targets, as the nature of their occupation requires them to allow strangers into their vehicles and to drive them to any destination the stranger chooses. The same applies to prostitutes, who are forced by the nature of their profession to accompany clients, and those pretending to be clients, to hotel rooms and other private places in the intimacy of which they are extremely vulnerable and completely unprotected. The marketing strategy used by department stores is to encourage impulse buying through an attractive display of goods and by making it possible and tempting for the customer to physically touch, handle, and examine the merchandise. Making the goods accessible to customers also means making them accessible to potential shoplifters. Target accessibility is an equally important consideration in both burglary and robbery.

We may distinguish between "physical accessibility," such as the amount and level of restrictions placed in the way of those who want to gain unauthorized entry to the target, and "temporal accessibility," that is, the length of time during which the target is readily accessible to the potential robber. Targets such as convenience stores, gas stations, and fast-food outlets, which are open twenty-four hours a day, are more temporally accessible than commercial establishments, which open only for limited business hours. Two aspects of physical accessibility that seem particularly relevant to target selection are the site (geographical location) and the physical layout.

Temporal Accessibility

Most commercial establishments limit their business to certain hours and close on Sundays or on weekends. By so doing they become inaccessible to potential robbers. A robber who wants to commit a holdup late at night is restricted to a choice of targets that are open late or twenty-four hours a day. The extended hours of operation allow the robber greater flexibility in timing the offense and make it possible to attack only when the robber feels the time is right. In Wilson's (1987) study of convicted robbers, financial establishments, such as banks and credit unions, were considered to have very limited temporal accessibility. Several robbers stated that the relatively short operating hours of the banks and the fact that they close in the afternoon meant that any robbery has to be perpetrated during the daylight hours; a prospect they did not particularly like.

Physical Accessibility

The limited temporal accessibility of most commercial establishments is in contrast to their easy physical accessibility. Robbers of commercial establishments interviewed by Wilson (1987) appreciated the ease with which they could enter and exit financial institutions. Such free access enables the robber to be fast and efficient. Jewelry stores, drug stores, liquor stores, and gas stations were also considered "easy-access" targets. Residential targets were viewed negatively because of their restricted access. Not only must the robber find an excuse or pretence to gain access, but some unpleasant surprises might also be encountered.

Because of the different nature of robbery and burglary, ease of access is a more important selection criterion in the latter than in the former. Thus, in Reppetto's (1974) study of residential burglary, accessibility proved to be the primary consideration. Close to half the subjects (44 percent) cited it as the reason for their choice of a particular target. Other studies of burglars (Maguire and Bennett, 1982; Scarr, 1973; Bennett and Wright, 1984) report similar findings. The Bennett and Wright study analyzed burglars' comments related to whether the offender could get into the dwelling. The statements were mainly nonspecific and related to the general ease or difficulty of entering a particular building. Other comments concerned either the nature or condition of the windows or doors. In this context, the size of the windows was often mentioned as affecting the ease of entry. Small windows were usually preferred to larger ones because they were easier to break or open. Judgments about doors usually concerned their strength or the quality of the locks.

Location

In many cases, the geographical location of the target is closely linked to its accessibility to the burglar or the robber. We have already discussed the distance the potential offender has to travel to reach the target. In addition to the target's proximity or distance, other features can increase the target's attractiveness and accessibility. Bevis and Nutter (1977), cited by Rengert and Wasilchick (1985), found that residential burglary victimization is closely related to the degree of access afforded by street design. Streets that are easiest to drive through (not into) are the streets that burglars chose as burglary sites. Burglary rates were higher on a cross street than in a cul-de-sac. Rengert and Wasilchick discovered that houses within a block or two of a major highway are more likely to be selected as burglary targets than houses farther away. They concluded that burglars do not want to travel farther from a familiar highway than is necessary to locate a good site to burgle.

Some of Wilson's (1987) robbers sought targets in close proximity to an underground parking lot, where they could discreetly leave their get-away car; adjacent to alleys, where the vehicle could be left out of sight; or situated on corners, which offer a number of alternative escape routes. These same features seem to appeal to burglars. Walsh (1980) reports that 44 percent of the burgled houses in his study had passages, alleyways, or footpaths abutting or adjoining the property. In another study, Walsh (1986) detected a marked preference among the robbers of commercial establishments he interviewed for edge as opposed to center targets. This confirms the findings of Brantingham and Brantingham (1975). Maguire and Bennett (1982), whose study was limited to burglary in a dwelling, noticed that corner properties were favored because they offered at least three escape routes.

Layout

One aspect of the physical layout considered by the robbers in Wilson's study (1987) is the number of entrances and exits. Multiple entries and exits present an advantage to the robber, who is not restricted to coming and going through a single opening. They also provide more than one escape route should something go wrong during the robbery. Banks with one set of entry doors, were preferred to those with two sets. Robbers also preferred targets that provide only limited visibility to the external viewer or passerby. Tinted windows, blinds, screens, other window coverings, and large advertisements stuck to the windows prevent those on the outside from seeing what is taking place on the inside. Another aspect of the physical layout deemed important by the robbers was the location of the money. Some robbers admitted to Wilson that certain commercial establishments, such as liquor stores and convenience stores, have the tills or the safe directly adjacent or in close proximity to the front doors of the building. This allows swift access to the money and reduces the risk of apprehension. Department stores, on the other hand, usually keep the money in a financial office located on the top floor, thus making it difficult for the robber to escape with the loot.

Residential burglars find it an advantage to be able to get to the rear of the property. This explains their preference for dwellings with easy rear-access. Bennett and Wright (1984) found terraced houses to be frequently disliked because of the difficulty of obtaining access to the rear. Detached houses, on the other hand, were often praised as targets because it was easy to get around to the back of them. Houses with rear or side exits were considered desirable by some because they offered an alternative means of getting away if anything went wrong. The absence of these convenient escape routes renders high-rise apartments less attractive targets for experienced burglars. The finding that residential burglars prefer detached houses to terraced ones is confirmed by Wright and Logie (1988), who also found that burglars were greatly attracted to houses with a hedge or fence, but were put off by those with a car in the drive.

Since burglars try to avoid confrontation with the victim, nonoccupancy of the target is an important selection factor. The absence of guardians is, therefore, one important dimension of accessibility. It is also a low-risk factor. British Crime Survey data led Hough (1987) to conclude that accessibility factors are often taken into account in the choice of targets, since homes frequently left empty and those with rear access were found to be more vulnerable than others.

MANAGEABILITY

Certain crimes, such as rape, robbery, or mugging, involve face-to-face confrontation with the victim, and their successful completion requires that the attacker be able to coerce and control the victim and to neutralize whatever resistance the victim may offer. When selecting a victim in such offenses, the potential offender takes into account factors such as the ease with which the prospective victim can be intimidated, the likelihood of victim resistance, and the possibility of forcing the victim into compliance. Manageability of the victim may also be considered an attractiveness feature. Thus, a victim who is unlikely to resist, who can be easily intimidated and forced to comply with the demands of the offender, is a more attractive victim than one who cannot be easily managed.

The attempt to manage and control the mugging situation before the encounter with the victim is a constant preoccupation of muggers, and this preoccupation is always revealed in accounts by those who have engaged in acts of muggings (Lejeune, 1977). The choice of a weak, vulnerable, easy-to-frighten, and easily intimidated victim is a reflection of the mugger's conscious, or subconscious, attempt to minimize the danger and the risks of the confrontation. For the mugger who is acting alone, manageability of the victim is clearly a more important selection criterion than for those who are acting in a pair or in a group. It is also likely to be of more significance to the unarmed mugger than to the armed one, especially when the threatening weapon used is a firearm.

Manageability of the victim and of the situation is also an important selection variable in commercial robbery. The would-be robber or holdup offender usually assesses this manageability by considering three factors: (1) the size of the establishment; (2) the number of people likely to be on the premises when the robbery is carried out; and (3) the likelihood of resistance on the part of the victim. The preference for small-size establishments, with a single victim, over larger ones (even though the yield is likely to be lower) is probably a good indication of the robbers' concerns over their ability to control the situation and to manage the victim.

National crime surveys in the United States consistently report that the vast majority of robbery incidents are committed against lone victims. This finding simply corroborates what many researchers have been reporting over the years (McClintock and Gibson, 1961; Conklin, 1972; Weir, 1973; Block, 1977; Normandeau, 1981).

Canadian robbers interviewed by Wilson (1987) expressed a general preference for businesses with few people. Even those who, for other considerations such as lucrativeness, choose targets likely to have a number of people in them, tried to time the robbery to coincide with the period or hour when the number was smaller. Although some did not mind a large crowd, most disliked the prospect of having to deal with a large number of people. In addition to such situations being unpredictable and difficult to control, there is also the greater chance of being later identified by one of those who was present during the robbery.

Rapists seem to avoid, at any cost, accompanied females. Chappell and James (1986) report that a key element in the contact situation, from the rapist's perspective, is whether the woman is alone. Ninety-six percent of the sample reported that they always checked to see whether a woman was, in fact, by herself before implementing an attack. And when the location was the woman's own home, they mentioned looking through windows, checking cars in the driveway, or knocking at the door and asking questions. Even when breaking into a home, the rapists interviewed said they walked through the house checking for other persons before approaching the victim. If the initial contact was to be made on the street or in a social setting like a tavern, they would observe the victim for some period to ensure she was alone. The rapists' distinct preference for committing rapes in the late evening period was based on their belief that their chances of discovering a vulnerable victim were greater at this time and that fewer persons would be likely to observe the offender or interfere during the evening hours.

While rapists have an overwhelming tendency to seek a lone victim, burglars try to avoid any contact with their victims. Their marked predilection for times when occupants are away or targets left unattended can be explained not only by their wish to avoid face-to-face confrontation, with all the risks and dangers involved, but also by their desire not to be interrupted while searching for money and valuables. Studies of burglars (Maguire and Bennett, 1982; Walsh, 1980; Scarr, 1973) reveal that most burglars think it is very important to have the house to themselves. Reppetto (1974) found the overwhelming majority of burglaries to be committed against unoccupied premises. Households with low occupancy-levels had an average annual rate of burglaries over three times (94 per 1,000 dwelling units) that of medium (27 per 1,000) and high (28 per 1,000) occupancy-level homes.

Another selection factor in robbery is the likelihood of resistance on the part of the victim. Most of the robbers in Wilson's study (1987) who expressed a preference for commercial robberies over residential or street robberies cited as the reason for their preference the smaller chance of resistance by the commercial victim and, hence, the lower risk of potential violence. There seemed to be a consensus that employees in commercial establishments would not try to foil a robbery. Robbers were aware that in many businesses employees are unlikely to resist, since the money is not their own and is insured. Many robbers seemed to shy away from corner grocery stores and taxicabs because of the higher likelihood of resistance by the owners or the drivers.

RISK

Not all potential victims/targets within a would-be offender's awareness or search space are good or appropriate victims/targets. As Brantingham and Brantingham (1984), writing about potential targets, point out, although the characteristics of a target that make it "good" or "bad" might be diverse, they have to include an assessment of the risk associated with the choice of a particular target together with the difficulty of actually succeeding. Brantingham and Brantingham (1984), suggest that most criminals are normal and are bound, therefore, to assess the risks to which they are exposed:

There are irrational criminals—those who commit offenses without regard to risk or in the hopes of being apprehended—but most criminals are psychologically normal. Some offenses are so emotional or affective that consideration of risk does not occur, but in most offenses it is clear that the people committing the offenses take some precautions. (p. 363)

When planning the offense and when choosing the victim/target the offender has two primary concerns: the chances of success or failure in achieving the criminal objective, and the risks and dangers of the criminal situation.[3] It is only natural that predatory criminals will try to work out a plan and select a victim/target with the potential to maximize their chances of success and minimize the risk of failure and of being caught. The choice of a vulnerable, unprotected victim/target is one way of reducing the probability of a negative outcome. The choice of a victim/target from which or whom the offender can easily get away after committing the crime or when something goes wrong is another way of lowering the risks involved. The underlying premise of current policies of target hardening as a means of crime prevention, is that easy targets are preferred, and are more attractive and more often selected than harder ones.

Security

Alarm systems, security locks, videocameras, watchdogs, and other security measures are meant to render the target unattractive to the potential burglar or robber by making it harder for the criminal to successfully achieve the criminal goal and by enhancing the chances of apprehension. While these target-hardening measures may deter the amateur or opportunistic offender, they do not seem to be very effective in dissuading the few who are experienced and determined. They rarely present any problems for the professional burglar, and some may even take a perverse pride in beating them (Maguire and Bennett, 1982). Maguire and Bennett agree that factors such as occupancy, size and style of the house, possible exits and escape routes, cover and visibility, and the presence of alarms, dogs, and security locks, do play some part in influencing burglars' choices of which particular houses they enter and which they avoid. They stress, however, that the importance of these factors is highly subjective and may be outweighed by a strong urge, optimism, or overconfidence. Maguire and Bennett (1982) make the following statement in support of this view:

Personal preferences and reasoning on such matters vary considerably among burglars, and an individual's mood on any one day may cause him to take more or less risk than usual. The general belief among thieves that burglary is "easy" and their knowledge that few burglars are caught in the act mean that, although they are aware of risk factors and may think about them in detail, in practice they often feel safe enough to break their own safety rules and do not spend a great deal of time selecting the optimum target. (p. 87)

Maguire and Bennett (1982) further assert that factors of "access" and "surveillance" are more important in explaining patterns of victimization than levels of household security. In other words, even if a house has good locks and bolts but is situated in a high-risk position with regard to easy and unnoticed access, then it may be more likely to be burgled than a home with little "security" less conveniently situated in terms of burglar access.

Further doubt about the significance of one particular security measure, namely dead bolt locks, comes from another study. In a study of how young burglars choose their targets, Wright and Logie (1988) used a control group of nonburglars. Both offenders and nonoffenders agreed that the presence of a dog or burglar alarm makes a house an unattractive target. The two groups disagreed, however, about dead bolt locks. The control group believed that these houses would be less attractive than those without dead bolts, but for the young burglars the presence of a dead bolt did not influence the choice.

Another security measure, which has grown in popularity in recent years, is the marking of objects to make them less desirable for theft (Operation Identification). In this security measure, items usually stolen from residences or cars are encoded with a unique identity number through the use of an engraving pen or an invisible-ink pen. The idea behind Operation Identification is to make houses taking part in the program unattractive targets for potential burglars as marked items are more difficult to dispose of or to sell to a fence. Evaluations of various Operation Identification programs have been carried out in different countries with varying results. In a Swedish study (Knutsson, 1984), no crime prevention effect of Operation Indentification could be documented, nor was it found to have any effect on either the flow of stolen goods or the crime clearance rate. Heller, Stenzel, Gill, Kolde, and Schimerman (1975) surveyed several American studies, some of which point to a crime-reducing effect. Gabor (1981) reached a positive conclusion in a Canadian study. Usually, it is difficult to tell whether the positive results reported are due to a net reduction in the incidence of burglary or simply to a displacement to other areas and houses not participating in the program.

General security measures do not seem to pose a big problem for robbers and are usually considered a hurdle that needs to be overcome. Wilson (1987) points out that while financial institutions were viewed as largely attractive in many respects, including the potential payoff, they were quite unattractive in terms of security precautions, such as alarms, visible or hidden cameras, marked bills, and armed guards. The presence of such security measures, however, did not seem to deter many robbers. Except for the presence of an armed guard(s), most offenders tried either to neutralize the security features or simply ignored them. Therefore, Wilson (1987) writes:

> *Security was expected by the offenders, and they dealt with it accordingly. For example, if the bank had an alarm, the robbers made sure that they would have escaped from the bank by the time the police arrived at the scene. If the bank had a camera, the robbers would wear a disguise and/or keep their backs to the camera during the robbery. This would reduce the likelihood of identification. (p. 198)*

Surveillability

Whereas common security measures do not seem to particularly deter the experienced, professional, or determined burglar, surveillance of the target by people or mechanical means appears to have a strong bearing upon the choice of targets. Walsh's (1986) interviews of forty-five commercial burglars incarcerated at a local prison revealed a strongly identifiable concentration on the issue of surveillability, thus confirming the findings of Bennett and Wright (1984).

There is a set of cues that burglars usually use to assess the level of surveillability of any given target. Among the popular ones are the distance of the house from neighboring houses and the distance of the house from the road. Houses very close to others are afforded some protection and are thus less preferred than those that are beyond the normal vision of attentive neighbors. Whether the house is hidden or exposed is also important. Visual seclusion provides the burglar with a sense of security when forcing a way into the house (Rengert and Wasilchick, 1985). The amount of visual seclusion or exposure is generally judged by the presence or absence of trees, hedges, bushes, and other obstructions that block the view from the street or from the neighbors' houses and, thus, allow unnoticed entry.

Risk factors most frequently mentioned by the burglars interviewed by Bennett and Wright (1984) related to the risk of being seen. The houses they found suitable for burglary were more often judged in terms of the amount of cover they offered than in terms of any other single variable. Houses found unsuitable were also most frequently judged in terms of their visual seclusion or exposure, although the presence of neighbors and signs of occupancy were also mentioned relatively often as important factors in the decision.

By far, the most important situational variable for the burglar is occupancy. The vast majority of burglars seek a house that is unoccupied. However, there are exceptions. One is where the burglary is committed in the small hours of the morning, and the second, much rarer, is where the burglar deliberately takes risks in order to provide excitement (Maguire and Bennett, 1982). Before forcing their way in, residential burglars go to great lengths to ensure that no one is in the house. Here, as well, they rely upon a set of popular signs: lights on, a car in the driveway, music being played, sounds from a television set, voices of people talking, and so on. Visual clues suggesting that the house is unoccupied include a pile of mail in the mailbox or delivered newspapers and magazines stacked by the entrance, which suggest that the occupants have been away for some time. Even when convinced that no one is inside, most burglars will knock or ring the doorbell in a final attempt to avoid a surprise.

Danger

The burglar's attempt to ensure that no one is inside the home is one of the precautions taken to minimize the danger. Confrontation with the victim, or with any third party, represents at least three risks for the burglar. First, there is the danger that the burglary attempt will be foiled. Second, there is the danger of the burglar being injured or even killed by an armed victim or by someone coming to the help of the victim. Third, there is the danger of being caught. Unoccupied houses and the absence of guardians provide reasonable assurances to the burglar that the robbery and the search for any specific objects will not be interrupted.

In offenses that require face-to-face confrontation with the victim, such as rape, robbery, and mugging, there are three potential sources of danger to the offender: the victim, others, and the police. To reduce the danger, the offender is likely to seek and to choose a victim unlikely to be armed or offer strong resistance. An additional safety measure is to choose a victim, such as a fence, drug dealer, prostitute, or homosexual, who is unlikely to report the victimization to the police. Avoidance of confrontation with an armed victim or guard seems to be foremost in the mind of robbers. Wilson (1987) believes that the presence of armed guards discourages most robbers and is the main reason why armored trucks were considered one of the least attractive commercial targets. Taxi drivers, as victims, were equally low on the list of preference because of the probability that they might be armed. One reason why commercial robberies were preferred over residential ones or over mugging is that they were perceived to be less threatening and more predictable. It is common knowledge that employees in financial institutions, large department stores, and even in jewelry stores are not armed. Furthermore, they are not likely to resist an armed robber, not only because the money and the goods are not theirs, but also because it is insured. In contrast, small grocery stores and convenience stores are often operated by the owner or family members. Many are not willing to part with their money as easily as, for example, a bank teller; some may want to resist, even when common sense militates against it; and some might have armed themselves as a means of protection. Thus, despite the general lack of adequate security measures in these stores, their attractiveness is reduced by the potential threat of violent confrontation and the dangers inherent in such confrontation.

The possibility of intervention from third parties looms large in certain robbery situations and is quite real whenever there is more than one person at the scene. This renders certain potential targets, such as restaurants, taverns, and bars, "off limits" for some robbers. One robber confided to Wilson (1987), "I won't touch anything where liquor is served. There's too many unpredictable people." Another commented on licensed establishments by saying, "There's way too many people. You're gonna get some asshole playing the hero because he is smashed" (p. 190). Some robbers' choice of closing time to commit their crime in these commercial establishments and others is yet another way of reducing the risks of intervention by one or more of the patrons.

Robbers also try to avoid confrontation with the police. The reasons are obvious. However, the fear of being shot, injured, or killed by the police is difficult to disentangle from the fear of being arrested. Both dangers are imminent when the police arrive before the robber has managed to get away. When selecting a target, the robber or the burglar can assess the probability of police intervention by considering factors such as the distance of the target to the nearest police station, the estimated response time, and the frequency of police patrols in the area where the target is located.

There is some empirical evidence that distance to the nearest police station is one of the factors considered by robbers (Servay and Rehm, 1986; Wilson, 1987) and in burglary (Bennett and Wright, 1984). The frequency of police patrols was also mentioned by some robbers in Wilson's study. Some conceded that they avoided convenience stores because they are usually heavily patrolled by the police. Others stated a preference for commercial targets located in residential areas because there are relatively fewer police patrols leading to a longer response time.

Sanctions

Estimates of the likely sanctions the offender may get are yet another factor that might lead some offenders to select certain targets and to avoid others. Predatory crimes are high-risk activities. Therefore, it is reasonable to expect that involvement in these crimes will be influenced by considerations similar to the ones that influence people's involvement in other high-risk activities, in particular by the balance of the potential risks against the potential rewards. Though theoretically plausible, such a logical proposition might not be that important in practice. Even the deadliest of risks is often overlooked when the urge to commit the crime is too powerful and can easily be dismissed by an overly confident or optimistic offender.

One of the risks facing the offender who is contemplating a crime is the risk of being caught and punished. Offenders, especially experienced ones, have more or less accurate perceptions of the general level of sanctions meted out for certain offenses, and the likely variations in the penalties when specific victims or groups of victims are involved. It does not require any particular knowledge of, or experience with, the criminal justice system to realize, for example, that vulnerable victims, such as children or the elderly, or victims who are handicapped, such as the blind or the deaf, evoke more sympathy among the police, prosecutors, and judges. Their criminal victimization is likely, therefore, to draw heavier penalties from the courts than the victimization of a less vulnerable person.

Some of the robbers in Wilson's study (1987) were convinced that judges handed out harsher sentences for residential and personal robberies than for commercial ones. The reason, they believed, is that robbing a "human being" is viewed as more serious and more contemptible than robbing a commercial establishment. Robbing a dwelling is widely held to be a violation of the sanctity of the home. One specific reason cited by some robbers for their view of taxi and bus drivers as particularly unattractive targets is the knowledge that their victimization often draws a prison or a penitentiary sentence, while the potential payoff, in most cases, is quite modest. The same reason was mentioned by some robbers in regard to small retail stores as the prospect of the low reward was not worth the prospect of a stiff penalty.

If it is true that these reasons are more than mere rationalizations, that these considerations do cross the mind of the robber, the burglar, or the rapist when contemplating their crimes and when deciding upon a victim/target, then it is possible and plausible that socially stigmatized groups would be preferred victims because of the relative leniency their victimizers are likely to receive.

Summary

Risks and rates of criminal victimization are not evenly divided within the general population. This suggests that victims/targets are not chosen at random, that certain victims/targets are preferred to others, and that some are often picked while others are frequently avoided. The study of victim/target selection has important theoretical and practical implications and there is a need for more research on what offenders look for and what criteria they use when selecting a target from among several others.

Although the selection criteria are diverse and although "target attractiveness" and "target appropriateness" are relative and subjective concepts, available research enables us to identify and classify a large number of factors likely to influence or contribute to the offender's choice, as shown in Table 9-1.

The factors in Table 9-1 have been grouped under five general headings: proximity, attractiveness, accessibility, manageability, and risk. Proximity is important because most offenders do not travel large distances to commit their crimes.

TABLE 9-1 **Victim/Target Choice Factors**

Proximity	**Attractiveness**	**Accessibility**	**Manageability**	**Risk**
Distance to travel.	Lucrativeness/ profitability: potential yield, likely payoff.	Temporal accessibility.	Ability to control situation.	Level of security.
Awareness: victim/ target within offender's awareness space.	Appropriateness: negative attributes facilitating neutralization.	Physical accessibility.	Size of establishment.	Level of surveillance.
Familiarity: victim/ target within offender's search space.	Physical attractiveness: (sex crimes).	Location, site.	Number of people.	Degree of situational danger from the victim, third parties, and the police.
Safety/security/ confidence: victim/ target within offender's action space.	Personal traits of the victim.	Layout.	Ease of generating compliance.	Estimate of potential sanctions.
		Ease of access.	Likelihood of co-operation.	
			Likelihood of resistance.	

Their search for a suitable victim/target is normally confined to their awareness space. Familiarity with the area as well as familiarity with the victim/target are likely to enhance the offender's feelings of safety and security and to boost his or her confidence. Victim/target attractiveness varies from offense to offense and from offender to offender. It is comprised of factors such as the personal characteristics of the victim, physical attractiveness (particularly in sexual crimes), profitability/lucrativeness (in crimes committed for financial gain), vulnerability, appropriateness, and suitability. Accessibility of the victim/target, both temporal and geographical, is also a selection factor. The geographical location, the site, the physical layout, and the ease of access to the victim/target are some of the features to which consideration might be given by the offender when choosing among several available victims/targets. Manageability of the victim is likely to be an important factor in crimes where there is face-to-face confrontation between the protagonists, such as in rape, robbery, and mugging. In deciding on a particular victim/target, offenders are likely to contemplate their ability to control the situation, to coerce the victim, and to generate compliance. In so doing, they are bound to consider factors such as the size of the establishment, the number of people present, the ease or the difficulty of generating compliance, and the likelihood of cooperation or resistance on the part of the victim. There is a host of risk factors associated with any given victim/target that may be grouped somewhat arbitrarily under the general heading of "risk." These include the following: (1) the level of security of the target; (2) the kind of protection or lack of it the target has; (3) the degree of surveillability of the target; (4) the dangers inherent in attacking the target, such as the likelihood of the victim being armed, likelihood of the offender being injured or killed by the victim, and likelihood of interruption by a third party or by the police; (5) the likelihood of police intervention; and (6) the offender's estimate of potential sanctions if arrested and convicted.

These selection variables are not of equal significance and do not carry the same weight in the choice of a victim/target. The relative importance of each category and of each of the discussed factors, as well as the relative weight assigned to it vary from offense to offense, offender to offender, and from incident to incident.

TEN

Victims' Personal Characteristics

In recent years, increasing attention has been paid to ways in which victims of crime (in the legal sense of that term) may play a part in the causation of crime. It has been noted that some kinds of people are especially vulnerable to crime and that they may, because of certain attributes or the nature of their interaction with offenders, be especially likely to become victims; in some cases, the person who is legally regarded as the victim of a crime may actually have caused the crime to happen. For certain types of crimes, at least, the probability of becoming a victim is not uniform but varies among different types of persons, groups, organizations, etc. To the extent that this is true, it is necessary to include some facts about the victims of crime in any adequate explanation of the spatial, temporal, or social distribution of crime.

Richard F. Sparks (1982, p. 6)

Etiological Explanations of Criminal Victimization

Explaining victimization was the major preoccupation of pioneers in victimology. The earliest victimological studies, both theoretical and empirical, were attempts to answer questions such as, Why do certain individuals become victims while others do not? What differentiates the victims of crime from the rest of the population? Do certain personal characteristics, attitudes, or behaviors enhance the chances of becoming a victim? Are certain individuals or groups more prone to criminal victimization than others? Attempts to find definitive and conclusive answers to these questions were hampered by the dearth of empirical data on victims. The wealth of data generated through victimization surveys renewed the interest in explaining victimization. In particular, the realization that criminal victimization is not a random occurrence was bound to lead many researchers to try to explain this nonchance phenomenon and to develop etiological models and theories of victimization. The purpose of the last three chapters is to provide a synthesis of the various micro and macro explanations that have been advanced by a number of researchers in recent years.

Although etiological explanations of criminal victimization are distinct from the etiological explanations of criminal behavior, there are, inevitably, certain parallels. The search for the correlates of victimization parallels the search for the correlates of crime. The search for the personal characteristics that increase the risk of being victimized is similar to the search for the personal characteristics that enhance the chances of becoming a young delinquent or an adult offender. Notions such as proneness or vulnerability to criminal victimization correspond more or less to the notions of predisposition or propensity to delinquency and crime. Despite their variety, the multitude of criminogenic factors encountered in all criminological theories may be grouped into three categories: predisposing factors, situational factors, and triggering (or actualizing) factors. By far the most popular criminological theories have been the ones that try to explain the etiology of criminal behavior by reference to the offender's personal characteristics and background. Early attempts to explain criminal victimization have also tried to find the causes of victimization in the personal characteristics, such as attractiveness, vulnerability, and proneness, of those who are victimized, or in the victim's contributing, facilitating, or triggering behavior (provocation, precipitation, negligence, carelessness, recklessness, etc.). More recent theoretical formulations have paid more attention to other situational determinants of criminal victimization such as exposure, life-style, accessibility, and opportunity.

Explaining Victimization by Reference to the Personal Characteristics of the Victim

That the likelihood and actual rates of criminal victimization are linked to the personal characteristics of victims and vary according to certain sociodemographic factors is beyond question (see Chapter 4). As Gottfredson (1981) points out, the available data on victimization consistently show that the likelihood of victimization from common theft and assault varies dramatically depending on people's characteristics. For example, in the United States, victimization rates for personal crimes are consistently higher for those who are poor, males, blacks, young, single, and urban residents. The importance of these personal characteristics has been confirmed over and over again by the victimization surveys conducted in different countries such as Canada, Australia, and the countries of Europe. But these personal characteristics of victims are simply correlates of criminal victimization. They are not the *causes* of this victimization. Their exact victimogenic role remains unclear. As many of these personal characteristics are simultaneously determinants of life-style, routine activities, and, thus, of exposure, it is quite possible that their victimogenic role is not a direct one. In other words, they might not be able to explain victimization if looked at on their own, but might explain it through other intervening variables, such as attractiveness, accessibility, vulnerability, proneness, and exposure.

ATTRACTION/REPULSION

In Chapter 9 we discussed victim/target attractiveness from the point of view of the victimizer and the role such attractiveness may play in the process of target selection. While the notion of attraction may be important in sexual crimes and property offenses, the opposite notion of "repulsion" may play a certain role in acts of expressive violence. The terms "victim attractiveness" or "repulsiveness" neither imply the passing of a value judgment nor the assignment of blame. Both concepts are borrowed from the animal kingdom in which the universality of attraction and repulsion has led to the belief that they are, at least in some cases, instinctive or inborn. Such is the proverbial antagonism between cats and mice or the irresistible attraction the lamb has for the wolf.

Gratus (1969) finds the way mutual attraction or repulsion operates hard to explain, just as it is difficult to explain why two people fall in love or why two strangers instinctively feel repelled by one another.

The highly personal and relative nature of the concepts of attraction/repulsion limits the extent to which these notions may explain the differences in the rates of victimization. At a micro level they might be useful in explaining why a particular act of victimization occurred and why a specific victim/target was chosen rather than another. They may also eventually explain why some cases of victimization are repeat or multiple. It is difficult, however, to incorporate them in macro explanations of criminal victimization.

Empirical studies of the role attraction/repulsion play in the etiology of criminal victimization are extremely rare. One such study was done by Grayson and Stein (1981), and published in the *Journal of Communication* under the provocative title "Attracting Assault: Victims' Nonverbal Cues." The authors started with the unusual premise that some individuals have a higher potential for attracting assault than others and may even be signaling their vulnerability to would-be assailants through gestures, posture, and exaggerated movements. The authors then set out to verify whether there are specific movements or behaviors that identify a potential victim of an assault. To do so, the authors videotaped persons selected at random walking through one of the highest assault areas of New York city. They subsequently showed the videotapes to offenders who had been incarcerated for assault and asked them to rate the vulnerability of potential victims. The analysis revealed that certain physical characteristics such as stride length, body movement, and type of walk were interpreted by the interviewed offenders as providing nonverbal cues to victim vulnerability. Based on their findings, Grayson and Stein suggest that movement should be considered an important component of potential victimization, and they conclude by offering this rather controversial proposition:

> *A nonverbal dialogue seems to exist between criminal and victim through which the victim communicates his or her vulnerability to the criminal in much the same way that releasor mechanisms operate in the animal world. (p. 75)*

Without further research it is difficult to agree or disagree with the authors' conclusion. What we can do is to recommend this unexplored area for future studies.

PROXIMITY/DISTANCE

The commission of certain crimes requires the offender to get physically close to, but stay emotionally remote from, the victim in order to decrease the geographical distance while increasing the affective distance that separates them.

Milgram's (1974) laboratory experiments, in which he explored his subjects' readiness and willingness to inflict pain through electrical shocks on fellow human beings when ordered to do so, provide empirical evidence on the effects of victims' physical proximity. Milgram correctly hypothesized that by bringing the victim closer to the subject, thus enhancing the subject's awareness of the victim's suffering and distress, the subject's performance could be regulated to some degree and obedience to the experimenter would decrease. The experiments confirmed the hypothesis and revealed that obedience declined as the victim was rendered more immediate to the subject. Thirty-five percent of the subjects defied the experimenter in the remote condition, 37.5 percent in voice-feedback, 60 percent in proximity, and 70 percent in touch-proximity. Commenting on his findings, Milgram points out that in the remote situation the victim's suffering possesses an abstract, remote quality for the subject. The subject is aware in a conceptual sense that his or her actions cause pain to another person. The remote condition allows the subject to put the victim out of his or her mind. When the victim is close it is more difficult to exclude him or her from thought. In the proximity condition, the subject may sense that she or he has become more salient in the victim's field of awareness and, consequently, becomes more self-conscious, embarrassed, and inhibited when punishing the victim (Milgram, 1974, p. 39).

Hurting the victim at a distance is therefore easier to do and evokes less guilt than hurting him or her at close proximity or in a face-to-face confrontation. Individuals who would never hurt, let alone kill, anyone in a personal interaction may not lose much sleep over killing hundreds of helpless people when it is done on orders, and at a distance, by dropping bombs from an airplane. The stronger inhibitions that result from the physical proximity of the victim explain why certain types of criminals avoid, at any cost, face-to-face confrontation with their victim. This is also why some sexual offenders make persistent attempts to calm and reassure the victim during the process of victimization.

Because sympathetic concern for the victim and heightened awareness of the victim's suffering are inhibiting forces, and because depersonalizing the victim and denying the injury are popular techniques of desensitization, a new way of preventing recidivism was developed in recent years. The idea is to bring the victim and victimizer together so that they may see each other as persons and so that the victimizer may be sensitized to the pain and suffering inflicted upon the victim.

If it is true that proximity and emotional attachment are inhibiting forces, how then can we explain that many violent victimizations such as killings and assaults occur within the intimate social sphere against persons to whom the victimizers are socially and emotionally related? The answer is that violent crimes are crimes of interaction, and the motives and situations that usually give rise to them develop mostly between people who live in close social and emotional contact. We do not get angry or terribly upset at people to whom we are totally indifferent or with whom we never or rarely interact (see Chapter 7).

PRONENESS/VULNERABILITY

The notion of proneness, in the sense of some general or specific susceptibility to a particular kind of negative outcome, is not really new. It is similar to the medical concept of "diathesis."[1] The idea that some people are "accident-prone" and that others are "suicide-prone" has been accepted for some time.[2] To try, then, to explain phenomena such as "variation in risk," "repeat victimization," and "multiple victimization" by referring to the victim's proneness or vulnerability does not seem farfetched or out of line. According to Smith (1986), it is not uncommon to draw a parallel between being a victim of crime and having an accident, for both are popularly attributed to chance. Yet, just as close inspection reveals systematic variations in accident-proneness, so detailed analyses reveal social and spatial bias in victim proneness (Smith, 1986, p. 87). In fact, there is a distinct possibility that a special kind of proneness or a specific type of vulnerability might be responsible, at least partially, for some of the extreme variations in the likelihood of victimization. How else could we explain, for instance, findings such as those of Sparks, Genn, and Dodd (1977) in which 60 percent of the 582 victimization incidents recorded in their London, England, survey were directed at only 13 percent of the sample, or those of Smith (1986) who discovered in a survey conducted in north central Birmingham that 26 percent of the sample accounted for 59 percent of the victimizations?

The Difference Between Proneness and Vulnerability

Although the terms "proneness" and "vulnerability" are often used interchangeably, some authors have suggested a subtle distinction between them. Reiss (1980) views victim proneness and victim vulnerability as two related but competing major explanations for differences in the risk of victimization and repeat victimization. Each uses a different set of explanatory variables. The victim proneness explanation, suggests Reiss, selects (1) personal, social, and behavioral characteristics of persons as potential victims and (2) their relationships to offenders as explanatory variables, while the victim vulnerability explanation selects (1) situations and characteristics of offenders, their networks, and their behavior and (2) relationships to potential victims as explanatory variables. Reiss (1980) adds the following:

> *Simply put, victim proneness models explain high risk of victimization and repeat victimization by victim behavior and relationships with potential offenders that precipitates crimes or increases their vulnerability to potential offenders. The vulnerability models are more offender oriented, explaining repeat victimization in terms of such factors as the offender's prior relationship with victims, selection of criminal opportunities and the organization of networks of offending. The considerable overlap of the models not only makes it difficult to test them as competing explanations but argues for a more general model. A more precise general model, however, depends upon yet to be acquired information on the behavior of both victims and offenders. (p. 41)*

Variations in the risk of victimization are generally reasonable indicators of differences in the levels of proneness. However, the concept of "proneness" is just one way of presenting what amounts to nothing more than a statistical probability. It does not imply in any shape or form some kind of fatalism or inevitability. It does not mean that every member of the highly prone group will necessarily be victimized nor that every member of the less prone group will be spared. Many factors, including chance factors, intervene to determine the actual happenings. As a result, some high-risk individuals may not, or may never, become victims, while some low-risk group members may become victims and may even become repeat or recidivist victims during the same reference period or during their lifetime.

The idea that certain individuals, and groups, are more prone to criminal victimization than others enjoys a fair degree of popular and empirical support. It has been suggested, for example, that once sufficient information is available on victims of crime it would be possible to construct a "vulnerability index" that could indicate the relative probability of an individual's becoming the victim of crime (Lamborn, 1981).

After reviewing the evidence, one author concluded that the available research supports the idea that some people are more victim prone than others (Gottfredson, 1981). Both the clustering of criminal victimization in certain groups and the phenomenon of repeat victimization lend credence to the belief in victim proneness. The idea is further corroborated by recent observations confirming the existence of an empirical relationship between accidents, mishaps, and criminal victimizations. Gottfredson's (1984) analysis of the British Crime Survey data reveals that the likelihood of being the victim of a personal victimization was twice as high for those who report any one of other misfortunes, such as motor vehicle accidents, household fires, and other accidents serious enough to cause injury and suffering, as it was for those reporting that they had never experienced one such misfortune. Gottfredson's comment on the findings leaves no doubt as to the existence of what may be described, for the absence of a better word, as victim proneness. Gottfredson writes:

> *It would appear, therefore, that not only does criminal victimization cluster (i.e. household, personal and auto crime are interrelated to some degree) but a variety of misfortunes are disproportionately suffered by those who are also crime victims. (p. 17)*

There have been few attempts to empirically test the explanatory power of the concept of victim proneness. In a study by Thissen and Wainer (1983), the authors drew two samples, each of five hundred households, from the data gathered by the National Crime Survey. Utilizing a nonlinear response model, they found that the resulting victimization fit a theoretical construct of victim proneness well. They also discovered that some aspects of proneness could be predicted from the social characteristics of the households.

Despite empirical evidence suggesting the existence of a cluster of variables that combine to enhance the likelihood of victimization, the loose and somewhat indiscriminate use of the notion of victim proneness/vulnerability has led to some severe criticism. In its final report entitled *Surveying Crime*, the Panel for the

Evaluation of Crime Surveys appointed by the United States National Research Council (National Research Council, 1976) distinguished several types of vulnerability: "ecological vulnerability" (e.g., living in a high crime area); "status vulnerability" arising from such attributes as sex, race, occupation, or social class; and "role vulnerability," arising from relationships from which the individual cannot readily withdraw, such as marriage or tenancy. Sparks (1981) is highly critical of such use of the concept of vulnerability. He feels it is too broad a use since it fails to specify *how* particular roles, statuses, or environments lead to higher risk of victimization. Sparks also feels that at times, the Panel's use of the term "vulnerability" seems equivalent to the notion of proneness. Like Reiss (1980), Sparks believes that the two terms (vulnerability and proneness) are not identical, and states that vulnerability is just one dimension of proneness. Proneness, according to Sparks, is a function of six concepts: precipitation, facilitation, vulnerability, opportunity, attractiveness, and the possibility of victimizing the target with impunity. Sparks (1981) is also critical of the notion of proneness, suggesting that it needs very careful interpretation. He fears that it may be extremely misleading where criminal victimization is concerned:

> *The term is harmless enough, if it is understood to refer merely to variations in the probability of experiencing a certain event in a given time period. But there is a danger that it may be understood to imply something more, namely, that such variations in risk are caused by inherent attributes of persons, such as clumsiness. This is certainly not the case. While variations in risk may be associated with particular groups or categories of persons, the causes of those variations may lie in the social situations of those persons, or places to which they usually go, rather than in anything inherent in the persons themselves. (p. 768)*

Having offered this warning, Sparks (1981) continued to use the term "proneness" "because there is no equally convenient alternative term." He then goes on to explain that the probability of a person actually being victimized is a function of his or her proneness as well as a random element not dependent on the attributes or social situation of the victim. According to Sparks (1981), the calculation of the net proneness of a given population is possible:

> *Given sufficient information about the attributes and behavior of a population, calculation of their "net proneness" to criminal victimization would in principle be possible, i.e., the probability of victimization in a given time period. That would permit us to calculate an expected level of victimization around which there should merely be random stochastic variation. Then, if the relevant characteristics of the population were to change (e.g., people go out less often, barricade themselves behind dozens of locks, get divorced, give away all their money, quit dealing cocaine), their proneness, and thus the expected rate of victimization in the population, should decrease accordingly. (p. 776)*

Is There a Positive Association Between Vulnerability and Victimization?

To differentiate between vulnerability and proneness to victimization and to view the former as one of the dimensions of the latter along the lines suggested by Sparks (1981), is both useful and necessary. Only by making such a distinction would it be possible to understand why vulnerability and proneness do not always go hand in hand, and why certain individuals or groups may be highly vulnerable but less prone to victimization than others. It also makes it possible to understand why the relationship between vulnerability and victimization is not always in the expected direction. The following examples will help illustrate this.

Normally we would expect vulnerability and victimization to be linked by a positive linear relationship: the higher the vulnerability, the higher the likelihood of victimization and the rates of actual victimization. This, however, is not always the case. Those who are most vulnerable are not necessarily those most often victimized. The elderly and women are two cases in point. The elderly would seem to be highly vulnerable to victimization because of weakened defenses and a reduced capacity to resist. Women would also seem to be more vulnerable than men because of their generally lesser physical strength. Despite this the relationship between advancing age and victimization is a negative one rather than the positive one we might expect (Fattah and Sacco, 1989). And for women, the rates of victimization (except for sexual victimization) are consistently lower than the rates for males (see Chapter 5). Both these observations are at odds with the assumption of a positive link between vulnerability and victimization. How can we explain this apparent paradox? The explanation is relatively simple. It is proneness and not vulnerability that is positively linked to actual victimization. Since proneness has several dimensions other than vulnerability it is not surprising to find that a group that scores high on vulnerability and low on other dimensions, such as exposure, accessibility, attractiveness, facilitation, and precipitation, will have low rather than high rates of criminal victimization. This raises the question of the relative importance of vulnerability as compared to the other dimensions of proneness. Unfortunately, in the present state of our knowledge, it is not possible to answer the question or to assign a relative weight to each dimension. It is, however, fair to assume, in view of the two examples discussed above, that vulnerability could be easily outweighed by the other components of proneness.

The Dimensions of Vulnerability

Vulnerability itself may be thought of as having separate dimensions. Mawby (1988) suggests that vulnerability to victimization has at least three dimensions: (1) a risk dimension, (2) a state of mind dimension, and (3) an impact dimension. Thus, we may talk about vulnerability in terms of a greater risk or higher probability of victimization, thus implying that those who are vulnerable have a greater likelihood of being victimized than others. Alternatively, vulnerability may be considered a state of mind rendering those who are vulnerable or very vulnerable more afraid of victimization and its consequences than those who are not vulnerable or are less vulnerable. Vulnerability might also be considered in terms of the impact victimization is likely to have on the victim, in the sense that the greater the vulnerability, the stronger and more serious is the impact.

Mawby (1988, p. 101) explains how these three dimensions of vulnerability can be applied to the study of the elderly. In studying the vulnerability of the elderly we may equate it with risk and consider the extent to which the elderly are victimized compared with younger populations. Considering vulnerability as a state of mind can lead us to focus on fear of crime and its implications for the quality of life of the elderly population. Finally, vulnerability may be examined in terms of the impact of crime on the victims, that is, we may ask how elderly victims perceive "their" crime and how it affects them.

Sacco and Glackman (1987) focused on vulnerability as a state of mind and tried to examine its relationship not to the risks or the rates of victimization, but to fear and worry about crime. To them, the concept of vulnerability is meant to emphasize the feelings of susceptibility and openness to attack that influence the process by which definitions of criminal danger are constructed and regarded as salient bases for action. They further consider powerlessness as a form of vulnerability and suggest that subjective powerlessness, like physical and social vulnerability, is indicative of a particular type of predisposition toward the risks, threats, and worries that individuals associate with crime. Sacco and Glackman's reasoning makes it easy to explain and to understand why it is that groups with relatively low victimization rates, such as women and the elderly, exhibit relatively high levels of fear of crime. The central concept is vulnerability. To the degree that people believe they are vulnerable, they may define the threat and risk of crime with a level of trepidation that does not, and would not be expected to, correspond in any precise way to the objective realities of threat and risk (Sacco and Glackman, 1987, p. 101). Sacco and Glackman (1987) write:

> *Thus, the concept of vulnerability encourages a view of the fearing-crime process that places an analytic emphasis upon an understanding of the ways in which some people (and not others) acquire a sense of susceptibility. (p. 101)*

Different Types of Proneness

SPATIAL PRONENESS

The findings of victimization surveys make it possible to link different levels of criminal victimization risks to certain ecological variables, thus suggesting the existence of what may be described as "spatial proneness" to victimization. City dwellers, for example, run a higher risk of criminal victimization than rural residents and, within a large city, people living or working in certain areas are more vulnerable to victimization than others (Braithwaite and Biles, 1984; Gottfredson, 1984). Gottfredson (1984) convincingly shows that residence in the inner city interacts with life-style-related variables to place some groups of people in positions of extremely high risk.

After reviewing various studies that examined the ecological distribution of victimization risks, Smith (1986) concluded that there is some agreement that place of residence has a significant effect on an individual's likelihood of victimization. These findings, plus her own survey conducted in Birmingham, led Smith (1986, p. 97) to suggest that "the odds of victimization are associated with *in situ* deprivation, not merely with personal vulnerability." Smith adds that the relatively affluent within an absolutely deprived community seem to be the most vulnerable to crime. This indicates that, even though certain disadvantages may be assessed in terms of the structural position occupied by people living near to each other, multiple deprivation has social consequences that must be appreciated in specifically spatial terms (p. 97). She further believes that the relative risks of victimization attendant on place of residence within the inner city are compounded by exposure to the risks of delinquent involvement (and the higher likelihood of official censure) and to the risks of household or personal accident.

Sampson and Lauritsen (1990) found ecological proximity to violence to be an important structural determinant of victimization. This, they believe, provides support to the recent revision of life-style theory, which argues that the structural constraint of residential proximity to crime has a direct effect on victimization that is unmediated by life-style.

STRUCTURAL PRONENESS

Criminal victimization clusters not only spatially but socially as well. Such clustering, according to certain sociodemographic variables, such as age, gender, race, marital status, social class, and employment status, suggests the existence of what may be designated as "structural proneness" to criminal victimization. When discussing the general characteristics of the victim population (see Chapter 5), we examined the relationship of some sociodemographic variables to the risks and the rates of victimization. Here, we will illustrate the meaning of the term "structural proneness" using three specific examples: being of a young age, being female, and having minority status.

Young Age as Structural Proneness: Victimization of Children as a Case Study

Young children are particularly prone to victimization. They are weak, frail, helpless, and highly vulnerable. Under a certain age, they are incapable of defending themselves, retaliating, or even complaining, and constitute, therefore, ideal targets for victimization. Victimization of children is as old as the human race itself. Infanticide was probably one of the earliest forms of victimization. It is the ultimate victimization: the annihilation of a helpless, unaware, and unsuspecting victim. Though infanticide is probably the most serious crime that may be committed against a child, it is but a single form of child victimization. Throughout history and until the present day, children have been and are being subjected to a wide variety of abuses, neglect, and maltreatments. Bakan (1971) reminds us:

> *Children have been whipped, beaten, starved, drowned, smashed against walls and floors, held in ice water baths, exposed to extremes of outdoor temperatures, burned with hot irons and steam pipes. Children have been tied and kept in upright positions for long periods. They have been systematically exposed to electric shock; forced to swallow pepper, soil, feces, urine, vinegar, alcohol, and other odious materials; buried alive; had scalding water poured over their genitals; had their limbs held in open fire; placed in roadways where automobiles would run over them; placed on roofs and fire escapes in such a manner as to fall off; bitten, knifed, and shot; had their eyes gouged out. (p. 4)*

Despite the well-documented fact that beating, torturing, and other victimization of children have taken place throughout the ages, the last three decades have witnessed a growing awareness of, and mounting interest in, child victimization, and these three decades saw the emergence of child abuse as a major social issue. The treatment of child victimization as a distinct criminological phenomenon proves once again the relevance of victim characteristics to the explanation, control, and prevention of specific types of crime. It is not difficult to understand why infants and young children are particularly prone to victimization. The relative lack of viability of the human infant and the helplessness and defenselessness of young children make them easy targets for attack, abuse, and destruction. Even in 1948, Von Hentig drew attention to this extreme vulnerability of children and youth:

> *Youth is the most dangerous period of life. Young creatures under natural conditions are the ideal prey, weak and easy to catch and savory. (p. 404)*

Several factors contribute to making the child an easy prey: the helplessness and undeveloped defensive mechanisms of infants and the very young; their inability to resist or oppose the attacker, to retaliate or even complain, to communicate (at all or effectively), and to express their wishes and explain their needs; their total dependence on adults for the satisfaction of their needs; and their accessibility as ready targets for the projection of anger, frustration, hostility, or sexual desires. These factors act, in many cases, as stimulants for adults which incite them to engage in physical and sexual abuse.

Proneness to physical abuse seems to be at its peak from birth until the ages of three or four (Gil, 1970; Fergusson et al., 1972; Johnson, 1974). Vulnerability is also at its highest point during the critical age when the child's irritating behaviors, such as incessant crying, uncontrolled natural functions, and temper-abrading and -eroding activities, combined with the parents' lack of parenting skills and self-control, are likely to elicit violent and aggressive responses from the adult against the child.

While male children seem to be slightly more prone to physical abuse than their female counterparts (Gil, 1970), the latter's vulnerability to sexual abuse is far greater than that of boys.[3] Moreover, vulnerability to sexual abuse follows a different age distribution. The most critical age for sexual abuse is understandably higher than that for physical abuse, with girls in the preadolescent and early adolescent years constituting the most prone age-group. Vulnerability seems to increase at the beginning, and with the progress of, sexual maturity (Maisch, 1973; Mohr et al., 1962; De Francis, 1969).

In addition to the general vulnerability related to age, specific attributes and particular qualities of the child may increase the potential for physical abuse. Justice and Justice (1976) use the term "high-risk children" to describe those particular children who are especially prone to abuse. Gil (1970) cites findings from several studies suggesting that some children, because of unusual congenital or acquired characteristics may occasionally be more prone to provoking abusive attacks against themselves than other more "normal children." Among the children who are particularly disposed to victimization are, according to Kempe (1971), the hyperactive and precocious, the premature, the adopted, the stepchild, and the child who, from the earliest day, seems to be singularly unrewarding to the mother no matter how hard she tries. Flynn (1970) describes what he calls the "obnoxious child" whom he sees as a natural stimulus for abuse. Bishop (1971) identifies six groups of children who are in specific risk of abuse: (1) illegitimate children, (2) premature babies, (3) congenitally malformed babies, (4) twins, (5) children conceived during the mother's depressive illness, and (6) children of mothers with frequent pregnancies and excessive work loads.

Friedrich and Boriskin (1977) point to mounting evidence suggesting that any perception of the child as strange, different, damaged, or abnormal increases the risk of that child being subjected to abusive treatment. Such children might then suffer not from one but from a double handicap (Friedrich and Boriskin, 1977):

> *Prematurity and low birth weight are important factors, as are mental retardation and physical handicaps. In effect, therefore, the child is victimized twice over, bearing both a physical burden of deprivation or damage and the anger this provokes in those responsible for its care. (p. 405)*

Other categories of children who are particularly prone to abuse are those overly difficult, aggravating, and hard to handle. Kempe and Kempe (1978) report that at least a quarter of the young children who have been abused, and probably more of the older ones, are negative, aggressive, and often hyperactive as well.

Justice and Justice (1976) offer several explanations for the high risk to which certain children are exposed. Regarding the disproportionate number of premature or low birth-weight babies among abused children, they note that prematurity predisposes a baby to anoxia, which in turn causes irritability and fussiness. Another explanation is that babies who weigh less than 5.5 pounds at birth may have subtle dysfunctions of the central nervous system which result in restlessness and distractability. Low birth-weight babies are also unlikely to be picked up as often as infants of normal weight, and this possibly has an unfortunate influence on the neonate's development, resulting in unresponsive behavior. Another theory cited by Justice and Justice is that because premature infants are separated from their parents for the first several weeks of life, the establishment of the child-caretaker bond is delayed, which in turn adversely affects the interaction between baby and parents—especially the mother's response to the infant. As to the higher incidence of abuse of illegitimate children, Justice and Justice point to the mother's rejection of the child resulting from her not wanting or being ashamed of him or her.

Young age proneness continues (and probably increases) into the teenage years.[4] The nature of victimization changes somewhat, with property victimization being added to physical violence and to sexual exploitation. The exposure to others outside the home environment also means that teenage victimization is not perpetrated exclusively or predominantly by the caretakers, as is the case with child abuse. Victimization data provide empirical support to the particular proneness of teenagers. A United States National Crime Survey report on teenage victims (United States, 1986) indicates that teenage (twelve to nineteen years old) victimization rates for violent crimes and theft from 1982 through to 1984 were about twice as high as those of the adult population of twenty years of age and older. The average annual violent crime victimization rate was 60.1 per 1,000 teenagers compared to 26.9 for the adult population. For crimes of theft, the teenage rate was 123.5; the adult rate, 65.6. Within the teenage population itself, older teens (ages sixteen to nineteen) had higher violent crime victimization rates than did younger teens (ages twelve to fifteen). However, the two groups had similar victimization rates for crimes of theft. Violent crimes against teenagers were more likely to be committed by other teenagers than by adults. Most of these crimes against younger teenagers were committed by offenders under eighteen years old. Close to half of the violent crimes against older teenagers were committed by offenders under twenty-one. By contrast, 70 percent of the violent crimes against adults were committed by offenders aged twenty-one or older.

The finding that juveniles and teenagers suffer an extensive and disproportionate amount of criminal victimization confirms earlier findings obtained from smaller scale surveys such as those by Feyerherm and Hindelang (1974) and Mawby (1979).

Powerlessness as Proneness: Female Victimization as a Case Study

The concept of "powerlessness" is central to feminist explanations of the victimization of women. Females are vulnerable to male violence because power relations in a patriarchal society place women in a subservient and subordinate role. Gates (1978), for example, argues that victimization of women by men is a consequence of the disparate power relationship between the two genders. Feminist writers have staunchly defended the position that crimes like rape and incest, among others, are not sex crimes but crimes of power motivated not by the quest for sexual pleasure, but by the desire to subjugate, humiliate, dirty, and defile the female victim. These arguments have been influential in bringing about legislative changes in many countries, including Canada, where the old term "rape" has been replaced by the term "aggravated sexual assault."

After reviewing feminist literature on domestic violence, Lorna Smith (1989) concluded that at the core of feminist explanations is the view that all violence is a reflection of unequal power relationships; domestic violence reflects the unequal power of men and women in society and also, therefore, within their personal relationships. This view, writes Smith, is propounded by sociologists (for example, Dobash and Dobash, 1979; Edwards, 1985), psychologists (for example, Walker, 1984), lawyers (for example, Freeman, 1979, 1984), and practitioners in the criminal justice system (for example, Pence, 1985) alike.

The writings of many feminists (Russell, 1975; Stanko, 1985; Gates, 1978) express the view that it is not gender as such, but rather gender inequality that is responsible for female victimization at the hands of men, and, in particular, for intrafamily violence. They insist that women's vulnerability to intimidating and violent male behavior is not due to their biological position, but to their social position. It is the powerlessness of women, not their gender, that explains why physical and/or sexual intrusions can happen with little or no interference, or even, to some extent, encouragement from others (Stanko, 1985). According to Stanko, the commonality of women's experiences exposes a process whereby men's physical and sexual intimidation toward women is permitted, with only minimum efforts to curb it. This process, one that significantly contributes to the maintenance of women's powerlessness and subjugation to men, operates on two levels. On one level, that of individual reactions, women's feelings of violation serve as an effective internal silencer of their experiences of men's threatening, intimidating, or violent behavior. The second level, the wider social reaction to male violence, effectively makes women who complain about men's behavior feel unrespectable, impure, tarnished, and shamed. Both levels ensure silence concerning the detrimental effects of male behavior on women's physical, sexual, and emotional autonomy. Both levels deny the effect of male violence on all women's lives.

Another feminist writer, Marrs (1990), affirms that the systemic violence women experience cannot be blamed on biological differences between males and females, but on the conditions that maintain and perpetuate women's subordination in society. The origin of this systematic violence against women and other disadvantaged groups lies in the existing power relations, which are based on gender, class, or race.

While most feminists express the view that it is powerlessness, not gender, and social condition, not biology, that are at the heart of female victimization, there are occasional references to the biological differences between men and women. Brownmiller (1975), for example, ties rape to the biological and anatomical gender differences. She argues that men's structural capacity to rape and women's corresponding structural vulnerability are as basic to the physiology of both sexes as the primal act of sex itself (Brownmiller, 1975):

> *Had it not been for this accident of biology, an accommodation requiring the locking together of two separate parts; penis into vagina, there would be neither copulation nor rape as we know it ... we cannot work around the fact that in terms of human anatomy the possibility of forcible intercourse incontrovertibly exists. This single factor may have been sufficient to have caused the creation of a male ideology of rape. (p. 14)*

Both the Schwendingers (1976) and Box (1983) are critical of Brownmiller's historical analysis of rape and her attempt to impose a biological explanation on what is essentially a social phenomenon. Box insists that it is an historical conjuncture of "sexist male culture" coupled with gross inter- and intra-gender inequalities in wealth, power, and privileges, and sustained by techniques of neutralization and a legal system in which institutionalized sexism is embedded, that forms the basis of rape. Schwendinger and Schwendinger (1976) criticize Brownmiller for her sex stereotyping of men, a stereotyping originating in sexist ideologies, where both sexes are caricatured. In so doing she wrests the typification of men from its original ideological context, which refers to dominant as well as submissive relations. They go on to blame her for using these typifications to rationalize a radical, bourgeois, feminist view of social reality. Rape, in that view, cannot be attributed to any cause other than natural law; men are oppressive by nature and rape maintains male supremacy and privilege.

What we said above about the victimization of women by men is a good illustration of a typical case of structural proneness. The structural proneness of females is a result of several factors that render women attractive, legitimate, accessible, and highly vulnerable targets for a variety of victimizations. To summarize, we can say that women are the visible and invisible victims of different types of victimizations. Their structural proneness to victimization can be traced to their social condition and lack of power in a patriarchal society. This powerlessness is a result of a combination of historical, cultural, economic, and political factors, which include among others, sexual division of labor, sexist male and female roles, gender inequality, lack of autonomy, systemic discrimination, and so forth. What follows is a very brief review of the main factors that contribute to women's proneness to victimization:

Women are less powerful than men. In her introduction to the book *Victimization of Women*, Gates (1978) points out that the simplest explanation for the maltreatment of women by men is the obvious fact that most men are physically stronger than most women, so that when it comes to fights, women are more often the losers. An extension of this explanation, adds Gates, is that most women anticipate their own defeat and are, therefore, intimidated by, and make themselves subservient to, men. This disparate power relationship has been recognized, sanctioned, and reinforced over time by all our social institutions.

Economic dependency. The institution of marriage in patriarchal societies places women in a state of economic dependency on men. It creates a master-serf type of family where the roles are not equal. This type of family, according to Martin (1981), is characterized by the husband/father as head of the household who, as the breadwinner, gives his wife and children what they need, as he defines their needs. This "stay-in-your-place" family, she points out, depends upon each member following preconceived roles and respecting the authority of the husband/father, who metes out punishment when the wife or children do not stay in their places. Martin explains that in many American states the husband still has exclusive authority of "community" property, including all the wife's earnings, and can dissipate or use the family assets without the wife's prior knowledge or consent. This leaves the wife at the mercy of her husband whom the state's legal system presumes to be a benevolent despot. If he decides to give her no money and refuses to buy her clothing she has no legal recourse.

Gender inequality. One important factor contributing to the structural vulnerability of women is gender inequality. In a sexist society, gender roles are not equal. The socialization process prepares girls for their inferior role in the hierarchy of power and reinforces the values of a male sexist culture. By so doing, it helps perpetuate the myth of male superiority and to maintain existing power relationships, making it almost impossible to change the power structure of the patriarchal society. This process is described by Martin (1981) as follows:

> *The superior role of men is maintained by definition of "masculinity" as strong, active, rational, aggressive, and authoritarian and "femininity" as submissive, passive, dependent, weak, and masochistic. These roles are incorporated into the culture by its philosophy, science, social and psychological theory, morality, and law. The inequality of the roles is obscured by calling them "natural" or "normal" and by training women to dependency upon men in order to maintain the nuclear family as the basic unit of society. (p. 196)*

The way girls acquire their female gender identity, an identity considered inferior to that of the male, is explained by Stanko (1985):

> *Women, as part of growing up in a male-dominated society, learn that the two genders—male and female—occupy different value positions in society. Men, as men, occupy a higher one. Power, prestige, and credibility too are awarded on a gender basis; men, as men, have greater access to the benefits of power, prestige, and credibility. It is likely that female children, as part of growing up*

> *in an unequal, thus—gendered position, learn that they are less valued and have less prestige than their male counterparts. In acquiring a gender identity, a little girl* ***knows*** *she is a girl; she has been taught about and has observed her world for gender differences and roles. She incorporates a complex set of values and behaviors geared towards becoming and being recognized as a competent female. (p. 72)*

System inequity. The criminal justice system is a system created and run mainly by men. It incarnates the inequalities, the injustices, the prejudices, and the sexist attitudes of the larger society. It is not surprising, therefore, that the victimization of women is treated differently by the system than that of men. The system continues to exhibit greater tolerance, more acceptance, less indignation, and less condemnation of criminal acts whose victims are exclusively or mainly women. This results in lower reporting rates, lesser charges, milder sanctions, and a higher acquittal rate for crimes committed by males against females. Such systemic discrimination contributes to the structural proneness of women to victimization (see Chapter 7). As Martin (1981) points out, adherence to, and reinforcement of, stereotypical sex roles by legal and social sanctions obscure the patriarchal nature of society, which depends upon the subjugation and control of women.

Minority Status as Proneness: Canadian Native Indians as a Case Study

One type of structural proneness worthy of particular attention is the victimization of disadvantaged ethnic or religious minorities. Throughout history these minorities have been the primary candidates for serious acts of mass victimization, most notably genocide. Yet, even for ordinary types of criminal victimization, minority groups exhibit a particular proneness.

In the United States, for example, the risks of criminal victimization, particularly violent victimization, are far greater for blacks and Hispanics than they are for white Americans. The same pattern is true for many other ethnic minorities such as the aborigines in Australia, the native Indians in Canada, and the gypsies in some European countries.

Elias (1986) offers some comparative victimization data for blacks and whites in the United States to show that the black minority suffers much higher rates of criminal victimization. He states that the risks of homicide measure 9.3 per 100,000 people for whites and 77.9 per 100,000 for blacks. He also cites one study that shows black victimization to be seven times higher for assaults and twenty-five times higher for robberies with assaults than for whites. Another study he quotes reports that blacks suffer 89 percent of all violent crimes, 80 percent of all personal robberies, and six to eight times the total victimization of whites. He concludes that to be poor and a member of a minority substantially increases one's risks of victimization.

The extent to which Canada's natives are structurally prone to victimization may be easily seen from a study by Griffiths et al. (1989) that tried to draw attention to the horrendous consequences of sociostructural deprivation. The authors suggest that the victimization of natives in Canada is largely a direct result of their minority status, the structural arrangements in Canadian society, and the majority/minority relationships between the white and Indian populations. They present nationwide Canadian data indicating that the sociostructural conditions of registered Indians in Canada result in extensive victimization of native peoples, as manifested by poverty, high infant-mortality rates, a lower life expectancy, high rates of accidents, poisoning and violence, high suicide rates, and alcoholism. Among the registered Indian population, deaths from accidents, poisonings, and violence accounted for 35 percent of all deaths, compared to only 9 percent among the Canadian population as a whole. The crude death rate of these three causes among the registered Indians is over 250 per 100,000 population in the group of those whose ages range from birth to one year compared to a rate of under 50 per 100,000 for the same age group among the general Canadian population. The suicide rate per 100,000 for registered Indians is nearly three times the national Canadian rate.

Rates for criminal victimization would no doubt show patterns similar to those revealed by the study, thus confirming the existence of a structural proneness related to the minority status. The data, however, are not available. Because of the small size of the Canadian native population (as well as their poverty and the lack of telephones), their numbers in any given sample constructed for a victimization survey are likely to be too small to allow any statistically significant comparison to the rates of the general population.

As for official crime statistics (with the exception of those on criminal homicide), they provide no breakdown of victims according to their ethnic origin, thus precluding the possibility of assessing the importance of the minority status as a victimogenic variable.

DEVIANCE-RELATED PRONENESS

Although the dark figure makes it difficult (or even impossible) to adequately compare the criminal victimization rates of deviant groups with those of the general population to ascertain whether they are victimized more or less, there seems to be little doubt that various forms of deviance are positively associated with a high degree of victim proneness. This deviance-related proneness is attributable to offenders' perceptions, to the nature of the deviant activities, and to the laxity of the criminal justice system when the victim is a member of a negatively labeled deviant group. Deviant transactions are generally high-risk activities, and the potential for victimization is strong and ever present. This is because most of these transactions, whether they have to do with sex, drugs, or other illicit goods and services, are characterized by distrust, mistrust, conflict, or outright antagonism. The extent of the proneness of the deviant depends largely on the degree of exposure, since all deviants are not equally exposed. The difference is well described by Karmen (1983):

> *When streetwalkers solicit strangers, they expose themselves to greater danger than the more privileged call girls who work the suites. When addicts loiter late at night on dimly lit corners with money in their pockets or enter abandoned buildings seeking their "connection" to buy drugs, they run greater risks than wealthy abusers who pay intermediaries to deliver the substances. When homosexuals cruise downtown areas or enter "tea rooms" (bathrooms) to find partners for brief sexual escapades, they subject themselves to threats not borne by monogamous gay couples ... But in general, the fundamental aspects of the deviant identity—carrying cash to purchase drugs, trading sex for money with strangers, begging money from passersby, hanging out with criminally inclined people, becoming active at night—are the causes of (presumably) higher victimization rates. (pp. 241-242)*

Another important determinant of deviance-related proneness is the lack of protection. Because of their deviant status and, often, the illegality of their deviant behavior, members of these groups lack the social resources necessary to protect them against the occurrence of criminal victimization, and they cannot rely on the official protective agencies to afford them the same kind of protection provided to conforming citizens. The fact that they cannot (or are not likely to) complain when victimized, combined with the fact that if they do complain they are not listened to, means that they can often be victimized with impunity. This is what Harry (1982) calls "derivative deviance." He defines it as "that subset of all victimizations which is perpetrated upon other presumed deviants who, because of their deviant status, are presumed unable to avail themselves of the protections of civil society without threat of discrediting" (p. 546).

Deviance-related Proneness: Drug Addicts as a Case Study

One form of deviance that predisposes those involved to various kinds of victimization is alcoholism and drug addiction. One of the most dramatic examples of alcoholic victimization are the skid-row men and women whose vulnerability to robbery by "jackrollers" has been described by Sutherland (1937) and others (Kelly, 1983). Kelly (1983) makes it abundantly clear that alcoholics and drug addicts occupy high-risk categories as potential victims. He explains that the biochemical and psychological effects of the substances they take and the typical environments in which alcohol and drugs are consumed increase the risks of victimization by others, as well as increasing the risk of self-victimization through injury, accident, and negligence. Kelly (1983) adds:

Because heroin is illegal, intensified police and law enforcement efforts make buying, selling, distribution, and use of it underground activities: dealing goes on clandestinely, in out-of-the-way places that are free of police surveillance. Consequently, the seller/pusher is very vulnerable to robberies and extortions by those who populate the drug culture. (p. 61)

Kelly points to two factors that are particularly important in understanding the victimization of the heroin addict. First, the illegal status of heroin precludes conventional methods of recourse (the police, the courts) in the event of robberies and thefts of their drugs. Second, the subculture and environment that addicts inhabit are filled with criminals and others who are operating outside the bounds and controls of the law. Together, these two factors combine to create a life-style and a set of circumstances in which the risk of victimization is quite high (Kelly, 1983, p. 62).

Drug addicts and drug traffickers are particularly vulnerable to criminal homicide. Drug-related homicides have been a fact of life in many North American cities for many years. Unfortunately, the studies documenting and analyzing these killings remain rather sparse. Two studies conducted in the early 1970s (Zahn and Bencivengo, 1974, 1975) suggest that the drug business is becoming riskier and riskier every year. The findings reveal that in the years from 1969 to 1972, drug users in Philadelphia were increasingly becoming victims of homicide. In 1972 alone, 30.8 percent of the homicide victims in Philadelphia were, according to the authors, drug users, primarily heroin users. In addition, the studies showed that young black male drug users are especially high-risk candidates for such deaths. As an explanation, the authors cite the transactional risks, which are high for drug users in a society where drug use is illegal. These risks include involvement in thefts, which may result in lethal involvement with law officers or with the victims; altercations, such as "getting burned," over drug-related transactions; control of drug-traffic turf; and other arguments related to securing or maintaining a supply of drugs in a highly competitive market.

The emergence of crack in the 1980s and its becoming the drug of choice for poor young blacks and ghetto dwellers has led to waves of drug-related killings in cities like New York, Los Angeles, and Washington, D.C.

Deviance-related Proneness: Homosexuality as a Case Study

The negative stereotyping, the cultural labeling, and the moral and religious prejudices that prevail in our society toward homosexuals render them extremely prone to a wide variety of criminal victimizations ranging from homicide to blackmail, from robbery and extortion to public ridicule. In most large North American cities, there are gangs of young males who prey exclusively or predominantly upon homosexual men. These activities have acquired a name of their own: "fag-bashing." The term refers to a declaration of virtual extralegal, vigilante-type warfare against persons of known or supposed homosexuality. This bashing is sometimes accompanied by robbery, and it may even include forced sodomy or rape (Maghan and Sagarin, 1983, p. 155). Gagnon (1974) suggests that many of these young victimizers are recruited from delinquent or quasi-delinquent communities. The victimization, he points out, takes different forms and in most cases goes unreported. In the few instances where it is reported, the official response is, more often than not, inadequate. So, acccording to Gagnon (1974), the following results:

> *The legal status of homosexuality makes the homosexual vulnerable to victimization and makes a law enforcement response to that victimization, even if well intended, extremely difficult. Homicides, robberies, and assaults that arise out of homosexual relationships are concealed or badly investigated because the victim is unable to establish a sense of trust in the police. If the homosexual has been involved in what is considered to be a sexual crime, there is a minimal likelihood that he will report being robbed during a criminal act. Further, there is no guarantee to the victim that there will be no further reprisals against him or his friends. (p. 256)*

Humphreys (1970) believes that the stigmatized status of homosexuality in general and the difficulties of integrating it into an otherwise conventional life-style promotes sexual contacts under conditions of relative sexual and personal degradation, and of high risk to the participants.

One of the best explanations of the proneness of homosexuals is offered by Sagarin and MacNamara. The authors (Sagarin and MacNamara, 1975) give eight different reasons why members of subsocietal groups run a much higher risk of becoming victims of crime than other citizens:

> *(1) They are more likely to have what the criminal wants—or the criminal so believes; (2) they are more frequently present in high-crime areas, in situations in which plots are hatched and crimes committed, or where there are temptations that lead to victimization; (3) they are defined as physically weaker than others and hence are liable to be "chosen" as easy targets by offenders; (4) they are believed to have relatively little access to law enforcement agencies and seats of power; (5) they are viewed as persons unlikely to use law enforcement agencies; (6) they are engaged in activities that lend themselves to manipulation by predators; (7) they participate in high-risk activities either because of personality traits or because of goals that make the risk a necessity for assurance of success; and (8) they live on the periphery of society and receive so little social support for their activities that the normal constraints of ordinary persons are neutralized, because the latter define the victim as worthless. (p. 73)*

Having enumerated these eight factors, Sagarin and MacNamara go on to explain that some of them are present in homosexual activities to a large extent, while others are present to a modified extent, making many of the participants in such acts particularly prone to victimization. They add that the proneness to victimization increases with each of four elements: casualness of relationship; anonymity; prostitutional character of the understanding; and age discrepancy of the participants, that is, the younger the partner, the more likely that he will be an offender.

In a subsequent paper, written with Jess Maghan (1983), Sagarin dwells further on the reasons for the vulnerability of the homosexual to criminal victimization, noting that this vulnerability derives from several sources so intertwined that they are hardly separable. Maghan and Sagarin (1983) explain the particular vulnerability of the homosexual in the following manner:

> *There is, above all else, the cultural impact on impressionable heterosexuals of the almost incessant propaganda that derides and dehumanizes homosexuals. Taught to despise, many heterosexuals see the victim as deserving of his fate and themselves as performing an acceptable and just service. To this is added the secrecy and fragility of the homosexual life-style that can so easily be shattered, subjecting persons to blackmail, on the one hand, and to interaction with marginal people, on the other. Patterns of homosexual behavior, furthermore, may for many be inherently less than stable, and this instability can result in vulnerability to victimization. (p. 153)*

OCCUPATIONAL PRONENESS

Many occupations carry with them a potential for criminal victimization. Victimization, in varying forms, is one of the occupational hazards facing those who work in many different sectors. Bank tellers run the risk of being held up, and pharmacists and those working in corner and convenience stores or gas stations could be robbed. For foreign diplomats there is always a danger of being kidnapped or held hostage, and for airpilots there is the risk of having the aircraft hijacked or even blown up. Those people, such as policemen, sheriffs, and prison guards, whose jobs bring them into contact or confrontation with criminals, are prone to violent victimization. Taxi drivers are particularly prone as their job requires them to pick up anonymous strangers in their vehicles and to drive them to wherever they desire. Those who are engaged in illegal or illicit activities, such as fencing, drug trafficking, gambling, procuring, black marketing, racketeering, or bootlegging, run a much higher risk of being victimized than the average citizen. The nature of the occupational proneness resulting from the involvement in illegal activities is somewhat similar to deviance-related proneness.

A recent Swedish study has brought to light the occupational proneness of those engaged in the public entertainment sector. In his study of everyday violence in contemporary Sweden, Wikström (1985) found that people working in public entertainment and in places where alcohol is consumed are not infrequently involved in violent confrontations. Nearly one-third of all violent crimes involving victims who were assaulted during work occurred at places of public entertainment. Public transport and shops/service institutions were other frequent scenes of crime. He points out that although alcohol intoxication plays an important role in all kinds of violence, it is particularly prevalent in situational conflicts arising in the course of public entertainment. The occupational proneness observed by Wikström extends to those who have contact with leisure activities. Wikström (1985) notes:

> *As regards those involved in violent crimes during work, it is mainly persons who have contact with leisure activities as part of their work e.g., employees of public establishments, those having as work to keep the peace (policemen, watchguards), those transporting people to and from public entertainment (bus and taxi drivers) and those taking care of injuries to people as a result of public entertainment (personnel at hospitals' casualty departments). (p. 94)*

In their study of crime victimization rates for incumbents of 246 occupations, Block, Felson, and Block (1985) found that amusement and recreation workers are among the five highest risk occupations for all five offenses of robbery, assault, burglary, larceny, and auto theft. The rates for all five offenses place certain restaurant occupations, including busboys, dishwashers, and servers (a category including females), among the five most victimized jobs. The authors think that the hours of work are perhaps the cause. Other findings reported in the study include sheriffs and police having the highest assault risk. Taxi drivers and newspaper deliverers were among the most often robbed. Those who most suffered property victimization included athletes and demonstrators, both of whom are presumably away from home often, while peddlers had very high auto-theft rates, presumably because they park their cars among strangers.

Increasing attention is being paid to criminal victimization on the job and to work-related criminal victimization, as evidenced by a number of empirical investigations published in the past few years (Collins, Cox, and Langan, 1987; Lynch, 1987; and Mayhew, Elliott, and Dowds, 1989). Lynch (1987) used data from the *Victim Risk Supplement* to the National Crime Survey to model victimization incidents that occurred at work or while commuting to and from work. In so doing, he went a step further than the simple taxonomies of risky and safe occupations that characterized earlier studies. The findings indicate that what people do at work does affect their chances of being victimized while on the job. Lines of work involving face-to-face contact with large numbers of persons on a routine basis involve a higher risk of criminal victimization than those with less accessibility to the public. Workers whose occupations require them to handle money are at greater risk than workers who do not. Jobs that involve more than a single work site or routine travel (local and extralocal) expose those who work in them to a greater risk of victimization than persons working in jobs at a single location. Lynch also found that work-related risks are cumulative. Thus, people whose occupation involves all the risk factors of public accessibility, mobility, and handling money, run the greatest risk of victimization.

Collins, Cox, and Langan (1987) went yet another step further by dichotomizing criminal victimization into two separate categories: (1) violent victimization and (2) victimization by personal theft or property damage. The first category contained assault (including sexual assault), robbery, and threat to injure. Theft or property damage included personal larceny, with or without contact, and vandalism. The data for the study was collected using methodology modeled after the National Crime Survey. Trained personnel conducted telephone interviews with a population sample of 5,542 civilian, noninstitutionalized persons aged twelve and over residing in the District of Columbia Standard Metropolitan Statistical Area in 1983.

The findings of the study by Collins, Cox, and Langan (1987) confirmed those reported by Lynch (1987) and offered additional insights on the relationship between occupational activities and criminal victimization. Collins, Cox, and Langan found that delivery of passengers or goods, out-of-town travel, and face-to-face public dealings in connection with work were directly associated with victimization. Individuals whose jobs included one of these three activities were approximately one and one-half times more likely to have experienced violent victimization in comparison to those whose jobs did not include such activities. As in Lynch's (1987) study, the effects of the different risk factors were cumulative. In other words, each work activity added significantly to the risk of violent victimization when all the activity types were included in the model. One factor that was not associated with increased violent victimization risk was working irregular hours. On the other hand, only one work activity was clearly associated with an increased risk of theft-damage victimization. Thus, those traveling in connection with work were found to be 1.38 times more likely to have been victimized. The association of other risk factors, such as dealing with the public and irregular working hours, with theft-damage victimization did not reach statistical significance.

Another study that looked at victimization at work is the 1988 British Crime Survey (Mayhew, Elliott, and Dowds, 1989). The 1988 survey included questions that were not part of the previous one in an attempt to explore this specific aspect of victimization. The survey also probed the respondents for verbal abuse at work in addition to the usual types of victimization: violence, threats, and theft. Although the survey revealed that criminal victimization was not infrequent at work, it confirmed the pattern reported previously in the United States, Canada, and Australia, namely that victimization risks are highest among the unemployed. The survey revealed further that work is the scene of much crime, a finding that could largely be explained by the amount of time people spend at work. Thus, seven out of ten thefts of workers' personal property took place at work, though the victims were understandably uncertain as to who was responsible—colleagues or the public. Verbal abuse by the public over a period of rather more than a year was reported by 14 percent of the workers. The frequency of abuse declined with age, but in relation to gender both men and women seemed to be equally prone. Workers reported that one-quarter of violent offenses and over one-third of the threats they experienced were due to the work they did. The pattern for threats was more pronounced for women than for men, with a full one-half of threats against female workers being job-related. Certain occupations proved to be more hazardous in terms of criminal victimization than others. For example, welfare workers and nurses reported comparatively high levels of violence and threats due to their job. The same was also true for security personnel and those who managed places of entertainment, such as pubs. Teachers were not vulnerable to violence, though they were vulnerable to threats, verbal abuse, and thefts.

In addition to their important contribution to the understanding of the differential risks of criminal victimization, findings of research on victimization risks related to, or associated with, certain job activities can have significant practical implications. Were we to consider the risk of victimization at work in the same way we look upon labor accidents, a great deal could be done to reduce or minimize those risks. This could be achieved, as Lynch (1987) points out, by changing the tasks of certain occupations or modifying the work environment. Naturally, to do this requires that the specific attributes of certain occupations that contribute to victimization risks be clearly identified and accurately measured.

Occupational Proneness: Prostitution as a Case Study

Street prostitution is without doubt one of the most hazardous occupations in which a female can be involved. The occupational proneness associated with street prostitution shares several similarities with deviance-related proneness. Street prostitutes engage in high-risk activities that lend themselves to manipulation by predators. They are accessible and easy targets who cannot afford to be too selective about their customers. They are generally physically weaker than their male clients. Their activities are characterized by the casualness and anonymity of the encounters and the privacy in which the sexual practices are usually performed. Their victimization can be easily rationalized because of their marginal status and the negative label attached to prostitution. And, finally, they enjoy no social protection and have little or no access to the protective agencies, notably the police. As a result they have to rely on pimps for protection, thus increasing their susceptibility to exploitation and abuse.

Boyer and James (1983) found, through observing and interviewing prostitutes, that violence is a constant in street life. It was difficult for them to find a street prostitute who had not been assaulted by a customer, beaten by a pimp, or robbed because of lack of protection. They attribute the popularity of prostitutes as targets of violence to the fact that they possess money, are least able to defend themselves, and are perceived as being beyond police protection.

Further evidence on the prevalence and extent of the victimization of prostitutes comes from several studies cited by Hatty (1989). Milman (1980) reports that over three-quarters of the prostitutes she interviewed claimed to have been injured by clients or police while working. Edwards (1984) noted that many prostitutes who spoke to her had experienced serious physical violence. Erbe (1984) concluded that over 70 percent of the prostitutes she surveyed had been sexually assaulted by clients, with an average of thirty-one times per woman. In a study of street and brothel prostitutes in Sydney, Australia, (Perkins and Bennett, 1985), over one-third of the prostitutes said that they had been sexually assaulted while working. Research with street prostitutes in Melbourne, Australia, found that almost half of those interviewed claimed to have been sexually assaulted during the course of their work (Hatty, 1989).

The victimization of prostitutes comes from various sources, the two main ones being the pimps and the clients. Client victimizers have acquired a name in the jargon of prostitution: "bad tricks." The most common forms of victimization to which prostitutes are particularly prone are homicide, rape, indecent assault, assault, wounding, and robbery.

The police are a third source of victimization. Gilfus (1987) maintains that the incarcerated prostitutes she interviewed "talked at length of the sexual and physical violence they experienced at the hands of pimps, customers and police officers" (p. 6). Hatty (1989) cites evidence presented before the Fitzgerald Commission into police corruption in Queensland, Australia, which suggests that sexual assault by police officers and coercion by brothel managers to provide sex to officers have been a routine aspect of prostitution in that state.

The vulnerability of prostitutes to criminal homicide was made famous by notorious cases such as that of Jack the Ripper, who is believed to have been responsible for the killing of several prostitutes in London, England, in the nineteenth century. More recent cases of serial killers who prey exclusively or predominantly on prostitutes include the Green River Killer who is supposedly responsible for taking the lives of at least forty prostitutes in the Seattle area. Another case (cited in Lowman, 1989) came recently to light in California. On October 9, 1988, the Vancouver newspaper *The Province* reported that the bodies of forty prostitutes and "street people" were found in rural areas of San Diego county in California.

Accurate and reliable statistics are difficult to come by. However, Lowman (1989) reports that in a three-year period from 1985 to 1988, at least ten Vancouver prostitutes were murdered. None of these murders has been solved. The real number could be much higher, since some homicide victims whose bodies have not been found may be listed as having disappeared or having left the city or the province. Lowman quotes a spokeswoman for POWER (Prostitutes and Other Women for Equal Rights) who, in December 1987, put the number of murdered Vancouver prostitutes at fifteen.[5]

More recent figures provide an even more sombre picture. In an article published in the Vancouver *Sun* (Pemberton and Bell, 1990), the authors give a list containing the names and ages of twelve Vancouver prostitutes who were killed during a two-year period, from April 3, 1988 to August 28, 1990. Even in the absence of accurate figures on the number of prostitutes active in the city of Vancouver, these numbers suggest that prostitution is one of the most dangerous (perhaps *the* most dangerous) occupations with regard to the risk of being intentionally killed.

Hatty (1989) contends that the discriminatory attitude toward violence against prostitutes is especially obvious in instances in which prostitutes are killed. In these cases, prostitutes are often portrayed as expendable objects, and their deaths are considered less worthy of attention than those of nonprostitutes. In support of her contention she quotes Sir Michael Havers, the Attorney-General of Britain who, commenting on Peter Sutcliffe's (the Yorkshire Ripper) victims, said "some were prostitutes, but perhaps the saddest part of this case is that some were not."

Lowman's (1989) research of the impact of the Canadian Bill C-49 suggests that the new legislation is likely to enhance the vulnerability of prostitutes to violence in at least five ways:[6]

> *First, because women might feel the need for more protection once the communicating law was in effect, they would turn increasingly to pimps to provide it. The result would be more pimp violence perpetrated against prostitutes. Second, if prostitutes were forced into off-street locations, it would be easier for pimps to gain control over them. Third, because women who did work on the street might become more dispersed and forced to operate more covertly, they would become more susceptible to "bad tricks." Fourth, because Section 195.1 serves to consolidate the criminal status of prostitution, this social marginalization might help some men to more easily rationalize acts of violence against prostitutes. Fifth, prostitutes would be even less likely to report crimes against them to the police than they already were for fear that they would have to admit working the street, and be charged under Section 195.1 as a result of doing so. As a result, serial bad tricks would be able to operate with less likelihood of apprehension. (p. 125)*

Lowman adds that every policeman interviewed for the study was well aware that prostitutes are frequently the victims of criminal offenses, and he thought that only a small portion of the victimizations were ever reported to the police.

Further support for the link between the way prostitution is regulated and the vulnerability of prostitutes to various types of victimization comes from Australia. Hatty (1989) believes that legal approaches to prostitution, irrespective of the progressive flavor of some of these approaches, may not benefit or protect prostitutes. Some may further marginalize women who work on the streets and thus expose them to greater risk of physical and sexual violence. Hatty (1989) adds:

> *Indeed, it is possible to argue that the dominant legal approaches to prostitution (prohibition and regulation) institutionalize physical and sexual violence against women—in this case, female prostitutes ... Both approaches*

provide significant scope for the undetected victimization of prostitutes and prejudice women's access to criminal justice protection ... The prohibition and regulation of prostitution may thus function to perpetuate the oppression of an extremely vulnerable group of women. (p. 242)

SITUATIONAL VULNERABILITY

Structural proneness stemming from minority status or young age as well as occupational proneness associated with a certain profession is a state that lasts for many years or even a lifetime. There are, on the other hand, temporary or transitory conditions that render the person vulnerable to victimization for a brief and limited period of time. These are termed states of "ephemeral vulnerability." The tourist in a foreign city, the freshman in college, and the young inmate experiencing prison for the first time are all vulnerable to victimization for as long as they remain in that state. Still, there are other states of vulnerability that may exist for even shorter periods of time and last only for few hours. They are states of "situational vulnerability." One such state is the state of chemical vulnerability resulting from drug or alcohol intoxication.

Ephemeral Vulnerability: A Case Study of Alcohol as a Victimogenic Factor

As early as 1948, Von Hentig drew attention to the specific vulnerability of the alcoholic and of the ordinary person who is under the influence of alcohol. Then came the classic study undertaken in Finland by Verkko (1951) that revealed that nearly half of the victims of nonnegligent manslaughter (49.5 percent) during the years from 1920 to 1929 were intoxicated at the moment of the crime. This was followed by the Philadelphia studies of Wolfgang and Strohm (1956) and Wolfgang (1958) where it was established that either or both the victim and the offender had been drinking immediately before the slaying in nearly two-thirds of the cases of criminal homicide they studied. In 11 percent alcohol was present in the offender only, in 9 percent it was present in the victim only, and in 44 percent alcohol was present in both the victim and the offender. Wolfgang (1958) further found a significant association between victim-precipitated homicide and presence of alcohol in the victim. Wolfgang explains that, in many of the cases of victim-precipitated homicides, the victim was intoxicated, or nearly so, and lost control of his own defensive powers. He frequently was a victim with no intent to harm anyone maliciously. Nonetheless, he struck the friend, the acquaintance, or wife who later became his assailant. Impulsive, aggressive, and often dangerously violent, the victim was the first to slap, punch, or commit an asault in another manner. Perhaps, suggests

Wolfgang (1958), the presence of alcohol in this kind of homicide victim played no small part in his taking the first and major physical step toward victimization:

> *Perhaps if he had not been drinking he would have been less violent, less ready to plunge into an assaultive state of interaction. Or, if the presence of alcohol had no causal relation to his being the aggressor, perhaps it reduced his ability to defend himself from retaliatory assault, and contributed in this way to his death. (p. 262)*

Subsequent empirical research provided further evidence confirming the initial findings of Verkko (1951) and of Wolfgang (1958) (Voss and Hepburn, 1968; Haberman and Baden, 1978; Centers for Disease Control, 1984). Further confirmation of the role of alcohol as a victimogenic factor comes from a California study, which used a large population rather than a small sample. Goodman et al. (1986) used data from the Los Angeles City Police Department and the Los Angeles Medical Examiner's Office to study 4,950 victims of criminal homicide in the period from 1970 to 1979. Alcohol was detected in the blood of 1,883 (46 percent) of the 4,092 victims who were tested. In 30 percent of those tested, the blood alcohol level was ≥ 100 mg/100 ml, the level of legal intoxication in most states. Blood alcohol was present most commonly in victims who were male, young, and Latino. More recent studies have tried to assess the victimogenic role alcohol plays in assault cases. A study of everyday violence in the Swedish town of Gavle (Wikström, 1985) reports that 75 percent of the offenders and 54 percent of the victims were intoxicated. In 46 percent both the offender and the victim were intoxicated, while in 37 percent one of the parties was intoxicated, and in 17 percent both the victim and offender were sober.

A recent British field study (Shepherd et al., 1989) used innovative methodology and reports interesting findings. All 539 adult victims of assault who attended an inner-city Accident and Emergency Department in 1986 were interviewed. Seventy-four percent of male victims and 42 percent of female victims reported alcohol consumption in the six hours before the assault. Thirty percent of males and 4 percent of females had consumed more than >ten units. Forty percent of males and 25 percent of females exceeded established safe levels of consumption, while 16 percent of males and 26 percent of females demonstrated abnormally high gamma-GT levels.

A victimogenic factor is a factor which predisposes the person to becoming a victim or contributes to his or her actual victimization. A factor that was relevant in the choice of a specific person as a victim or which contributed in some way to the commission of the crime against that particular victim may be described as a victimogenic factor. Alcohol may be considered a victimogenic factor if the victim was chosen because he or she had imbibed some alcohol, was drunk or intoxicated, or, as a result of the alcohol intoxication, had precipitated or facilitated the act of victimization. Alcohol may contribute to the victimization in a variety of different ways—some subtle and some not so subtle. It can do this by attracting people to high-risk entertainment places where alcohol is served and consumed; by creating conflict situations and helping to inflame the conflict into violent actions; by reducing or eliminating the resistance and the vigilance of the potential victim; by slowing the defensive reflexes of the victim or by weakening the victim's critical judgment; by increasing the imprudence, recklessness, or impulsiveness of the future victim or by reducing the person's control over his or her words and deeds; and by lowering the person's inhibitions and releasing his or her provocative, aggressive, and violent potential. As Wolfgang (1958) puts it, lowered inhibitions due to ingestion of alcohol may cause an individual to give vent more freely to pent-up frustrations, tensions, and emotional conflicts that have either built up over a prolonged period of time or that arise within an immediate emotional crisis (Wolfgang, 1958, p. 261).

Summary

Since the beginning of criminology, criminologists have tried to explain criminal behavior by reference to the personal characteristics of the offender. Similarly, victimologists have tried to explain victimization by reference to the personal characteristics of the person being victimized. The impetus for such research came from the undisputable fact that the risks of criminal victimization are not evenly distributed within the general population and that the likelihood (and actual rates) of victimization are linked to the personal characteristics of victims and do vary according to certain sociodemographic variables. There was also the realization that a variety of other misfortunes are disproportionately suffered by those who are crime victims. All this suggests a certain vulnerability or proneness. These notions, however, carry with them certain dangers. They might be construed as implying some sort of fatalism or inevitability, whereas they are simply meant to indicate variations in risk and in statistical probabilities of victimization. There is also the danger that such variations in risk might be seen as having as their cause some inherent personal attributes, such as clumsiness, whereas risk differences are most likely the result of such differences as social situations, areas of residence, exposure, and accessibility. Another problem is that the concepts of vulnerability and proneness have been used interchangeably, although they are not the same. Vulnerability is just one dimension of proneness and is by no means the most important dimension.

We were able to identify various types of proneness; spatial proneness, structural proneness, deviance-related proneness, occupational proneness, and situational proneness. These types are suggested by variations in the risks of victimization. City dwellers, for example, run a higher risk of criminal victimization than rural residents, and, within a large city, people living or working in certain areas are more prone to victimization than others. Criminal victimization clusters not only spatially but socially, which suggests the existence of what may be described as "structural proneness." To illustrate structural proneness we used young age, female gender, and minority status as three case studies. Deviance-related proneness was examined by focusing on two groups: drug addicts/traffickers and homosexuals. It was suggested that the negative labeling, the lack of protection, the nature of the activities, and the conditions under which these activities take place, are important factors leading to the proneness of the members of these groups. We gave examples of certain occupations that carry with them a risk (or a higher risk) of criminal victimization, and we used prostitution as a case study to illustrate what is meant by occupational proneness. Factors contributing to the proneness of prostitutes were shown to be similar in many ways to those endangering other deviant groups. Certain conditions of proneness are temporary or transient and may thus be qualified as states of "ephemeral vulnerability." One such state is the state of chemical vulnerability resulting from alcohol consumption. Alcohol may be considered an important victimogenic factor and may contribute in different ways to the risk of victimization. This is confirmed by a growing body of empirical evidence showing a high percentage of victims of violence to have consumed alcohol in the hours preceding their victimization.

ELEVEN

Victim Behavior as a Situational Variable

Understanding victim precipitation has many valuable uses. It helps us better understand the origin of particular criminal events. It allows us to examine the kinds of victim-offender interactions that lead to victimization. It suggests, from a sociological perspective, that victims have a "functional responsibility" for victimization that develops not because victims have necessarily provoked the crime, but rather from their being necessary for the criminal transaction to have occurred. Clarifying the victim's role in crime can also help us devise strategies for reducing risks and predicting victimization.

Robert Elias (1986, p. 85)

If retaliation is a key principle in violence, then the behavior of one antagonist is crucial in determining the behavior of the other. The more aggressive is a participant, the more aggression one expects from his or her adversary. In the case of criminal violence, verbal and physical attacks by the victim should be correlated with verbal and physical attacks by the offender. One might also hypothesize that the more aggressive the victim, the more likely it is that he or she will be killed.

Richard B. Felson and Henry J. Steadman (1983, p. 60)

Explaining Victimization by Reference to the Behavior of the Victim

The beginnings of victimology were characterized by sustained efforts to explain victimization by reference to the behavior of the person who has been victimized. Von Hentig's (1940, 1948) pioneering work was a serious attempt to show that victims of crime are not simply passive objects who fall prey to aggressive predators. Von Hentig (1948) stressed the interactionist nature of many crimes, making repeated reference to "the victim's contribution to the genesis of crime," and "the duet frame of crime," and he insisted that "in the long chain of causative forces the victim may assume the role of the determinant" (pp. 383, 384). Through these statements and several others Von Hentig made it clear that the search for the causes of crime would neither be successful nor complete unless it thoroughly analyzed the interaction between criminal and victim and the role played by both protagonists in the drama of crime.

Because most crimes of violence and the majority of sex offenses involve a brief or prolonged interaction between victim and victimizer, an analysis of these interactions is clearly indispensable for an adequate understanding of these victimizations. The attention of researchers, however, seems to have been largely focused upon the act of criminal homicide. Luckenbill (1977), for example, analyzed seventy transactions ending in murder and tried to reconstruct these transactions. His investigation covered all forms of criminal homicide but felony murder, where death occurs in the commission of other felony crimes, and contract murder, where the offender conspires with another to kill on his or her behalf for payment. His conclusion leaves no doubt as to the inadequacy of traditional explanatory formulations. On the basis of the research, he found that criminal homicide is not a one-sided event with an unwitting victim assuming a passive, noncontributory role. Rather, it was clear that murder is the outcome of a dynamic interchange between an offender, victim, and, in many cases, bystanders.

In their study of the situational factors in disputes leading to criminal violence, Felson and Steadman (1983) found that victims of homicide were more likely to have displayed (i.e., actually drew, threatened, or used) some type of weapon (gun, knife, or other object) than were victims of assault, which suggested that offenders were more likely to kill the victim if the latter had a weapon. In addition, victims of homicide were significantly more likely to have been intoxicated with drugs or alcohol, which suggested that offenders were more likely to kill intoxicated victims. They found significant effects of both victim aggression and victim intoxication on the severity of the outcome. This led Felson and Steadman (1983) to the following conclusion:

> *The evidence then, is consistent with an interactionist viewpoint, in that the behavior of the victim appears to have affected the behavior of the offender in*

these incidents ... These results suggest that the successive behaviors of a participant are more a function of the antagonist's behavior than they are of his or her own earlier actions, demonstrating again the importance of interaction in these incidents. (pp. 65, 69)

Probably the most important finding of Felson and Steadman's study is that victims who were aggressive were more likely to be killed even when they did not use a weapon. There was also some evidence that victims who were aggressive and used a weapon were particularly likely to be killed. This suggests that killing the victim was, to some extent, a strategic, physical self-defense move by the offender.

Victim Behavior as a Situational Variable

Although the victim's functional role can take several forms, one form in particular, victim-precipitation, has generated the strongest interest as well as the fiercest criticism.

PROVOCATION/PRECIPITATION

Because of the criticism the concept of "victim-precipitation" has generated over the years, it is necessary not only to clarify this concept and its various operationalizations, but also to distinguish the legal notion of provocation from the behavioral concept of precipitation. It is important to stress at the outset that provocation is an *exculpatory* concept whereas precipitation is an *explanatory* concept. Explanatory concepts such as precipitation, facilitation, and participation, to name but a few, also need to be distinguished from popular expressions by which the respective responsibility of the parties involved is assessed and apportioned. Expressions such as "He was asking for it" or "She had it coming to her" clearly are not meant to explain what happened but are meant simply to attribute to the victimized party a share of the guilt and a part of the blame. The frequent use in victimological writings of words borrowed from legal terminology, such as "guilt," "culpability," "responsibility," and "blame," has only added to the confusion. In what follows we will try to clear up some of the confusion by clarifying the concepts and by stressing the difference between them.

Provocation in Canadian Law

Modern criminal codes recognize "provocation" sometimes as a legal excuse, and other times as an extenuating circumstance. Section 215 of the Canadian Criminal Code stipulates that "culpable homicide that otherwise would be murder may be reduced to manslaughter if the person who committed it did so in the heat of passion caused by sudden provocation." The section goes on to explain what constitutes and what does not constitute provocation in a legal sense. Thus "a wrongful act or insult that is of such a nature as to be sufficient to deprive an ordinary person of the power of self-control is provocation enough for the purposes of this section if the accused acted upon it on the sudden and before there was time for his passion to cool." Section 215 of the Canadian Criminal Code stipulates further that "no one shall be deemed to have given provocation to another by doing anything that he had a legal right to do, or by doing anything that the accused incited him to do in order to provide the accused with an excuse for causing death or bodily harm to any human being."

Canadian jurisprudence cited in *Snow's Annotated Criminal Code* (Heather, 1979) makes it clear that provocation has a precise legal meaning. The test to be applied in order to determine whether homicide, which would otherwise be murder, is "manslaughter" by reason of provocation "is whether the provocation was sufficient to deprive a reasonable man of his self-control by reason of the provocation which he received" (pp. 6-13, 6-14). This is done in two steps: (1) the decision must be made as to whether an "ordinary" man would have been deprived of his self-control by the wrongful act or insult and (2) whether, in fact, the accused actually acted upon the provocation "on the sudden." For example, in a case cited in *Snow's Annotated Criminal Code* (Heather, 1979, pp. 6-14.1 - 6-15), it was decided that a subsequent mention by a wife to her husband of her adultery did not constitute provocation and the accused husband's murder of her could not be reduced to manslaughter.

The Difference Between Provocation and Victim-precipitation

The legal concept of provocation is used in criminal courts for determining and measuring the criminal responsibility of the accused, for settling the issue of guilt, and for choosing the optimal criminal sanction. The behavioral concept of victim-precipitation is used by social scientists in an attempt to explain the etiology of victimization. The main criterion for determining whether there is provocation in the legal sense is the state of mind of the accused and the offender's loss of self-control measured against the abstract concept of the "reasonable man." The sole criterion for victim-precipitation in a victimological sense is the behavior of the victim, whether or not the victim's behavior was a direct, positive precipitator of the crime. That the two concepts "provocation" and "precipitation" are quite distinct may be demonstrated by the fact that several types of victim behavior, which may fit the legal definition of provocation, do not fit the behavioral definition of victim-precipitation, and vice-versa. There are also behaviors that qualify neither as provocation nor precipitation. Wolfgang (1958) gives some examples:

> *Infidelity of a mate or lover, failure to pay a debt, use of vile names by the victim, obviously means that he played an important role in inciting the offender to overt action in order to seek revenge, to win an argument, or to defend*

> *himself. However, these mutual quarrels and wordy altercations do not constitute sufficient provocation under law, nor are they included in the present interpretation of victim-precipitated homicide ... Primary demonstration of physical force by the victim, supplemented by scurrilous language characterizes the most common victim-precipitated homicides. (pp. 252-253)*

Finally, the legal concept of provocation, being an exculpatory concept, implies that the person responsible for the provocation shares a part of the responsibility for the act and the ensuing guilt. Victim-precipitation and other behavioral explanations of the causative forces engendering the act of victimization do not involve attributions of fault or imputations of guilt. Referring to "victim-precipitation" should not be construed as an attempt to blame the victim or to hold him or her responsible for what happened.[1] What it does is to emphasize the importance of situational and triggering factors and the role they play in the etiology of criminal victimization. Victim-precipitation enables the researcher to understand and explain the motives of the crime and to analyze the chain of events that led to, or culminated in, the victimizing act. As Kinberg (1960) puts it, when analyzing the genesis of an action to determine its causes, it is not possible to regard certain facts or groups of facts as separate entities. The logical intellectual process requires that the researcher take an overall view of the intricate web of factors that form a tight causal chain, the last link of which is the action being analyzed.

After all, gratuitous violence is the exception rather than the rule. Unless the motive for the aggression is robbery or sex, or unless the attacker is a mentally deranged individual shooting or stabbing anyone who passes by, it is unlikely that a person would be killed or assaulted without any precipitating action on his or her part. While this action may take varying forms, its role in triggering the victimization is a crucial one. Once such triggering behavior reaches a certain degree of seriousness, and once it meets the legal requirements, it might fit the law's definition of "provocation." And if it meets the operational criteria of the researcher's definition it might be considered "precipitation." The typical context in which everyday nonacquisitive, nonsexual violence occurs is that of an altercation, a quarrel, a dispute between two persons, or a squabble or a row involving several people. The person who gets beaten, hit, injured, or killed is only rarely an uninvolved bystander. Most of the time, this person is a party to the dispute and an involved participant. As Palmer (1974) points out, in interpersonal disputes, the complaining witness who files the criminal affidavit is frequently the party who won the race to the police station and was the first to file.

The criminal law and the criminal courts operate on the basis of theoretical and abstract legal assumptions and presumptions. Social and behavioral scientists, in contrast, are not interested in what should or would normally have happened, but in what actually happened, not in presumptive roles and behavior, but in actual roles and behavior. This is particularly the case in situations where a brief or prolonged personal interaction took place between victim and victimizer before the victimization. In such situations it is imperative to establish the effective role each party played in the transaction.

Victim-precipitation: Justified and Unjustified Criticisms

Most of the criticism leveled at the concept of victim-precipitation can be traced to the failure of the critics to grasp the subtle distinction between exculpatory concepts and explanatory concepts. When correctly understood, victim-precipitation is nothing other than a legitimate effort to understand the motives of the crime, to analyze the dynamics of victim-offender interaction, and to explain the chain of events that ultimately led to the act of victimization. In such an explanatory model there is no place for normative or value judgments such as guilt or blame. Still, from the very beginning, critics of the concept of victim-precipitation did not accept it for what it really is and what it is meant to explain, but insisted that it was designed and used to blame the victim. Surprisingly, the feminists who led the campaign against victim-precipitation saw nothing wrong in using the abuse, battering, and maltreatment to which many women were subjected to explain, and even to justify, the violence that was finally used by a few women against abusive lovers and spouses.[2] Cases of homicide, attempted murder, or assault were invariably explained by reference to the abusive behavior of the male victim.

Some critics did not limit their attacks to the concept of victim-precipitation but extended their criticism to the entire discipline of victimology. Clark and Lewis (1977), for example, offered the following proposition:

> *In the social sciences, victim blaming is becoming an increasingly popular rationalization for criminal and "deviant" behaviour ... Over the past few years, victim blaming has become institutionalized within the academic world under the guise of victimology ... The male researcher finds his escape in victimology. He seeks the problem's cause in the behaviour of its victim, and goes on to persuade himself and the public at large that by changing that behaviour, the problem can be controlled. In this way, the study of victimology becomes the art of victim blaming. (pp. 147, 148, 150)*

The ideological and gender biases underlying this criticism are too obvious to require a rebuttal.[3] If there is a problem with the concept of victim-precipitation, then the problem does not lie in the concept itself (and has nothing to do with victim blaming), but in the way the concept was operationalized in some studies, particularly in Amir's study of forcible rape in Philadelphia (Amir, 1967, 1971). Silverman (1973) shares the view that most of the operationalizations of victim-precipitation leave much to be desired. He believes that with the exception of Wolfgang's definition of victim-precipitated homicide, there has been no adequate operational definition of the concept. The problem, as he sees it, is that the measures used have been highly unreliable from a methodological point of view because they are largely dependent on the researcher's interpretation rather than on fixed criteria. Yet, the fact that the concept has been defined too broadly or operationalized too loosely in one (or several studies) is not a good reason to dismiss it altogether or to challenge its inherent validity and its potential utility, when correctly applied, to the explanation of the dynamics of criminal victimization (Fattah, 1979). Wolfgang's definition of victim-precipitated homicide is a clear indication that it is not impossible to operationalize victim-precipitation using objective and unequivocal behavioral criteria that do not imply any attribution of guilt or assignment of blame.

With a growing emphasis in criminology in recent years on the dynamics of criminal behavior, victim-offender interactions, situational and triggering variables, environmental stimuli and opportunities, differential risks of victimization, and repeat and multiple victimization, one would have expected the victim-precipitation debate to quietly come to an end. However, this is not the case. The debate seems to be regaining momentum with new critics emerging from the new political right. Surprisingly, victim advocates and spokespersons for the victim movement are being joined by some radical criminologists. Victim-precipitation, it seems, creates strange bed fellows!

Among recent critics of victim-precipitation are Timmer and Norman (1984) who claim that victim-precipitation functions as an ideology which blames the victim and diverts attention from the structural causes of crime. They argue that the "ideology of victim-precipitation," as expressed in both academic criminology and criminal justice practice, serves to legitimate existing criminogenic structural and institutional arrangements in American society. This, in turn, leads to more of the "ideology" of "victim-precipitation." Since structure is not responsible for crime, individuals must be. Once again we see here a good example of a widespread misconception, namely, that any attempt to explain the victimization at a micro level, by reference to the behavior of the victim, is an effort to blame the victim and to stress the individual rather than the structural causes of crime. The fallacy of this contention should now be clear: victimology does not seek to explain crime but to explain victimization. It does not seek to explain why some people become criminals but why some people (targets) become victims and others do not. This obviously cannot be adequately done without looking at the characteristics, the behavior, and the life-style of those who are victimized. To claim that by so doing attention is diverted from the structural causes of crime is unjustified. Explaining the differential risks of victimization requires that we look not only at the individual characteristics of the victim, but also at the structural factors that enhance vulnerability and proneness such as age, gender, minority status, unemployment, and poverty. It sheds light on the role these structural factors play in the etiology of victimization. Such macro explanations need, however, to be supplemented by others capable of explaining victimization in individual cases, explaining why this particular victim was chosen, why the victimization occurred in this specific situation, at that specific time and place, and in the circumstances it did. Hence, the need for concepts such as victim-precipitation and victim-participation.

Continuing with their earlier critique, Timmer and Norman (1984) then claim that focusing on victim-offender interaction—on "situational variables" and "environmental opportunities" only—cannot go far to increasing our understanding of the etiology of crime. They add (Timmer and Norman, 1984):

> *The ideology of victim precipitation blames neither the structure of society nor the individual offender for crime. Instead it blames the victim who precipitates crime. (p. 66)*

Finally, it is not true, as some critics (Franklin II and Franklin, 1976) claim, that victim-precipitation reduces the offender to a passive actor who is set into action by the victim's behavior. What is true is that victim-precipitation, according to both its original definition (Wolfgang, 1958) and its current definitions (Gobert, 1977), is a form of overt, aggressive, and provocative behavior by the victim that *triggers* the action of the criminal. It is an actualizing factor, the stimulus that elicits the violent response. Thus, what may be considered, if viewed unilaterally, as an "action" would be regarded, when viewed in the dynamic, interactionist perspective of victim-precipitation, as a "reaction," or more accurately an "overreaction." To establish victim-precipitation, then, is to demonstrate that had it not been for the precipitating actions of the victim, the victimization would not have occurred against that particular victim in that particular situation.

Some Empirical Evidence on Precipitated Victimization

One of the first attempts to assess the extent of the victim's situational involvement is Wolfgang's study of criminal homicide in Philadelphia (1958). Based on his definition of victim-precipitation (see Chapter 4), Wolfgang concluded that of the 588 criminal homicides he studied, 150, or 26 percent, may be designated as victim-precipitated cases. Male victims and black victims showed greater involvement than did female victims and white victims. Nearly 80 percent of victim-precipitated cases compared to 70 percent of cases not victim-precipitated involved blacks, which was a proportional difference resulting in a significant association between race and victim-precipitated homicide. Males comprised 94 percent of victim-precipitated homicides, but only 70 percent of homicides not victim-precipitated, which showed a significant association between sex of the victim and victim-precipitated homicide.

Females were much less likely to precipitate their own victimization than males. However, females were twice as frequently offenders in victim-precipitated slayings (29 percent) as they were in slayings not victim-precipitated (14 percent)—a proportional difference that is also highly significant.

The 1967 American National Survey (done for the National Commission on the Causes and Prevention of Violence) covered seventeen cities and tested the empirical validity of victim-precipitation in criminal homicide, aggravated assault, forcible rape, and robbery. Guided by Wolfgang's definition and those of others, the survey tailored a definition of the term "victim-precipitation" to each of the violent crimes studied (Curtis, 1974b). On the basis of the definitions used, precipitation was not uncommon in homicide and assault, appeared less frequently, but was still empirically noteworthy, in robbery, and was least relevant in rape.

For many, it is difficult to conceive and to believe that children can be deliberately provocative or that they can, through misbehavior, trigger acts of victimization directed against them. Psychiatrists, psychologists, social workers, and criminal justice practitioners do encounter such cases in their professional practice. Barbara Bender (1976) relates how the behavior pattern of two boys, aged eight and ten, who had been battered as young children, had an impact on her. This behavior pattern seemed to her to be directly related to the abusive treatment they had received from their parents. The two boys had a compulsive need to provoke punishment from everyone with whom they came in contact, both peers and adults. Bender labeled this type of compulsive violence-eliciting behavior "scapegoating behavior." She tells how the ten-year-old boy spent months, while in casework, in desperate attempts to provoke the worker into hitting him by insulting her mother and grandmother, screaming names, spitting, breaking toys, and attempting, in a multitude of other ways, to provoke retaliation. In the midst of these scenes he would scream, "Hit me! Go ahead and hit me!" Bender reports that one of the visible characteristics of the two boys was a low self-esteem and a sense of inferiority. The ten-year-old frequently screamed, "I hate myself! I hate myself!" The paper, too long to be summarized here, gives several examples of deliberately provoking behavior in which the two boys regularly engaged for the sole purpose of evoking violent retaliation, either from their parents or their peers.

Other Types of Victim Functional Behavior

The victim's involvement in the causal chain leading to victimization may take forms other than precipitation. Certain behaviors by the victim may not attain extreme levels of precipitation but may still play a major or a minor causal role. And whereas victim-precipitation is usually (and justly) confined to conscious, deliberate, and active behavior, the functional role of the victim may be in the form of inadvertent behavior or the failure to act (nonfeasance). In other words, acts of negligence, carelessness, recklessness, and imprudence, which create a temptation or opportunity situation or make it easier for the potential offender to commit a certain crime, are contributing factors, even though they may not fit a narrow operational definition of victim-precipitation.

It is also important to emphasize that the interest in a victim's functional behavior is not purely theoretical. Analyzing the causal role such behavior plays in the etiology of many crimes can have very important practical implications. Mention has been made of the implications of the victim's behavior to legal issues, such as laying charges, conviction, sentencing, and compensation. But the implications for criminal policy are no less important. The modern approaches to crime prevention, such as those aimed at reducing the opportunities for crime and making targets harder to victimize, are largely victim-centered and cannot be effective unless they can manage to bring about a change in the victim's contributory behaviors. This preventative approach is predicated on the premise that simple and minor changes in the behavior of potential victims can bring about a reduction in the number of many common crimes.

FACILITATION/PARTICIPATION/COOPERATION

Contrary to popular stereotypes, which portray crime victims as passive, uninvolved, and unlucky individuals who are at the receiving end of criminal actions, victims can and do participate and cooperate in offenses committed against them. Examples of these facilitating/participating/cooperating victims are not rare, that is why few examples only will be given.

Some consensual sex acts are punishable by law despite the fact that both parties are willing, consenting participants. The consent may not be recognized by the criminal code if one of the partners is a minor, mentally handicapped, or under the authority, and thus the subtle coercion, of the other, and so forth. A minor wishing to escape her parent's home to marry or to live with her lover might conspire, plan, and fully participate in her own kidnapping, thus fitting the role of a facilitating/participating/cooperating victim.

Even in crimes against the person, willing victims are encountered who are fully cooperating participants. The classic example here is that of mercy killing, where a terminally ill patient who initiates the act might literally beg the reluctant physician, spouse, relative, or friend to put an end to his or her intolerable suffering. A somewhat similar situation is that of individuals who are deeply depressed about their lives and want to die but who have strong inhibitions or religious convictions that prevent them from committing suicide. These people may, therefore, seek to provoke their own death using another person as the medium. Wolfgang (1959) suggests that some cases of victim-precipitated homicide might, in reality, be masked suicides. In a paper entitled "Suicide by Means of Victim-precipitated Homicide," he reports that certain persons wanting to die but unwilling to commit suicide may bring about their own deaths by indirectly provoking another person into killing them.

It is probably in property crime that the largest number of facilitating/participating/cooperating victims is encountered. Many forms of swindle and fraud require not only the cooperation, but also the active participation of the person (or the business) being swindled or defrauded. Without such facilitation/cooperation/participation the scheme would not be successful, and the fraud or swindle would not take place. Most notable among these fraudulent activities are confidence games (Sutherland, 1937), marriage swindle (Padowetz, 1954), and medical quackery. We might add that many victims of fraud are cheated while trying themselves to cheat the criminal.

The victim's facilitating behavior may be active, though more often it is in the form of negligent, reckless, imprudent, or inadvertent behavior. An example of active behavior occurs when a victim hands the potential offender a weapon, which will ultimately be used by the offender to assault or murder the victim, and challenges him or her to use it. Wolfgang (1958) cites a case in which a drunken husband, beating his wife in their kitchen, gave her a butcher knife and dared her to use it on him. She warned him that if he should strike her once more she would use the knife, whereupon he slapped her in the face, and she fatally stabbed him.

The explanatory nature of the concepts of facilitation, participation, and cooperation should be reiterated here. These concepts are not meant to blame or to hold the victim responsible for the victimization. This is a matter for the courts and for compensation boards to decide. Social scientists are interested in explanations, not in assessing responsibility or establishing and apportioning guilt. The use of these explanatory concepts is meant to show the temptation/opportunity situation created by the victim, making it particularly propitious, or at least possible, to commit the crime.

When a victimization is neither premeditated nor planned, but is perpetrated on the spur of the moment by the offender to take advantage of an opportunity created by the deliberate, negligent, or inadvertent behavior of the victim, then the victim's behavior may (and should) be considered as a contributory factor in the sense that, were it not for such behavior, the victimization would not have occurred.[4] These cases should be distinguished from those of exchangeable victims where the behavior of the victim does not play a causal role, but simply influences the choice of a particular victim/target over another.

Many authors (Fooner, 1966; Lamborn, 1981; Joutsen, 1987) adopt broader definitions of victim-facilitation. They speak of facilitation whenever victims have failed to take reasonable precautions to protect themselves or their property or reasonable measures to prevent the victimization from taking place. Sparks (1982) also suggests that anyone who fails to take precautions against crime that would be regarded as reasonable in the circumstances may be said to have facilitated a subsequent crime committed against him or her. Sparks cites some examples to illustrate the concept of facilitation: (1) persons who sign contracts without reading the fine print and who, therefore, run the risk of being cheated by bogus repairmen and (2) "Good Samaritans" who intervene in crimes being committed against others, thus facilitating their own victimization.

Sparks (1982) also points out the difference between precipitation and facilitation. With the former it is the victim's behavior in interaction with the offender that counts, whereas with the latter, the creation of special risks is involved; these may arise either from the attributes or usual behavior of the victim, but do not involve a bilateral transaction with the offender (Sparks, 1982, p. 28).[5] He adds that facilitation is both context-dependent and culture-dependent, that is, the standards of "due care" differ from one area to another and from one culture to another.

Victim-facilitation in Property Offenses

In Normandeau's study of robbery in Philadelphia (1968) and Curtis's analysis of violent crimes in seventeen American cities (1975, 1981) the victim's role in armed and unarmed robbery was defined in terms of creating "temptation-opportunities where the victim clearly had not acted with reasonable self-protective behavior in handling money, jewelry or other valuables" (1975, p. 104). Curtis reports that careless, precipitating behavior was present in 11 percent of the armed clearances, 5 percent of the nonclearances, 6 percent of the unarmed clearances, and 10 percent of the nonclearances. Normandeau found a roughly comparable 11 percent of the robberies he examined to fit the temptation/opportunity definition.

An earlier study of robbery in London, England, (McClintock and Gibson, 1961) led the authors to conclude that analyzing the behavior of the offenders and the victims "leaves little doubt that a number of offences would have been prevented if certain elementary precautions had been taken to avoid giving obvious opportunities to potential offenders" (p. 23).

Nkpa (1976) studied victims of armed robbery in post-civil-war Nigeria, analyzing their attitudes, actions, and behavior. He discovered that most victims create dangerous situations that lead to their victimization. Only 43.6 percent could be considered nonparticipatory, nonprecipitating, or, as Nkpa calls them, "neutral victims." The rest displayed various forms of negligence or carelessness and imprudent or reckless behavior that placed them in a situation of vulnerability advantageous to the commission of robbery.

A study of common property offenses in Sheffield, England, (Baldwin, 1974) revealed some interesting patterns of victims' contributory behavior:

—Almost one-third of houses attacked had been left insecure to at least a marked degree.

—A substantial proportion of all houses entered were left in a marked or serious state of insecurity.

—Carelessness on the part of the victims proved to be a very common characteristic of housebreaking offenses, suggesting that such negligence may well be an important contributory factor in offenses of this type.

—Thirty-nine percent of cars, for which there were details of security available, had been left insecured. The findings further suggest that the failure of the victims to adequately secure their property is at least as important in these offenses as it was found to be in the case of housebreaking offenses.

—Of the 760 cars for which information was available (32.6 percent), 240 involved thefts from vehicles that had been left unattended in an insecured condition, either with doors unlocked or with windows open. Surprisingly, cars of higher value were more often left insecured.

—Cars left insecured by their owners were approximately seven times more likely to be removed and approximately five times more likely to have property stolen from them than cars that were left secured.

On the basis of these findings, Baldwin (1974) concludes:

Given the close correspondence between levels of criminality and the extent of opportunities for crime commission, minimizing extreme degrees of carelessness might be seen as a simple but effective means of crime prevention. (p. 358)

Findings similar to those reported by Baldwin in his Sheffield study are provided in a United States document on household burglaries (United States, 1979). The document confirms that unlawful entry without force is a crime of opportunity in which the victims, through their own negligence in securing dwellings and other residential structures, provide offenders with the opportunity to carry out burglaries with relative ease. Thus, entry into residential structures was most frequently through unlocked doors or windows. Naturally, not all households were equally vulnerable. An interesting finding, however, was that while some persons were almost regularly preyed upon by criminals, many others did not experience a single victimization and perhaps never would. Like Baldwin (1974), the study concludes that burglary in dwellings and other residential structures is a *preventable* crime that can be deterred by using minimal household security devices such as door or window locks. The authors also stress most emphatically that effective prevention of unlawful entry may, in many cases, be as simple as locking doors and windows before leaving home.

The situation in Canada is strikingly similar. In their study of burglary in Toronto, Waller and Okihiro (1978) found several indications suggesting that offenders tend to take advantage of the carelessness of householders. For example, in a large number of cases in their study, the offender simply opened an unlocked door, and in several cases the door was wide open. In an attempt to measure the level of carelessness, the authors constructed a scale based on responses to a number of questions that could be answered by the responses of "usually," "sometimes," or "never," and scores of "one," "two," and "three" were given for each response respectively. The total scores formed the scale. Forty-eight percent of victims compared to 28 percent of nonvictims in apartment buildings had above-average scores on carelessness. There was no difference between victims and nonvictims in houses. The reasons for this difference between apartment and house dwellers are not clear, and the authors offer no explanation.

Victim-facilitating Behavior: Hitchhiking as a Case Study

Karmen (1984) views victim-facilitation as a catalyst in a chemical reaction, which, given the right ingredients and conditions, speeds up the interaction. One concrete example of victim-facilitating behavior is hitchhike victimization. Hitchhiking is particularly popular among young people but people of all ages have to resort to hitchhiking during transportation strikes. Hitchhiking is a common practice not only in North America but in many other parts of the world. It is also a dangerous practice, both for the hitchhikers and for the drivers. Either can end up becoming a victim of rape, sexual assault, robbery, and occasionally homicide. There seems to have been no studies comparing victimization figures for hitchhikers to those of the drivers to find out who is victimized more often. Attention is usually focused on the hitchhiking victim rather than on the driver, who is sometimes victimized by the hitchhiker. Intuitively, it would seem that rape victimization is more common against female hitchhikers than it is against female drivers for the simple reason that more women are picked up by male drivers than men by female drivers. Robbery, on the other hand, seems to be more often committed by the hitchhiker against the driver. Probably, the reason for this is that the car driver is more likely to have money or other valuable possessions than the hitchhiker. Robbery in these incidents is very similar to that committed against taxi drivers and, when planned, is usually planned in the same manner.

The dangers of hitchhiking have been too often and too well publicized to need a detailed explanation or discussion, but these well-known dangers make the act of hitchhiking a classic example of a potential and highly vulnerable victim willingly placing himself or herself in the hands, and at the mercy, of a possible victimizer. This applies as much to the hitchhiker as to the driver. The driver who gives a ride to a male hitchhiker (or more than one) who might have a concealed weapon, can hardly prevent being victimized if that is what the hitchhiker has planned. There are countless incidents where such drivers have been threatened, beaten, sexually assaulted, robbed of money, robbed of their vehicles, and left on the road or in some secluded place to which they were forced to drive. Cases of drivers being killed by hitchhikers are not rare. Out of fifty cases of murder for robbery in a study in Austria (Fattah, 1971), three were committed against taxi drivers and a fourth was perpetrated by a hitchhiker on the driver who gave him a ride. Once the driver was killed, the murderer hid the body in the trunk of the car. He then drove the car for several days before abandoning it.

Allowing a stranger into the tight space of a car so as to be totally at the mercy of that stranger (who is free to act while the driver is concentrating on the driving) fits the definition of "facilitating behavior" very well. In either situation, whether it is the driver or the hitchhiker who becomes the victim, it is the victim who creates the opportunity that makes it possible for the potential offender to commit the crime. While many hitchhike victimizations are planned in advance, either by the hitchhiker or the driver, others are committed on the spur of the moment, and are motivated and inspired by an advantageous situation and triggered by a favorable or unique opportunity. There are rapists who search for female hitchhikers, and there are also hitchhike robbers who have planned to rob whomever would stop and agree to let them in the car, van, or truck. However, there are other incidents that do not start with any preconceived ideas and where the original intention is simply to hitch a ride or to give a ride. Some of these incidents may later culminate in a rape or robbery situation, motivated or triggered by some favorable circumstances or by the behavior of the prospective victim.

As interesting as the hitchhiking situation is to victimologists, there have been very few empirical studies analyzing the elements of the situation, the reciprocal attitudes of victim and victimizer, and the interaction between them leading to the victimization. Because of the dearth of studies on this topic, the study by Nelson and Amir (1975) of hitchhike victims of rape in Berkeley, California, is of particular interest, despite the fact that the study is limited to heterosexual rape and to those cases in which the hitchhiker is the victim. The study covered a three-year period and revealed that hitchhike rape represented an average of 20 percent of the total reported rapes occurring in Berkeley. In other words, one in every five rapes reported in Berkeley was a hitchhike rape. The study shows that hitchhike rapes are different from other rapes in several respects and that the hitchhike situation contains several elements that render it particularly dangerous for the single female hitchhiker as (1) hitchhike rape is an offense that occurs between strangers, one of whom is transient; (2) the offender is able to isolate his victim in the course of choosing the location of the offense; and (3) the offender is able to escape safely by automobile following the attack. Additional factors include the reluctance of many victims to report their victimization to the police and the inability of the hitchhiker to be too selective in choosing with whom she rides. Another situational element discussed by Nelson and Amir is that the offender, if apprehended, is able to claim that the victim entered the vehicle willingly and agreed to have sexual intercourse with him. In fact, one specific characteristic of the hitchhike rapes studied by Nelson and Amir is that they involved a voluntary social contact between victim and offender, frequently initiated by the victim herself. This does not mean that there were no incidents in which the victim had been kidnapped, but Nelson and Amir excluded such instances from the material as they did not fit their definition of hitchhike rape. Based on their data they were able to make three generalizations: (1) the victim's behavior contributes to her victimization; (2) the victim is generally submissive; and (3) the victim appears to be fatalistic regarding the hazards involved in hitchhiking. Nelson and Amir found that in 82 percent of the rapes, the victim was hitchhiking by herself, thus removing herself from any possibility of assistance. In 60 percent of the events the victims initiated the contact which led to their being raped. Nelson and Amir report further that the victims usually submitted rather than resisted. In only 15 percent of the hitchhike rapes did the victim resist the offender. This despite the fact that the amount of force exerted by the offender was usually, according to the authors, minimal. They also found that in 75 percent of the hitchhike rape events, physical force or some type of weapon was involved. In 52 percent of the events, physical force, usually consisting of slapping or arm twisting, was used. Although the amount of force varied, in none of the instances was the victim hospitalized. Nelson and Amir were surprised at the fatalism with which the victims of hitchhike rape regarded their victimization. This fatalism resulted in many victims not being disturbed about what happened to them. Nelson and Amir quote one victim who told the investigating officer, "Rape is one of the risks the hitchhiker must be willing to accept." One hitchhiker told another officer that she had been in California for six months and during that period had been raped four times. Although most victims did not express these views they were *all* aware of the hazards involved in hitchhiking. Probably, the facilitating behavior of the victim would not have been that important had it not been for the misconception that many male drivers have of female hitchhikers. One element that adds to the vulnerability of the hitchhiker as a potential victim is the widely held stereotype of female hitchhikers. Nelson and Amir (1975) report that for certain groups the hitchhiking woman presents an image of promiscuity:

> *This image is conveyed by the solicitation of contact with strangers; her apparel and also as a result of the popular folklore regarding the promiscuity of hippies ... The female hitchhiker is assumed to be unchaste and contemptuous of the societal double standard of sexual contact; as a result, she is believed to be beyond the protection of society. A popular belief is that the hippy girl will easily agree, or succumb to sexual flirtation, exploitation or sheer pressure. (p. 48)*

TEMPTATION/INITIATION/INSTIGATION

The victim's behavior may play a role in the pre-victimization phase by creating the motives for the crime that is later committed. The English language is rich in verbs meant to describe the functional role of the offender and/or the motivational role of the victim, such as tempting, seducing, inducing, inspiring (the idea of the crime), attracting, arousing, inviting, initiating, instigating, inciting, enticing, and luring. Typical cases where the temptation, instigation, or initiation comes from the victim rather than the offender are those of minors and members of other protected groups who act against their self-interest and who try persistently to get others to violate the laws intended to protect them. By highlighting the functional or the motivational role these "victims" play, we simply want to draw attention to the conflict that sometimes exists between the protective function of the law and the unwillingness of some potential victims to be protected as well as their disregard for laws designed for their own protection. The laws intended to protect minors, mentally handicapped persons, and others judged unable to distinguish sexual exploitation are a case in point. For example, minors who are months or days away from the age of legal consent do have sex drives and desires and might try to satisfy them independent of any initiation by adults and despite the legal prohibition. In such cases, the course of events is likely to be at odds with the legal presumption which has the adult as the seducer and the child as the seduced victim.

The Role of the Victim in Nonviolent, Noncoercive Sex Offenses

Psychiatrists (Boven, 1943; Bender and Gruggett, 1952; Gebhard et al., 1965; Gagnon, 1965; Körner, 1975, 1977; Schönfelder, 1965, 1968; Virkkunen, 1975, 1980; Wolf, 1957) who examined young victims and the men charged with sexually victimizing them realized that while the legal presumption established by the criminal law in favor of the child did, in most cases, reflect what really happened, in a few cases it did not. Occasionally, the legal victim was not, as presumed, a pressured, seduced, corrupted, or bribed sex partner, but was someone who took part in initiating or instigating the sexual behavior forbidden by the law. Psychiatrists found that claims made by some of the accused were not merely apologies and defenses aimed at reducing their responsibility or excusing them in the eyes of the law and the community, but were a true account of the events that led to the sexual episode.

Despite the general presumption of an adult seducer and seduced child, the legislator is cognizant of the possibility that some minors might initiate, invite, or instigate the forbidden sexual behavior. Thus Subsection 146(2) of the Canadian Criminal Code punishes the male who has sexual intercourse with a female person who is not his wife, who is of previously chaste character, and who is fourteen years of age or more, but is under the age of sixteen years. Subsection 146(3) stipulates that where an accused is charged with an offense under Subsection 146(2), the court may find the accused not guilty if it is of the opinion that the evidence does not show that, as between the accused and the female person, the accused is more to blame than the female person. Subsection 146(3) is therefore an admission that the general presumption may, at least in cases of girls over fourteen but less than sixteen years old, be reversed.

The psychiatric and criminological literature contains reported cases of "prostitutes" of both genders, below the age of consent, soliciting elderly males, who, because of their weakness and their desperate need to satisfy their fading sexual drive, might be easier to entice than younger customers (Pollak, 1941). Three such cases are reported by Wolf (1957), a German psychiatrist. Three elderly men were accused, in unrelated cases, of having committed sexual offenses involving two minor girls. In the three cases the victims were the same, suggesting that the instigation and initiation of the acts had probably come from the victims themselves and thus confirming the version of the three accused who had no criminal record and no previous history of child molestation.

Although the possibility that an under-age child might initiate, encourage, or even consent to sexual acts is vehemently denied by many, several empirical studies have shown that this possibility does exist (Gebhard et al., 1965; Gagnon, 1965; Maisch, 1973; Körner, 1975, 1977; Schönfelder, 1965; Virkkunen, 1975, 1980). In their extensive study of sex offenders, Gebhard et al. (1965) point out that in sexual offenses against children, except for aggression offenses, there was encouragement, or at least passive behavior in well over three-quarters of the cases.

In Germany, where the role of the victim in sex offenses is systematically examined, Dr. Thea Schönfelder, a psychiatrist, has written extensively on the role played by young female victims in sex offenses. Schönfelder (1965) offers some quantitative data on the issue in a study based on 175 cases of convicted sex offenders and involving 309 child victims (245 girls and 64 boys). Schönfelder found active participation on the part of 31 percent of the girls and 28 percent of the boys. She further found that the active behavior of the child increased with the age of the offender. In cases where the sexual offender was over sixty years old, the percentage of actively participating victims was 47 percent. In cases where the offenders were under forty years old, the corresponding percentage was only 20 percent.

Further information on the role of the victim in sex offenses committed by elderly men comes from the doctoral research carried out by Körner (1975, 1977). Körner examined 483 cases of men over fifty-five years old who were charged with sex offenses against children in the district court of Frankfurt am Main in the years from 1960 to 1969. Although official records, Körner points out, tend to emphasize the victim's resistance and to downplay the victim's encouragement and/or participation, he found that in no less than 35 percent of the cases there was active participation from the victim. Körner notes that, since voluntary sexual contacts are rarely reported to the authorities and since a higher percentage of cases where the victim is a willing or initiating partner is likely to remain undetected, the real percentage of actively participating victims should be far higher than 35 percent. In contrast to Schönfelder's findings, Körner found that active participation of child male victims was slightly higher than that of their female counterparts. To illustrate the points he makes, Körner cites detailed case histories from his material to show how some of the elderly sex offenders were actively and persistently seduced and even pursued by precocious, promiscuous children. Such incidents, of course, are difficult to prevent when prevention, treatment, and rehabilitation efforts are geared to the offenders alone. Körner quotes another researcher, Paulsen who, like Wolf (1957), wondered how it was possible to prevent such sexual offenses when the statistics showed that almost 59 percent of the so-called victims were, in fact, the seducers.

Finnish psychiatrist Matti Virkkunen (1975, 1980) defined victim-precipitated pedophilia cases as ones where the victim's behavior had a positive effect on initiation of the sexual offense. He considered precipitating behavior to be involved when the victim repeatedly, *on his or her own initiative*, visited the offender despite the fact that the latter committed unchaste acts and/or when the victim displayed some kind of initiative in the offense itself. Cases where it could be verified that there was, at any level, some resistance or even a passive attitude, were taken as controls. The data for the study consisted of sixty-four cases of pedophilia. These were all the pedophilia cases subjected to mental examination at the Psychiatric Clinic of the Helsinki University Central Hospital during the years from 1951 to 1972. The subjects totaled thirty-one and there were thirty-three controls for a total of sixty-four. Female victims numbered forty-one, and males, twenty-three. The average age of the victims was from nine to ten years and no clear difference emerged between the subjects and the controls. The age was recorded at the beginning of the offenses, as, in some cases, the acts had continued for several years. The offenders were naturally much older, with those in the precipitated cases having a significantly higher average (41.3 years) than that of the controls (30.7 years). Having noted the high percentage of victim-precipitated cases in his material (48.4 percent), Virkkunen suggests that the real percentage might be even higher. This is because the dark figure in pedophilia offenses is high, and cases where the offense is minor and the victim's precipitation is very strong have a greater likelihood of remaining undetected than others.

Confirmation of the high incidence of victim involvement in nonviolent noncoercive sex offenses committed against minors comes from other studies. Using a number of studies of child victims of sex offenses as their source, Gibbens and Prince (1963) estimated that two-thirds of the victims (a percentage that appears astoundingly high) may be considered "participant" victims, that is, "they cooperate in an assault more than once or with more than one assailant" (p. 7). They add that of this main group, a minority consists of those for whom being a sex assault victim is only one of a large number of indications of maladjustment:

They are promiscuous or provocative, they steal, play truant, run away from home and show other behavior disorders. Their families tend to be disorganized "problem" families, with parents so negligent, extremely inconsistent or cruel that the child seeks more affectionate and consistent relationships outside the home, especially perhaps with the offender. (p. 7)

Writing in the 1960s, at a time when there was no sex education in schools and when knowledge about sex was not as widespread as it is now, Gibbens and Prince (1963) observed that many little girls knew a great deal about sex behavior from observation from an early age, and it held no great surprises for them. They state that the girls "may not participate emotionally in sex offences, but they certainly precipitate them" (p. 5). The authors add that, if supported by another child of the same age, the girls will blackmail adults to pay them weekly for the repetition of the same indecent act. Gibbens and Prince also suggest that in some cases the attitude of adults may transform a romantic and pleasurable experience for the minor into a highly traumatic one. A good example of this is the following case which Gibbens and Prince (1963) describe in some detail:

An attractive but emotionally immature girl of 15, from a respectable but restrictive home, began to be interested in boys; she was told firmly that she was far too young to accept any dates. She met a young man of 23 secretly. He probably pursued her fairly relentlessly, for she said later that he always wanted to go somewhere where they could kiss and cuddle, while she only wanted to go dancing or to the pictures. Her parents found out and forbade her to see him. As so often, this led to protest and rebellion and had the effect of making her start to have sexual intercourse with him. When this was discovered, there was a family crisis; she ran away, was brought before the court as in need of care or protection, and sent to a hostel to remove her from this association. The young man was prosecuted, no doubt mainly because of the father's relentless insistence. In the hostel the girl appeared very anxious and unsettled, and after many weeks had to go and give evidence against her lover, much against her will. She was still very much in love with him, and never had the slightest resentment against him. The warden of the hostel who accompanied her remembered how cool and self-possessed she was during the trial. Her lover was sent to prison for a year. On return to the hostel the girl was much more unsettled. Two older girls exposed her to a great deal of pseudosophisticated talk about lesbian habits, and may have taken her to lesbian clubs. She became completely confused and paranoid about friendship with other girls, imagined herself about to be seduced homosexually, and after a few weeks, in an hysterical scene, rushed from the hostel and tried to throw herself under a bus. The report to the court recommended that she be sent home and referred for psychiatric treatment. Her breakdown, very unusual in a case of seduction which does not lead to court, was attributed to having to give evidence against her lover. She had not only to submit completely to the discipline of parents against whom she was rebelling, but to make a public confession of rejecting all that was most worth while in her experience (however romantic and misguided it may have been). It is not surprising that this led temporarily to a rejection of heterosexuality altogether and a state of acute emotional confusion which had quite dangerous results. (pp. 5-6)

Gibbens and Prince conclude that in this case, as in many others, it is perfectly clear that the behavior of *parents* is the main source of difficulty.

While some children might initiate the sex offenses committed against them, it is the minor in statutory rape who is, without doubt, the prototype of the willing, participating victim. As Brieland (1967) points out, in these cases we are faced with situations in which the child sex victim (as seen socially and legally) may be the "active provocateur." Many such girls, he believes, are children only under the law. He adds that the problem caseworkers encounter in these cases is to try to protect an adolescent who is herself aggressively seeking sexual satisfaction and who may be quite unwilling to recognize the problem as a problem. In jurisdictions where the age of consent to homosexual acts is set at eighteen or twenty-one, boys as old as seventeen or even twenty might be considered incapable of giving informed, enlightened consent, thus being classified as victims when, in fact, they might have been the pursuers, not the pursued, and the seducers, not the seduced.

It must be noted that the possibility of victim-initiation, -instigation, -precipitation, or -participation applies *only* to nonviolent, noncoercive sexual acts. This obviously excludes forced and forcible nonconsensual sexual victimizations such as rape, incest, and sexual assault by those in positions of power on children under their authority. It also excludes a variety of sex offenses committed against very young children who are too young to initiate or even to understand the sexual nature of what is being done to them. Even where initiation, instigation, precipitation, or participation by the victim was present, it does not in any way excuse the behavior of the sex offender, nor does it affect his or her legal responsibility. Examining and analyzing these behaviors, however, is necessary and invaluable for the understanding of sexual victimization.

But why do we adamantly reject any suggestion that a minor in a sex encounter could be anything but a totally passive victim? And why do we use derogatory adjectives such as promiscuous, lewd, licentious, and lascivious, to describe normal sexual behavior by "minors"? Part of the refusal to acknowledge and accept any role played by the minor is due to the tendency of adults to deny that children or minors can experience sexual feelings and can try, out of curiosity or craving for affection, to seek some sexual satisfaction. In the case of females, the forceful suppression of any sexual expressions by young, unmarried girls is only a part of the much larger oppression of the female gender in a patriarchal society. In the case of boys, cultural and legal prohibitions are motivated by society's strict and strong condemnation of homosexual practices. The violations of such prohibitions are, however, commonplace, and the motivations for these violations are strong and varied (see Chapter 4).

Rossman (1980) used a nonrandom snowball sample to study sexual relations between adult men and young boys. He reports how distressed he was to find that large numbers of boys, particularly twelve to fourteen year olds, were being prostituted. While admitting that he could not interview a truly representative sample of children, he insists that he talked with older boys and young men who had been lovers of pederasts, as well as with boy prostitutes. He was anxious to know what the motives of the boys were and was able to identify the following four main reasons (or combinations of them) that lead boys to respond to men's overtures or even seek men out (Rossman, 1980):

> *(1) Some boys are hungry for affection, (2) some mainly want money and gifts (and not always because of poverty), (3) some want adventure, new experiences, kicks other than sexual ones. Some at a rather young age see "playing the queers" as an exciting game to play until they are old enough for girls, (4) mostly, however much they may hide behind other reasons, boys indulge in sexual activity with men because they greatly enjoy being fellated. They are highly aroused by a sexually stimulating culture, and they want sex education and sexual kicks. (p. 346)*

Rossman adds that in nearly all cases the boys were first seduced by youngsters of their own age or slightly older.

Summary

In Chapter 10 we summarized the various efforts to explain criminal victimization by looking at the personal characteristics of the victim. In this chapter we reviewed the different attempts to incorporate the behavior of the victim into a dynamic, interactionist model of criminal victimization. Victim-precipitation is one of the first concepts victimologists used in their analysis of victim-victimizer interactions. It is also one of the concepts that generated a great deal of criticism. Precipitation is a behavioral concept, whereas provocation is a legal concept. The former is an explanatory concept, while the latter is an exculpatory one. The two concepts are distinct. Certain victim behaviors may qualify as provocation but not precipitation, and the opposite is also true.

Critics of victim-precipitation have claimed that it was designed and is being used to blame the victim. Others have suggested that, by emphasizing the behavior and contribution of the individual victim, victim-precipitation diverts attention from the structural causes of crime. These criticisms overlook the fact that the concept is not meant to explain crime but to explain victimization. It is not meant to explain why some people become criminals, but why some people (targets) become victims while others do not.

The victim's involvement in the causal chain leading to victimization may also take forms other than precipitation. It may consist of inadvertent behavior or the failure to act. Negligence, carelessness, recklessness, and imprudence may create a temptation/opportunity situation or make it easier for the potential offender to commit the crime. Facilitation, participation, and cooperation may be encountered in crimes against the person and in sex and property offenses. Initiation, instigation, and temptation are other forms of a victim's contributory behaviors and are encountered in some cases of nonviolent, noncoercive sexual acts with minors. Although the possibility that an underage child might initiate, instigate, or even consent to sexual acts is vehemently denied by some, there is sufficient empirical evidence suggesting that such behaviors are much more common than we are willing to admit.

TWELVE

Macro Explanations of Variations in Criminal Victimization

Why is it that the elderly have such low likelihoods and the young such high ones? Is it because the young are more active out of the home than are the elderly? Is it because of where they are likely to go when out, or who they are likely to come into contact with? Or does it have more to do with area of residence, with the elderly less likely to live in age-heterogeneous housing? Why does being married apparently reduce the risk of personal crime? Is it, perhaps, because a married lifestyle in contrast to a single one is associated with fewer out-of-the-home activities and different forms of activities when out? How do alcohol and people's own offending patterns figure into the victimization equation?

Michael R. Gottfredson (1984, pp. 8-9)

Repeat and Multiple Victimization

As mentioned earlier in Chapter 2, most respondents in crime surveys do not report any victimization, a minority report a single victimization during the reference period, while a very small minority report being frequently victimized. This last group offers exciting possibilities for victimological research. Within this group of repeatedly victimized individuals (or households) we can distinguish two distinct subgroups: those subjected to types of victimization that, by their very nature, tend to recur; and those who fall victim to offenses that normally do not occur in series.

Wife beating, child battering, physical abuse of the elderly, and incest may happen only once, thus remaining an isolated incident in the life of both victim and victimizer. However, more often than not, they recur at long or short intervals. Victims of these types of family violence or sex offenses, therefore, tend to be repeat victims, and there is nothing surprising about the fact that their victimizations recur over and over again. It is all part of the typical pattern of these types of victimization. More surprising are the experiences of those individuals, households, or businesses who report types of victimizations that are usually nonrecurring, such as burglary, car theft, vandalism, and robbery, happening to them more than once during the reference period. The victimization may be of the same kind or of different kinds covered by the survey. This phenomenon has come to be known in the language of victimization research as "multiple victimization." Multiple victimization raises a number of interesting questions, some theoretical, others of practical relevance: Why are some individuals, households, or businesses frequently or repeatedly victimized while others are never victimized or are victimized only once? Is multiple victimization a random phenomenon or are there specific variables that account for this repeat victimization? Are repeat victims different from nonvictims or from those who are victimized only once, and if so, in what way? In addition to these theoretical questions there are other more practical ones raised by the phenomenon of multiple victimization: Does repeat victimization produce cumulative or diminutive effects on the victim? Is every subsequent victimization more or less traumatic than the previous one(s)? Are repeat victims more or less afraid of victimization than nonvictims or victims of a single victimization? What can those who have been victimized several times do to minimize their chances of future victimization? Research in this area is still in an embryonic stage, and we do not have, therefore, any satisfactory answers to most of these questions. It is not surprising that Sparks (1981) has identified "multiple victims" as one of the highest priority groups for future research. He writes the following:

> *They may illuminate more general causal processes, and thus help to show how far, and in what ways, the attributes or behavior of victims themselves may help to explain their victimization ... Clearly, the consequences of one-time victimization generally are not relatively serious. Such incidents (even*

occurring in a fairly short time period) are relatively unimportant from the victim's point of view and the standpoint of public policy. But those whose lives are frequently or chronically affected by crime are another matter. For many such persons, the social meaning of crime and victimization likely is very different from what it is to one-time victims. (pp. 765-766)

MULTIPLE VICTIMIZATION REVEALED BY SURVEY RESEARCH

The United States

Hindelang, Gottfredson, and Garofalo (1978) analyzed victimization data from twenty-six American cities to establish the frequency and patterns of repeat and multiple victimization. Repetitive personal victimization during the reference period of one year proved to be extremely rare, with only an estimated seven-tenths of 1 percent of the population suffering two or more nonseries personal victimizations, and only one-half of 1 percent suffering one or more series crimes.[1]

Multiple victimization of households was more common than multiple personal victimization. Hindelang, Gottfredson, and Garofalo (1978) report that 4 percent of the households in the twenty-six cities they studied suffered more than one nonseries household victimization. Furthermore, the authors discovered a certain interdependency between the different types of victimization covered by the survey. For example, the overall risk of being the victim of a robbery at least once during the reference period was 22 out of 1,000. However, among those who reported being victims of aggravated assault during the reference period, 95 out of 1,000 also reported being victims of robbery at least once during the reference period. A similar pattern was observed for household victimization. Thus, for each type of household victimization, the likelihood was substantially greater for those households reporting having been victims of another household crime during the reference period (p. 133). More surprising still was the intersection of personal and household victimizations the authors discovered. They found, for example, that overall, regardless of the age, marital status, or sex of the respondent, the likelihood of having been a victim of at least one personal crime was about twice as great for members of households that were victims of household crimes as for members of households that were not victims of household crimes (pp. 136, 138). They report further that within all six race and income groups, persons residing in victimized households had a substantially greater likelihood of personal victimization than those residing in nonvictimized households (p. 138). Personal victimization increased, in a similar manner, the likelihood of household victimization. Hindelang, Gottfredson, and Garofalo (1978) report that overall, the likelihood of household victimization was about twice as great for households in which a member was a victim of a personal crime than for households in which no member was the victim of a personal crime (p. 141). Another interesting finding was the increased likelihood of a personal victimization for respondents residing in a victimized household in which another member has suffered a personal victimization. Controlling for age, sex, and marital status, persons residing in households that reported a household victimization and in which at least one other household member reported a personal victimization had a likelihood of personal victimization that was generally three to four times greater than that for persons residing in households that did not report a household victimization and in which no other household member reported a personal victimization (p. 146).

The findings of Hindelang, Gottfredson, and Garofalo (1978), which have been confirmed in subsequent surveys, lead to some important conclusions:

—There is a definite clustering of risks for both personal and household victimizations. This clustering lends empirical support to the theoretical concept of proneness to victimization, which was discussed earlier. They indicate beyond any doubt that certain individuals and certain households run a higher risk of victimization than others.

—If it is true that the probability of victimization depends in whole or in part on, or is related in one way or another to, a certain proneness—personal or environmental—then it is reasonable to expect the risks of victimization to be higher for prone persons and households than for others who are randomly selected from the general population. We can further expect that one victimization will enhance the likelihood of a subsequent victimization and so forth.

—Victimization risks seem to vary not only according to the personal characteristics of the target but also according to certain environmental variables. This finding, as Hindelang, Gottfredson, and Garofalo (1978) point out, suggests that it is important to include ecological variables among the risk factors in theoretical models designed to account for variations in victimization (p. 149).

Canada

The tenth and final issue of the *Canadian Urban Victimization Survey Bulletin* (Canada, 1988) is devoted to the issue of multiple victimization. The distortion that multiple victimization can cause to the general rate of victimization is vividly illustrated in the information the bulletin provides. While there were 141 incidents of personal crime victimization per 1,000 persons in 1981, there were only 115 victims of personal crime per 1,000 persons (p. 1). There were 369 household incidents per 1,000 households but only 256 households victimized per 1,000. The lower values for victimization rates as compared to incident rates reflect multiple counting of survey respondents who were victims of a criminal incident on more than one occasion during the reference period (pp. 1-2).

Multiple assault clearly shows the inflationary effects of multiple victimization and the extent to which global victimization rates can be misleading as a result. The survey revealed that over 5 percent of all individuals were victims of assault and that 21 percent of these victims experienced more than one such incident. These multiple assault victims, however, accounted for 60 percent of all assault victimizations when each incident in a series is counted separately. Series incidents alone, experienced by 6 percent of all assault victims, accounted for 39 percent of all assault incidents when each incident is counted separately (p. 4).

The *Canadian Urban Victimization Survey Bulletin* (Canada, 1988) reports that more than one-quarter of all households were victimized by household property crime, and, of these, one-third experienced more than one incident of victimization during the survey reference period. Of all individuals aged sixteen and older, 12 percent were victims of personal crime and one-quarter of these victims experienced more than one incident. Households experiencing more than one victimization incident may have been subject to several events of the same type (repeat victimization), a number of events characterized by quite different types of crime (cross-crime victimization), or a combination of both (p. 2).

The *Canadian Urban Victimization Survey Bulletin* (Canada, 1988) provides a relatively detailed analysis of multiple victimization. The analysis yielded some interesting findings:

— The risk of at least one repeat victimization was considerably higher among victimized households than was the overall risk of victimization among all households (p. 2).

— The risk of repeat victimization increases as the probability of victimization in general decreases (p. 2).

— In every case, households victimized by a particular crime were more likely than were households in general to have also experienced victimization of other types of crime. One striking example is motor vehicle theft victims for whom the likelihood of a second household victimization of any type was approximately double the likelihood of victimization among all households in the population (p. 3).

— Although personal crimes were far less prevalent than household crimes, they exhibited the same pattern as household offenses. Thus, repeat victimization for victims of personal offenses was higher than was victimization in the population in general. The increased likelihood of repeat victimization was four times greater for victims of assault, nine times greater for robbery victims, and perhaps as high as thirty-five times greater for sexual assault victims than was the overall likelihood of being a victim in the general population (p. 3).

— As with household crime, many victims of personal crime were also victims of at least one incident of a different type of personal crime during the twelve-month reference period. In general, the increased likelihood of cross-crime victimization for *personal* crime victims over the general population is many times greater than was the case for *household* cross-crime victimization (p. 3).

—Domestic violence is characterized by repeated victimization, or by a continuing condition of victimization eventually classified as a series incident. One-third of domestic-assault victims, compared to one in five victims of other assaults, experienced multiple incidents (p. 4).

These findings suggest, as the *Canadian Urban Victimization Survey Bulletin* (Canada, 1988) points out, that some households have particular characteristics that increase their vulnerability to certain types of victimization. They also suggest that there are significant factors at play that put certain individuals at risk for repeat victimization. They further indicate that a relatively small number of victims experience a disproportionate level of crime victimization. Such concentration, the authors believe, provides an opportunity for crime prevention strategies to focus their limited resources on a relatively small but highly victimized population. Such strategies, they argue, could have, at a reasonable level of effectiveness, a comparatively large impact on the causes and consequences of crime victimization on some sectors of Canadian society (p. 8).

STATISTICAL EXPLANATIONS OF MULTIPLE VICTIMIZATION

The phenomenon of multiple victimization can be explained by a number of simple probabilistic models using different explanations (Sparks, 1982). Sparks groups these statistical explanations under two headings: (1) the heterogeneity model and (2) the contagion models. Sparks gives his preference to the former over the latter. The following is a summary of Sparks's description of the models:

The Heterogeneity Model

One such model was first discussed by Greenwood and Yule (1920). Its starting point is the assumption that the population at risk to a certain phenomenon consists of persons or other entities with differing degrees of "proneness" or susceptibility to the phenomenon in question, and this "proneness" is itself distributed in the population in a certain way. According to Sparks, the Greenwood and Yule statistical model fits observed distributions of criminal victimization from several surveys in different countries fairly well. He also feels that quite apart from its fairly accurate fit, the model has a certain intuitive plausibility where the explanation of such incidents as accidents or illnesses is concerned. He writes the following:

In such a model, differences in susceptibility or proneness are conceived of as relatively invariant, in the sense of being unaffected by the number of times a person has previously suffered the thing in question. Thus, in the case of accidents, it is assumed that some persons are just naturally clumsy or are given to taking imprudent risks in the course of their work; others are naturally adept or cautious. These two groups' different experiences are then conceived of as being caused by their basic attributes. Though this is an oversimplification, it is a reasonable first step toward an explanation of the observed facts. (p. 117)

Sparks (1982) believes that, subject to some modifications, this approach to the explanation of multiple victimization is more plausible than other statistical models that have been used to explain multiple happenings and are based on an idea usually, and somewhat loosely, called "contagion."

The Contagion Models

Sparks points out that the so-called "contagion" models are based on the assumption that an event's having happened once increases the subsequent probability that it will happen a second time; its happening a second time increases the probability of its happening a third, and so on. This is somewhat similar to what has been posited by labeling theorists who have hypothesized that the more often an offender is arrested, convicted, or otherwise stigmatized as "deviant," the more likely he or she is to go on offending in the future. Sparks (1982) offers the following critique of the contagion models:

Several such probability models now exist in the statistical literature, and there are many social situations in which they may seem intuitively reasonable. Criminal victimization, however, does not strike me as one of them. We might imagine, for example, that a burglar breaks into a house or store and finds many things worth stealing and a few precautions against theft; and that he tells other burglars about it or plans to return himself, thus increasing the probability of second and subsequent burglaries. Or, again, a man who has been assaulted may become paranoid and belligerent, take lessons in self-defence, etc. and thereby increase the probability that he will be assaulted again. But these examples are obviously pretty farfetched; and it is not easy to think of others. In particular, it is not easy to apply the concept of "contagion" to repeated or frequent victimization of different types, e.g., burglary followed by robbery followed by car theft. (p. 118).

EMPIRICAL EXPLANATIONS OF MULTIPLE VICTIMIZATION

Very little empirical research has been done on the factors that might explain, totally or partly, the phenomenon of repeat and multiple victimization. One such study was undertaken by Lasley and Rosenbaum (1988). The authors examined the relationship between certain routine activities and the likelihood of becoming the victim of multiple personal-crime. To do so, they used data from the 1982 British

Crime Survey. The sample was comprised of all British Crime Survey respondents having reported one or more personal victimizations (N=916). Independent measures of routine activities included occupational status, weekend nights out, and self-reported drinking. The study provided preliminary evidence that the social processes involved in producing single personal-victimization are quite similar to those producing multiple personal-victimization. They concluded that three routine activity traits that increase the chance of repeated convergence of suitable crime targets and motivated offenders are as follows: (1) nonparticipation in the work force, (2) spending weekend nights away from home, and (3) consuming high levels of alcohol.

Macro Explanations of the Differential Risks of Criminal Victimization

The two previous chapters dealt with what may be considered as micro explanations of the differential risks of victimization. In what follows we will deal with some more general explanatory models. It should be made clear, however, that the distinction between micro and macro explanations is neither absolute nor clear cut. For example, the reference to structural proneness related to gender, age, or minority status could very well be regarded as a macro level explanation. On the other hand, many of the explanatory components of two of the models we will be discussing, the life-style model and the routine activities approach, may be seen as micro level explanations. It should also be stressed that the models to be discussed share a great many similarities and overlap to a large extent. Life-style and routine activities may be considered, for example, opportunity models, and both use the idea of exposure in their attempt to explain the differential risks of victimization. The concepts of life-style and routine activities largely overlap. In fact, in their original formulation of the life-style model, Hindelang, Gottfredson, and Garofalo (1978) explicitly indicated that "life-style refers to routine daily activities, both vocational activities (work, school, keeping house, etc.) and leisure activities" (p. 241). The Dutch model incorporates elements, such as proximity, attractiveness, and exposure, from the life-style and routine activities models. It is not surprising, therefore, that these models are sometimes treated in the literature as one or simply as variations on the same theme. As many readers will not be familiar with these theoretical formulations we will discuss the models separately and will try to point out the similarities and differences between them.

AN OVERVIEW OF THE VARIOUS MODELS

The major task of theoretical victimology is to develop models and formulate theories to explain the differential risks of criminal victimization, that is, to explain why certain individuals, groups, households, and businesses are victimized while others are not, or why they are more frequently victimized than others. Without the information on victims made available through victimization surveys, such a task would have been impossible. As more and more data were collected, researchers were able to map out the distribution of criminal victimization and to explore the factors that increase or decrease the risks of becoming victim to different types of crime (Cohen, Kluegel, and Land, 1981). The result is a variety of explanatory models: lifestyle (Hindelang, Gottfredson, and Garofalo, 1978); routine activity (Cohen and Felson, 1979; Felson and Cohen, 1980); opportunity (Cohen, Kluegel, and Land, 1981); and social structure (Smith and Jarjoura, 1988). Since the causes for differential victimization are probably as complex as those of differential delinquency, it is understandable that all models developed to date are partial models meant to explain only certain types of criminal victimization but not others. Moreover, none of these models fully succeeds in incorporating the micro explanations of individual risks that we discussed in Chapters 10 and 11 with the more macro type explanations of general risks. Also, some models, for example routine activity, were not even meant originally to explain the uneven distribution of victimization risks but to explain the changes in crime rates over time (particularly predatory offenses). A major reason for the weaknesses in the current models is the lack of information necessary to the development of comprehensive models of victimization.

To be able to explain the differential risks of victimization and to answer the question regarding whether some households and persons in a population are more vulnerable or prone to victimization than others, one would need to model the distribution and behavior of both victims and offenders. But as Reiss (1980) points out, too little information is available at present to construct such a model. There is too little information on the distribution of offenders in a population and almost none on their networks or selection of victims. Thus, Reiss (1980) asks the following:

> *Do offenders, for example, select victims for their vulnerability to victimization? Similarly, while it is known that the risk of victimization varies considerably across territorial space, among different social aggregates, and over time, there is too little information on repeat victimization and the behavior proneness of victims. (p. 41)*

The difficulties outlined by Reiss explain to some extent why the models developed to date to account for differential victimization patterns are tentative and far from perfect. The fact that these attempts are pioneering efforts should be kept in mind and they should not, therefore, be judged too harshly. We should also remember that, despite their limitations and shortcomings, these models represent real progress and an important step on the way to developing an integrated theory of criminal victimization.

The Typological Approach

In Chapters 10 and 11 we reviewed several explanations that use victim characteristics such as age, gender, ethnicity, occupation, sexual orientation, alcohol consumption, or victim behavior such as precipitation, facilitation, negligence, and so forth, to explain the variations in victimization probabilities and why it is that the risks are not evenly distributed within the general population. These explanations belong to what Gottfredson (1981) calls the "typological approach." This approach, he explains, sees distinct causal mechanisms operating for different victimization events. Some may be caused by simple carelessness, others by active provocation; some may be the result of physical impairments, and others the result of greed. The starting point of the typological approach is that the determinants of victimization events are diverse and range from biological factors (e.g., infirmity due to age) to psychological factors (e.g., predisposed to perceive a wide variety of stimuli as requiring a violent response) to physical factors (e.g., apparent wealth) to situational factors (e.g., the john who is robbed by the prostitute because he is unlikely to report the offense to the police). Gottfredson adds that a productive theory must acknowledge these numerous causative factors, perhaps through the development of distinctive explanatory mechanisms. Research agendas faithful to this view would seek factors that distinguish victims from one another rather than only searching for what they have in common (p. 724).

This typological approach, popular in the early days of victimology, is being gradually overshadowed by the macro level explanations such as "routine activities" and "life-style." Gottfredson (1981) makes a good case for using both the typological approach and the routine activities and life-style approaches rather than opting for one or the other. Gottfredson (1981) writes the following:

> *This is not to argue that a variety of causes should not be studied—indeed, the life-style-exposure model both permits and encourages multiple-factor research. The point is that, in this very early stage of theorizing about criminal victimization, there is no logical need to abandon a search for a theory capable of accounting for distinct causes, nor any reason to argue the futility of a common criterion. As a consequence, there is incentive, with respect to future research agendas, to continue to search for what victims may have in common—and how they differ from those who are not victimized. (pp. 724-725)*

Life-style as an Explanatory Concept

Using life-style to explain variations in risk is neither a novel nor a unique approach. It has been known for a long time that the probability of accidental death or injury is in many respects related to people's life-style and the kind of activities in which they are involved. Physicians have repeatedly stressed the close link between life-style and routine activities and the risk of suffering certain diseases such as cancer, high blood pressure, and cardiovascular ailments. As a matter of fact, the life-style concept permeates the explanations of a higher or lower susceptibility to a wide variety of diseases. We refer to life-style when we maintain that those who smoke have a higher risk of lung cancer than those who do not; that those who expose themselves, unprotected, to the sun have a greater probability of skin cancer; that those who drink heavily have a greater susceptibility to liver disease. Life-style is also the central concept in explanations linking dietary habits, the lack of exercise, and a sedentary way of life to heart disease. More recently, life-style has been identified as a major risk factor in contracting Aids. The belief that life-style can influence the probabilities of victimization by increasing or decreasing people's chances of becoming victims of certain crimes may be seen as a simple, and in many ways logical, extension of the concept to the social sphere. We have alluded to the relationship between life-style and victimization on several occasions, for example, when explaining that a deviant or criminal life-style greatly enhances the probability of being victimized.

The Life-style Model (Hindelang, Gottfredson, and Garofalo)

One of the first attempts to develop a theoretical model using life-style to explain the variations in the risks of personal victimization was undertaken by Hindelang, Gottfredson, and Garofalo (1978). To develop this explanatory model, the authors used empirical data gathered from an eight-city survey conducted by the United States Bureau of Census in the cities of Atlanta, Baltimore, Cleveland, Dallas, Denver, Newark, Portland (Oregon), and St. Louis in 1972. Hindelang et al. (1978) synthesized the findings and put forth some propositions to account for variations in risk and consequences of personal victimization. Their model posits that the likelihood an individual will suffer a personal victimization depends heavily on the concept of life-style. The life-style model is constructed on the basis of several premises. The most important are the following:

- The uneven distribution of criminal victimization across space and time. This means that there are high-risk locations and high-risk time periods.
- Offenders do not constitute a representative sample of the general population. Certain characteristics are more frequently present among offenders than within the general population. This means there are high-risk persons.
- Life-style determines the likelihood of personal victimization through the intervening variables of *association* and *exposure*.
- People are not equally exposed to high-risk places and times, and they vary in the degree to which they associate with persons who are likely to commit crimes. Life-style influences the amount of exposure and the prevalence of associations with high-risk persons.

—What is meant by association are the more or less sustained personal relationships that evolve as a result of similarities in life-style and interests shared by these individuals. It is posited that in the course of vocational and leisure pursuits, individuals are likely to spend a large part of time with others who have similar life-styles.

—Associations are also influenced by age and age-linked roles. Throughout life, people tend to associate with, and to come into contact with, others who occupy similar age-linked roles: students with students, workers with workers, homemakers with homemakers, and retired persons with retired persons.

Hindelang et al. (1978) summarize the life-style model and how it affects the chances of personal victimization in the following manner:

> *For a personal victimization to occur, several conditions must be met. First, the prime actors—the offender and the victim—must have occasion to intersect in time and space. Second, some source of dispute or claim must arise between the actors in which the victim is perceived by the offender as an appropriate object of the victimization. Third, the offender must be willing and able to threaten or use force (or stealth) in order to achieve the desired end. Fourth, the circumstances must be such that the offender views it as advantageous to use or threaten force (or stealth) to achieve the desired end. The probability of these conditions being met is related to the life circumstances of members of society. Lifestyle is the central component in our theoretical model. In our view, the centrality of lifestyle derives primarily from its close association with* ***exposure*** *to victimization risk situations. Victimization is not a phenomenon that is uniformly distributed; it occurs disproportionately in particular times and places; it occurs disproportionately by offenders with particular demographic characteristics; it occurs disproportionately under certain circumstances (e.g., according to whether or not the person is alone); it occurs disproportionately according to the prior relationship between the potential victim and the potential offender; and so forth. Because different lifestyles imply different probabilities that individuals will be in particular places, at particular times, under particular circumstances, interacting with particular kinds of persons, lifestyle affects the probability of victimization. (pp. 250-251)*

The authors then offer eight propositions to explain how and why life-style has a direct impact on the risks of victimization:

1. The probability of suffering a personal victimization is directly related to the amount of time that a person spends in public places (e.g., on the street, in parks, etc.) and particularly in public places at night (p. 251).
2. The probability of being in public places, particularly at night, varies as a function of life-style (p. 253). (Younger more than older, males more than females, single persons more than married persons....)

3. Social contacts and interactions occur disproportionately among individuals who share similar life-styles (p. 255).
4. An individual's chances of personal victimization are dependent upon the extent to which the individual shares demographic characteristics with offenders (p. 257).
5. The proportion of time that an individual spends among nonfamily members varies as a function of life-style (p. 259).
6. The probability of personal victimization, particularly personal theft, increases as a function of the proportion of time that an individual spends among nonfamily members (p. 260).
7. Variations in life-style are associated with variations in the ability of individuals to isolate themselves from persons with offender characteristics (p. 262). (Changing one's residence to a low crime area, using private cars instead of public means of transportation, access to private environs of recreation, etc.)
8. Variations in life-style are associated with variations in the convenience, the desirability, and vincibility of the person as a target for personal victimizations (p. 264).
   - From the offender's perspective, it is *convenient* to wait for a potential victim to come to a place (at a time) that is suitable to the offender for victimization (p. 264).
   - Offenders tend to commit their crimes within short distances of their residence (p. 265).
   - From the offender's perspective, not all individuals are equally desirable targets (p. 265).
   - A person's vincibility to personal victimization increases to the extent that the potential victim is seen by the offender as less able to resist the offender successfully—persons who are unaccompanied or under the influence of drugs or alcohol are relatively vincible to personal victimization (p. 266).

Findings of the Canadian Urban Victimization Survey (Canada, 1983) suggest that life-style is an important component of overall risk of victimization. One measure of life-style used by the survey is the number of evening activities outside the home each month. A strong relationship was found between the number of activities outside the home and rates of assault, robbery, and theft of personal property, and a less dramatic, but still positive relationship, was shown for rates of sexual assault.

A similar pattern was revealed by the Canadian General Social Survey (Sacco and Johnson, 1990). Patterns of evening activity were found to have important implications for the risk of personal victimization, with the risk rising steadily as the number of evening activities increased. This held true for both males and females.

The significance of evening activities for the rates of personal victimization was illustrated by the fact that the rates associated with the highest activity level were approximately five times those associated with the lowest activity level.

The Routine Activity Approach (Cohen and Felson)

The routine activity approach, formulated by Cohen and Felson, was developed at about the same time as the life-style model. Cohen and Felson (1979) define routine activities as the following:

> *Any recurrent and prevalent activities which provide for basic population and individual needs, whatever their biological or cultural origins. Thus routine activities would include formalized work, as well as the provision of standard food, shelter, sexual outlet, leisure, social interaction, learning and childrearing. (p. 593)*

The focus in Cohen and Felson's approach is on "direct-contact predatory violations," which are those "involving direct physical contact between at least one offender and at least one person or object which that offender attempts to take or damage" (Cohen and Felson, 1979, p. 589).

Cohen and Felson (1979) argue that the occurrence of these types of victimization is the outcome of the convergence in space and time of three minimal elements: motivated offenders, suitable targets, and absence of capable guardians. The central factors underlying the routine activity approach are opportunity, proximity/exposure, and facilitating factors. For example, an abundance of goods that can be stolen leads to higher rates of property victimization (opportunity). The dispersion of routine activities in the United States since the end of World War II has led to a substantial increase in predatory crime. This shift of routine activities away from the home and the greater interaction between people who are not members of the same household result in greater exposure of people to potential offenders outside the home and, thus, increases the risks of direct-contact predatory crime (proximity/exposure). Concomitantly, the increasing absence from home leaves the residences insufficiently protected and renders them suitable and easy targets for the common types of household victimization (facilitating factors: the absence of capable guardians).

The concept of opportunity is central to the routine activity approach, as may be seen from the following excerpt from Cohen and Felson's (1979) article:

> *It is ironic that the very factors which increase the opportunity to enjoy the benefits of life also may increase the opportunity for predatory violations. For example, automobiles provide freedom of movement to offenders as well as average citizens and offer vulnerable targets for theft. College enrollment, female labor force participation, urbanization, suburbanization, vacations and*

new electronic durables provide various opportunities to escape the confines of the household while they increase the risk of predatory victimization. Indeed, the opportunity for predatory crime appears to be enmeshed in the opportunity structure for legitimate activities to such an extent that it might be very difficult to root out substantial amounts of crime without modifying much of our way of life. Rather than assuming that predatory crime is simply an indicator of social breakdown, one might take it as a byproduct of freedom and prosperity as they manifest themselves in the routine activities of everyday life. (p. 605)

The Opportunity Model (Cohen, Kluegel, and Land)

In a subsequent study, Cohen, Kluegel, and Land (1981) offer what they call an "opportunity model" of predatory victimization. This model incorporates elements from both the life-style and routine activity perspectives and posits that the risk of criminal victimization depends largely on people's life-style and routine activities that bring them and/or their property into direct contact with potential offenders in the absence of capable guardians. Cohen, Kluegel, and Land (1981, pp. 508-509) identified five factors that they claim are strongly related to the risk of predatory criminal victimization. These factors are exposure, proximity, guardianship, target attractiveness, and definitional properties of specific crimes. Having defined these five factors, the authors then went on to formulate five assumptions or hypotheses that explain differences in victimization risks. The five assumptions are as follows:

1. Exposure. All else equal, an increase in exposure leads to an increase in victimization risk.
2. Guardianship. All else equal, offenders prefer targets that are less well-guarded to those that are more well-guarded. Therefore, the greater the guardianship, the lesser the risk of criminal victimization.
3. Proximity. All else equal, the closer the residential proximity of potential targets to relatively large populations of motivated offenders, the greater the risk of criminal victimization.
4. Attractiveness. All else equal, if a crime is motivated by instrumental ends, the greater the attractiveness of a target, the greater the risk of victimization.
5. Properties of crime. The strength of the partial effects of exposure, guardianship, and proximity on victimization risk depends upon the degree to which properties of crimes themselves constrain strictly instrumental action. Specifically, the more constrained strictly instrumental action is, the stronger will be the effects of exposure, guardianship, and proximity on victimization risk relative to the effect of target attractiveness.

The Dutch Model (Steinmetz)

The life-style model, the routine activity approach, and the opportunity model were all developed in the United States. A very similar model was developed by a researcher at the Research and Documentation Center of the Dutch Ministry of Justice (Steinmetz, undated). A first attempt to determine the factors related to the objective risk of petty crime in the Netherlands was undertaken by Van Dijk and Steinmetz (1979) using data from the Dutch victim surveys between 1974 and 1979. The authors defined risk "as the *objective* chance of becoming the direct or indirect victim of a punishable offense (a chance of one equals 100 percent risk)" (Steinmetz, undated, p. 6). The model was developed further by Steinmetz (undated) who identified three main factors—proximity, attractiveness, and exposure—as important determinants of differential victimization risks. What follows is a summary of Steinmetz's description of these three factors.

Proximity factor. Proximity has two dimensions, one geographic (spending time with or living in close proximity to potential offenders), and the second, social (the volume of contacts a person has with potential offenders as a result of that person's life-style). Geographical proximity to potential offenders enhances the risk of criminal victimization due to the fact that offenders generally prefer to operate close to home. Social proximity, on the other hand, is mainly determined by life-style, individual or collective. Certain life-styles result in more contacts with potential offenders than others. Steinmetz (undated) indicates, for example, that adolescents and young people in the Netherlands spend an average of sixty hours per week in leisure activities, of which forty-seven hours are spent outside the home going out in the evening. It was found that in the three largest Dutch cities, these evenings out take young people to places of entertainment, such as pubs, dances, and bars, where they are exposed to the nightlife subculture and where they are with unknown people who prefer to remain anonymous. Steinmetz (undated) explains that the importance of social proximity and individual life-style as factors in the risk of victimization varies according to the type of offense. It is more likely to affect the chances of becoming a victim of street crimes, such as assault or indecent assault, than the chances of becoming a victim of residential crimes such as burglary or car theft.

Steinmetz (undated) identifies three social developments as particularly relevant to the factor of social proximity: (1) the amount of leisure, particularly that of young people; (2) the emancipation of women, which will likely lead to an increased number of contacts between potential female victims and potential male offenders; and (3) growing urbanization, which inevitably leads to more contact with strangers and, thus, with offenders. He also insists that the proximity factor alone does not account for the risk of being the victim of crime. There must be a motive and opportunity for the crime to be committed. The second and third factors—attractiveness and exposure—as explained by Steinmetz, are related to the characteristics of potential victims and to opportunity.

Attractiveness factor. The attractiveness factor on the part of the victim is the counterpart of the motive factor on the part of the offender. It designates the extent to which someone or something clearly represents an attractive target for potential offenders. Thus, according to the type of victimization, attractiveness could be determined by the possession of valuables, particular sexual characteristics, or characteristics that may arouse aggression. The importance of the attractiveness factor varies as well with the type of crime. Possession of valuables, for example, will largely be a factor in property crimes, such as burglary and theft, while certain physical features might be a factor in sexual offenses.

Exposure factor. This third factor, identified by Steinmetz (undated), is the extent to which an offender is given an opportunity to commit an offense when he or she comes into contact with an attractive target. Steinmetz makes a distinction between the technical and the social aspects of the exposure factor. The technical aspects include facilitating behaviors by the potential victim, such as the failure to lock up the house or to secure the car or to ensure that one's purse is not left visibly on the top of a shopping bag or cart. Among the important social aspects is the degree to which some form of protection or guard is present. Preventive patrols by the police are cited as an example of guardianship, while being away from home or absent on holiday is given as a factor facilitating burglary victimization. Steinmetz (undated) points out that the prospects for this kind of protection and informal social controls in urban areas are rather poor. The widespread anonymity and impersonality that characterize the urban environment weaken or eliminate social control, formal and informal.

As may be seen from the above, the Dutch model borrows elements from both the life-style model and the routine activity approach and draws heavily on both. The theoretical and practical implications of the model are outlined by Steinmetz (undated) as follows:

> *The theoretical framework outlined above (proximity factor, attractiveness factor, and exposure factor) reveals a large number of widely varying backgrounds to the interactions between potential offenders and potential victims. The range of significant interactions between the different elements of the model is such that for future analyses a systems theory approach will have to be used. This is the only approach which would seem to offer adequate possibilities for describing optimally the dynamics of the social and physical ecology involved. We may also conclude that this theoretical framework provides starting points for primary crime prevention. It will make it possible to*

systematically determine the socioeconomic, physical and social components in the structure of society which generate crime, and to see at which points barriers might be placed between potential offenders and potential victims, or at least greater obstacles created. (pp. 11-12)

LIMITATIONS OF THE LIFE-STYLE/ROUTINE ACTIVITY/OPPORTUNITY MODELS REVEALED BY EMPIRICAL RESEARCH

The Absence of Direct Measures for Key Life-style Variables in the Original Life-style Model

The data originally used by Hindelang et al. (1978) to develop the life-style model did not contain direct measures for key variables in the model such as the amount of out-of-home leisure activities for various demographic groups. The popularity and plausibility of the model led to the inclusion of questions related to life-style in subsequent victimization surveys conducted in countries such as Canada and Britain. These empirical data made it possible to test some of the premises that the model uses.

To do so, Corrado et al. (1980) used data from the Greater Vancouver Victimization Survey, which was conducted in 1979 by Statistics Canada for the Ministry of the Solicitor General of Canada. The data provided strong support for the significant relationship between the demographic variables of sex, age, and marital status and the rate of violent personal victimization. Young, primarily unmarried males had the highest rate. However, the analysis of a behavioral indicator of the life-style model, namely "nights out," suggested that this was not an intervening variable, as implied by Hindelang et al. Rather, it appeared to be another important independent variable with its own impact on violent victimization rates. The authors conclude that their findings highlight the need for more direct measures of the behaviors and attitudes related to life-style if the model is to be of use in enhancing our understanding of the nature of violent victimization.

Ignoring the Possible Association Between Delinquent Activities and Victimization

Jensen and Brownfield (1986) outline four limitations that have constricted prior theory and research on the opportunity/routine activity/life-style models of victimization. These four limitations are as follows:

1. Research seeking to explain victimization and variations in victimization risk failed to directly assess the contribution of routine activities or life-styles to victimization. Instead, the variables used as opportunity variables were

presumed to account for the correlation between background variables and victimization. The reason is that the models had been formulated and tested using National Crime Survey data, which concentrate on demographic variables. A better assessment of the contribution of different activities to victimization requires a more direct analysis of those activities.

2. There is an artificial dichotomy created in the models between victims and offenders. Consequently, interaction with offenders or proximity to them are used as key explanatory variables. And yet, as Jensen and Brownfield (1986) point out, criminal or delinquent life-styles/routines may be the most victimogenic of all routines. Hence the similarity in background characteristics of victims and offenders could be, at least partly, a product of that correlation. Jensen and Brownfield (1986) add that contrary to some authors (Gottfredson, 1984) who dismissed offending as a potential intervening life-style variable or routine, one may consider offense activity as a life-style characteristic or as a type of routine activity that enhances the risk of victimization.
3. Jensen and Brownfield (1986) are critical of opportunity theory for its passive interpretation of life-styles as enhancing victimization solely through exposure and guardianship. Such interpretation, they feel, does not fully capture the potential relevance of life-styles, particularly when it comes to violent crimes. The authors point out that certain routines involving the active pursuit of excitement and fun can be seen as indicative of particular life-styles. As examples they cite activities such as frequenting taverns and bars, cruising, and partying as ones that are likely to increase the risk of victimization because of exposure and lack of protection. For Jensen and Brownfield (1986), the primary victimogenic importance of such activities lies in the motivations of both potential victims and offenders involved in such routines.
4. Jensen and Brownfield (1986) argue that attempts to test the opportunity model have concentrated on three demographic variables, namely age, race, and income, but little attention has been paid to what they believe is the most persistent and prominent correlate of victimization—gender. The authors argue that if the opportunity model were to become an adequate, general theory, it would have to explain the gender difference. Obviously female and male life-styles differ. Females are less likely to be exposed to potential offenders and more likely to be guarded against victimization, but it cannot be claimed that they are less attractive targets for crime. Jensen and Brownfield (1986) contend that one key factor that may be contributing to the gender difference in victimization risks is that females are far less likely than males to be involved in deviant routines.

To counter the problems and to overcome the limitations they identified in prior research, Jensen and Brownfield (1986) used data from a national survey called the Monitoring the Future Study and a 1977 study of delinquency in middle-class high school students in Tucson, Arizona, to test four hypotheses about gender, routine activities, and delinquent activities as correlates of teenage victimization. The findings were consistent with the hypotheses and suggest that (1) activities that involve the mutual pursuit of fun are more victimogenic than activities that passively put people at risk; (2) delinquent activity is positively related to victimization; (3) delinquent activity is more strongly related to victimization than nondelinquent activities; and (4) gender differences in victimization are reduced considerably by controls for delinquent activity (p. 85). Jensen and Brownfield admit that since their data were cross-sectional, it was not possible to demonstrate that offense activity preceded victimization. They note, however, that the results do demonstrate the potential importance of delinquent activity in explanations of victimization among youths.

The linkage between offending and victimization was also examined by Sampson and Lauritsen (1990) who used data from two British Crime Surveys conducted in 1982 and 1984. They found that offense activity—whether of a violent or a minor deviance such as drinking or drug use—directly increases the risk of personal victimization. These results were generally replicated across time and across type of victimization (e.g., crimes by strangers versus crimes by acquaintances), and they were independent of major demographic and individual-level correlates of victimization. The following is a summary of their findings:

—A significant relationship was found between the risk of victimization and involvement in violence, vandalism, and theft offending—regardless of type of victimization. Persons who engage in criminal offending sharply increase their overall risk of victimization (pp. 120, 126).

—A fairly strong relationship exists between violent offending behavior and victimization risk (p. 121). Of all the variables in the model, violent offending has the second largest ratio of coefficient to standard error for assault victimization (p. 126).

—Overall, assault risk showed a monotonic increase as drinking frequency increases from abstention to occasional use to moderate drinking to heavy alcohol consumption. Twice as many heavy drinkers were assaulted as abstainers (19 percent versus 7 percent). Alcohol consumption was also found to increase the overall risk of total victimization (p. 121).

—Proximity to violence (and hence to violent offenders) proved to be a salient risk factor and an important structural determinant of victimization. There was a monotonic increase in the risk of all types of victimization as the actual rate of neighborhood violence increased. Overall, living in high-violence areas approximately doubles the risk of suffering a victimization (p. 123). Sampson and Lauritsen (1990) report that the effect of proximity to violence on assault is due mostly to violence by acquaintances. They report further that their research findings point to three broad factors—violent offending, deviant life-styles, and ecological proximity to crime and violence—as warranting further investigation and inclusion in theoretical and empirical accounts of victimization (p. 132).

Poor Performance in Explaining Violent Victimization

Miethe, Stafford, and Long (1987) assessed the mediational effects of routine activities/life-style variables (major daytime activity, frequency of nighttime activity) on the demographic correlates of victimization using a sample of 107,678 residents in thirteen United States cities. Their findings were consistent with predictions about the direct and mediational effects of routine activity/life-style variables for the risk of property victimization but not for violent victimization. Based on their findings, the authors suggest that routine activity/life-style approaches may only be appropriate for explaining the likelihood of property victimization. Even for these, they believe that differences in routine activities/life-styles that affect target suitability, guardianship, and exposure to motivated offenders may not be able to account for the relative risk of victimization for all subsets of persons. Miethe et al. (1987) offer several explanations for the alleged poor performance of routine activity/life-style variables in explaining violent victimization. They are summarized below:

— There is the possibility that the aggregate measures of violent victimization Miethe et al. used may have suppressed the impact of activity/life-style variables given that acts of interpersonal violence commonly occur near the home and are committed by persons who are related or by other primary group members (e.g., friends, coworkers). However, they dismiss this possibility, as separate analyses for persons victimized by strangers and nonstrangers, as well as the location of victimization (near home or away from home), yielded results similar to those obtained by using the aggregated measures (p. 192).

— The poor performance of the model used by Miethe et al. in explaining violent victimization could not have been due to problems with the validity of measures of activities/life-styles because these measures exhibited the expected direct and mediational effects on the likelihood of property victimization (p. 192).

— One plausible reason for the poor performance could be the nature of most violent victimizations. Many violent crimes are expressive acts (spontaneous, impulsive) that defy the rational characterization of criminal motivation underlying routine activity/life-style approaches. Violent crimes are also relatively infrequent acts and involve a direct confrontation between victims and offenders. This spontaneous and situational nature of violent crimes may account for the poor performance of routine activity/life-style theories. If so, Miethe et al. believe that it is unlikely that more refined measures of routine activities and situational data on the context of victimization would improve our ability to explain this type of victimization (p. 192).

Using their findings, Miethe et al. (1987) outline some of the limitations of the routine activity/life-style models:

— The models are incapable of explaining why the risk of victimization is stable across activity categories for some social groups but varied for others. They ask, for example, why the predicted odds of violent victimization are fairly uniform across activity levels for females, younger persons, and older persons, but vary considerably across levels of activity outside the home for whites, low-income persons, and high-income persons (p. 192).

— The models are incapable of explaining why there is relative stability of property victimization across activity levels for households in which the head is black, high-income, married, young, or old, whereas there is notable variation across levels of activity outside the home among other groups of persons (p. 192).

— The models are incapable of explaining why persons who may be more suitable as targets and generally lack guardianship are not necessarily those who are more likely to be victimized by property or violent crimes (p. 193).

— The models do not explain why some persons who are in close residential proximity to motivated offenders and who spend relatively more time outside the household do not have a greater likelihood of victimization (p. 193).

— Although offender motivation is largely neglected or assumed to be constant, routine activities/life-style theories adopt a rational conception of criminal behavior. While this image may be consistent with the etiology of instrumental crimes such as property offenses, the expressive and spontaneous nature of many violent crimes is largely inconsistent with the "rational behavior" postulate underlying routine activity/life-style theories (pp. 193-194).

Findings at odds with those of the previous study come from research undertaken by Kennedy and Forde (1990) who used data from the Canadian Urban Victimization Survey conducted in 1981 that contain detailed measures of routine activities not available in American survey data used by Miethe et al. Kennedy and Forde found contrary evidence suggesting that personal crime is contingent on the exposure that comes from following a certain life-style. Findings for property crimes such as breaking and entering and vehicle theft were similar to those reported by American studies and support the view that people are vulnerable to property crime because of the absence of guardians from the target (their home in break-and-entry, their vehicle in vehicle theft). Kennedy and Forde's findings on personal crime are quite different from those of Miethe et al. (1987) and are consistent with the predictions of the routine activities theory. For example, when looking at assault, the authors found that all demographic variables significantly predict victimization, although there is a poor fit to the data. Once routine activities variables are added there is an improved fit to the data. Thus, in accordance with what the routine activities theory predicts, the most vulnerable groups are young unmarried males who frequent bars, go to movies, go out to work, or spend time out of the house walking or driving around (p. 143). The pattern for robberies is similar: young unmarried males who frequent bars and who are out walking and driving around are likely to be victims of this crime (p. 144). Kennedy and Forde's comment on their findings is as follows:

> *It appears that it is this public life-style that creates exposure to risk and, although it may be the case that violent crime is spontaneous, the targets of violent crime are more likely to be people who are in places where conflict flares up. This does not explain motivation, but it does explain exposure to crime and identifies those groups that are most likely to experience this exposure. (pp. 143-144)*

In contrast to Miethe et al., Kennedy and Forde believe that routine activities variables contribute significantly to the explanation of personal victimization.

Further support for the link between "leisure time activities" and violent victimization comes from Sweden and England. In Sweden, Wikström (1985) found that human activities can be divided into work and leisure, and that crimes of violence are greatly related to the latter, not the former. Wikström notes that work is not likely to be a particularly conflict-free human activity, yet very few conflicts at work result in violent actions. Public entertainment, on the other hand, is the scene of many violent confrontations. Strangers, with different behavioral customs meet within small areas. One of the major activities in places of public entertainment is meeting persons of the opposite sex: a process in which disappointments and frustrations are often encountered. Alcohol, Wikström points out, is a major ingredient in public entertainment and may contribute to the development of conflicts into violent crimes. All this indicates why the opportunities for confrontation between people are comparatively great in places of public entertainment. Wikström's study of violence in Gävle, Sweden, amply demonstrates how a single area in a small city can be a truly "hot spot" (Sherman et al., 1989) for violence. The highest incidence of outdoor crimes of violence in the city occurred in a small cross street. On one side of the street was the entrance to a restaurant, often frequented by pupils of upper-secondary schools, and one high-class dance-restaurant, frequented by somewhat older people. On the other side was a hot-dog stand, a place in and around which many of the rockers of the city spent some of their time at night. The location of the two public entertainment spots and the hot-dog stand on that particular cross street created many opportunities for confrontation between different kinds of people.

To illustrate how life-style can, at an individual level, lead a person to become involved in violence as a victim or offender, Wikström (1985) gives the following description of a "normal" activity pattern for some of those living outside conventional society:

A usual meeting place to start the day's activities is the city center. Hanging around and meeting "friends," perhaps entering a department store, getting into conflict with the personnel or guards. Meeting in a park to drink alcohol, perhaps being approached by the police, occasional conflicts with them or other conventional citizens who comment upon some behavior. Going with "friends" to someone's flat, generally in the outer-city areas, perhaps a confrontation with a taxi-driver over the payment. Heavy drinking parties in the apartment, perhaps confrontation with the others about alcohol, girl-friends, (illegal) affairs or whatsoever. An occasional confrontation with a complaining neighbor. Perhaps the police turn up and there is confrontation with them. In the evening, if not still in the apartment, going down town to a public entertainment. Getting into conflict with other people, perhaps commenting upon something or not approving of being passed in a queue. Occasional conflicts with personnel at restaurants. Needless to say, a description like this is likely to be very superficial and, of course, all mentioned confrontations are not likely to occur during a single day, but I believe it grasps some essential aspects of a life-style highly related to violence. (pp. 95-96)

In North Central Birmingham, England, Smith (1986) found that variations in susceptibility were apparently influenced by the *type* of spare-time socializing that is undertaken. Victims were more likely to engage in more types of activity than nonvictims, but a considerably larger proportion of those victimized engaged in regular visits to the cinema, theater, dances, or bingo. Respondents who tended to meet with friends in pubs or cafes were also twice as likely to have been victims during the reference year as those who did not.

Ignoring the Possible Link Between Community Structure and Victimization

Sampson and Wooldredge (1987) contend that models of criminal victimization have ignored a major theoretical factor that is crucial to explaining victimization, that is the community context of everyday activities. They explain the significance of this particular factor with two reasons: (1) one of the major assumptions of the opportunity model is that there is a positive association between victimization risks and the ecological proximity of potential targets to motivated offenders and (2) there is also the macro level assumption of an important role that the spatial structure of routine activities and opportunities plays in determining the frequency with which motivated offenders encounter suitable targets in the absence of capable guardians. Motivated offenders, Sampson and Wooldredge argue, may be influenced by the criminal-opportunity structure of entire areas, not just by individuals and their households. Hence, regardless of a household's family composition and even proximity to offenders, living in a community with low guardianship and surveillance may increase victimization (p. 373). In an attempt to explore the importance of linking the micro and macro level dimensions of household and personal victimization, Sampson and Wooldredge (1987) used the British Crime Survey data to measure the extent to which differences in victimization risks are associated with demographic characteristics, life-style/routine activities, and community context.

Sampson and Wooldredge (1987) report that the results of their study provide support for a multilevel opportunity theory of victimization risk. Like all previous studies, victimization risks were found to be highest for the young, the singles, and those who frequently go out at night or leave their homes unattended. In addition, they found burglary victimization to be related to age, household family type, and guardianship. Yet independent of these micro level effects, burglary risk increased directly with community family disruption, percentage of singles, unemployment, and housing density, with the latter two factors having very large effects. Burglary risk was also inversely related, though not in the same magnitude, to community social cohesion (p. 390). Similar observations were also made for personal theft both with and without contact. Despite these findings, the data generally showed that demographic and structural variables have the largest impact on victimization. The authors contend that the results demonstrate clearly that an individual or community model in isolation is insufficient to explain patterns of victimization.

Smith and Jarjoura (1988) also set out to study the effect of social structure on criminal victimization. Using victimization data from fifty-seven neighborhoods, they examined the relationship between neighborhood characteristics and rates of violent crime and burglary. The study relied on three measures of social disorganization—poverty, residential mobility, and racial heterogeneity—as well as variables from the subculture of violence, social control, and opportunity perspectives.

The authors found that although social disorganization variables are important in explaining neighborhood victimization rates, their influence is more conditional than additional and varies by type of crime. For example, increasing residential mobility is associated with higher rates of violent crime, but only in neighborhoods characterized by high levels of poverty (p. 46). Residential instability and social heterogeneity were associated with high burglary rates. These variables, suggest the authors, may be indicators of weak neighborhood integration (p. 46). And while residential mobility was significantly associated with rates of violent crime and burglary, poverty was associated with violent crime rates but not burglary rates. Racial heterogeneity, on the other hand, was significantly associated with rates of burglary but not violent crime. Three other community characteristics were identified as important sources of variation in neighborhood victimization rates: percentage of single-parent households, percentage of the population between the ages of twelve and twenty, and population density (p. 47). The authors conclude that while variables related to a neighborhood's capacity for social control are central elements in explaining variation in community victimization, the intervening mechanisms among variables, such as community family structure or population mobility and rates of violent crime and burglary, remain unknown.

Taking a Simplistic View of the Association Between Demographic Variables and Criminal Victimization

Cohen, Kluegel, and Land (1981) tried to find out whether certain dimensions of social stratification—income, race, and age—relate to the risk of predatory criminal victimization. Their analysis was based on National Crime Surveys of households within the United States. They employed data from two years of the survey, 1974 and 1977, and they analyzed each sample separately and in merged form. The types of victimization they examined were burglary, assault, and/or personal larceny. The analysis led Cohen and his coresearchers to suggest that the relationship between the variables of income, race, and age and the risk of predatory crime is a much more complex one than that assumed by current models of victimization. It also led them to conclude that, other things being equal, those usually thought to be most vulnerable economically and socially—the poor, the nonwhite, and the old—are *not* the most likely victims of crime. Many of the bivariate and multivariate findings were contrary to the conventional wisdom that "street crimes," which include assault and personal larceny, occur disproportionately among low-income persons. Cohen, Kluegel, and Land (1981) report the following:

> *Our data, however, indicate that, at the bivariate level, income is inversely related to risk of assault, directly related to risk of personal larceny, and parabolically related to risk of burglary victimization. Also, at the bivariate level, (and contrary to conventional wisdom), we find race to have little direct effect on victimization risk for any of the crimes studied here. Age, on the other hand, is inversely related to each type of victimization at the bivariate level of analysis. When we control for proximity, guardianship, and exposure (introduced as factors associated with risk in our theory), the income-victimization relationship changes. Most notably, the affluent have the highest risk of victimization for each crime studied here. (p. 522)*

Some researchers, for example, Collins, Cox, and Langan (1987), believe that the associations usually reported between certain demographic variables and victimization risks might be spurious. Collins, Cox, and Langan (1987) assume that the use of direct life-style measures might weaken or even completely wash out the relationship between victimization risk and demographic characteristics. In support of their contention they quote the London, England, survey conducted in the 1970s by Sparks, Genn, and Dodd (1977), which showed that a direct measure of life-style could largely explain the negative relationship between old age and violent victimization. The results indicated that the amount of time respondents went out in the evenings "largely" explained the low rate of violent victimization among older respondents. Collins, Cox, and Langan's (1987) own findings suggest that the relevance of demographic factors either disappears or is reduced when controls are introduced for life activities. This is similar to Lynch's (1986) results, which indicated that sex and race were not associated with victimization once life-activity variables were controlled.

Collins, Cox, and Langan (1987) suggest further refinement to the concept of exposure by differentiating between the risk of victimization where there is face-to-face contact with an offender and the risk of offenses where no contact is involved. While exposure to potential offenders is likely to increase the risk of face-to-face victimization, there is no reason to believe that it enhances the risk of no-contact victimization.

LIMITATIONS OF THE LIFE-STYLE/ROUTINE ACTIVITY/OPPORTUNITY MODELS: A SUMMARY

As we mentioned earlier, the life-style/routine activities/opportunity models are pioneering efforts and therefore should not be judged too harshly. Their great merit is to have generated much interest and enthusiasm among researchers and to have opened the door to some of the most exciting empirical research conducted in criminology in recent years. As with all pioneering efforts, they were not devoid of problems and flaws. Empirical research conducted to test the models revealed certain weaknesses and limitations in the original versions. Each of the studies reviewed above drew attention to one or more problems in the models as originally formulated. The following is a very brief summary of some of the weaknesses and limitations pointed out by different authors:

— The opportunity theory and its life-style and routine activities variants, are essentially passive theories because differences in victimization are explained by the characteristics of victims that make them vulnerable. They are available, unprotected, and unguarded (Jensen and Brownfield, 1986).

— Many of the basic premises of both models are simplistic, bordering on the axiomatic. Saying that the more evenings and weekends individuals spend outside the home, the more vulnerable they are to personal crime, or saying that the more evenings a week a home is left unguarded, the more likely it is to be burglarized, amounts to saying that those who do not ski are less vulnerable to ski accidents, or that those who do not drive or ride motor vehicles are less vulnerable to traffic accidents.

— In both models, offender motivation and inclination are assumed or are taken as a given. In addition, both deal with patterned behavior among population aggregates rather than with variability in individual characteristics, such as the psychological propensity to "precipitate" violent interaction (Garofalo, 1986; Miethe, Stafford, and Long, 1987).

— The life-style concept can be used in a way that makes the theory true by definition and, therefore, uninformative and trivial (Garofalo, 1986).

— The life-style model creates a strong temptation for *ex post facto* explanations. Given the vagueness of the life-style concept it is easy to claim that some of the factors showing a positive association with victimization are indicators of life-style. This makes the theory virtually unimpeachable (Garofalo, 1986; Miethe, Stafford, and Long, 1987).

— Although the relevance of the life-style model and its exposure-to-risk thesis is indisputable, the model is neither well developed as a theory of victimization, nor sufficient in itself as an explanation of the incidence of crime in modern society (Smith, 1986).

— The scope of activity labeled as routine is, for most people, very broad. Most people engage in different domains of activity and face varying levels of risk in each domain. Hence, there is a need for more analysis of victimization risks in specific domains (Maxfield, 1987).

— Central theoretical concepts such as life-style and exposure are operationalized using very crude indicators. Some substitute measures of factors such as marital status for measures of behavior. For example, at the individual level, life-style differences, that is, differences in the way people spend their time, where they go, and with whom they associate, have been assumed to be reflected in major demographic characteristics such as age, sex, race, income, and "major activity." Some studies (for example, Messner and Tardiff, 1985) used sociodemographic characteristics as proxy indicators of routine activity variables, while others (for example, Cohen, Kluegel, and Land, 1981) used the proxy measures of marital status and employment to operationalize the guardianship and exposure concepts into a life-style indicator. (Gottfredson, 1981; Collins, Cox, and Langan, 1987; Corrado, Roesch, Glackman, Evans, and Leger, 1980; Skogan, 1981).

— The absence of refined and direct measures of life-style and exposure has impeded significant and unequivocal tests of the model as well as further theoretical development (Gottfredson, 1981; Collins, Cox, and Langan, 1987).

— The absence of multiple measures of each theoretical concept, coupled with the reliance on single indicators of key concepts, may result in errors of specification due to the exclusion of relevant variables (Miethe and Meier, 1990).

—Progress in understanding the link between victimization and life-style requires much more detailed analysis of the timing and location of those activities that render participants more vulnerable (Gottfredson, 1984).

—Life-style is just one manifestation of more fundamental social and economic processes. Life-style measures used by Cohen and Felson (1979), for example, are ultimately a reflection of the nature of income inequality in American society (Carroll and Jackson, 1983).

—The models do not explain the differences in victimization rates of males and females who lead similar life-styles as measured by the indicators used in most studies or whose routine activities are quite similar. They do not explain why, at constant levels of exposure, victimization risks are different.

—The models do not explain why persons who may be more suitable targets and generally lack guardianship are not necessarily those who are more likely to be victimized by property or violent crime (Miethe et al., 1987).

—The models do not explain why some persons who are in close residential proximity to motivated offenders and who spend relatively more time outside the household do not have a greater likelihood of victimization (Miethe et al., 1987).

—The expressive and spontaneous nature of many violent crimes is largely inconsistent with the "rational behavior" postulate underlying routine activities and life-style theories (Miethe et al., 1987).

—The models overlook or minimize the importance of other structural variables such as community context (Sampson and Wooldredge, 1987), social inequality (Cohen, Kluegel, and Land, 1981), and social disorganization (Smith and Jarjoura, 1988) to variations in the probabilities of victimization.

—The models do not consider involvement in delinquent activities as a routine activity, thus ignoring the importance of these activities as a victimogenic factor (Jensen and Brownfield, 1986).

—The models are inadequate for explaining a good part of assault victimization that occurs in the home, namely, the various forms of family violence.

Having thus outlined some of the important criticisms leveled at the life-style/routine activity/opportunity models, we need to draw attention to two things:

1. Empirical research testing the life-style/routine activity/opportunity models is by no means perfect. Some of it suffers from methodological problems, sometimes serious. Some of these problems are related to the difficulty in properly operationalizing many of the research concepts. Others have to do with such problems as the use of aggregate data and the lack of detailed information on some key variables.

2. Although existing data, research, and theory suffer from several major deficiencies, the situation is changing rapidly. The early theoretical models have been subjected to a number of improvements in recent years. Among the significant advances signaled by Maxfield (1987) are (1) better measurement of behavior; (2) linking of life-style and opportunities for offending; (3) contextual analysis of neighborhood opportunities and individual life-style; and (4) development of a domain, specific routine activity theory (p. 279).

Explaining the Differential Risks of Criminal Victimization

A TENTATIVE INTEGRATIVE SCHEMA

Having reviewed the various micro and macro explanations of the differential risks of victimization and the models that have been developed to explain the etiology of victimization, the explanatory elements contained in the models will now be synthesized and presented in an integrative schema. To make the schema easier to comprehend, forty propositions have been grouped, somewhat arbitrarily, under the following ten headings: opportunities, risk factors, motivated offenders, exposure, associations, dangerous times/dangerous places, dangerous behaviors, high-risk activities, defensive/avoidance behaviors, structural/cultural proneness.

Opportunities

—Criminal victimization is not a random occurrence. Probabilities of victimization are a function of the available opportunities to victimize. Variations in opportunities can thus explain, at least partially, the uneven distribution of victimization and the differences in victimization risks and rates. By the same token, increasing or decreasing opportunities over time can produce fluctuations in the risks and rates of victimization.

—The temporal and spatial clustering of opportunities produces an uneven distribution of the risks and rates of victimization in time and space. There are, therefore, days, times, areas, and places that are more dangerous than others.

—Opportunities for criminal victimization are closely linked to the characteristics of potential targets (persons, households, businesses) and to the activities and behavior of those targets. There are, therefore, hard and easy targets. The absence of capable guardians is an important opportunity factor for several types of victimization and it increases the ease with which the target can be victimized.

Risk Factors

— Probabilities of victimization are determined by a number of risk factors. Risk factors, such as attractiveness, suitability, accessibility, and vulnerability, are not independent from one another. It is the convergence of certain risk elements in time and space that accounts for the occurrence of victimization.

— Differential probabilities of victimization are strongly related to sociodemographic characteristics. The young, the unmarried, the unemployed, and blacks in the United States run much greater risks of victimization than the old, the married, the employed, and whites in the United States. Females run a much greater risk of sexual victimization than men do. These different risks are due, among other things, to different levels in structural proneness, as well as to differences in routine activities and life-style.

— Differences in probabilities of victimization associated with sociodemographic characteristics, such as age and gender, are rather stable across regions, areas, cities, and over time.

— Victimization risks are closely linked to area of residence. As household (and personal) victimizations are clustered in certain areas, "the hotspots of predatory crimes" (Sherman et al., 1989), those who reside in, or in close proximity to, high crime areas will have a greater likelihood of being victimized than those living in low delinquency and crime areas.

— Victimization rates are usually higher in the inner city than in the peripheral areas of the urban environment. Residence in the inner city, in conjunction with other variables, places some groups of people in extremely high-risk positions as regards criminal victimization.

— Households in the vast majority of cases are victimized when nobody is at home. Thus, the amount of time people leave their residences unguarded affects their chances of becoming victims of burglary and other household crimes.

— Alcohol is a high-risk factor in violent victimization. Hence, people's drinking patterns can significantly influence their chances of victimization. The setting in which people drink can also affect their risks of violent victimization.

Motivated Offenders

— Probabilities of victimization are dependent upon the numbers of motivated offenders. Fluctuations in the numbers of those offenders are bound to produce changes in victimization risks and rates.

— Many offenders, particularly reasoning property offenders, select their targets. Hence, targets considered attractive by potential offenders run a higher risk of being victimized than others. Attractiveness, however, is a very relative and subjective feature of the target.

— Physical visibility, proximity, availability, and accessability are important target selection criteria. Hence, targets that are visible, available, and accessible, as well as targets in close proximity to where large numbers of potential offenders reside, have a greater chance of being victimized than others.

— People living in densely populated, weakly integrated neighborhoods with higher percentages of males in the delinquency-prone ages of twelve to twenty run a higher risk of being victimized than those living in less densely populated and more cohesive neighborhoods with relatively higher percentages of middle-age and elderly persons.

Exposure

— Exposure to potential offenders and to high-risk situations and environments enhances the risks of criminal victimization. The higher the exposure, the greater the risk; the lower the exposure, the lesser the likelihood of being victimized.

— The level and degree of exposure to potential offenders and to high-risk situations and environments vary according to sociodemographic characteristics such as age, gender, marital status, occupation, and income. Such variation in exposure contributes to the differential risks of criminal victimization.

— Certain social activities, such as alcohol consumption in public entertainment places, increase the level of exposure by bringing potential targets in close proximity to a large pool of unknown, anonymous potential offenders. Hence, the probability of personal victimization is related to the frequency of evenings out for leisure and social activities and to the amount of time a person spends in public places at night (Hindelang, Gottfredson, and Garofalo, 1978).

Associations

— The homogeneity of the victim and offender populations suggests that differential association is as important to criminal victimization as it is to crime and delinquency. Thus, individuals who are in close personal, social, or professional contact with potential delinquents and criminals run a greater chance of being victimized than those who are not.

— Persons who share potential offenders' sociodemographic characteristics are more likely to interact socially with those potential offenders. In so doing, their chances of being victimized by those offenders increase (Cohen, Kluegel, and Land, 1981).

Dangerous Times/Dangerous Places

—Personal victimization, particularly violent victimization, occurs more frequently in the evening and early night hours and on weekends. Hence, people's activity patterns, particularly out-of-home activities, can have a strong bearing upon their chances of being victimized.

—A good part of personal victimization, particularly predatory victimization, takes place on the street or in other public places during hours of darkness. Thus, the more people are, or have to be, on the street or in public places during the late evening or early night hours, the higher are their chances of being victimized.

—Personal victimization, particularly assault victimization, occurs with a certain frequency in or close to places of public entertainment. Hence, the frequency with which people visit these places or congregate in their vicinity can affect their risks of victimization.

—More personal victimization is associated with the use of public means of transportation than with the use of private vehicles. Thus, people who have to rely on those means for their mobility run a greater risk of personal victimization than those who do not. Those who use private vehicles, on the other hand, have a higher risk of becoming victims of theft of, or from, their car than the others.

Dangerous Behaviors

—Situational variables play an important role in certain types of criminal victimization. Therefore, individuals whose aggressive behavior is likely to trigger a violent response have a greater risk of becoming victims of violence than others.

—Individuals whose negligent/careless behavior is likely to attract or tempt potential offenders and/or to facilitate the commission of certain property offenses run a higher risk of being victimized than those whose behavior is more circumspect and less inviting.

—Certain behaviors place those who engage in them in dangerous situations where their ability to defend and protect themselves against attacks is greatly reduced. For example, the behavior of hitchhiking alone can be dangerous for both driver and hitchhiker. The risks of being victimized for those practicing these dangerous behaviors are greater than for those who do not.

High-risk Activities

—Activities that involve the mutual pursuit of fun involve a higher risk of victimization than do activities that passively put people at risk (Jensen and Brownfield, 1986).

—Certain occupations carry with them a higher than average potential for criminal victimization. Members of these occupations run a higher risk of becoming victims than those in less dangerous occupations. Delivery of passengers or goods and dealing with the public are, for example, strongly associated with violent victimization (Collins, Cox, and Langan, 1987).

—Some deviant and illegal activities, such as dealing in illicit goods and services, fencing, trafficking in drugs, bootlegging, racketeering, gambling, loan sharking, trading sex for money, and cruising or seeking sex partners in tearooms, lead those who engage in them to dangerous places at dangerous times and get them involved with marginal individuals in dangerous transactions and situations. The casualness and anonymity of some of these contacts, the potential for conflict, and the lack of social and police protection create excellent opportunities for criminal victimization and place those involved in greater risk of being victims than others.

—Delinquent and criminal activities are more strongly and positively related to criminal victimization than nondelinquent activities. Hence, criminals/delinquents run a higher risk of victimization than noncriminal/nondelinquent individuals.

Defensive/Avoidance Behaviors

—Many risks of criminal victimization can be easily avoided. People's attitudes to those risks can, therefore, influence their chances of being victimized. Risk-takers are bound to be victimized more often than risk-avoiders.

—There are risk-avoidance behaviors as well as risk-management activities. The former limit a person's exposure to potential offenders while the latter reduce the chances of being victimized when people are exposed to potential offenders (Skogan, 1981).

—People provide varying levels of opportunity for victimization by choosing to recognize or ignore the threat of victimization in structuring their daily actions (Cook, 1985, quoted in Maxfield, 1987). Those who choose to ignore the threat increase their chances of being victimized.

—Vulnerability may lead to less rather than to more victimization. Perceptions of high vulnerability and overestimation of the risks (and consequences) of criminal victimization normally lead to greater caution and more precautions against victimization. These are bound to reduce the risks of becoming a victim.

—Fear of crime can lead to less victimization by inducing those who are fearful to take certain precautions against crime and to curtail the pursuit of their day and nighttime activities, thus reducing their exposure and vulnerability to the risks of victimization. This is one of the reasons why groups that exhibit the highest levels of fear are sometimes the least victimized.

— Sociodemographic characteristics such as age, gender, race, marital status, income, and socioeconomic status are intimately related to the attitude to victimization risks and to the levels of fear of victimization. Thus, variations in victimization risks and rates along sociodemographic variables can be a reflection of the defensive/avoidance measures that members of various groups take to protect themselves against victimization.

Structural/Cultural Proneness

— There is a negative association between power and proneness to criminal victimization and a positive correlation between deprivation and victimization. Probabilities of victimization for members of the powerless and deprived groups and those low in the power hierarchy are greater than for those high on the power ladder.

— Odds of victimization are associated with *in situ* deprivation. The relatively affluent within an absolutely deprived community are the most vulnerable to victimization (Smith, 1986).

— Those who are structurally prone to criminal victimization exhibit a higher proneness than others to other kinds of mishap and misfortune. The same factors that contribute to the higher risk of victimization also contribute to higher risks of such misfortunes as accidents.

— Marginalizing and stigmatizing certain minorities or deviant groups designate them as appropriate and legitimate targets, thus promoting or facilitating their victimization. Being perceived as "fair game," members of these groups run a higher risk of being victimized than members of dominant and conventional groups whose victimization is strongly condemned by the culture.

Concluding Remarks

Integrating the Micro and Macro Level Approaches and Linking Criminological and Victimological Theories

Victimology has come a long way since Von Hentig (1948) published his book *The Criminal and His Victim.* Although originally designed to provide an estimate of the dark figure of crime, victimization surveys played a major role in promoting theoretical victimology. The methodological refinements they underwent in the past twenty-five years and the broadening of their scope have generated an unprecedented interest in the study of crime victims. New avenues have been opened and useful, exciting insights have been gained into the phenomenon of criminal victimization. Due to the novelty of the field and the inevitable imperfections from which all pioneering efforts suffer, the findings of victimization research are still inconclusive. The different, and sometimes inconsistent, results reported by many studies certainly have much to do with the data and methodologies being used and, above all, with the varying ways in which the key concepts have been defined and operationalized and with the proxy measures that have been employed as indicators of the various concepts. Despite this, it is undeniable that the approach is very promising, much more promising, in fact, than the sterile and static studies that have always been the trademark of traditional criminology. It is also undeniable that a great deal of research remains to be done before the current tentative theoretical formulations and constructions can be developed into a full-fledged theory of criminal victimization and before we are able to come up with models capable of predicting criminal victimization with a fair degree of accuracy. The countless criticisms of present models, which we have summarized in Chapter 12, are indicative of the kind of research problems that need to be overcome. Most of the problems have to do with conceptual and measurement issues. The criticisms also suggest new directions for future research. At present, there seems to be two urgent needs in theoretical victimology: first, the need to integrate the micro and macro level explanations of criminal victimization; and second, the need to link criminological theories with theories of victimization.

The wealth of data, which became available in the last two decades through victimization surveys, has transformed theoretical victimology from the micro level analysis of the characteristics and behavior of small groups of victims into a macro level analysis of the characteristics, the life-styles, and routine activities of the general victim population (Fattah, 1979). The dominance of this macro, and inevitably static, perspective has overshadowed the early modest attempts to develop a dynamic and interactionist model of victimization behavior, a model that pays equal attention to the victim and the victimizer, their relationships, their reciprocal attitudes, their actions and reactions. And yet, such a dynamic approach is indispensable to a better understanding of face-to-face victimization. It is, of course, possible to study target selection criteria using victimization survey data (Hough, 1987) or to examine some situational variables, such as opportunity or guardianship, at the macro level. However, this quantitative, abstract approach cannot yield information as rich, elaborate, concrete, or as lively and enlightening as that gained through qualitative, micro level studies such as Lejeune's (1977) study of mugging or Sutherland's (1937) study of the professional thief. A great deal more of this type of research will have to be done if we are to be able to complement the somewhat superficial data of victimization surveys with more in-depth information and to integrate the micro and macro approaches into a comprehensive theoretical model of criminal victimization.

There is also another problem. There have been very few endeavors to link victimological and criminological theories. One such endeavor is Felson's (1986) valiant attempt to link criminal choices, routine activities, informal control, and criminal outcomes. Generally, victimization research has been moving independently from, and almost in a parallel fashion to, criminological theory. As we mentioned earlier, none of the current models of victimization tries to explain criminal inclinations or the motivations of offenders. Criminal inclinations and motivations seem to be assumed or taken as a given! The models constantly talk about "potential" offenders or motivated offenders without describing the characteristics of these potential offenders (except for some vague references to their age group), without searching for what it is that renders them so, or without specifying who it is that fits into this nebulous category. Criminal victimization involves offenders and victims and, as we have seen in Chapter 5, the two populations are similar and homogeneous. Traditional criminology completely ignored the victim. Modern victimology cannot afford to ignore the victimizers. Explaining the crime/victimization phenomenon requires the pooling and linking of criminological and victimological knowledge so that we may better understand who victimizes whom and why. We should not lose sight of the fact that what we are studying, that is crime and victimization, are not parallel phenomena but are one and the same phenomenon. The study of the phenomenon of crime would not be complete if it excluded the victims and the study of the victimization phenomenon would not be whole if it excluded the victimizers. What we need is a holistic approach, a comprehensive model where the theoretical tenets of criminology and victimology are incorporated and integrated. This realization should, it is hoped, put to rest the current debate about the present and future status of victimology and whether it will become a separate discipline or remain as an integral part of criminology.

And what of the tremendous and far-reaching practical implications of the theoretical study of victims of crime? These implications can never be overestimated. The failure of traditional strategies of crime prevention, based as they are on punishment and deterrence, is too well documented to need any elaboration. Despite the manifest unwillingness to do away with this ineffective policy and to abandon these deeply entrenched but largely futile practices, there can be no doubt that crime policies of the future will be geared more and more toward environmental and situational prevention. Crime prevention through environmental design, situational prevention, reduction of the opportunities, and target-hardening are approaches whose time has come and that are gaining more attention and more acceptance every day. Victimological research provides the knowledge base necessary to implement these concepts and to translate these ideas into practice. The role of the victim in all of these approaches is pivotal. This is victim-based not offender-centered crime prevention. And whether the aims are to reduce vulnerability, better protect against victimization, modify attitudes and behaviors that facilitate, instigate, or precipitate victimization, the target population is potential victims. This is why we need as much information as we can possibly get on the characteristics, attitudes, and behaviors of those who are victimized. Furthermore, solid scientific knowledge about the victims of various types of crime is a prerequisite for efficient and effective programs and services designed to help, assist, and meet the needs of crime victims. All this signals the dawning of a new era in criminology: the era of VICTIMOLOGY.

Notes

Chapter 1. On Victimization, Criminal and Otherwise

1. Some overlap between the groups seems to be inevitable whenever a grouping or a typology is attempted. For example, if one tries to group victimizations by their nature, as is common in criminology, some overlap will still exist. The popular four-group division of criminal victimization into violent victimization, sexual victimization, property victimization, and other victimizations illustrates well this unavoidable overlap. Rape (sexual assault) fits into the first and second categories. Robbery, extortion, and ransom kidnapping fit into the first and third categories. The same is true with murder for robbery, and so on.
2. See Avery, M. (1983). See also Viano, E. (1990).
3. There is no doubt that deaths, injuries, and losses from criminal victimization are relatively minor when compared to those caused by other forms of victimization. Unfortunately, there are no accurate statistics for several victimization types. To give a rough idea of how deaths (and injuries) from criminal victimization compare with those from some other types we give here figures quoted from two different sources: Waller (1969) reports that 112,000 deaths a year in the United States are attributed to accidents, 21,000 to suicide, and 12,000 to homicide. In addition, an estimated 50 million nonfatal accidents are believed to occur annually, whereas there are 200,000 to 500,000 suicide attempts and at least one-half million nonfatal assaults. It should be noted that most of these figures have increased dramatically in the following two decades.

   According to Elias (1986), there were 20,000 homicides in the United States in 1974 contrasted with 14,200 deaths from workplace accidents, 100,000 deaths from workplace diseases, 219,000 to 328,500 pollution deaths, 16,000 deaths from unnecessary surgery, over 20,000 deaths from improper emergency care, 200 to 10,000 deaths from unnecessary prescriptions, and untold tens of thousands of deaths from symptoms of poverty such as malnutrition and poor health care. Most of these figures, we should point out, are estimates rather than actual statistics.

   A major study of medical malpractice in the United States released in 1990 (the Vancouver *Sun*, March 1, 1990) and reported by Reuter, provides some startling figures. The study, conducted by researchers at the Harvard Medical School, reports that in 1984 there were about 7,000 hospital deaths and 27,000 injuries due to the negligence of doctors or hospital staff at fifty-one hospitals in the state of New York alone. The study further found that 99,000 patients out of 2.7 million in New York hospitals in 1984 suffered injuries during their hospital stay, and 28 percent of those suffered injuries caused by negligence. The study shows that only 2 percent of the patients who suffered malpractice injuries that year sued a doctor or a hospital.

4. Whether criminal victimization is qualitatively different from noncriminal victimization is debatable. Some believe it is not. Others feel that certain features are unique to the experience of being the victim of a crime and that these therefore warrant special attention by researchers. Van Dijk (1986) quotes the British philosopher, Jeremy Bentham, who observed that even a dog can distinguish between being kicked and being stumbled over (an observation often attributed to Justice Holmes). Van Dijk adds that the authorities and public react differently to road accidents or natural disasters than to crime, since the response to the latter contains an element of moral indignation toward the perpetrator. He feels that the very existence of extensive social institutions whose raison d'être is this sense of moral outrage (the criminal justice system) is reason in itself to study crime victims as a separate category.
5. For a more elaborate discussion of criminology's nonnormative character, see Fattah, E. A. (1985).

Chapter 2. Sources of Data on Criminal Victimization

1. The sample used for the Canadian Urban Victimization Survey was much larger than the one used for the General Social Survey. The latter survey collected information from 9,870 persons in the ten provinces (Sacco and Johnson, 1990). Sample sizes for the Canadian Urban Victimization Survey ranged from 6,910 in one city to 9,563 in another, with more than 61,000 interviews completed by Statistics Canada interviewers overall (Canada, 1984a).
2. Selected findings of the Canadian Urban Victimization Survey are reported in the *Canadian Urban Victimization Survey Bulletin*, which is published at irregular intervals. Ten issues have been published, with the first appearing in 1983 and the tenth, and last, issue appearing in 1988.

Chapter 3. Extent and Patterns of Criminal Victimization

1. Another useless technique for presenting risks of criminal victimization is the so-called "crime clock" invented by the FBI under Edgar Hoover in an attempt to highlight the seriousness of the American crime problem. Aggregate daily data on index crimes for the whole country are divided by time units, and the frequency of each crime, such as homicide, rape, or robbery, is presented in terms of minutes or seconds. Due to the enormous variations in the risks of victimization between regions, states, cities, and between areas within the city, the message communicated to the American public that there is a homicide every twenty-three minutes or a robbery every minute in the United States is totally devoid of any informational value. The sole aim of this questionable technique seems to be to heighten anxiety and to raise the level of concern about crime and victimization, which is already quite high in the United States, to still higher levels.
2. The issue of seasonality remains unsettled and is likely to be for some time to come. Statistics Canada asked three independent teams to search for seasonality in Canadian homicides using different statistical techniques and data for the years 1961 to 1980. The results were far from conclusive. McKie (1985) found "no evident seasonality" in any Canadian homicide series. McLeod et al. (1985) arrived at a mixture of conclusions, sometimes finding seasonality, sometimes not. Their preferred technique showed that all three quarterly series exhibited significant seasonality, but that the only monthly series to exhibit seasonality was the one for nondomestic, noncriminal homicide. Nakamura and Nakamura (1985) discovered that certain homicides increase on Fridays, but found no increase on Saturdays, in times of high unemployment, or in hot weather. They found weak evidence suggesting that certain homicides decrease in cold weather.

   In the United States, Michael and Zumpe (1983) used the cosinor method (a method that has not been applied previously to data on human violence derived from many different locations) to analyze fifty thousand police-recorded rapes in sixteen different locations. Their analysis revealed statistically significant annual rhythms in fourteen locations, with maxima in the summer. Changes in numbers of rapes and assaults showed similar seasonal patterns. In contrast, there was a virtual absence of seasonal changes in numbers of murders. A close relationship emerged between crimes of assaults and rapes and the temperature in different geographical locations. This is interpreted by Michael and Zumpe (1983) as suggesting that rape comprised a subcategory of aggressive behavior. They conclude:

> *The link between temperature and human behavior is now placed on a firm basis. If this were due simply to the obvious fact that higher temperatures facilitate increased social interaction, it might be expected that locations with higher mean annual temperatures ... would have higher assault and rape rates than locations with lower mean annual temperatures ... but this was not the case ... Thus, the old notion that human aggression is more prevalent in hotter climates was not generally substantiated. (p. 885)*

Chapter 4. Who are the Victims of Crime?

1. See Grayson and Stein (1981).
2. See Fattah, E.A. (1976).
3. Ibid.
4. For the importance of situational factors see Wikström, P. (1985).
5. For the impact of the victim on criminal justice decisions, see the following: Hall, D.J. (1975) and Williams, K. (1976).
6. See Black, D.J. (1970).
7. See Mayhew, P. et al. (1976).

Chapter 5. The Homogeneity of the Victim/Offender Populations

1. See Canada (1983).
2. See United States (1985).
3. Ibid. p. 2.
4. See Statistics Canada (1981).
5. See Singer (1981), Sparks (1982), and Smith (1986).

6. See in particular, Hindelang et al. (1978), Gottfredson (1984), Braithwaite and Biles (1984), and Singer (1980,1981).
7. See Fattah and Raic (1970).
8. See Savitz, Lalli, and Rosen (1977). (Also quoted in Singer [1981] p. 780.)

Chapter 6. The Victims and Their Victimizers

1. The terms cannon and slave are defined as follows:

    Cannon: The pickpocket racket; a member of a mob engaged in the racket of picking pockets.

    Slave: A workingman, wage earner.

Chapter 7. Victim-Offender Relationships

1. See, for example, Section 395 of the Belgian Criminal Code or Sections 299 and 302 of the French Criminal Code.
2. See, for example, Section 380 of the French Criminal Code (added on August 2, 1950), which stipulates that theft between spouses as well as theft by children against parents and other ascendants are to be treated as a civil matter.
3. Victimization surveys such as the Canadian Urban Victimization Survey usually use one category for nonsexual assault, grouping both its aggravated and simple forms. According to the survey's definition, assault involves the presence of a weapon or an attack or threat. Assault incidents may thus range from face-to-face verbal threats to an attack resulting in extensive injuries. In its study of violence among friends and relatives, the United States Bureau of Justice Statistics (United States, 1980) gives the following definition of aggravated assault: "attack with a weapon resulting in injury (e.g., broken bones, loss of teeth, internal injuries, loss of consciousness) or in undetermined injury requiring 2 or more days of hospitalization." The definition also includes attempted assault with a weapon (p. 51).
4. Wikström uses the term "everyday violence" to designate confrontations between people in their daily living excluding such violent acts that are carried out as part of stealing (robbery) or sexual offenses (rapes). Wikström also excludes from his study violence or threats against officials.

Chapter 8. The Dynamics of Criminal Victimization

1. Hepburn uses Lofland's (1969) definition of encapsulation: "A constriction of the range of perceptible action alternatives and a foreshortening of the time span to which Actor refers his conduct in order to judge its propriety."
2. According to the study, victims were classified as having been seriously injured if they sustained at least one of the following injuries: gunshot or knife wounds; one or more broken, chipped, or cracked bones; knocked-out teeth; internal injuries; loss of consciousness; or undetermined injuries requiring two or more days in the hospital. Actually, the most frequent injuries revealed by the survey (85 percent) were bruises, black eyes, cuts, scratches, swelling, chipped or cracked teeth, or undetermined injuries requiring less than two days hospitalization.
3. The definition of injury varies from one study to the other. The definitions of what constitutes a serious or nonserious injury are also not uniform. This renders the comparisons of the findings of different studies rather difficult, hence, the impossibility of drawing any general or definitive conclusions.
4. This confirms an earlier study by the Bureau of Justice Statistics (1987a), which revealed that a weapon is more likely to be present in crimes committed by strangers than in crimes committed by nonstrangers. Offenders had a weapon in one-fourth of the crimes by nonstrangers compared to over one-third of the crimes by strangers.
5. "Forceful resistance" includes cases in which the respondent reported that he had "used or brandished a weapon" and cases in which he had used or tried physical force. In 1973 and 1974 the latter category was divided into two types of action: "hit, kicked, or scratched offender" or "held onto property." "Nonforceful resistance" includes all other actions taken to protect self or property during the incident (Cook, 1986).
6. Zimring and Zuehl (1986) note that victims of robbery killings are predominantly male. Excluding residential robbery killings, female victims are rare. Much of the difference by gender, they explain, is related to differences in perceived and actual victim resistance. They note that robbers may think that women are likely to offer less resistance to robbery and, thus, they will use less force at the outset of a robbery. Further, the large difference in death rate by sex and the persistence of this pattern in gun robbery suggest that actual resistance is much less frequent among female robbery victims.
7. Symonds (1975) suggests that victims who fight back and are not hurt seem to have a minimum amount of psychological trauma. They feel exhilarated and

strong. Those who fight back and are hurt still feel supported by society. They easily find sympathetic responses, though some might feel annoyed by police reactions.

8. Symonds (1975) is of the view that men and women who grow up from middle-class backgrounds tend to freeze and propitiate the aggressor while those who have working-class backgrounds tend to be action oriented and fight back. In my own readings I have not come across empirical studies that have examined and analyzed the reaction of the victim in relation to the victim's socioeconomic and sociocultural background. Race, age, and gender are the three demographic variables most often discussed in this context.

Chapter 9. Victim/Target Selection

1. In 1966, when I started writing my doctoral dissertation on the factors that determine, influence, or contribute to the choice of the victim in cases of murder for robbery, I was unable to find one single study on victim selection.
2. Houses in Britain owned by the local council are usually lived in by people who cannot afford to own their own homes.
3. As mentioned earlier, our discussion of target selection is not concerned with offenses committed as a spontaneous reaction to a specific opportunity that presents itself. Our focus is on offenses where there is a degree of planning and a choice of a specific target from several possible ones.

Chapter 10. Victims' Personal Characteristics

1. Diathesis, according to *Webster's New Twentieth Century Dictionary*, is used in medicine to refer to a congenital susceptibility or liability to certain diseases.
2. Studies of accident-proneness were done by psychologists as early as 1959. See, for example, Mayer, K. (1959) and Mayer, K. (1960). Underlying the studies was a belief that there is a specific relationship between personality and accident-proneness, and that there is a specific psychological makeup that characterizes those who are accident-prone.
3. Freeman-Longo (1990) believes that the dark figure for the sexual victimization of male children is higher than that for female children. The

author cites a number of studies whose findings suggest that the number of sexual crimes committed against male children may be greater than those committed against female children.

4. The likelihood that certain personality traits and character attributes enhance the potential for victimization applies to adults as well as to children. The violent, abusive, aggressive, provocative, and impulsive types are capable of arousing antipathy and generating animosity and are therefore more liable to be recipients of violence than others. There is also evidence suggesting that quarrelsome, nagging, scolding, or irritating types are more likely to be assaulted than others. We have already explained that those who are extremely credulous or naive are particularly vulnerable to all kinds of swindle and fraud, and we have pointed out that dishonesty is a dominant character of victims in confidence games (see Chapter 9).
5. On June 9, 1989, Kim Pemberton, a Vancouver *Sun* reporter, reported that eight Vancouver prostitutes had been slain over the previous fourteen months, including two killed the week before (Pemberton, 1989).
6. Bill C-49 had its first reading in the Canadian Parliament in the summer of 1985 and was enacted on December 20, 1985. Its main purpose was to change Section 195.1 of the Canadian Criminal Code to reduce the impact of the Supreme Court decision in R. V. Hutt (1978) 2 S.C.R. 476, which made it difficult for police to enforce the law against soliciting. One of the changes was to include a motor vehicle in Section 195.1 to counteract the ruling that a car was a private, not a public, place.

Chapter 11. Victim Behavior as a Situational Variable

1. When researchers point to the Good Samaritan's intervention as behavior contributing to his or her victimization, they are not blaming him or her for this commendable conduct. They are simply emphasizing the risks that such highly desirable behavior involves for the intervener.

   When researchers point to the link between smoking and lung cancer and/or cardiovascular disease, they are not blaming the sick person for his or her illness or holding him or her responsible for it. They are simply stressing the causal role that smoking plays in the etiology of the disease.
2. See Gillespie (1989) and Watts (1989).
3. The reader who is interested in a response to this critique is referred to Fattah (1979).

4. It is reasonable to say that the victim has played a causal role and has contributed to the genesis of crime whenever it is unequivocally established that the crime would not have been committed were it not for that specific behavior(s) by the victim. By so defining victim contribution our purpose is to make it absolutely clear that no explanatory model would be complete without incorporating such contributory action by the victim.
5. It would be absurd to consider attributes over which the victim has no control but which increase the likelihood of victimization (e.g., physical weakness, feeblemindedness) as precipitating factors. They are predisposing factors, not precipitating factors.

Chapter 12. Macro Explanations of Variations in Criminal Victimization

1. Series crimes are defined by Hindelang, Gottfredson, and Garofalo (1978, p. 126) as three or more similar victimizations that occur to the same person during the reference period and for which the victim cannot recall details of individual events.

References

Chapter 1. On Victimization, Criminal and Otherwise

Avery, M. (1983). The Child Abuse Witness: Potential for Secondary Victimization. *Criminal Justice Journal*, *7*(1), 1-48.

Bartollas, C. et al. (1975). Staff Exploitation of Inmates: The Paradox of Institutional Control. In I. Drapkin and E.C. Viano (Eds.), *Victimology: A New Focus: Vol. V. Exploiters and Exploited*. Lexington, MA: D.C. Heath.

Bartollas, C. et al. (1976). Organizational Processing and Inmate Victimization in a Juvenile Training School. In E.C. Viano (Ed.), *Victims and Society* (pp. 569-578). Washington, D.C.: Visage Press.

Bassiouni, C. (1988). The Protection of "Collective Victims" in International Law. In C. Bassiouni (Ed.), *International Protection of Victims* (pp. 181-198). Association Internationale de Droit Pénal.

Biderman, A. (1981). Sources of Data for Victimology. *Journal of Criminal Law and Criminology*, *72*(2), 789-817.

Bohannan, P. (1969). Cross-cultural Comparison of Aggression and Violence. In D.J. Mulvihill, M.M. Tumin and L. Curtis (Eds.), *Crimes of Violence*, A Staff Report to the National Commission on the Causes and Prevention of Violence (Vol. 13, pp. 1189-1239). Washington, D.C.: Superintendent of Documents.

Bowker, L.H. (1980). *Prison Victimization*. New York: Elsevier.

Canada. (1988). *Multiple Victimization, Canadian Urban Victimization Survey Bulletin* (No. 10). Ottawa: Ministry of the Solicitor General.

Dinitz, S. et al. (1975). Inmate Exploitation: A Study of the Juvenile Victim. In I. Drapkin and E.C. Viano (Eds.), *Victimology: A New Focus: Vol.V. Exploiters and Exploited*. Lexington, MA: D.C. Heath.

Dinitz, S. et al. (1976). The Exploitation Matrix in a Juvenile Institution. *International Journal of Criminology and Penology*, *4*, 259-270.

Drapkin, I. (1976). The Prison Inmate as Victim. *Victimology*, *1*(1), 98-106.

Elias, R. (1986). *The Politics of Victimization: Victims, Victimology and Human Rights*. New York: Oxford University Press.

Fattah, E.A. (1985). *Introduction to Criminology: A Study Guide*. Vancouver: Simon Fraser University—Centre for Distant Education.

(1989). Victims of Abuse of Power: The David/Goliath Syndrome. In E.A. Fattah (Ed.), *The Plight of Crime Victims in Modern Society*. London: Macmillan.

Fattah, E.A., and Sacco, V. (1989). *Crime and Victimization of the Elderly*. New York: Springer Verlag.

Flynn, E.E. (1982). Theory Development in Victimology: An Assessment of Recent Progress and of Continuing Challenges. In H.J. Schneider (Ed.), *The Victim in International Perspective* (pp. 96-104). Berlin: de Gruyter.

Fuller, D., and Orsagh, T. (1977). Violence and Victimization Within a State Prison System. *Criminal Justice Review*, *2*(2), 35-55.

Galvin, D. (1976). Concepts in Victimization and the Slave. In E. Viano (Ed.), *Victims and Society*. Washington, D.C.: Visage Press.

Goffman, E. (1961). *Asylums*. Chicago: Aldine.

Kiefl, W., and Lamnek, S. (1986). *Soziologie des Opfers: Theorie, Methoden und Empirie der Viktimologie*. München: Wilhelm Fink Verlag.

Porporino, F.J., and Doherty, P. (1986). *Characteristics of Homicide Victims and Victimizations in Prisons: A Canadian Historical Perspective* (mimeograph, 24 pages). Ottawa: Ministry of the Solicitor General of Canada.

Reiman, J.R. (1975). Aging as Victimization: Reflections on the American Way of (Ending) Life. In J. Goldsmith and S.S. Goldsmith (Eds.), *Crime and the Elderly* (pp. 77-82). Lexington, MA: Lexington Books.

(1979). *The Rich Get Richer and the Poor Get Prison*. Toronto: J. Wiley and Sons.

Reiss, A., Jr. (1974). Citizen Access to Criminal Justice. *British Journal of Law and Society, 1*.

Sellin, T., and Wolfgang, M.E. (1964). *The Measurement of Delinquency*. New York: John Wiley and Sons Inc.

Silverman, R. (1974). Victim Typologies: Overview, Critique and Reformulation. In I. Drapkin and E. Viano (Eds.), *Victimology* (Vol. 1). Lexington, MA: Lexington Books.

Sparks, R.F. (1981). Multiple Victimization: Evidence, Theory, and Future Research. *The Journal of Criminal Law and Criminology*, *72*(2), 762-778.

Sutherland, E.H. (1949). *White Collar Crime*. New York: Holt, Rinehart & Winston.

Van Dijk, J.J. (1986). Introductory Report. In *Research on Victimization*. Strasbourg: Council of Europe.

Viano, E. (1990). *Crime and Its Victims: International Research and Public Policy Issues*. New York: Hemisphere Publishing Corporation.

Von Hentig, H. (1948). *The Criminal and His Victim*. New Haven: Yale University Press.

Walklate, S. (1989). *Victimology: The Victim and the Criminal Justice Process*. London: Unwin Hyman.

Waller, J.A. (1969). Accidents and Violent Behavior: Are They Related? In D.J. Mulvihill, M.M. Tumin and L. Curtis (Eds.), *Crimes of Violence*, A Staff Report to the National Commission on the Causes and Prevention of Violence (Vol. 13, Appendix 33, pp. 1525-1558). Washington, D.C.: Superintendent of Documents.

Walsh, D., and Poole, A. (1983). *A Dictionary of Criminology*. London: Routledge and Kegan Paul.

Wolfgang, M.E. (1967). Analytical Categories for Research and Theory on Victimization. In A. Mergen and H. Schafer (Eds.), *Kriminologische Wegzeichen* (pp. 169-185). Hamburg: Kriminalistik Verlag.

Wolfgang, M.E., and Singer, S.I. (1978). Victim Categories of Crime. *Journal of Criminal Law and Criminology*, *69*, 379-394.

Chapter 2. Sources of Data on Criminal Victimization

Anttila, I. (1964). The Criminological Significance of Unregistered Criminality. *Excerpta Criminologica*, *4*, 411.

Anttila, I., and Jaakkola, R. (1966). *Unrecorded Criminality in Finland* (Series A:2). Helsinki: Institute of Criminology.

Aromaa, K. (1974). Victimization to Violence: A Gallup Survey. *International Journal of Criminology and Penology*, *2*(4), 333-346.

(1984). Three Surveys of Violence in Finland. In R. Block (Ed.), *Victimization and Fear of Crime: World Perspectives* (pp. 11-21). Washington, D.C.: United States Department of Justice, Bureau of Justice Statistics.

Belson, W.A. et al. (1970). *The Development of a Procedure for Eliciting Information from Boys about the Nature and Extent of Their Stealing*. London School of Economics—Survey Research Centre.

(1975). *Juvenile Theft: The Causal Factors*. New York: Harper and Row.

Biderman, A.D. (1967). Survey of Population Samples for Estimating Crime Incidence. *The Annals of the American Academy of Political and Social Science*, *374*, 16-33.

(1981). Sources of Data for Victimology. *Journal of Criminal Law and Criminology*, *72*(2), 789-817.

Biderman, A.D., and A.J. Reiss, Jr. (1967). On Exploring the Dark Figure of Crime. *The Annals of the American Academy of Political and Social Science*, *374*, 1-15.

Braithwaite, J., and Biles, D. (1980). Overview of Findings from the First Australian National Crime Victims Survey. *Australian and New Zealand Journal of Criminology*, *13*, 41-51.

(1984). Victims and Offenders: The Australian Experience. In R. Block (Ed.), *Victimization and Fear of Crime: World Perspectives* (pp. 3-10). Washington, D.C.: United States Department of Justice, Bureau of Justice Statistics.

Canada. (1983). *Victims of Crime, Canadian Urban Victimization Survey Bulletin* (No. 1). Ottawa: Ministry of the Solicitor General.

(1984a). *Reported and Unreported Crime, Canadian Urban Victimization Survey Bulletin* (No. 2). Ottawa: Ministry of the Solicitor General.

(1984b). *Crime Prevention: Awareness and Practice, Canadian Urban Victimization Survey Bulletin* (No. 3). Ottawa: Ministry of the Solicitor General.

(1985). *Female Victims of Crime, Canadian Urban Victimization Survey Bulletin* (No. 4). Ottawa: Ministry of the Solicitor General.

(1985). *Cost of Crime to Victims, Canadian Urban Victimization Survey Bulletin* (No. 5). Ottawa: Ministry of the Solicitor General.

(1985). *Criminal Victimization of Elderly Canadians, Canadian Urban Victimization Survey Bulletin* (No. 6). Ottawa: Ministry of the Solicitor General.

(1986). *Household Property Crimes, Canadian Urban Victimization Survey Bulletin* (No. 7). Ottawa: Ministry of the Solicitor General.

(1987). *Patterns in Violent Crime, Canadian Urban Victimization Survey Bulletin* (No. 8). Ottawa: Ministry of the Solicitor General.

(1988). *Patterns in Property Crime, Canadian Urban Victimization Survey Bulletin* (No. 9). Ottawa: Ministry of the Solicitor General.

(1988). *Multiple Victimization, Canadian Urban Victimization Survey Bulletin* (No. 10). Ottawa: Ministry of the Solicitor General.

Chambers, G., and Tombs, J. (Eds.). (1984). *The British Crime Survey Scotland*, A Scottish Office Social Research Study. Edinburgh: Her Majesty's Stationery Office.

Christie, N. et al. (1965). A Study of Self-Reported Crime. In K.O. Christiansen (Ed.), *Scandinavian Studies in Criminology* (Vol. 1). London: Tavistock Publications.

Clinard, M. (1978). *Cities with Little Crime: The Case of Switzerland*. Cambridge: Cambridge University Press.

Corrado, R. et al. (1980). Life Styles and Personal Victimization: A Test of the Model with Canadian Survey Data. *Journal of Crime and Justice*, *3*, 129-139.

Courtis, M.C., and Dussuyer, I. (1970). *Attitudes to Crime and the Police in Toronto: A Report on Some Survey Findings*. Toronto: Centre of Criminology, University of Toronto.

Doleschal, E. (1970). Hidden Crime. *Crime and Delinquency Literature*, *2*(5), 546-572.

Doleschal, E., and Klapmuts, N. (1973). Toward a New Criminology. *Crime and Delinquency Literature*, *5*(4), 607-625.

Elmhorn, K. (1965). Study in Self-Reported Delinquency Among School Children in Stockholm. In K.O. Christiansen (Ed.), *Scandinavian Studies in Criminology* (Vol. 1, pp. 117-146). London: Tavistock.

Ennis, P.H. (1967a, June). Crime, Victims and the Police. *Trans-Action*, 36-44.

(1967b). *Criminal Victimization in the United States: A Report of a National Survey*. Washington, D.C.: United States Government Printing Office.

Evans, J., and Leger, G. (1979). Canadian Victimization Surveys: A Discussion Paper. *Canadian Journal of Criminology*, *21*(2), 166-183.

Fiselier, J.P.S. (1978). *Victims of Crime: A Study of Unreported Crime.* (In Dutch.) Utrecht, Netherlands: Ars Aequi Libri.

Garofalo, J., and Hindelang, M. (1977). *An Introduction to the National Crime Survey.* Washington, D.C.: United States Government Printing Office.

Gottfredson, M.R., and Hindelang, M.J. (1977). A Consideration of Memory Decay and Telescoping Biases in Victimization Surveys. *Journal of Criminal Justice, 5*, 202-216.

Hauge, R., and Wolf, P. (1974). Criminal Violence in Three Scandinavian Countries. In K.O. Christiansen (Ed.), *Scandinavian Studies in Criminology* (Vol. 5, pp. 25-33). Oslo: Universitetsforlaget.

Hindelang, M.J. (1976). *Criminal Victimization in Eight American Cities: A Descriptive Analysis of Common Theft and Assault.* Cambridge, MA: Ballinger.

Hood, R., and Sparks, R. (1970). *Key Issues in Criminology.* London: Weidenfeld and Nicolson (World University Library).

Hough, M. (1986). Victims of Violent Crime: Findings from the British Crime Survey. In E.A. Fattah (Ed.), *From Crime Policy to Victim Policy* (pp. 117-132). London: Macmillan.

Hough, M., and Mayhew, P. (1983). *The British Crime Survey: First Report.* London: Her Majesty's Stationery Office.

Klecka, W.R., and Tuchfarber, A.J. (1978). Random Digit Dialing: A Comparison to Personal Surveys. *Public Opinion Quarterly, 42*, 105-114.

Koenig, D. (1974). *Correlates of Self-Reported Victimization and Perceptions of Neighbourhood Safety* (mimeographed). Also printed (1977). In L. Hewitt and D. Brusegard (Eds.), *Selected Papers from the Social Indicators Conference.* Edmonton: Alberta Bureau of Statistics.

Leblanc, M. (1975). Middle Class Delinquency. In R. Silverman and J. Teevan (Eds.), *Crime in Canadian Society* (pp. 213-222). Toronto: Butterworth & Co.

(1975). Upper Class vs. Working Class Delinquency. In R.A. Silverman and J.J. Teevan (Eds.), *Crime in Canadian Society* (pp. 102-118). Toronto: Butterworth & Co.

(1977). *La Délinquance juvénile au Québec.* Québec: Ministère des Affaires Sociales.

Levy, R., Perez-Diaz, C., Robert, P., and Zauberman, R. (1986). *Profils sociaux de victimes d'infractions: Premiers Resultats d'une enquête nationale.* Paris: Centre de Recherches Sociologiques sur le droit et les institutions pénales.

Murphy, L.R., and Cowan, C.C. (1976). Effects of Bounding on Telescoping in the National Crime Survey. *American Statistical Association Proceedings of the Social Statistics Section* (Part II, pp. 633-638).

O'Brien, R.M. (1985). *Crime and Victimization Data.* Beverly Hills: Sage Publications.

Penick, B.K., and Owens, M.E.B. (Eds.). (1976). *Surveying Crime.* Washington, D.C.: National Academy of Sciences.

Reiss, A., Jr. (1981). Foreword: Towards a Revitalization of Theory and Research on Victimization by Crime. *Journal of Criminal Law and Criminology*, *72*(2), 704-710.

Sacco, V.F. (1989). *Victimization and Fear of Victimization in Canada*. A brief submitted to the European and North American Conference on Urban Safety and Crime Prevention (mimeographed).

Sacco, V.F., and Johnson, H. (1990). *Patterns of Criminal Victimization in Canada*, General Social Survey Analysis Series (No. 2). Ottawa: Statistics Canada.

Schur, E. (1971). *Labeling Deviant Behavior: Its Sociological Implications*. New York: Harper and Row.

Sellin, T. (1951). The Significance of Records of Crime. *The Law Quarterly Review*, *67*, 489-504.

Short, J.F., and Nye, F.I. (1958). Extent of Unrecorded Juvenile Delinquency. *Journal of Criminal Law, Criminology and Police Science*, *49*, 296-302.

Sirén, R. (1980). *Victims of Violence: Results of the 1976 National Surveys* (Publication No. 40). Helsinki: Research Institute of Legal Policy.

Sirén, R., and Heiskanen, M. (1985). *Victimization to Violence — Results from a National Survey 1980*. Helsinki: National Research Institute of Legal Policy.

Skogan, W.G. (1975). Measurement Problems in Official and Survey Crime Rates. *Journal of Criminal Justice*, *3*, 17-32.

(1976). Crime and Crime Rates. In W.G. Skogan (Ed.), *Sample Surveys of the Victims of Crime*. Cambridge, MA: Ballinger.

(1981). *Issues in the Measurement of Victimization*. Washington, D.C.: United States Department of Justice, Bureau of Justice Statistics. United States Government Printing Office.

(1982). Methodological Issues in the Measurement of Crime. In H.J. Schneider (Ed.), *The Victim in International Perspective*. Berlin: Walter de Gruyter.

(1986). Methodological Issues in the Study of Victimization. In E.A. Fattah (Ed.), *From Crime Policy to Victim Policy* (pp. 80-116). London: Macmillan.

Sparks, R.F. (1981). Surveys of Victimization: An Optimistic Assessment. In M. Tonry and N. Morris (Eds.), *Crime and Justice: An Annual Review of Research* (Vol. 3, pp. 1-60).

(1982). *Research on Victims of Crime: Accomplishments, Issues and New Directions*. Rockville, MD: United States Department of Health and Human Services.

Sparks, R.F., Genn, H., and Dodd, D. (1977). *Surveying Victims: A Study of the Measurement of Criminal Victimization*. London: John Wiley and Sons.

Statistics Canada. (1990). *Patterns of Criminal Victimization in Canada*, General Social Survey Analysis Series (Catalogue 11—612E, No. 2 [authors, V. Sacco and H. Johnson]). Ottawa: Minister of Supply and Services.

Stephan, E. (1976). *Die Stuttgarter Opferbefragung*. Wiesbaden: Bundeskriminalamt. Forschungsreihe Bd. 3.

Sutherland, E.H. (1949). *White Collar Crime*. New York: Dryden.

Tuchfarber, A.J., and Klecka, W.R. (1976a). *Measuring Crime Victimization: An Efficient Method*. Washington, D.C.: The Police Foundation.

(1976b). *Random Digit Dialing: Lowering the Cost of Victimization Surveys*. Washington, D.C.: The Police Foundation.

Tuchfarber, A.J., Klecka, W.R., Bardes, B.A., and Oldendick, R.W. (1976). Reducing the Cost of Victim Surveys. In W.G. Skogan (Ed.), *Sample Surveys of the Victims of Crime*. Cambridge, MA: Ballinger.

United States. (1972). *San Jose Methods Test of Known Crime Victims*. Washington, D.C.: United States Department of Justice, Law Enforcement Assistance Administration. United States Government Printing Office.

(1976). *Criminal Victimization in the United States: A Comparison of 1973 and 1974 Findings*. Washington, D.C.: Department of Justice, Law Enforcement Assistance Administration. United States Government Printing Office.

(1979). *Criminal Victimization in the United States: 1973-1978 Trends*. Washington, D.C.: Department of Justice, Law Enforcement Assistance Administration. United States Government Printing Office.

(1981). *Crime and the Elderly*. Washington, D.C.: Department of Justice, Bureau of Justice Statistics. United States Government Printing Office.

(1983). *Criminal Victimization in the United States: 1973 - 1982 Trends*, Bureau of Justice Statistics Special Report. Washington, D.C.: Department of Justice, Bureau of Justice Statistics. United States Government Printing Office.

Van Dijk, J., and Mayhew, P. (1989). *Criminal Victimization Across the World: An Outline of the 1989 International Crime Survey* (mimeograph).

Van Dijk, J., Mayhew, P., and Killias, M. (1990). *Experiences of Crime Across the World—Key Findings of the 1989 International Crime Survey*. Deventer: Kluwer Law and Taxation Publishers.

Van Dijk, J., and Steinmetz, C.H.D. (1984). The Burden of Crime in Dutch Society, 1973-1979. In R. Block (Ed.), *Victimization and Fear of Crime: World Perspectives* (pp. 29-43). Washington, D.C.: United States Department of Justice, Bureau of Justice Statistics.

Vaz, E.W. (1965). Middle-Class Adolescents: Self-Reported Delinquency and Youth Culture Activities. *Canadian Review of Sociology and Anthropology*, *2*(1), 52-70.

(1966). Self-Reported Delinquency and Socio-Economic Status. *Canadian Journal of Corrections*, *8*, 20-27.

(1967). Juvenile Delinquency in the Middle-Class Youth Cultures. In *Middle-Class Juvenile Delinquency* (pp. 131-147). New York: Harper and Row Publishers.

Waller, I., and Okihiro, N. (1978). *Burglary: The Victim and the Public*. Toronto: University of Toronto Press.

Wallerstein, J.A., and Wyle, C.J. (1947). Our Law-Abiding Lawbreakers. *Federal Probation*, *25*, 107-112.

Zauberman, R. (1986). Report. In *Research on Victimization*. Strasbourg: Council of Europe.

Chapter 3. Extent and Patterns of Criminal Victimization

Amir, M. (1971). *Patterns in Forcible Rape*. Chicago: University of Chicago Press.

Bensing, R., and Schroeder, O. (1960). *Homicide in an Urban Community*. Springfield, IL: Charles C. Thomas.

Block, R. (1977). *Violent Crime*. Lexington, MA: D.C. Heath & Co.

Boggs, S.L. (1965). Urban Crime Patterns. *American Sociological Review, 30*, 899-908.

Brantingham, P.J., and Brantingham, P.L. (1984). *Patterns in Crime*. New York: Macmillan Publishing Company.

Büchler, H., and Leineweber, H. (1984). Raubüberfälle auf Geldinstitute und Täterwissen. *Kriminalistik, 38*, 476-477.

(1986). *Bankraub und Technische Prävention*. Wiesbaden: Bundeskriminalamt.

Bullock, H.A. (1955). Urban Homicide in Theory and Fact. *The Journal of Criminal Law, Criminology and Police Science, 45*, 565-575.

Chambers, G., and Tombs, J. (Eds.). (1984). *The British Crime Survey Scotland*, A Scottish Office Social Research Study. Edinburgh: Her Majesty's Stationery Office.

Ciale, J., and Leroux, J.P. (1984). *Armed Robbery in Ottawa: A Descriptive Case Study for Prevention* (Working Paper No. 23). Ottawa: Ministry of the Solicitor General.

Clarke, R.V.G. (1981). The Prospects of Controlling Crime. *Home Office Research Unit Research Bulletin* (12), 12-19. London: Her Majesty's Stationery Office.

Coburn, G.M.B. (1988). *Patterns of Homicide in Vancouver: 1980-1986.* Master's Thesis, Simon Fraser University, Burnaby, B.C.

Fattah, E.A. (1967). Die Stellung des Raubmordes in der Gliederung der Verbrechen. *Monatsschrift für Kriminologie und Strafrechtsreform, 50*(2), 49-60.

(1971). *La Victime est-elle Coupable?* Presses de l'Université de Montréal.

Fattah, E.A., Bissonnet, F., and Geoffrion, G. (1972). *Études de Criminologie Écologique* (Vol. I). Montréal: École de Criminologie, Université de Montréal.

Fattah, E.A., Bissonnet, F., and Scholtes, A.C. (1973). *Études de Criminologie Écologique* (Vol. II). Montréal: École de Criminologie, Université de Montréal.

(1974). *Études de Criminologie Écologique* (Vol. II, Partie 2). Montréal: École de Criminologie, Université de Montréal.

Gottfredson, M.R. (1984). *Victims of Crime: The Dimensions of Risk*, Home Office Research and Planning Unit Report (No. 81). London: Her Majesty's Stationery Office.

Hough, M., and Mayhew, P. (1983). *The British Crime Survey: First Report*. London: Her Majesty's Stationery Office.

Jackson, P.I. (1984). Opportunity and Crime: A Function of City Size. *Sociology and Social Research, 68*, 172-193.

Letkemann, P. (1973). *Crime as Work*. Englewood Cliffs: Prentice Hall Inc.

Lundsgaarde, H.P. (1977). *Murder in Space City*. New York: Oxford University Press.

Mayhew, P., Elliott, D., and Dowds, L. (1989). *The 1988 British Crime Survey*, A Home Office Research Studies Report (No. 111). London: Her Majesty's Stationery Office.

McDermott, J. (1979). *Rape Victimization in 26 American Cities* (United States Department of Justice, Law Enforcement Assistance Administration, Analytic Report SD-VAD-6). Washington, D.C.: Government Printing Office.

McKie, C. (1985). Seasonality in Canadian Homicides, 1961-1980. *Canadian Journal of Statistics, 13*(4), 266-268.

McLeod, I. et al. (1985). Seasonal Effects in Canadian Murders. *Canadian Journal of Statistics, 13*(4), 269-271.

McPheters, L.R., and Stronge, W.B. (1973). Testing for Seasonality in Reported Crime Data. *Journal of Criminal Justice, 1*, 125-134.

Michael, R., and Zumpe, D. (1983). Sexual Violence in the United States and the Role of Season. *American Journal of Psychiatry, 140*, 883-886.

Mulvihill, D.J., Tumin, M.M., and Curtis, L.A. (1969). *Crimes of Violence*, A Staff Report Submitted to the National Commission on the Causes and Prevention of Violence (Vol. 11). Washington, D.C.: Government Printing Office.

Nakamura, A., and Nakamura, M. (1985). A Search for Monthly Fluctuations in Canadian Homicides: 1965-1980. *Canadian Journal of Statistics, 13*(4), 271-276.

Normandeau, A. (1968). *Trends and Patterns in Crimes of Robbery*. Ph.D. Dissertation, University of Pennsylvania.

(1981). Armed Robbery in America. *Canadian Police College Journal, 5*, 1-12.

Parmelee, M. (1926). *Criminology*. New York: The Macmillan Company.

Pittman, D.J., and Handy, W. (1964). Patterns in Criminal Aggravated Assault. *Journal of Criminal Law, Criminology and Police Science, 55*(1), 462-469.

Pratt, M. (1980). *Mugging as a Social Problem*. London: Routledge and Kegan Paul.

Pyle, G.F. (1976). Spatial and Temporal Aspects of Crime in Cleveland, Ohio. *American Behavioral Scientist, 20*, 175-197.

Quetelet, A.J. (1842). *Treatise on Man*. Excerpts reprinted (1972). In S.F. Sylvester, Jr. (Ed.), *The Heritage of Modern Criminology*. Cambridge, MA: Schenkman Publishing Company.

Reppetto, T.A. (1974). *Residential Crime*. Cambridge: Ballinger Publishing Co.

Roesch, R., and Winterdyk, J. (1985). *The Vancouver Convenience Store Robbery Prevention Program* (Final report). Ottawa: Ministry of the Solicitor General.

Roncek, D. (1981). Dangerous Places: Crime and Residential Environment. *Social Forces*, *60*, 74-96.

Sacco, V.F. (1989). *Victimization and the Fear of Victimization in Canada.* A brief submitted to the European and North American Conference on Urban Safety and Crime Prevention (mimeograph).

Sacco, V.R., and Johnson, H. (1990). *Patterns of Criminal Victimization in Canada*, General Social Survey Analysis Series (No. 2). Ottawa: Statistics Canada.

Skogan, W.G. (1976). Crime and Crime Rates. In W.G. Skogan (Ed.), *Sample Surveys of the Victims of Crime* (pp. 105-120). Cambridge, MA: Ballinger.

Smith, L.J.F. (1989). *Concerns About Rape*, Home Office Research Study (No. 106). London: Her Majesty's Stationery Office.

Smith, S.J. (1986). *Crime, Space, and Society.* Cambridge: Cambridge University Press.

Sparks, R.F. (1980). Criminal Opportunities and Crime Rates. In S.E. Fienberg and A.J. Reiss, Jr. (Eds.), *Indicators of Crime and Criminal Justice: Quantitative Studies.* Washington, D.C.: Government Printing Office.

(1981). Surveys of Victimization: An Optimistic Assessment. In M. Tonry and N. Morris (Eds.), *Crime and Justice: An Annual Review of Research* (Vol. 3, pp. 1-60). Chicago: University of Chicago Press.

(1982). *Research on Victims of Crime: Accomplishments, Issues and New Directions.* Rockville, MD: United States Department of Health and Human Services.

Statistics Canada. (1990). *Patterns of Criminal Victimization in Canada*, General Social Survey Analysis Series (Catalogue 11 — 612E, No. 2. [authors, V. Sacco and H. Johnson]). Ottawa: Minister of Supply and Services.

Steinmetz, C.H.D. (1979). *An (Empirically Tested) Analysis of Victimization Risks.* The Hague, Netherlands: Ministry of Justice.

Stipak, B. (1988). Alternatives to Population-Based Crime Rates. *International Journal of Comparative and Applied Criminal Justice*, *12*(2), 247-260.

United States. (1980). *Crime and Seasonality*, National Crime Survey Report (NCJ-64818). Washington, D.C.: Department of Justice, Bureau of Justice Statistics. Superintendent of Documents.

(1985, January). Household Burglary. *Bureau of Justice Statistics Bulletin.* Washington, D.C.: Department of Justice, Bureau of Justice Statistics. Superintendent of Documents.

(1985, March). The Crime of Rape. *Bureau of Justice Statistics Bulletin.* Washington, D.C.: Department of Justice, Bureau of Justice Statistics. Superintendent of Documents.

(1985, May). *The Risk of Violent Crime — Special Report.* Washington, D.C.: Department of Justice, Bureau of Justice Statistics. Superintendent of Documents.

(1988). *The Seasonality of Crime Victimization* (NCJ-111033). Washington, D.C.: Department of Justice, Bureau of Justice Statistics. Superintendent of Documents.

(1989, June). *Criminal Victimization in the United States, 1987*, A National Crime Survey Report (NCJ-115524). Washington, D.C.: Department of Justice, Bureau of Justice Statistics. Government Printing Office.

Voss, H.L., and Hepburn, J.R. (1968). Patterns of Criminal Homicide in Chicago. The *Journal of Criminal Law, Criminology and Police Science, 59*, 499-508.

Wikström, P-O.H. (1985). *Everyday Violence in Contemporary Sweden.* Stockholm: The National Council for Crime Prevention.

Wilkins, L. (1964). *Social Deviance.* London: Tavistock Publications.

Wilt, G.M. (1974). *Towards an Understanding of the Social Realities of Participants in Homicides.* Wayne State University: Xerox University Press.

Wolfgang, M.E. (1958). *Patterns in Criminal Homicide.* Philadelphia: University of Pennsylvania Press.

Chapter 4. Who are the Victims of Crime?

Anttila, I. (1974). Victimology: A New Territory in Criminology. In *Scandinavian Studies in Criminology* (Vol. 5, pp. 7-10). Oslo: Universitetsforlaget.

Aromaa, K. (1974a). Victimization to Violence: A Gallup Survey. *International Journal of Criminology and Penology, 2.*

(1974b). Our Violence. In *Scandinavian Studies in Criminology* (Vol. 5, pp. 35-46). Oslo: Universitetsforlaget.

Beynon, E.D. (1935). Crime and Custom of the Hungarians in Detroit. *Journal of the American Institute of Criminal Law and Criminology, 25*, 755-774.

Black, D.J. (1970). Production of Crime Rates. *American Sociological Review, 35*, 733-748.

Blumenthal, M., Kahn, P., Andres, M., and Head, K. (1972). *Justifying Violence: Attitudes of American Men.* University of Michigan, Ann Arbor: Institute for Social Research.

Cameron, M.O. (1964). *The Booster and the Snitch.* London: Free Press of Glencoe.

Christie, N. (1977). Conflicts as Property. *The British Journal of Criminology, 17*(1), 1-15.

(1986). The Ideal Victim. In E.A. Fattah (Ed.), *From Crime Policy to Victim Policy.* London: Macmillan.

Conklin, J. (1975). *The Impact of Crime.* New York: Macmillan.

Curtis, L. (1975). Victim Precipitation and Violent Crime. *Social Problems, 21*, 594-605.

Ellenberger, H. (1955). Psychological Relationships Between Criminal and Victim. *Archives of Criminal Psychodynamics, 2*, 257-290.

Fattah, E.A. (1967). La Victimologie: Qu'est-elle, et quel est son avenir? *Revue Internationale de Criminologie et de Police Technique, XXI* (2), 113-124.

(1967). La Victimologie: Qu'est-elle, et quel est son avenir? *Revue Internationale de Criminologie et de Police Technique, XXI* (3), 193-202.

(1967). Towards a Criminological Classification of Victims. *International Review of Criminal Police*, (209), 162-169.

(1976). The Use of the Victim as an Agent of Self-Legitimization: Towards a Dynamic Explanation of Criminal Behavior. *Victimology, 1*(1), 29-53.

Fattah, E.A., and Williams, J.E.H. (1973). Crimes Sans Victimes. In D. Szabo (Ed.), *La Criminalité Urbaine et la Crise de l'Administration de la Justice* (pp. 83-118). Montreal: University of Montreal Press.

Gibbens, T.C.N., and Prince, J. (1962). *Shoplifting*. London: Institute for the Study and Treatment of Delinquency.

Goode, W.J. (1969). Violence Between Intimates. In D.J. Mulvihill, M.M. Tumin and L. Curtis (Eds.), *Crimes of Violence*, A Staff Report to the National Commission on the Causes and Prevention of Violence (pp. 941-977). Washington, D.C.: Superintendent of Documents.

Grayson, B., and Stein, M.I. (1981, winter). Attracting Assault: Victims' Nonverbal Cues. *Journal of Communication*, 68-75.

Hall, D. (1975). The Role of the Victim in the Prosecution and Disposition of a Criminal Case. *Vanderbilt Law Review, 28*(5), 932-985.

Hinrichs, R. (1987). *Das Chronische Opfer*. Stuttgart: Georg Thieme Verlag.

Huxley, A. (1928). *Point Counter Point*. London: Chatto and Windus.

Johnson, J. et al. (1973). The Recidivist Victim: A Descriptive Study. *Criminal Justice Monographs, 4*(1). Huntsville, Texas: Sam Houston State University.

Kennedy, L.W. (1990). *On the Borders of Crime—Conflict Management and Criminology*. New York: Longman.

Mayhew, P. et al. (1976). *Crime as Opportunity*, Home Office Research and Planning Unit Report (No. 34). London: Her Majesty's Stationery Office.

Mendelsohn, B. (1956). Une nouvelle branche de la science bio-psychosociale: La Victimologie. *Revue Internationale de Criminologie et de Police Technique, 11*(2), 95-109.

Packer, H. (1968). *The Limits of the Criminal Sanction*. Stanford: Stanford University Press.

Quinney, R. (1972). Who is the Victim? *Criminology, 10*(3), 314-323.

Rubin, S. (1971). Developments in Correctional Law. *Crime and Delinquency, 17*(2), 213.

Schur, E. (1965). *Crimes Without Victims: Deviant Behavior and Public Policy*. Englewood Cliffs, NJ: Prentice Hall.

(1969). *Our Criminal Society*. Englewood Cliffs, NJ: Prentice Hall.

Smigel, E.O., and Ross, H.L. (1970). *Crimes Against Bureaucracy*. New York: Van Nostrand.

Spitzer, S. (1975). Towards a Marxian Theory of Deviance. *Social Problems, 22*, 638-651.

Sykes, G., and Matza, D. (1957). Techniques of Neutralization: A Theory of Delinquency. *American Sociological Review, 22*, 664-670.

United States. (1981). *Victims of Crime*. Washington, D.C.: Bureau of Justice Statistics. Superintendent of Documents.

Von Hentig, H. (1941). Remarks on the Interaction of Perpetrator and Victim. *Journal of Criminal Law and Criminology, 31*(3), 303-309.

(1948). *The Criminal and His Victim*. New Haven: Yale University Press.

Walklate, S. (1990). *Researching Victims of Crime: Critical Victimology*. Paper presented to the Realist Criminology Conference held in Vancouver, BC, May 1990 (31 pages).

Weis, K., and Borges, S. (1973). Victimology and Rape: The Case of the Legitimate Victim. *Issues in Criminology, 8*(2), 71-115.

Wikström, P-O.H. (1985). *Everyday Violence in Contemporary Sweden: Situational and Ecological Aspects*. Stockholm: The National Council for Crime Prevention.

Williams, K. (1976). The Effects of Victim Characteristics on the Disposition of Violent Crimes. In W.F. McDonald, (Ed.), *Criminal Justice and the Victim*. Beverly Hills: Sage Publications.

Wolfgang, M.E. (1958). Victim-Precipitated Criminal Homicide. *Journal of Criminal Law, Criminology and Police Science, 48*(1), 1-11.

Ziegenhagen, E. (1976). The Recidivist Victim of Violent Crime. *Victimology: An International Journal, 1*(4), 538-550.

Chapter 5. The Homogeneity of the Victim/Offender Populations

Anttila, I. (1974). Victimology—A New Territory in Criminology. In K.O. Christiansen (Ed.), *Scandinavian Studies in Criminology* (Vol. 5, pp. 7-10). Oslo: Universitetsforlaget.

Aromaa, K. (1974). Our Violence. In K.O. Christiansen (Ed.), *Scandinavian Studies in Criminology* (Vol. 5, pp. 35-46). Oslo: Universitetsforlaget.

Blomquist et al. (1980). Arga katter får rivit skinn. Konsekvenser av knivvåldet i Stockholm. *Läkartidningen*, (25).

Braithwaite, J., and Biles, D. (1979). On Being Unemployed and Being a Victim of Crimeå. *Australian Journal of Social Issues*, *14*, 192-200.

(1980). Overview of Findings from the First Australian National Crime Victims Survey. *Australian and New Zealand Journal of Criminology*, *13*, 41-51.

(1984). Victims and Offenders: The Australian Experience. In R. Block (Ed.), *Victimization and Fear of Crime: World Perspectives* (NCJ-93872, pp. 3-10). Washington, D.C.: United States Department of Justice.

Brantingham, P.J., and Brantingham, P.L. (1984). *Patterns in Crime*. New York: Macmillan Publishing Company.

Canada. (1983). *Victims of Crime, Canadian Urban Victimization Survey Bulletin* (No. 1). Ottawa: Ministry of the Solicitor General.

(1984a). *Reported and Unreported Crime, Canadian Urban Victimization Survey Bulletin* (No. 2). Ottawa: Ministry of the Solicitor General.

(1984b). *Crime Prevention: Awareness and Practice, Canadian Urban Victimization Survey Bulletin* (No. 3). Ottawa: Ministry of the Solicitor General.

(1985). *Female Victims of Crime, Canadian Urban Victimization Survey Bulletin* (No. 4). Ottawa: Ministry of the Solicitor General.

(1985). *Cost of Crime to Victims, Canadian Urban Victimization Survey Bulletin* (No. 5). Ottawa: Ministry of the Solicitor General.

(1985). *Criminal Victimization of Elderly Canadians, Canadian Urban Victimization Survey Bulletin* (No. 6). Ottawa: Ministry of the Solicitor General.

(1986). *Household Property Crimes, Canadian Urban Victimization Survey Bulletin* (No. 7). Ottawa: Ministry of the Solicitor General.

(1987). *Patterns in Violent Crime, Canadian Urban Victimization Survey Bulletin* (No. 8). Ottawa: Ministry of the Solicitor General.

(1988). *Patterns in Property Crime, Canadian Urban Victimization Survey Bulletin* (No. 9). Ottawa: Ministry of the Solicitor General.

(1988). *Multiple Victimization, Canadian Urban Victimization Survey Bulletin* (No. 10). Ottawa: Ministry of the Solicitor General.

Chambers, G., and Tombs, J. (Eds.). (1984). *The British Crime Survey Scotland*, A Scottish Office Social Research Study. Edinburgh: Her Majesty's Stationery Office.

Cohen, L.E., and Felson, M. (1979). Social Change and Crime Rate Trends: A Routine Activity Approach. *American Sociological Review*, *44*, 588-608.

Congalton, A.A., and Najman, J.M. (1974). *Who Are The Victims?* Sydney: New South Wales Bureau of Crime Statistics and Research.

Fattah, E.A. (1989). Victims and Victimology: The Facts and the Rhetoric. *International Review of Victimology*, *1*(1), 43-66.

Fattah, E.A., and Raic, A. (1970). L'alcool en tant que facteur victimogène. *Toxicomanies*, *3*(2), 143-173.

Gottfredson, M.R. (1984). *Victims of Crime: The Dimensions of Risk*, Home Office Research and Planning Unit Report (No. 81). London: Her Majesty's Stationery Office.

Hindelang, M.J., Gottfredson, M.R., and Garofalo, J. (1978). *Victims of Personal Crime: An Empirical Foundation for a Theory of Personal Victimization*. Cambridge, MA: Ballinger.

Hochstedler, E. (1981). *Crime Against the Elderly in 26 Cities*. Washington, D.C.: United States Department of Justice, Bureau of Justice Statistics.

Hough, M., and Mayhew, P. (1983). *The British Crime Survey: First Report*. London: Her Majesty's Stationery Office.

(1985). *Taking Account of Crime: Key Findings from the 1984 British Crime Survey*, Home Office Research and Planning Unit Report (No. 85). London: Her Majesty's Stationery Office.

Johnson, J. et al. (1973). The Recidivist Victim: A Descriptive Study. *Criminal Justice Monographs*, (4). Huntsville, TX: Sam Houston University.

Lenke, L. (1973). Den dolda Våldbrottsligheten i Stockholm — en sjukhusrevy. *Nordisk tidskrift for kriminalvidenskab*.

Mayhew, P., and Elliott, D. (1990). *Self-Reported Offending, Victimization, and the British Crime Survey*. Paper scheduled to appear in the journal *Violence and Victims*.

Mayhew, P., Elliott, D., and Dowds, L. (1989). *The 1988 British Crime Survey*, A Home Office Research Report (No. 111). London: Her Majesty's Stationery Office.

Reiss, A., Jr. (1981, summer). Foreword: Towards a Revitalization of Theory and Research on Victimization by Crime. *The Journal of Criminal Law and Criminology*, *72*(2), 704-710.

Sacco, V.F., and Johnson, H. (1990). *Patterns of Criminal Victimization in Canada*, General Social Survey Analysis Series (No. 2). Ottawa: Statistics Canada.

Savitz, L., Lalli, M., and Rosen, L. (1977). *City Life and Delinquency — Victimization, Fear of Crime, and Gang Membership*. Washington, D.C.: United States Government Printing Office.

Singer, S. (1980). *Victims in a Subculture of Crime: An Analysis of the Social and Criminal Backgrounds of Surveyed Victims in the Birth Cohort Follow-Up*. Unpublished dissertation, University of Pennsylvania, Department of Sociology.

(1981, summer). Homogeneous Victim-Offender Populations: A Review and Some Research Implications. *The Journal of Criminal Law and Criminology*, *72*(2), 779-788.

Skogan, W. (1981). Assessing the Behavioral Context of Victimization. *The Journal of Criminal Law and Criminology*, *72*(2), 727-742.

Smith, S.J. (1986). *Crime, Space and Society*. Cambridge: Cambridge University Press.

Sparks, R.F. (1981). Multiple Victimization: Evidence, Theory and Future Research. *The Journal of Criminal Law and Criminology*, *72*(2), 762-778.

(1982). *Research on Victims of Crime: Accomplishments, Issues, and New Directions.* Rockville, MD: United States Department of Health and Human Services.

Sparks, R., Genn, H.G., and Dodd, D.J. (1977). *Surveying Victims.* Toronto: John Wiley and Sons.

Stanko, E.A. (1985). *Intimate Intrusions: Women's Experience of Male Violence.* London: Routledge and Kegan Paul.

Statistics Canada. (1981). Homicide Statistics—1980 (Catalogue 85-209, Annual). Ottawa: Minister of Supply and Services.

Sutherland, E., and Cressey, D. (1970). *Criminology* (8th ed.). Philadelphia: J.B. Lippincott.

Thornberry, T.P., and Figlio, R.M. (1972). *Victimization and Criminal Behavior in a Birth Cohort.* Paper presented at the meetings of the American Society of Criminology, Caracas, Venezuela.

United States. (1978). *A Partnership for Crime Control.* Washington, D.C.: Department of Justice, Bureau of Justice Statistics. Government Printing Office.

(1981). *Victims of Crime.* Washington, D.C.: Department of Justice, Bureau of Justice Statistics. Government Printing Office.

(1985). *The Risk of Violent Crime.* Washington, D.C.: Department of Justice, Bureau of Justice Statistics. Government Printing Office.

(1988). *Households Touched by Crime, 1987.* Washington, D.C.: Department of Justice, Bureau of Justice Statistics. Government Printing Office.

(1989). *Households Touched by Crime, 1988.* Washington, D.C.: Department of Justice, Bureau of Justice Statistics. Government Printing Office.

(1990). *Black Victims*, Bureau of Justice Statistics Special Report. Washington, D.C.: Department of Justice, Bureau of Justice Statistics.

Van Dijk, J., and Steinmetz, C. (1983). Victimization Surveys: Beyond Measuring the Volume of Crime. *Victimology: An International Journal, 8*, 291-301.

Walmsley, R. (1986). *Personal Violence*, Home Office Research and Planning Unit Report (No. 89). London: Her Majesty's Stationery Office.

Wikström, P-O.H. (1985). *Everyday Violence in Contemporary Sweden.* Stockholm: The National Council for Crime Prevention.

Wilson, P.R., and Brown, J. (1973). *Crime and the Community.* Brisbane: University of Queensland Press.

Wolfgang, M.E. (1958). *Patterns in Criminal Homicide.* Philadelphia: University of Pennsylvania Press.

Chapter 6. The Victims and Their Victimizers

Ben-David, S. (1982). Rapist-Victim Interaction During Rape. In H.J. Schneider (Ed.), *The Victim in International Perspective* (pp. 227-246). Berlin: De Gruyter.

Bercheid, E., and Walster, E.H. (1969). *Interpersonal Attraction*. Reading, MA: Addison-Wesley.

Beynon, E.D. (1935). Crime and Custom of the Hungarians in Detroit. *Journal of the American Institute of Criminal Law and Criminology*, *25*, 755-774.

Brock, T.C., and Buss, A.H., (1964). Effects of Justification for Aggression and Communication with the Victim on Postaggression Dissonance. *Journal of Abnormal Social Psychology*, *68*, 403-412.

Cialdini et al. (1976). Victim Derogation in the Lerner Paradigm: Just World or Just Justification? *Journal of Personality and Social Psychology*, *33*(6), 719-724.

Cleaver, E. (1968). *Soul on Ice*. New York: Dell Publishing Co.

Cohen, M., Garofalo, R., Bouscher, R., and Seghorn, T. (1971). The Psychology of Rapists. *Seminars in Psychiatry*, *3*, 307-327.

Cressey, D. (1953). *Other People's Money: A Study in the Social Psychology of Embezzlement*. Glencoe, IL: The Free Press.

Davis, J.A. (1974). Justification for No Obligation: Views of Black Males Toward Crime and the Criminal Law. *Issues in Criminology*, *9*(2), 69-87.

Debuyst, C., and Joos, J. (1971). *L'enfant et l'adolescent Voleurs*. Bruxelles: Dessart.

De Greeff, E. (1950). La Criminogénèse. *Actes du IIe Congrès International de Criminologie* (Tome VI). Paris: Presses Universitaires de France.

Diener, E. (1976). Effects of Prior Destructive Behavior, Anonymity, and Group Presence on Deindividuation and Aggression. *Journal of Personality and Social Psychology*, *33*(5), 497-507.

Diener, E., and Fraser, S.C. (1976). Effects of Deindividuation Variables on Stealing Among Halloween Trick-or-Treaters. *Journal of Personality and Social Psychology*, *33*(2), 178-183.

Fattah, E.A. (1971). *La Victime est-elle Coupable?* Montréal: Presses de l'Université de Montréal.

(1976). The Use of the Victim as an Agent of Self-Legitimization: Toward a Dynamic Explanation of Criminal Behavior. *Victimology: An International Journal*, 1(1), 29-53.

Gagnon, J. (1974). Sexual Conduct and Crime. In D. Glaser (Ed.), *Handbook of Criminology* (pp. 233-277). Chicago: Rand McNally.

Godfrey, B.W., and Lowe, C.A. (1975). Devaluation of Innocent Victims: An Attribution Analysis Within the Just World Paradigm. *Journal of Personality and Social Psychology*, *31*(5), 944-951.

Goode, W.J. (1969). Violence Among Intimates. In D.J. Mulvihill, M.M. Tumin and L. Curtis (Eds.), *Crimes of Violence*, A Staff Report Submitted to the National Commission on the Causes and Prevention of Violence (pp. 941-977). Washington, D.C.: Superintendent of Documents.

Göppinger, H. (1976). *The Victim as Seen by the Offender*. Paper presented at the 2nd International Symposium on Victimology, Boston, MA. Abstract published 1977. In *Victimology: An International Journal*, *2*(1), 63.

Hesnard, A. (1963). *Psychologie du Crime*. Paris: Payot.

Hijazi, M. (1966). *Délinquance et Réalisation de Soi*. Paris: Masson.

Inciardi, J. (1974). Vocational Crime. In D. Glaser (Ed.), *Handbook of Criminology*. Chicago: Rand McNally.

Kanin, E. (1970). Sex Aggression by College Men. *Medical Aspects of Human Sexuality*, *4*, 25-40.

Katz, I. et al. (1977). Ambivalence, Guilt, and the Denigration of a Physically Handicapped Victim. *Journal of Personality and Social Psychology*, *45*(3), 419-429.

Lerner, M.J. (1974). *Social Psychology of Justice and Interpersonal Attraction*. New York: Academic Press.

Menninger, K. (1966). *The Crime of Punishment*. New York: Viking.

Mills, C.W. (1940, December). Situated Actions and the Vocabulary of Motives. *American Sociological Review*, *5*, 904-913.

Redl, F., and Wineman, D. (1951). *Children Who Hate*. Glencoe, IL: The Free Press.

Robert, P. (1966). *Les Bandes d'Adolescents*. Paris: Editions Ouvrières.

Robert, P. et al. (1974). *Images du Viol Collectif et Reconstruction D'Objet*. Paris: Service des Études Pénales et Criminologiques.

Ryan, W. (1971). *Blaming the Victim*. New York: Pantheon Books.

Schwendinger, H., and Schwendinger, J. (1967). Delinquent Stereotypes of Probable Victims. In M.W. Klein and B.G. Myerhoff (Eds.), *Juvenile Gangs in Context* (pp. 91-105). Englewood Cliffs: Prentice Hall.

Scully, D., and Marolla, J. (1984). Convicted Rapists: Vocabulary of Motives: Excuses and Justifications. *Social Problems*, *31*(5), 530-544.

Singer, S. (1981). Homogeneous Victim-Offender Populations: A Review and Some Research Implications. *Journal of Criminal Law and Criminology*, 72(2), 779-788.

Sparks, R.F. (1981). Surveys of Victimization—An Optimistic Assessment. In M. Tonry and N. Morris (Eds.), *Crime and Justice: An Annual Review of Research* (Vol. 3, pp. 1-60). Chicago: University of Chicago Press.

(1982). *Research on Victims of Crime: Accomplishments, Issues, and New Directions*. Rockville, MD: Department of Health and Human Services.

Sutherland, E.H. (1937). *The Professional Thief.* Chicago: University of Chicago Press.

Sykes, G., and Matza, D. (1957). Techniques of Neutralization: A Theory of Delinquency. *American Sociological Review*, *22*, 664-670.

Thornberry, T.P., and Singer, S.I. (1979). Opfer und Täter: Zur Übereinstimmung zweir Populationen. In G.F. Kirchhoff and K. Sessar (Eds.), *Das Verbrechens Opfer* (pp. 321-335). Bochum: Studienverlag Brockmeyer.

Vaucresson, Centre de. (1962). La Délinquance des Jeunes en Groupe. Paris: Cujas.

Wolfgang, M.E., and Ferracuti, F. (1967). *The Subculture of Violence*. London: Tavistock.

Wright, R. (1945). *Black Boy: A Record of Childhood and Youth*. New York: Harper and Brothers Publishers.

Chapter 7. Victim-Offender Relationships

Agopain, M., Chappell, D., and Geis, G. (1972). *Interracial Rape in a North American City: An Analysis of 66 Cases*. Paper presented to the meeting of the American Society of Criminology in Caracas, Venezuela. Also published (1974). In I. Drapkin and E. Viano (Eds.), *Victimology*. Lexington, MA: D.C. Heath & Co.

Amir, M. (1971). *Patterns in Forcible Rape*. Chicago: University of Chicago Press.

Block, R. (1977). *Violent Crime*. Lexington, MA: D.C. Heath & Co.

Burgess, A.W., and Holmstrom, L.L. (1974). *Rape: Victims of Crisis*. Bowie, MD: Robert Brady.

Canada. (1983). *Victims of Crime, Canadian Urban Victimization Survey Bulletin* (No. 1). Ottawa: Ministry of the Solicitor General.

Cormier, B. (1962). Psychodynamics of Homicide Committed in a Marital Relationship. *Corrective Psychiatry and Journal of Social Therapy*, *8*(4), 187-194.

(1975). Mass Murder, Multicide and Collective Crime: The Doers and the Victims. In I. Drapkin and E. Viano (Eds.), *Victimology: A New Focus* (Vol. IV). Lexington, MA: D.C. Heath & Co.

Cormier, B. et al. (1971). The Psychodynamics of Homicide Committed in a Specific Relationship. *Canadian Journal of Criminology and Corrections*, *13*(1), 1-8.

Coser, L. (1964). *The Functions of Social Conflict*. New York: The Free Press.

Curtis, L. (1974). *Criminal Violence: National Patterns and Behavior.* Lexington, MA: D.C. Heath & Co.

Driver, E. (1961). Interaction and Criminal Homicide in India. *Social Forces, 40,* 153-158.

Ellenberger, H. (1955). Psychological Relationships Between the Criminal and His Victim. *Archives of Criminal Psychodynamics, 2,* 257-290.

Fattah, E.A. (1971). *La Victime est-elle Coupable?* Montréal: Presses de l'Université de Montréal.

Federal Republic of Germany. (1988). *Polizeiliche Kriminalstatistik.* Wiesbaden: Bundeskriminalamt.

Finkelhor, D. (1979). *Sexually Victimized Children.* New York: The Free Press.

Finkelhor, D. et al. (1983). *The Dark Side of Families—Current Family Violence Research.* Beverly Hills: Sage Publications.

Garfinkel, H. (1949). Research Note on Inter- and Intra-racial Homicides. *Social Forces, 27*(4), 370-381. Reprinted (1967). In M.E. Wolfgang (Ed.), *Studies in Homicide.* New York: Harper and Row.

Gelles, R.J. (1979). *Family Violence.* Beverly Hills: Sage Publications.

(1983). An Exchange/Social Control Theory. In D. Finkelhor et al. (Eds.), *The Dark Side of Families—Current Family Violence Research* (pp. 151-165). Beverly Hills: Sage Publications.

Gibson, E. (1975). *Homicide in England and Wales: 1967-1971,* Home Office Research Study (No. 31). London: Her Majesty's Stationery Office.

Gibson, E., and Klein, S. (1961). *Murder,* A Home Office Research Unit Report. London: Her Majesty's Stationery Office.

(1969). *Murder 1957 to 1968,* A Home Office Statistical Division Report on Murder in England and Wales, Home Office Research Study (No. 3). London: Her Majesty's Stationery Office.

Goode, W. (1969). Violence Among Intimates. In D. Mulvihill, M. Tumin, and L. Curtis, (Eds.), *Crimes of Violence,* A Staff Report to the National Commission on the Causes and Prevention of Violence (Vol. 13, pp. 941-977). Washington, D.C.: Government Printing Office.

Hayman, C.R. et al. (1968). Sexual Assault on Women and Children in the District of Columbia. *Public Health Report, 83*(12), 1021-1028.

Katz, S., and Mazur, M.A. (1979). *Understanding the Rape Victim: A Synthesis of Research Findings.* New York: John Wiley & Sons.

Kennedy, L., and Silverman, R. (1990). The Elderly Victim of Homicide: An Application of the Routine Activities Approach. *The Sociological Quarterly, 31*(2), 307-319.

Kratcoski, P.C., and Walker, D.B. (1988). Homicide Among the Elderly: Analysis of the Victim/Assailant Relationship. In B. McCarthy and R. Langsworthy (Eds.), *Older Offenders: Perspectives in Criminology and Criminal Justice*. New York: Praeger.

Messner, S.F., and Tardiff, K. (1985). The Social Ecology of Urban Homicide: An Application of the "Routine Activities" Approach. *Criminology*, *23*(2), 241-267.

Morris, T., and Cooper, L.B. (1964). *A Calendar of Murder: Criminal Homicide in England Since 1957*. London: Michael Joseph, Ltd.

Mulvihill, D., Tumin, M., and Curtis, L. (1969). *Crimes of Violence*, A Staff Report to the National Commission on the Causes and Prevention of Violence (Vol. 11). Washington, D.C.: Government Printing Office.

Normandeau, A. (1972). Violence and Robbery: A Case Study. *Acta Criminologica*, *2*, 11-96.

Palmer, S. (1970). Aggression in 58 Non-Literate Societies: An Exploratory Analysis. *International Annals of Criminology*, 1st semester, 57-69.

(1975). Characteristics of Homicide and Suicide Victims in Forty Non-Literate Societies. In I. Drapkin and E. Viano (Eds.), *Victimology: A New Focus* (Vol. 3). Lexington, MA: D.C. Heath & Co.

Pittman, D., and Handy, W. (1964). Patterns in Aggravated Assault. *The Journal of Criminal Law, Criminology and Police Science*, *55*(4), 462-470.

Pizzey, E., and Shapiro, J. (1981, April 23). Choosing a Violent Relationship. *New Society*, 133-135.

(1982). *Prone to Violence*. London: Hamlyn Paperbacks.

Schwendinger, H., and Schwendinger, J. (1983). *Rape and Inequality*. Beverly Hills: Sage Publications.

Sebastian, R.J. (1983). Social Psychological Determinants. In D. Finkelhor et al. (Eds.), *The Dark Side of Families—Current Family Violence Research* (pp. 182-192). Beverly Hills: Sage Publications.

Sessar, K. (1975). The Familiar Character of Criminal Homicide. In I. Drapkin and E. Viano (Eds.), *Victimology: A New Focus: Vol. IV. Violence and Its Victims*. Lexington, MA: D.C. Heath & Co.

Silverman, R.A., and Kennedy, L.W. (1987). Relational Distance and Homicide: The Role of the Stranger. *The Journal of Criminal Law and Criminology*, *78*(2), 272-308.

Smith, L.J.F. (1989). *Concerns About Rape*, A Home Office Research Study. London: Her Majesty's Stationery Office.

Stanko, E.A. (1985). *Intimate Intrusions: Women's Experience of Male Violence*. London: Routledge & Kegal Paul.

Statistics Canada. (1973). *Murder Statistics 1961-1970* (Catalogue 85-503 Occasional). Ottawa: Statistics Canada.

(1976). *Homicide in Canada: A Statistical Synopsis.* Ottawa: Ministry of Supply and Services. Also, P. Reed, T. Bleszynski, and R. Gaucher. (1978). Homicide in Canada: A Statistical Synopsis. In M.A.B. Gammon (Ed.), *Violence in Canada.* Toronto: Methuen Publications.

(1987). *Homicide in Canada 1976-1985: An Historical Perspective* (Catalogue No. 85-209). Ottawa: Ministry of Supply and Services.

Straus, M.A. (1973). A General Systems Theory Approach to a Theory of Violence Between Family Members. *Social Science Information, 12*, 105-125.

(1986). Domestic Violence and Homicide Antecedents. *Bulletin of the New York Academy of Medicine.*

Straus, M.A., and Gelles, R.J. (1986, August). Societal Change and Change in Family Violence from 1975 to 1985 as Revealed by Two National Surveys. *Journal of Marriage and the Family, 48*(4), 465-479.

Straus, M.A., Gelles, R.J., and Steinmetz, S.K. (1980). *Behind Closed Doors: Violence in the American Family.* Garden City, New York: Doubleday.

Svalastoga, K. (1956). Homicide and Social Contact in Denmark. *American Journal of Sociology, 62*, 37-41.

(1962). Rape and Social Structure. *Pacific Sociological Review, 5*, 48-53.

United States. (1980). *Intimate Victims: A Study of Violence Among Friends and Relatives,* A National Crime Survey Report (NCJ - 62319) Washington, D.C.: Department of Justice, Bureau of Justice Statistics.

Von Hentig, H. (1948). *The Criminal and His Victim.* New Haven: Yale University Press.

Wallace, A. (1986). *Homicide: The Social Reality.* New South Wales: Bureau of Crime Statistics and Research, Attorney General's Department.

Weiss, G. (1963). *Die Kinderschändung.* Hamburg: Kriminalistik Verlag.

Wikström, P-O.H. (1985). *Everyday Violence in Contemporary Sweden: Situational and Ecological Aspects* (Report No. 15). Stockholm: National Council for Crime Prevention.

Wolfgang, M.E. (1958). *Patterns in Criminal Homicide.* Philadelphia: University of Pennsylvania Press.

Chapter 8. The Dynamics of Criminal Victimization

Amir, M. (1967). Victim-Precipitated Forcible Rape. *Journal of Criminal Law, Criminology and Police Science, 58*(4), 493-502.

(1971). *Patterns in Forcible Rape.* Chicago: University of Chicago Press.

Bart, P., and O'Brien, P. (1985). *Stopping Rape: Successful Survival Strategies*. Oxford: Pergamon Press.

Block, R. (1977). *Violent Crime*. Lexington, MA: D.C. Heath & Co.

(1981). Victim-Offender Dynamics in Violent Crime. *Journal of Criminal Law and Criminology*, *72*(2), 743-761.

(1989). Victim-Offender Dynamics in Stranger to Stranger Violence: Robbery and Rape. In E.A. Fattah (Ed.), *The Plight of Crime Victims in Modern Society*. London: Macmillan.

Block, R., and Skogan, W.G. (1986). Resistance and Nonfatal Outcomes in Stranger-to-Stranger Predatory Crime. *Violence and Victims*, *1*(4), 241-253.

Blumberg, M. (1979). Injury to Victims of Personal Crimes: Nature and Extent. In W.H. Parsonage (Ed.), *Perspectives on Victimology*. Beverly Hills: Sage Publications.

Brodsky, S.L. (1976). Prevention of Rape: Deterrence by the Potential Victim. In M.J. Walker and S.L. Brodsky (Eds.), *Sexual Assault: The Victim and The Rapist*. Lexington, MA: Lexington Books, D.C. Heath & Co.

Burgess, A.W., and Holmstrom, L.L. (1974). *Rape: Victims of Crisis*. Bowie, MD: Robert Brady.

Chappell, D., and James, J. (1986). Victim Selection and Apprehension from the Rapist's Perspective: A Preliminary Investigation. In K. Miyazawa and M. Ohya (Eds.), *Victimology in Comparative Perspective*. Tokyo: Seibundo Publishing Co. Ltd.

Christie, N. (1952). Fangevoktere i Konsentrasjonsleire. *Nordisk Tidskrift for Kriminalvidenskap*, *41*, 439-458. Also published as a book in 1972.

Clark, L., and Lewis, D. (1977). *Rape: The Price of Coercive Sexuality*. Toronto: The Women's Press.

Conklin, J. (1972). *Robbery and the Criminal Justice System*. Philadelphia: J.P. Lippincott.

Cook, P.J. (1982). The Role of Firearms in Violent Crime. In M.E. Wolfgang and N.A. Weiner (Eds.), *Criminal Violence*. Beverly Hills: Sage Publications.

(1986, June). The Relationship Between Victim Resistance and Injury in Non-Commercial Robbery. *Journal of Legal Studies*, *XV*, 405-416.

Cooper, H.H.A. (1976). The Terrorist and the Victim. *Victimology*, *2*, 229-239.

Curtis, L. (1974). *Criminal Violence: National Patterns and Behavior*. Lexington, MA: D.C. Heath & Co.

(1976). Toward a Theory of Response to Rape: Some Methodological Considerations. In E. Viano (Ed.), *Victims and Society* (pp. 220-229). Washington: Visage Press.

Fattah, E.A. (1984). Victim's Response to Confrontational Victimization: A Neglected Aspect of Victim Research. *Crime and Delinquency*, *30*(1), 75-89.

Fattah, E.A., and Raic, A. (1970). L'alcool en tant que facteur victimogène. *Toxicomanies*, *3*(2), 143-173.

Felson, R.B., and Steadman, H.J. (1983). Situational Factors in Disputes Leading to Criminal Violence. *Criminology*, *21*(1), 59-74.

Finkelhor, D. (1979). *Sexually Victimized Children*. New York: The Free Press.

Fisher, W.S. (1980). Predicting Injury to Rape Victims. In B.R. Price and P.J. Baunash (Eds.), *Criminal Justice Research: New Models and Findings* (pp. 55-72). Beverly Hills: Sage Publications.

Gibson, L., Linden, R., and Johnson, S. (1980). A Situational Theory of Rape. *Canadian Journal of Criminology*, *22*(1), 51-65.

Goode, W. (1969). Violence Among Intimates. In D. Mulvihill, M. Tumin and L. Curtis (Eds.), *Crimes of Violence*, A Staff Report to the National Commission on the Causes and Prevention of Violence (Vol. 13, pp. 941-977). Washington, D.C.: Government Printing Office.

Haselwood, R.R., and Harpold, J.A. (1986, June). Rape: The Dangers of Providing Confrontational Advice. *FBI Law Enforcement Bulletin*, 1-5.

Hepburn, J.R. (1973). Violent Behavior in Interpersonal Relationships. *Sociological Quarterly*, *14*, 419-429.

Hindelang, M., Gottfredson, M., and Garofalo, J. (1978). *Victims of Personal Crime: An Empirical Foundation for a Theory of Personal Victimization*. Cambridge, MA: Ballinger.

Hochstedler, E. (1981). *Crime Against the Elderly in 26 Cities*. Washington, D.C.: Department of Justice.

Katz, S., and Mazur, M.A. (1979). *Understanding the Rape Victim: A Synthesis of Research Findings*. New York: John Wiley & Sons.

Kleck, G., and Sayles, S. (1990, May). Rape and Resistance. *Social Problems*, *37*(2), 149-162.

Lofland, J. (1969). *Deviance and Identity* (p. 50). Englewood Cliffs, NJ: Prentice Hall.

Lizotte, A.J. (1986). Determinants of Completing Rape and Assault. *Journal of Quantitative Criminology*, *2*(3), 203-217.

Luckenbill, D.F. (1977). Criminal Homicide as a Situated Transaction. *Social Problems*, *25*, 176-186.

(1981). Generating Compliance: The Case of Robbery. *Urban Life*, *10*, 25-46.

Marques, J.D. (1981). Effects of Victim Resistance Strategies on the Sexual Arousal and Attitudes of Violent Rapists. In R.B. Stuart (Ed.), *Violent Behavior: Social Learning Approaches to Prediction, Management and Treatment*. New York: Brunner/Mazel.

Massey, J.B. et al. (1971). Management of Sexually Assaulted Females. *Obstetrics and Gynecology*, *38*(1), 29-36.

McDermott, J.M. (1979). *Rape Victimization in 26 American Cities* (United States Department of Justice, LEAA Analytic Report SD-VAD-6). Washington: United States Government Printing Office.

Mezey, G. (1988). Reactions to Rape: Effects, Counselling and the Role of Health Professionals. In M. Maguire and J. Pointing (Eds.), *Victims of Crime—A New Deal.* Philadelphia: Open University Press.

Milgram, S. (1969). *Obedience to Authority: An Experimental View.* New York: Harper and Row.

Ochberg, F. (1978). The Victim of Terrorism: Psychiatric Considerations. *Terrorism: An International Journal, 1* (2), 147-167.

Peters, J.J. et al. (1976, June). *The Philadelphia Assault Victim Study* (Final Report ROIMH 21304). National Institute of Mental Health.

Prentky, R.A., Burgess, A.W., and Carter, D.L. (1986). Victim Responses by Rapist Type: An Empirical and Clinical Analysis. *Journal of Interpersonal Violence, 1*(1), 73-98.

Quinsey, U.L., and Upfold, D. (1985). Rape Completion and Victim Injury as a Function of Female Resistance Strategy. *Canadian Journal of Behavioral Science, 17*(1), 40-50.

Reppetto, T. (1974). *Residential Crime.* Cambridge, MA: Ballinger Press.

Selkin, J. (1975, January). Rape: When to Fight Back? *Psychology Today*, pp. 71-76.

Shapland, J., Willmore, J., and Duff, P. (1985). *Victims in the Criminal Justice System.* Aldershot: Gower Publishing Company.

Skogan, W.G. (1978). Weapon Use in Robbery. In J. Inciardi and A.E. Pottieger (Eds.), *Violent Crime: Historical and Contemporary Issues.* Beverly Hills, CA: Sage Publications.

Smith, L.J.F. (1989). *Concerns About Rape*, Home Office Research Study (No. 106). London: Her Majesty's Stationery Office.

Swift, C. (1985). The Prevention of Rape. In A. Burgess (Ed.), *Rape and Sexual Assault.* New York: Garland Publishing Inc.

Symonds, M. (1975). Victims of Violence: Psychological Effects and Aftereffects. *American Journal of Psychoanalysis, 35*, 19-26.

Time. (October 4, 1976). The Hijackee Syndrome. *Time*, p. 87.

United States. (1980, January). *Intimate Victims: A Study of Violence Among Friends and Relatives*, A National Crime Survey Report. Washington D.C.: Department of Justice, Bureau of Justice Statistics.

(1982, April). Violent Crime by Strangers. *Bureau of Justice Statistics Bulletin.* Washington, D.C.: Department of Justice, Bureau of Justice Statistics.

(1987a, January). *Violent Crime by Strangers and Nonstrangers*, Bureau of Justice Statistics Special Report. Washington, D.C.: Department of Justice, Bureau of Justice Statistics.

(1987b, April). *Robbery Victims*, Bureau of Justice Statistics Special Report. Washington, D.C.: Department of Justice, Bureau of Justice Statistics.

(1989a). *Criminal Victimization in the United States 1987* (NCJ-115524). Washington, D.C.: Department of Justice, Bureau of Justice Statistics.

(1989b). *Injuries from Crime*, Bureau of Justice Statistics Special Report (by Caroline Wolf Harlow). Washington, D.C.: Department of Justice, Bureau of Justice Statistics.

Waller, I. (1989). The Needs of Crime Victims. In E.A. Fattah (Ed.), *The Plight of Crime Victims in Modern Society*. London: Macmillan.

Waller, I., and Okihiro, N. (1978). *Burglary: The Victim and the Public*. Toronto: Toronto University Press.

Weis, K., and Weis, S. (1975). Victimology and the Justification of Rape. In I. Drapkin and E. Viano (Eds.), *Victimology: A New Focus* (Vol. V). Lexington, MA: D.C. Heath & Co.

Wikström, P-O.H. (1985). *Everyday Violence in Contemporary Sweden: Situational and Ecological Aspects* (Report No. 15). Stockholm: National Council for Crime Prevention.

Wolfgang, M.E. (1982). *Victim Intimidation, Resistance and Injury: A Study of Robbery*. Unpublished manuscript. Published (1986). In K. Miyazawa and M. Ohya, *Victimology in Comparative Perspective*. Tokyo: Seibundo Publishing Co. Ltd.

Wright, R. (1980). Rape and Physical Violence. In D.J. West, (Ed.), *Sex Offenders in the Criminal Justice System*. Cambridge: Institute of Criminology, Cropwood Conference Series No. 12.

Ziegenhagen, E.A., and Brosnan, D. (1985, November). Victim Responses to Robbery and Crime Control Policy. *Criminology, 23*(4), 675-695.

Zimbardo, P. (1972). Pathology of Punishment. *Trans-Action, 9*, 4-8.

Zimring, F. (1979). Determinants of the Death Rate from Robbery: A Detroit Time Study. In H.M. Rose (Ed.), *Lethal Aspects of Urban Violence*. Lexington, MA: D.C. Heath & Co.

Zimring, F., and Zuehl, J. (1986, January). Victim Injury and Death in Urban Robbery: A Chicago Study. *Journal of Legal Studies, XV*, 1-31.

Chapter 9. Victim/Target Selection

Alderman. (1979, November 3). KING CON: Has Tony Foster Got a Deal for You? *Weekend Magazine*. pp. 17-19.

Angel, S. (1968). *Discouraging Crime Through City Planning*. Berkeley: Center for Planning and Development Research, University of California.

Bennett, T., and Wright, R. (1984). *Burglars on Burglary: Prevention and the Offender*. Aldershot, Hants: Gower Publishing Co. Ltd.

Bevis, C., and Nutter, J.B. (1977). *Changing Street Layouts to Reduce Residential Burglary*. Paper read at the American Society of Criminology Meeting, Atlanta.

Bilking the Affluent Investor. (1970, August 24). *Montreal Star*.

Blazicek, D.L. (1979). The Criminal's Victim: A Theoretical Note on the Social Psychology of Victim Selection. *Journal of Crime and Justice, 1*, 113-131.

(1985, August 18-23). *Patterns of Victim Selection Among Robbers: A Theoretical and Descriptive Analysis*. Paper presented at the 5th International Symposium on Victimology, Zagreb, Yugoslavia.

Block, R. (1977). *Violent Crime*. Lexington, MA: D.C. Heath and Co.

Brantingham, P.J., and Brantingham, P.L. (1975). The Spatial Patterning of Burglary. *Howard Journal*, *14*, 11-23.

(1981). *Environmental Criminology*. Beverly Hills: Sage Publications.

(1984). *Patterns in Crime*. New York: Macmillan.

Chappell, D., and James, J. (1986). Victim Selection and Apprehension from the Rapist's Perspective: A Preliminary Investigation. In K. Miyazawa and M. Ohya (Eds.), *Victimology in Comparative Perspective*. Tokyo: Seibundo Publishing Co.

Clarke, R.V. (1980). Situational Crime Prevention: Theory and Practice. *British Journal of Criminology*, *20*, 136-147.

(1983). Situational Crime Prevention: Its Theoretical Basis and Practical Scope. In N. Morris and M. Tonry (Eds.), *Crime and Justice: An Annual Review of Research*. Chicago: University of Chicago Press.

Conklin, J.E. (1972). *Robbery and the Criminal Justice System*. Toronto: J.B. Lippincott and Co.

Costanzo, C.M. et al. (1986). Criminal Mobility and the Directional Component in Journeys to Crime. In R.M. Figlio, S. Hakim and G.F. Rengert (Eds.), *Metropolitan Crime Patterns*. Monsey, New York: Criminal Justice Press.

Cornish, D.B., and Clarke, R.V. (1986). *The Reasoning Criminal: Rational Choice Perspectives on Offending*. New York: Springer Verlag.

Curtis, L. (1974). *Criminal Violence*. Lexington, MA: D.C. Heath and Co.

Einstadter, W.J. (1969). The Social Organization of Armed Robbery. *Social Problems*, *17*, 64-83.

Fattah, E.A. (1971). *La Victime est-elle Coupable? Les Facteurs qui contribuent au choix de la Victime dans les cas de meurtre en vue de Vol*. Montréal: Presses de l'Université de Montréal.

(1980). Some Reflections on the Victimology of Terrorism. *Terrorism: An International Journal*, *3*(1-2), 81-108.

Feeney, F. (1986). Robbers as Decision-Makers. In D.B. Cornish and R.V. Clarke (Eds.), The *Reasoning Criminal*. New York: Springer Verlag.

Gabor, T. (1981, July). The Crime Displacement Hypothesis: An Empirical Examination. *Crime and Delinquency*, *27*(3), 391-403.

Goode, W. (1969). Violence Among Intimates. In D.J. Mulvihill, M.M. Tumin and L.A. Curtis (Eds.), *Crimes of Violence*, A Staff Report Submitted to the National Commission on the Causes and Prevention of Violence (pp. 941-977). Washington, D.C.: United States Government Printing Office.

Göppinger, H. (1974). Criminology and Victimology. In I. Drapkin and E. Viano (Eds.), *Victimology: A New Focus: Vol. I. Theoretical Issues in Victimology*. Lexington, MA: D.C. Heath and Co.

Heller, N.B., Stenzel, W.W., Gill, A.D., Kolde, R.A., and Schimerman, S.R. (1975). *Operation Identification Projects: Assessment of Effectiveness*. St. Louis: The Institute for Public Program Analysis.

Hepworth, M. (1975). *Blackmail: Publicity and Secrecy in Everyday Life*. London: Routledge & Kegan.

Hesnard, A. (1963). *La Psychologie du Crime*. Paris: Payot.

Hough, M. (1987). Offenders' Choice of Target: Findings from Victim Surveys. *Journal of Quantitative Criminology*, *3*(4), 355-369.

Inciardi, J. (1974). Vocational Crime. In D. Glaser (Ed.), *Handbook of Criminology*. Chicago: Rand McNally College Publishing.

Kitchen, G. (1973, August 15). Crime Biggest Worry for American Doctors. *Montreal Star*.

Knutsson, J. (1984). *Operation Identification –A Way to Prevent Burglaries?* (Research Division Report No. 14). Stockholm: National Council for Crime Prevention.

LeBeau, J.L. (1987). The Journey to Rape: Geographical Distance and the Rapist's Method of Approaching the Victim. *Journal of Police Science and Administration*, *15*(2), 129-136.

Lejeune, R. (1977). The Management of a Mugging. *Urban Life*, *6*(2), 123-148.

Letkemann, P. (1973). *Crime as Work*. Englewood Cliffs, NJ: Prentice Hall, Inc.

Maguire, M., and Bennett, T. (1982). *Burglary in a Dwelling*. London: Heinemann Educational Books Ltd.

Maxfield, M.G. (1987). Lifestyle and Routine Activity Theories of Crime: Empirical Studies of Victimization, Delinquency and Offender Decision-Making. *Journal of Quantitative Criminology*, *3*(4), 275-281.

McClintock, F.H., and Gibson, E. (1961). *Robbery in London*. London: Macmillan and Co. Ltd.

McIver, J.P. (1981). Criminal Mobility: A Review of Empirical Studies. In S. Hakim and G.F. Rengert (Eds.), *Crime Spillover*. Beverly Hills: Sage Publications.

Montreal Star. (1973, April 18).

Normandeau, A. (1981). Armed Robbery in Montreal and Its Victims. *Victimology: An International Journal*, *6*, 1-4.

Phillips, P. (1980). Characteristics and Typology of the Journey to Crime. In D. Georges-Abeyie and K.D. Harris (Eds.), *Crime: A Spatial Perspective*. New York: Columbia University Press.

Rengert, G.F. (1972). *Spatial Aspects of Criminal Behavior: A Suggested Approach.* Paper read at East Lakes Division, Association of American Geographers Annual Meeting.

Rengert, G.F., and Wasilchick, J. (1985). *Suburban Burglary—A Time and a Place for Everything.* Springfield: Charles C. Thomas.

Reppetto, T.A. (1974). *Residential Crime.* Cambridge, MA: Ballinger Publishing Co.

Rhodes, W.M., and Conly, C. (1981). Crime and Mobility: An Empirical Study. In P.J. Brantingham and P.L. Brantingham (Eds.), *Environmental Criminology.* Beverly Hills: Sage Publications.

Sampson, R.J., and Wooldredge, J.D. (1987). Linking the Micro- and Macro-Level Dimensions of Lifestyle—Routine Activity and Opportunity Models of Predatory Victimization. *Journal of Quantitative Criminology, 3*(4), 371-392.

Scarr, H.A. (1973). *Patterns of Burglary.* Washington: Government Printing Office.

Selkin, J. (1975, January). Rape: When to Fight Back? *Psychology Today*, 71-76.

Servay, W., and Rehm, J. (1986). *Bankraub aus Sicht der Täter.* Wiesbaden: Bundeskriminalamt.

Smith, D.A., and Jarjoura, G.R. (1988). Social Structure and Criminal Victimization. *Journal of Research in Crime and Delinquency, 25*(1), 27-52.

Smith, S.J. (1986). *Crime, Space and Society.* Cambridge: Cambridge University Press.

Sutherland, E. (1937). *The Professional Thief.* Chicago: University of Chicago Press.

Teske, R.H.C., Jr., and Arnold, H.R. (1988, September). *A Comparative Analysis of Factors Related to the Probability of Criminal Victimization.* Paper presented at the 10th International Congress of Criminology, Hamburg, Federal Republic of Germany.

Walsh, D. (1978). *Shoplifting: Controlling a Major Crime.* London: Macmillan.

(1980). *Break-Ins: Burglary from Private Houses.* London: Constable.

(1986). Victim Selection Procedures Among Economic Criminals: The Rational Choice Perspective. In D.B. Cornish and R.V. Clarke (Eds.), *The Reasoning Criminal: Rational Choice Perspectives on Offending.* New York: Springer Verlag.

Weir, A. (1973). The Robbery Event. In F. Feeney and A. Weir (Eds.), *The Prevention and Control of Robbery.* University of California: The Center for Administration of Justice.

Wilkins, L. (1964). *Social Deviance.* London: Tavistock Publications.

Wilson, D.A. (1987). *Target Selection in Robbery: An Exploratory Investigation.* Master's thesis, Simon Fraser University, Burnaby, B.C.

Wright, R., and Logie, R.H. (1988). How Young House Burglars Choose Targets. *The Howard Journal, 27*(2), 92-104.

Chapter 10. Victims' Personal Characteristics

Bakan, D. (1971). *Slaughter of the Innocents: A Study of the Battered Child Phenomenon*. Toronto: Canadian Broadcasting Corporation.

Bishop, R.I. (1971). Children at Risk. *Medical Journal of Australia*, *1*, 623-628.

Block, R., Felson, M., and Block, C.R. (1985). Crime Victimization Rates for Incumbents of 246 Occupations. *Sociology and Social Research*, *69*(3), 442-451.

Box, S. (1983). *Power, Crime, and Mystification*. London: Tavistock Publications.

Boyer, D.K., and James, J. (1983). Prostitutes as Victims. In D.E.J. MacNamara and A. Karmen (Eds.), *Deviants: Victims or Victimizers?* Beverly Hills: Sage Publications.

Braithwaite, J., and Biles, D. (1984). Victims and Offenders: The Australian Experience. In R. Block (Ed.), *Victimization and Fear of Crime: World Perspectives* (pp. 3-10). Washington, D.C.: United States Department of Justice, Bureau of Justice Statistics.

Brownmiller, S. (1975). *Against Our Will*. London: Secker and Warburg.

Centers for Disease Control. (1984). Alcohol and Violent Death—Erie County, New York, 1973-1983. *Morbidity and Mortality Weekly Report*, *33*, 226-227.

Collins, J.J., Cox, B.G., and Langan, P.A. (1987). Job Activities and Personal Crime Victimization: Implications for Theory. *Social Science Research*, *16*, 345-360.

De Francis, V. (1969). *Protecting the Child Victim of Sex Crimes Committed by Adults*, Final Report. Denver: The American Humane Association—Children's Division.

Dobash, R.E., and Dobash, R.P. (1979). *Violence Against Wives*. New York: The Free Press.

Edwards, S.S.M. (1984). *Women on Trial*. Manchester: Manchester University Press.

(1985). A Socio-Legal Evaluation of Gender Ideologies in Domestic Violence, Assault and Spousal Homicides. *Victimology: An International Journal*, *10*, 186-205.

Elias, R. (1986). *The Politics of Victimization: Victims, Victimology and Human Rights*. New York: Oxford University Press.

Erbe, S. (1984). Prostitutes: Victims of Men's Exploitation and Abuse. *Law and Inequality: Journal of Theory and Practice*, *2*, 607-623.

Fattah, E.A. (1989). The Child as Victim: Victimological Aspects of Child Abuse. In E.A. Fattah (Ed.), *The Plight of Crime Victims in Modern Society*. London: Macmillan.

Fattah, E.A., and Raic, A. (1970). L'Alcool en tant que facteur victimogène. *Toxicomanies*, *3*(2), 143-173.

Fattah, E.A., and Sacco, V. (1989). *Crime and Victimization of the Elderly*. New York: Springer Verlag.

Felson, R.B., and Steadman, H.J. (1983). Situational Factors in Disputes Leading to Criminal Violence. *Criminology*, *21*(1), 59-74.

Fergusson, D.M. et al. (1972). *Child Abuse in New Zealand.* Wellington: Research Division, Department of Social Work.

Feyerherm, H., and Hindelang, M. (1974). On the Victimization of Juveniles: Some Preliminary Results. *Journal of Research in Crime and Delinquency, 11*(1), 40-50.

Flynn, W.R. (1970). Frontier Justice: A Contribution to the Theory of Child Battery. *American Journal of Psychiatry, 127*(3), 375-379.

Freeman, M.D.A. (1979). *Violence in the Home*. Farnborough: Saxon House.

(1984). Legal Ideologies, Patriarchal Precedents and Domestic Violence. In M.D.A. Freeman (Ed.), *The State, the Law, and the Family*. London: Tavistock Publications.

Freeman-Longo, R.E. (1990). The Sexual Victimization of Males: Victim to Victimizer: Clinical Observations and Case Studies. In E.C. Viano (Ed.), *Crime and Its Victims: International Research and Public Policy Issues* (pp. 193-202). New York: Hemisphere Publishing Corporation.

Friedrich, W., and Boriskin, J. (1977). The Role of the Child in Abuse: A Review of the Literature. *American Journal of Orthopsychiatry, 46*(4). Also published as a summary in *Victimology: An International Journal*, *2*(2), 405-406.

Gagnon, J. (1974). Sexual Conduct and Crime. In D. Glaser (Ed.), *Handbook of Criminology* (pp. 233-277). Chicago: Rand McNally.

Gates, M. (1978). Introduction. In J.R. Chapman and M. Gates, (Eds.), *The Victimization of Women*. Beverly Hills: Sage Publications.

Gil, D.G. (1970). *Violence Against Children: Physical Child Abuse in the United States*. Cambridge, MA: Harvard University Press.

Gilfus, M.E. (1987). *Life Histories of Women in Prison*. Paper presented to the Third National Family Violence Conference, University of New Hampshire, July 6-9.

Goodman, R.A. et al. (1986). Alcohol Use and Interpersonal Violence: Alcohol Detected in Homicide Victims. *American Journal of Public Health, 76*(2), 144-149.

Gottfredson, M.R. (1981). On the Etiology of Criminal Victimization. *Journal of Criminal Law and Criminology, 72*, 714-726.

(1984). *Victims of Crime: The Dimensions of Risk.* London: Her Majesty's Stationery Office.

Gratus, J. (1969). *The Victims*. London: Hutchinson.

Grayson, B., and Stein, M.I. (1981). Attracting Assault: Victims' Nonverbal Cues. *Journal of Communication*, Winter, 68-75.

Griffiths, T. et al. (1989). Victimization of Canada's Natives: The Consequences of Socio-Cultural Deprivation. In E.A. Fattah (Ed.), *The Plight of Crime Victims in Modern Society*. London: Macmillan.

Haberman, P.W., and Baden, M.M. (1978). *Alcohol, Other Drugs and Violent Death.* New York: Oxford University Press.

Harry, J. (1982). Derivative Deviance: The Cases of Extortion, Fag-Bashing, and Shakedown of Gay Men. *Criminology*, *19*, 546-564.

Hatty, S. (1989). Violence Against Prostitute Women. *Australian Journal of Social Issues*, *24*(4), 235-248.

Hill, T. (1982). Rape and Marital Violence in the Maintenance of Male Power. In S. Friedman and E. Sarah (Eds.), *On the Problem of Men: Two Feminist Conferences*. London: The Women's Press.

Humphreys, L. (1970). *Tearoom Trade*. Chicago: Aldine Publishing Company.

Johnson, C.L. (1974). *Child Abuse in the Southeast: An Analysis of 1,172 Reported Cases*. Georgia University, Athens: Regional Institute of Social Welfare Research.

Justice, B., and Justice, R. (1976). *The Abusing Family*. New York: Human Sciences Press.

Karmen, A. (1983). Deviants as Victims. In D.E.J. MacNamara and A. Karmen (Eds.), *Deviants: Victims or Victimizers?* Beverly Hills: Sage Publications.

Kelly, R.J. (1983). Addicts and Alcoholics as Victims. In D.E.J. MacNamara and A. Karmen (Eds.), *Deviants: Victims or Victimizers?* Beverly Hills: Sage Publications.

Kempe, C.H. (1971). Pediatric Implications of the Battered Baby Syndrome (The Windermere Lecture, 1970). *Archives of Diseases in Childhood*, *46*(1), 28-37.

Kempe, C.H., and Kempe, R.S. (1978). *Child Abuse*. Cambridge, MA: Harvard University Press.

Lamborn, L. (1981). The Vulnerability of the Victim. In B. Galaway and J. Hudson (Eds.), *Perspectives on Crime Victims*. Toronto: The C.V. Mosby Company.

Lowman, J. (1989). *Street Prostitution: Assessing the Impact of the Law—Vancouver*. Ottawa: Department of Justice.

Lynch, J.P. (1987). Routine Activity and Victimization at Work. *Journal of Quantitative Criminology*, *3*(4), 283-300.

MacNamara, D.E.J. (1983). Prisoners as Victimizers and Victims. In D.E.J. MacNamara and A. Karmen (Eds.), *Deviants: Victims or Victimizers?* Beverly Hills: Sage Publications.

Maghan, J., and Sagarin, E. (1983). Homosexuals as Victims and Victimizers. In D.E.J. MacNamara and A. Karmen (Eds.), *Deviants: Victims or Victimizers?* Beverly Hills: Sage Publications.

Maisch, H. (1973). *Incest* (first published in German under the title Inzest). London: Andre Deutch.

Marek, Z. et al. (1974). Alcohol as a Victimogenic Factor of Robberies. *Forensic Science*, *4*, 119-123.

Martin, D. (1981). Battered Women — Scope of the Problem. In B. Galaway and J. Hudson (Eds.), *Perspectives on Crime Victims* (pp. 190-201). Toronto: The C.V. Mosby Company. Originally published in 1978 under the title *Battered Women: Issues of Public Policy*. Washington, D.C.: United States Commission on Civil Rights.

Marrs, C. (1990, January, February, March). Golden Lake Reserve Support Group. *Match News—News About Women and Development*, 6-7.

Mawby, R.I. (1979). The Victimization of Juveniles: A Comparative Study of Three Areas of Publicly Owned Housing in Sheffield. *Journal of Research in Crime and Delinquency*, *16*(1), 98-113.

(1988). Age, Vulnerability and the Impact of Crime. In M. Maguire and J. Pointing (Eds.), *Victims of Crime: A New Deal* (pp. 101-114). Milton Keynes: Open University Press.

Mayer, K. (1959). Zur Psychischen struktur des Unfällerpersönlichkeit. *Zeitschrift für Verkehrssicherheit.*

(1960). Unfallneigung und Persönlichkeit. *Zeitschrift für Psychotherapie und Medizinische Psychologie*, *10*(4), 167-173.

Mayhew, P., Elliott, D., and Dowds, L. (1989). *The 1988 British Crime Survey*, A Home Office Research and Planning Unit Report. London: Her Majesty's Stationery Office.

Milgram, S. (1974). *Obedience to Authority*. New York: Harper and Row.

Milman, J. (1980). New Rules for the Oldest Profession: Should We Change Our Prostitution Laws? *Harvard Women's Law Journal*, *3*, 1-35.

Mohr, J.H. et al. (1962). The Pedophiliacs: Their Clinical, Social and Legal Implications. *Canadian Psychiatric Association Journal*, *7*, 255-260.

National Research Council. (1976). *Surveying Crime—Report of the Panel for the Evaluation of Crime Surveys*. Washington, D.C.: National Academy of Science.

Pemberton, K. (1989, June 9). Pattern Ruled Out in Hooker Slayings. *Sun* (Vancouver).

Pemberton, K., and Bell, S. (1990, September 1). Man Held in Hooker Slaying Suspect in Other Deaths. *Sun* (Vancouver), pp. 1-2.

Pence, E. (1985). *Criminal Justice Response to Domestic Assault Cases: A Guide for Policy Development*. Duluth, MN: Domestic Abuse Intervention Project, Minnesota Program Development Inc.

Perkins, R., and Bennett, G. (1985). *Being a Prostitute*. Sydney: George Allen and Unwin.

Reiss, A., Jr. (1980). Victim Proneness in Repeat Victimization by Type of Crime. In S.E. Fienberg and A.J. Reiss, Jr. (Eds.), *Indicators of Crime and Criminal Justice: Quantitative Studies*. Washington, D.C.: United States Department of Justice, Bureau of Justice Statistics.

Russell, D. (1975). *The Politics of Rape*. New York: Stein & Day.

Sacco, V., and Glackman, W. (1987). Vulnerability, Locus of Control and Worry About Crime. *Canadian Journal of Community Mental Health*, *6*(1), 99-111.

Sagarin, E., and MacNamara, D.E.J. (1975). The Homosexual as a Crime Victim. In I. Drapkin and E. Viano (Eds.), *Victimology: A New Focus: Vol. V. Exploiters and Exploited: The Dynamics of Victimization*. Lexington, MA: D.C. Heath & Co.

Sampson, R.J., and Lauritsen, J.L. (1990). Deviant Lifestyles, Proximity to Crime, and the Offender—Victim Link in Personal Violence. *Journal of Research in Crime and Delinquency*, *27*(2), 110-139.

Schwendinger, H., and Schwendinger, J. (1976). A Review of Rape Literature. *Crime and Social Justice*, *6*, 79-85.

Shepherd, J. et al. (1989). Alcohol Consumption Among Victims of Violence and Among Comparable U.K. Populations. *British Journal of Addictions*, *84*(9), 1045-1051.

Smith, L.J.F. (1989). *Domestic Violence: An Overview of the Literature*, Home Office Research Study (No. 107). London: Her Majesty's Stationery Office.

Smith, S.J. (1986). *Crime, Space and Society*. Cambridge: Cambridge University Press.

Sparks, R.F. (1981). Multiple Victimization: Evidence, Theory, and Future Research. *The Journal of Criminal Law and Criminology*, *72*(2), 762-778.

(1982). *Research on Victims of Crime: Accomplishments, Issues and New Directions*. Rockville, MD: United States Department of Health and Human Services.

Sparks, R.F., Genn, H.G., and Dodd, D.J. (1977). *Surveying Victims*. Chichester: J. Wiley & Sons.

Stanko, E.A. (1985). *Intimate Intrusions: Women's Experience of Male Violence*. London: Routledge and Kegan Paul.

Sutherland, E. (1937). *The Professional Thief*. Chicago: University of Chicago Press.

Thissen, D., and Wainer, H. (1983). Toward the Measurement and Prediction of Victim Proneness. *Journal of Research on Crime and Delinquency*, *20*(2), 243-261.

United States. (1986). *Teenage Victims*, A National Crime Survey Report (NCJ-103138). Washington, D.C.: Department of Justice, Bureau of Justice Statistics. Superintendent of Documents.

Verkko, V. (1951). *Homicides and Suicides in Finland and Their Dependence on National Character*. Copenhagen: G.E.C. Gads Forlag.

Von Hentig, H. (1948). *The Criminal and His Victim*. New Haven: Yale University Press.

Voss, H.L., and Hepburn, J.R. (1968). Patterns in Criminal Homicide in Chicago. *Journal of Criminal Law, Criminology and Police Science*, *59*, 449-508.

Walker, L.E. (1984). *The Battered Woman Syndrome*. New York: Springer.

Wikström, P-O.H. (1985). *Everyday Violence in Contemporary Sweden: Situational and Ecological Aspects*. Stockholm: The National Council for Crime Prevention.

Wolfgang, M.E. (1958). *Patterns in Criminal Homicide*. Philadelphia: University of Pennsylvania Press.

Wolfgang, M.E., and Strohm, R. (1956). The Relationship Between Alcohol and Criminal Homicide. *Quarterly Journal of Studies on Alcohol, 17*, 411-425.

Zahn, M.A., and Bencivengo, M. (1974). Violent Death: A Comparison Between Drug Users and Non-Drug Users. *Addictive Diseases: An International Journal, 1*(3).

(1975). Murder in a Drug Using Population. In M. Reidl and T. Thornberry (Eds.), *Crime and Delinquency: Dimensions of Deviance*. New York: Praeger.

Chapter 11. Victim Behavior as a Situational Variable

Amir, M. (1967). Victim Precipitated Forcible Rape. *Journal of Criminal Law, Criminology and Police Science, 58*(4), 493-502.

(1971). *Patterns in Forcible Rape*. Chicago: University of Chicago Press.

Avison, N.H. (1975). Victims of Homicide. In I. Drapkin and E. Viano (Eds.), *Victimology: A New Focus: Vol. IV. Violence and Its Victims*. Lexington, MA: D.C. Heath & Co.

Baldwin, J. (1974, June). The Role of the Victim in Certain Property Offences. *Criminal Law Review*, 353-358.

Bender, B. (1976). Self-Chosen Victims: Scapegoating Behavior Sequential to Battering. *Child Welfare, LV*(6), 417-422.

Bender, L., and Gruggett, Jr., A.E. (1952). A Follow-Up Study of Children Who Had Atypical Sexual Experience. *American Journal of Orthopsychiatry, 22*, 825-837.

Boven W. (1943). Délinquants Sexuels: Corrupteurs d'enfants, Coupables et Victimes. *Schweizer Archiv für Neurologie und Psychiatrie, 51*, 14-25.

Brieland, D. (1967). The Child Sex Victim—Some Unanswered Questions. In S. Chaneles and D. Brieland (Eds.), *Sexual Abuse of Children: Implications for Casework*. Denver: Children's Division of the American Humane Association.

Clark, L., and Lewis, D. (1977). *Rape: The Price of Coercive Sexuality*. Toronto: Women's Press.

Curtis, L. (1974a). *Criminal Violence: National Patterns and Behavior*. Lexington, MA: D.C. Heath & Co.

(1974b). Victim Precipitation and Violent Crime. *Social Problems, 21*, 594-605.

(1975). Victim Precipitation. *The Aldine Crime and Justice Annual, 1974*. Chicago: Aldine Publishing Co.

(1981). Victim Precipitation and Violent Crime. In B. Galaway and J. Hudson (Eds.), *Perspectives on Crime Victims*. Toronto: The C.V. Mosby Company.

Elias, R. (1986). *The Politics of Victimization: Victims, Victimology and Human Rights*. New York: Oxford University Press.

Fattah, E.A. (1971). *La Victime est-elle Coupable?* Montreal: University of Montreal Press.

(1979). Some Recent Theoretical Developments in Victimology. *Victimology: An International Journal*, *4*(2), 198-213.

Felson, R.B., and Steadman, H.J. (1983). Situational Factors in Disputes Leading to Criminal Violence. *Criminology*, *21*(1), 59-74.

Fiedler, J. et al. (1989). *Anhalterwesen und Anhaltergefahren*. Wiesbaden: Bundeskriminalamt.

Fooner, M. (1966). Victim-Induced Criminality. *Science*, *153*(3740), 1080-1083.

Franklin II, C.W., and Franklin, A.P. (1976). Victimology Revisited: A Critique and Suggestions for Future Direction. *Criminology*, *14*(1), 177-214.

Gabor, T. et al. (1987). *Armed Robbery: Cops, Robbers, and Victims*. Springfield, IL: Charles C. Thomas.

Gagnon, J.H. (1965). Female Child Victims of Sex Offenses. *Social Problems*, *13*(2), 176-192.

(1974). Sexual Conduct and Crime. In D. Glaser (Ed.), *Handbook of Criminology* (pp. 233-277). Chicago: Rand McNally.

Gebhard, P.H. et al. (1965). *Sex Offenders: An Analysis of Types*. New York: Harper & Row.

Gibbens, T.C.N., and Prince, J. (1963). *Child Victims of Sex Offences*. London: Institute for the Study and Treatment of Delinquency.

Gillespie, C.K. (1989). *Justifiable Homicide: Battered Women, Self-Defence, and the Law*. Columbus: Ohio University Press.

Gobert, J.J. (1977). Victim Precipitation. *Columbia Law Review*, *77*(4), 511-553.

Greenley, J.R., and Rice, D.G. (1973). Female Hitchhiking: Strain, Control, and Subcultural Approaches. *Sociological Focus*, *7*, 87-100.

Heather, D.R.H. (1979). *Snow's Annotated Criminal Code*. Toronto: The Carswell Company Limited.

Joutsen, M. (1987). *The Role of the Victim of Crime in European Criminal Justice Systems*. Helsinki: Helsinki Institute for Crime Prevention and Control.

Karmen, A. (1984). *Crime Victims: An Introduction to Victimology*. Monterey: Brooks/Cole Publishing Company.

Kinberg, O. (1960). *Les Problèmes Fondamentaux de la Criminologie*. Paris: Cujas.

Körner, H.H. (1975). *Sexualentgleisungen Alternder Menschen in Umgang mit Minderjährigen*. Doctoral dissertation, Mainz University, Federal Republic of Germany.

(1977). *Sexualkriminalität im Alter*. Stuttgart: Ferdinand Enke Verlag.

Lamborn, L. (1981). The Culpability of the Victim. In B. Galaway and J. Hudson (Eds.), *Perspectives on Crime Victims*. Toronto: The C.V. Mosby Company.

Luckenbill, D.F. (1977). Criminal Homicide as a Situated Transaction. *Social Problems*, *25*(2), 176-186.

Maisch, H. (1973). *Incest* (first published in German under the title *Inzest*). London: Andre Deutch.

McClintock, F., and Gibson, E. (1961). *Robbery in London*. London: Macmillan.

Morgan, C.J. (1975). Hitchhiking—Social Signals at a Distance. *Bulletin of the Psychonomic Society*, *5*, 459-461.

Nelson, S., and Amir, M. (1975). The Hitchhike Victim of Rape: A Research Report. In I. Drapkin and E. Viano (Eds.), *Victimology: A New Focus: Vol. V. Exploiters and Exploited: The Dynamics of Victimization*. Lexington, MA: D.C. Heath & Co.

Nkpa, N.K.U. (1976). Armed Robbery in Post-Civil War Nigeria: The Role of the Victim. *Victimology: An International Journal*, *1*(1), 71-83.

Normandeau, A. (1968). *Trends and Patterns in Crimes of Robbery*. Ph.D. dissertation. Philadelphia: University of Pennsylvania Press.

Padowetz, M. (1954). *Der Heiratsschwindel*. Wien: Springer.

Palmer, J. (1974). Pre-arrest Diversion. *Federal Probation*. Reprinted in *The Aldine Crime and Justice Annual* (pp. 464-479). Chicago: Aldine Publishing.

Pollak, O. (1941). The Criminality of Old Age. *Journal of Criminal Psychopathology*, *3*, 213-235.

Rossman, P. (1980). The Pederasts. In Leroy G. Schultz (Ed.), *The Sexual Victimology of Youth*. Springfield, IL: Charles C. Thomas.

Schönfelder, T. (1965). Die Initiative des Opfers. In F.G.V. Stockert (Ed.), *Das Sexuell Gefährdete Kind*. Stuttgart: Ferdinand Enke Verlag.

(1968). *Die Rolle des Mädchens bei Sexualdelikten*. Stuttgart: Ferdinand Enke Verlag.

Silverman, R. (1973). Victim Precipitation: An Examination of the Concept. In I. Drapkin and E. Viano (Eds.), *Victimology: A New Focus* (Vol. 1). Lexington, MA: Lexington Books.

Sparks, R.F. (1982). *Research on Victims of Crime: Accomplishments, Issues and New Directions*. Rockville, MD: United States Department of Health and Human Services.

Sutherland, E. (1937). *The Professional Thief*. Chicago: University of Chicago Press.

Timmer, D., and Norman, W.H. (1984). The Ideology of Victim Precipitation. *Criminal Justice Review*, *9*, 63-68.

United States. (1979). *The Cost of Negligence: Losses from Preventable Household Burglaries* (NCJISS). Washington, D.C.: National Criminal Justice Information and Statistics Service, Government Printing Office.

Virkkunen, M. (1975). Victim-Precipitated Pedophilia Offences. *British Journal of Criminology*, *15*(2), 175-180.

(1980). *The Child as Participating Victim* (pp. 122-134). Reprint.

Von Hentig, H. (1940/41). Remarks on the Interaction of Perpetrator and Victim. *Journal of Criminal Law and Criminology*, *31*, 303-309.

(1948). *The Criminal and His Victim*. New Haven: Yale University Press.

Waller, I., and Okihiro, N. (1978). *Burglary: The Victim and the Public*. Toronto: University of Toronto Press.

Watts, T.J. (1989). *Justifiable Homicide or Manslaughter: The Battered Woman Defence in Murder Trials—A Bibliography*. Monticello: Vance Bibliographies.

West, D.J. (1985). *Sexual Victimization*. Aldershot: Gower.

Wolf, N. (1957). Sexualdelikte von Greisen. *Münchener Medizinische Zeitschrift*, 256-259.

Wolfgang, M.E. (1957). Victim-Precipitated Criminal Homicide. *Journal of Criminal Law and Criminology*, *48*(1), 1-11.

(1958). *Patterns in Criminal Homicide*. Philadelphia: University of Pennsylvania Press.

(1959). Suicide by Means of Victim-Precipitated Homicide. *Journal of Clinical and Experimental Psychopathology*, *20*(4), 335-349.

Chapter 12. Macro Explanations of Variations in Criminal Victimization

Balkin, S. (1979). Victimization Rates, Safety and Fear of Crime. *Social Problems*, *26*, 343-358.

Canada. (1983). *Victims of Crime, Canadian Urban Victimization Survey Bulletin* (No. 1). Ottawa: Ministry of the Solicitor General.

(1988). *Multiple Victimization, Canadian Urban Victimization Survey Bulletin* (No. 10). Ottawa: Ministry of the Solicitor General.

Carroll, L., and Jackson, P.I. (1983). Inequality, Opportunity and Crime Rates in Central Cities. *Criminology*, *21*, 178-194.

Clarke, R.V.G. et al. (1985). Elderly Victims of Crime and Exposure to Risk. *Howard Journal of Criminal Justice*, *24*, 81-89.

Cohen, L.E. (1981). Modelling Crime Trends: A Criminal Opportunity Perspective. *Journal of Research in Crime and Delinquency*, *18*, 136-164.

Cohen, L.E., and Cantor, D. (1980). The Determinants of Larceny: An Empirical and Theoretical Study. *Journal of Research in Crime and Delinquency*, *17*, 140-159.

(1981). Residential Burglary in the United States: Lifestyle and Demographic Factors Associated with the Probability of Victimization. *Journal of Research in Crime and Delinquency*, *18*, 113-127.

Cohen, L.E., and Felson, M. (1979). Social Change and Crime Rate Trends: A Routine Activities Approach. *American Sociological Review*, *44*, 588-608.

Cohen, L.E., Kluegel, J.R., and Land, K.C. (1981, October). Social Inequality and Predatory Criminal Victimization: An Exposition and Test of a Formal Theory. *American Sociological Review*, *46*, 505-524.

Collins, J.J., Cox, B.G., and Langan, P.A. (1987). Job Activities and Personal Crime Victimization: Implications For Theory. *Social Science Research*, *16*, 345-360.

Cook, P.J. (1985). *The Demand and Supply of Criminal Opportunities*. Working paper. Institute of Policy Science and Public Affairs, Duke University.

Corrado, R.R., Roesch, R., Glackman, W., Evans, J.L., and Leger, G.J. (1980). Lifestyles and Personal Victimization: A Test of the Model with Canadian Survey Data. *Journal of Crime and Justice*, *3*, 129-139.

Fattah, E.A. (1979). Some Recent Theoretical Developments in Victimology. *Victimology: An International Journal*, *4*(2), 198-213.

Felson, M. (1986). Linking Criminal Choices, Routine Activities, Informal Control, and Criminal Outcomes. In D.B. Cornish and R.V. Clarke (Eds.), *The Reasoning Criminal—Rational Choice Perspectives on Offending*. New York: Springer Verlag.

Felson, M., and Cohen, L.E. (1980). Human Ecology and Crime: A Routine Activity Approach. *Human Ecology*, *4*, 389-406.

Fienberg, S.E. (1980). Statistical Modelling in the Analysis of Repeat Victimization. In S.E. Fienberg and A.J. Reiss, Jr. (Eds.), *Indicators of Crime and Criminal Justice: Quantitative Studies*. Washington, D.C.: United States Department of Justice, Bureau of Justice Statistics. Government Printing Office.

Garofalo, J. (1986). Lifestyles and Victimization: An Update. In E.A. Fattah (Ed.), *From Crime Policy to Victim Policy*. London: Macmillan.

(1987). Reassessing the Lifestyle Model of Criminal Victimization. In M. Gottfredson and T. Hirschi (Eds.), *Positive Criminology*. Beverly Hills: Sage Publications.

Gottfredson, M. (1981). On the Etiology of Criminal Victimization. *Journal of Criminal Law and Criminology*, *72*(2), 714-726.

(1984). *Victims of Crime: The Dimensions of Risk*, Home Office Research Study (No. 81). London: Her Majesty's Stationery Office.

Greenwood, M., and Yule, G. (1920). An Inquiry into the Nature of Frequency Distributions Representative of Multiple Happenings with Particular Reference to the Occurrence of Multiple Attacks of Disease or Repeated Accidents. *Journal of the Royal Statistics Society*, *83*, 255-279.

Hindelang, M., Gottfredson, M., and Garofalo, J. (1978). *Victims of Personal Crime: An Empirical Foundation for a Theory of Personal Victimization*. Cambridge, MA: Ballinger Publishing Company.

Hough, M. (1987). Offenders' Choice of Target: Findings From Victim Surveys. *Journal of Quantitative Criminology*, *3*(4), 355-369.

Jensen, G.F., and Brownfield, D. (1986). Gender, Lifestyles, and Victimization: Beyond Routine Activity. *Violence and Victims*, *1*(2), 85-99.

Kennedy, L.W., and Forde, D.R. (1990). Routine Activities and Crime: An Analysis of Victimization in Canada. *Criminology*, *28*(1), 137-152.

Lasley, J.R., and Rosenbaum, J.L. (1988). Routine Activities and Multiple Personal Victimization. *Sociology and Social Research*, *73*(1), 47-50.

Lejeune, R. (1977). The Management of a Mugging. *Urban Life*, *6*(2), 123-148.

Lynch, J.P. (1986). Routine Activity and Victimization at Work. *Journal of Quantitative Criminology*, *3*(4), 283-300.

Maxfield, M.G. (1987). Lifestyle and Routine Activity Theories of Crime: Empirical Studies of Victimization, Delinquency, and Offender Decision-Making. *Journal of Quantitative Criminology*, *3*(4), 275-281.

Messner, S.E., and Blau, J.R. (1987). Routine Activities and Rates of Crime: A Macro-Level Analysis. *Social Forces*, *65*, 1035-1051.

Messner, S.E., and Tardiff, K. (1985). The Social Ecology of Urban Homicide. *Criminology*, *23*, 241-267.

Miethe, T.D., and Meier, R.F. (1990, August). Opportunity, Choice, and Criminal Victimization: A Test of a Theoretical Model. *Journal of Research in Crime and Delinquency*, *27*(3), 243-266.

Miethe, T.D., Stafford, M.C., and Long, J.S. (1987). Routine Activities/Lifestyle and Victimization. *American Sociological Review*, *52*, 184-194.

Reiss, A.J., Jr. (1980). Victim Proneness in Repeat Victimization by Type of Crime. In S.E. Fienberg and A. Reiss, Jr. (Eds.), *Indicators of Crime and Criminal Justice: Quantitative Studies*. Washington, D.C.: United States Department of Justice, Bureau of Justice Statistics. Government Printing Office.

Riely, D. (1986). Sex Differences in Teenage Crime: The Role of Lifestyle. *Home Office Research and Planning Unit Bulletin*, *20*, 34-38.

Sacco, V.F., and Johnson, H. (1990). *Patterns of Criminal Victimization in Canada*, General Social Survey Analysis Series (No. 2). Ottawa: Statistics Canada.

Sampson, R.J. (1983). Structural Density and Criminal Victimization. *Criminology*, *21*, 276-293.

(1985). Neighborhood and Crime: The Structural Determinants of Personal Victimization. *Journal of Research in Crime and Delinquency*, *22*, 7-40.

(1986). The Effects of Urbanization and Neighborhood Characteristics on Criminal Victimization. In R.M. Figlio, S. Hakim and G.F. Rengert (Eds.), *Metropolitan Crime Patterns*. Monsey, New York: Criminal Justice Press.

(1987). Personal Violence by Strangers: An Extension and Test of the Opportunity Model of Predatory Victimization. *Journal of Criminal Law and Criminology*, *78*, 327-356.

Sampson, R.J., and Castellano, T.C. (1982). Economic Inequality and Personal Victimization: An Areal Perspective. *British Journal of Criminology*, *22*(2), 363-385.

Sampson, R.J., and Lauritsen, J.L. (1990). Deviant Lifestyles, Proximity to Crime, and the Offender-Victim Link in Personal Violence. *Journal of Research in Crime and Delinquency*, *27*(2), 110-139.

Sampson, R.J., and Wooldredge, J. (1987). Linking the Micro- and Macro-level Dimensions of Lifestyle-Routine Activity and Opportunity Models of Predatory Victimization. *Journal of Quantitative Criminology*, *3*, 371-393.

Sherman, L.W. et al. (1989). Hot Spots of Predatory Crime: Routine Activities and the Criminology of Place. *Criminology*, *27*(1), 27-55.

Skogan, W.G. (1981). Assessing the Behavioral Context of Victimization. *Journal of Criminal Law and Criminology*, *72*, 727-742.

Smith, D.A., and Jarjoura, G.R. (1988). Social Structure and Criminal Victimization. *Journal of Research in Crime and Delinquency*, *25*(1), 27-52.

Smith, S.J. (1982). Victimization in the Inner City. *British Journal of Criminology*, *22*(2), 386-402.

(1986). *Crime, Space and Society*. Cambridge: Cambridge University Press.

Sparks, R. (1980). Criminal Opportunities and Crime Rates. In S.E. Fienberg and A.J. Reiss, Jr. (Eds.), *Indicators of Crime and Criminal Justice: Quantitative Studies*. Washington, D.C.: United States Department of Justice, Bureau of Justice Statistics. Government Printing Office.

(1981). Multiple Victimization: Evidence, Theory and Future Research. *Journal of Criminal Law and Criminology*, *72*(2), 762-778.

(1982). *Research on Victims of Crime: Accomplishments, Issues and New Directions*. Rockville, MD: United States Department of Health and Human Services.

Sparks, R.F., Genn, H.G., and Dodd, D.J. (1977). *Surveying Victims*. New York: John Wiley and Sons.

Steinmetz, C.H.D. (1979). *An (Empirically Tested) Analysis of Victimization Risks*. The Hague: Ministry of Justice.

(undated). *A First Step Towards Victimological Risk Analysis*. The Hague: Ministry of Justice.

Sutherland, E. (1937). *The Professional Thief.* Chicago: University of Chicago Press.

Teske, R.H.C., Jr., and Arnold, H.R. (1988, September). *A Comparative Analysis of Factors Related to the Probability of Criminal Victimization.* Paper presented at the 10th International Congress on Criminology, Hamburg, Federal Republic of Germany.

Van Dijk, J.J.M., and Steinmetz, C.H.D. (1979). *Victim Surveys 1974-1979* (Report No. XXXV). The Hague: Research and Documentation Center of the Dutch Ministry of Justice.

Von Hentig, H. (1948). *The Criminal and His Victim.* New Haven: Yale University Press.

Wikström, P-O.H. (1985). *Everyday Violence in Contemporary Sweden: Situational and Ecological Aspects.* Stockholm: The National Council for Crime Prevention.

Credits

1. Excerpt from *Black Boy* by Richard Wright. Copyright 1937, 1942, 1944, 1945 by Richard Wright. Reprinted by permission of HarperCollins Publishers.
2. Gagnon, J. Sexual Conduct and Crime. In D. Glaser (Ed.), *Handbook of Criminology* (pp. 233-277). (1974). Houghton Mifflin Company.
3. Cleaver, E. *Soul on Ice.* (1968). McGraw-Hill, Inc. Reprinted by permission of McGraw-Hill, Inc.
4. Fritz Redl and David Wineman. *Children Who Hate.* Copyright 1951 by The Free Press: copyright renewed 1979 by Fritz Redl and David Wineman. Reprinted by permission of the publisher.
5. From Rengert, G.F. and Wasilchik, J. *Suburban Burglary - A Time and Place for Everything.* (1985). Courtesy Charles C. Thomas, Publisher, Springfield, Illinois.
6. From Rossman, R. The Pederasts. In Leroy G. Schultz (Ed.), *The Sexual Victimology of Youth.* (1980). Courtesy of Charles C. Thomas, Publisher, Springfield, Illinois

Index

A

Abel Syndrome, 176
Abortion, as a victimless crime, 94
Accessibility, as a factor in victim/target selection, 240–43
Age: as a factor in victim response, 199–200;
and relationship to victimization rates, 51–52, 119;
as a risk factor in victimization, 337–38;
and victim-offender relationships, 165–66
Aggravated assault: intraracial patterns of, 181;
intrasex pattern of, 181;
and victim-offender relationships, 166–67.
See also Assault
Aggravated sexual assault. See Rape
Airline pilots: and occupational proneness, 277;
and reactions to hijackers, 198
Alcohol consumption: and day of the week, 66;
effects of, 284–85;
as a factor in crime, 66, 76, 118, 277–78;
as a factor in victimization, 118, 283–85, 319, 324, 331, 334;
and victim response, 205.
See also drugs
Alcoholics, and proneness to victimization, 274–5. See also Drunks
Alibi tricks, 148
Amusement/recreation workers, and occupational proneness, 278
Apartheid (South Africa), 10, 15
Armenian nationalists, 143
Assassination, political, 143
Assault: defined, 354 n.3;
inside and outside the home, 76–77;
resistance to, 198;
in rural vs. urban areas, 71–72;
and time of day, 70;
and victim-offender relationships, 167
Associated Press, 231
Athletes, and property victimization, 278
Attractiveness: as a factor in victim/target selection, 237–40, 326, 328;
as a personal characteristic of victim, 257–8
Auto-victimization, 8
Awareness, and victim/target selection, 236

B

"Bad tricks," and violence toward prostitutes, 281, 282
Bank robbery: and day of the week, 67;
and time of day, 69
Bank tellers: and occupational proneness, 277;
and reaction to robbery, 198
Bedroom, victimization in, 74, 75
Bentham, Jeremy, 351 n.4
Bill C-49 (Canada), and prostitution, 282, 357 n.6
Black Boy (Richard Wright, 1945), 144
Blackmail, selection of victim in, 229–30
Blacks: and feelings of injustice, 148–49;
and proneness to victimization, 272;
and risk of homicide, 59;
structural victimization of, 10;
and victimization rates, 121–22;

and victim response, 199.
See also Minority groups; Race
Blitz rape, 169. See also Rape
Born victim, 96
Brazil, domestic violence in, 99
British Crime Survey, 32–33
British Crime Survey Scotland, 29
Bureau of Social Science Research (U.S.), 31, 32
Burglary: and detached houses, 243;
and high-rise apartments, 243, 301;
injury in, 194;
location of houses as a factor in, 242;
and physical accessibility, 241–2;
in rural vs. urban areas, 72;
and sanctions on, 250–51;
and security measures on, 246–8;
sources of danger in, 249–50;
and surveillability on, 248–9;
and unoccupied houses, 245, 248–9
See also Robbery; Property offenses

C

Canadian Urban Victimization Bulletin, 315–17, 351 n.2
Canadian Urban Victimization Survey, 33, 351 n.2
"Cannon," defined, 354 n.1
Chernobyl, nuclear accident at, 9
Children: abuse of, 98, 150;
and alcohol, 104;
illegitimate, 268;
as instigators of nonviolent sexual acts, 304–309;
and pornography, 104;
sexual feelings of, 308–309;
and types most at risk for abuse, 267;
and victim-precipitation, 296;
and victim proneness, 265–68;
See also Infanticide; Sexual abuse of children
Cleaver, Eldridge, 145
Collective victimization, 14–15
Communication: in conflict situations, 189;
in rape, 189–91
Community structure and victimization, 335–37
Confidence games, 230
Confidence rape, 169
Consensual sex, 297
Continuing victimization, 17
Corporate victimization, 13–14
Crack, 275
Crime: and nonspecific victims, 92–93;
and potential victims, 93;
properties of, 326;
situational approach to, 187–89;
and specific victims, 92;
victimless, 93
Crime clock, 352 n.1
Crime statistics, problems of, 27–28
Crimes of passion: justiciary aspects of, 142–3;
victims of, 223–4
Crimes of relationships, 158
The Criminal and His Victim (Von Hentig, 1948), 347
Criminal victimization: 10–11, 23;
and day of the week, 65–67;
deaths, injuries, and losses from, 350–51 n.3;
defined, 10;
as different from noncriminal victimization, 351 n.4;
distribution of, 52–53;
etiological explanations of, 256–57;
geographical and spatial patterns in, 71–77;
indicators for, 49–50;
injuriousness of, 53;
rarity of, 52;
reporting of, 43–45, 51, 53–54;
risks of, 54–61;

rules governing frequency and visibility of, 50–52;
scope of, 19–21;
and seasonality, 61–65;
sources of data on, 28–43;
traumatic effects of, 215;
trends, 60–61;
trivial nature of, 53.
See also Victimization
Criminality, hidden, 27
Cultural victimization. See Structural victimization

D

Danger, as a factor in victim/target selection, 249
Dangerous behaviors, and victimization risk, 344
Dark figure, defined, 27
Date rape: and sexist attitudes, 191;
and victim-offender relationship, 169
See also Rape
Day of the week, as a factor in victimization, 65–67
Dead bolt locks, 247
Defensive/avoidance behaviors, 345–46
Delinquent activities, and victimization, 123–26, 329–31, 345
Demographic variables and victimization, 337–8
Department stores, as accessible targets, 106, 240–41
Desensitization techniques: 140–47;
and blaming the victim, 142–45;
and denial of injury to victim, 141–42;
and denial, reification, deindividuation, depersonalization, 140–41;
and devaluation of the victim, 145–46
Deviance, "derivative," 274
Deviant activities, and victimization, 345
Deviant groups: and degree of exposure, 274;
lack of protection for, 274.
and proneness to victimization, 273–7, 346;
See also Drug addicts; Homosexuals
"Diathesis," defined, 356 n.1 (Ch. 10)
A Dictionary of Criminology, 4
Differential risks of criminal victimization: 58–61;
and the Dutch model, 327–9;
and homicide, 58–59;
and the life-style model, 321–25;
macro explanations of 319–46;
and the opportunity model, 326;
and the routine activity approach, 325–26;
and the typological approach, 321
Diplomats, and occupational proneness, 277
Direct victimization, 17
Distance-decay factor, 127
Doctors, as victims of fraud, 231
Doer-sufferer, 94, 176
Domestic violence: and accessibility, 240;
in Brazil, 99;
as a criminal offense, 98–99;
and dominant wives, 173;
and homicide, 161–63;
and multiple victimization, 16, 313, 317;
reasons for, 158–60;
reporting of, 39;
theories of, 172–5.
See also Spousal violence
Drinking. See Alcohol consumption
Drug addicts: and police, 101;
and proneness to victimization, 274–75;
and victimless crime, 94;
and vulnerability to homicide, 275;

as "worthless" victims, 101
Drugs, as a victimogenic factor: 324;
and victim response, 205.
See also Alcohol consumption
Drunks: and susceptibility to mugging, 240.
as "worthless" victims, 101. See also Alchoholics
Dutch model of differential risks of victimization: 327–9;
and attractiveness factor, 328;
and exposure factor, 328–9;
and proximity factor, 327–8

E

Elderly: and homicide, 166;
indirect victimization, 17;
structural victimization of, 10;
and victim response, 199–200;
and vulnerability to victimization, 51–52, 264, 338
Ellenberger, Henri, 176
"Encapsulation:" 189; defined, 355 n.1 (Ch. 8)
Euthanasia (mercy killing): 134; and willing victims, 297
"Everyday violence," defined, 354 n.4
Exchangeable victim, 223–25
Exhibitionism, and strangers, 170
Exposure, as a factor in victimization, 326, 328–9, 343

F

Familiarity, and victim/target selection, 237
Family violence. See Domestic violence
FBI (Federal Bureau of Investigation), 352 n.1
Fear of crime, and victim vulnerability, 264, 345
Felony rape, 169. See also Rape
Foster, Tony, 231–2
Fraud, cooperation of victim in, 298
Freedman, Lawrence (psychiatrist), 213
Fun, pursuit of, and victimization risk, 344

G

Gender: as a factor in victim response, 199–200, 205;
and victimization risk, 330
Gender difference: and robbery killings, 59, 355 n.6;
and sexual assault, 120
Gender inequality: and violence toward women, 269;
and vulnerability of women, 271
General Social Survey (Canada), 34
Genocide: as collective victimization, 14;
legitimation of, 143–44;
as mass victimization, 272
Good Samaritan, 299, 357 n.1
Gossip, as noncriminal victimization, 11
Green River Killer, and prostitutes, 281
Guardianship, as a factor in victimization, 326

H

Harvard Medical School, 351 n.3
Havers, Michael, Sir (Attorney-General of Britain), 282
Hidden-delinquency studies, 28–29
Hijackee Syndrome, 213
Hijacking, 198, 212, 213
Hinrichs, Reimer, 107
Hispanics (U.S.): proneness to victimization, 272;
and victimization rates, 121
Hitchhike rape: 225, 302–303;
and accessibility, 240;
fatalism of victim in, 303;
and stereotype of female hitchhiker, 134, 303;

and victim-offender relationship, 169. See also rape
Hitchhiking: risks involved in, 344;
and victim-facilitation, 301–303
Homicide: and age of victim, 165–66;
and alcohol consumption, 283–85;
and day of the week, 65–67;
differential risks of, 58–59;
differential risks of (table), 59;
inside and outside the home, 74–75;
as interchange between victim and offender, 289;
intraracial pattern of, 180–81;
intrasex pattern of, 180, 181;
personal relationships in, 160–63;
and size of social group, 163–65;
and time of day, 68;
victim-precipitated, 103, 295–96, 298
Homosexuality: and age of consent, 93, 104, 308;
and rape, 180;
and relations between men and boys, 308–9
Homosexuals: as "appropriate" victims, 151;
and "fag-bashing," 275–76;
and police, 101, 151;
and proneness to victimization, 275–77;
and susceptibility to mugging, 240;
as "worthless" victims, 101
Hoover, J. Edgar, and "crime clock," 352 n.1
Hostage-taking, 211–12
Human rights, violations of, 143
Huxley, Aldous, 96

I

Ideal victim, 97–8
Incest: and accessibility, 240;
as a crime of power, 268–69;
defined, 157;
father-daughter, 171;
as a victimless crime, 93;
and victim-offender relationship, 170
Income level: as a risk factor in victimization, 337;
and victimization rates, 122–23
Indirect victimization, 17–18
Industrial pollution, 9
Industrial/technological victimization, 9
Infanticide: defined, 157;
and proneness of children, 265–66
Injury: defined, 355 nn.2, 3;
frequency of, 193–96;
instrumental, 209;
noninstrumental, 209
Instantaneous victimization, 17
Instigational potential, 159
Institute for Social Research of the Survey Research Center (U.S.), 32
Institutional victimization, 15–16
Interracial crime, and victim blame, 144
Intracity victimization rates, 71–2
Intraracial crime: 179–82; and aggravated assault, 181;
and homicide, 180–81;
and rape, 181–82;
and robbery, 182

J

Jack the Ripper, and prostitutes, 281
Journal of Communication, 258
"Just world" hypothesis, 147

K

Kidnapping, 211–12
Killers, stereotype of, 152–53
Kitchen, victimization in, 74

L

Layout, in victim/target selection, 242–43
Life-style: defined, 319;

as an explanatory concept, 321–2;
and relationship to victimization risk, 57
Life-style model: 322–5;
and association, 322–3;
and exposure, 322;
limitations of, 329–40
Living room, victimization in, 74
Location, in victim/target selection, 242, 344
Looting, 188
Lucrativeness/profitability, and victim/target selection, 238–39
Lynching, as legitimized victimization, 143

M

Mai Lai massacre (Vietnam), 188
Manageability, and victim/target selection, 243–5
Marital status: and injury risk, 194;
and victimization rates, 120–21
"Mark," 135
Matricide. See Patricide
The Measurement of Delinquency (Wolfgang and Singer), 14
Medical Times, 231
Men: and homicide risk, 59;
and injury risk, 193–94;
and victim-precipitated homicide, 295–96;
as victims of robbery killings, 355 n.6;
and vulnerability to victimization;
Mentally handicapped, 104
Mercy killing. See Euthanasia
Ministry of the Solicitor General (Canada), 33, 37
Minority groups: and police, 44;
proneness to victimization, 272–3, 346.
See also Blacks; Hispanics; Native Canadians
Miron, Murray (psycholinguist), 213
Montreal Star, 231
Motivated offenders and probability of victimization, 342–3
Motor vehicle theft, in rural vs. urban areas, 71
Mugging: and manageability of victim, 244;
and selection of victim, 228–29;
and victim characteristics, 239–40
Multiple (series) victimization: 16, 50, 260, 313–19;
in Canada, 315–17;
and the contagion model, 318;
empirical explanations of, 318–19;
and the heterogeneity model, 317–18;
statistical explanations of, 317–18;
in the U.S., 314–15
Murder. See Homicide
Mutual victimization, 13

N

National Crime Survey (U.S.): 31, 43;
sampling errors in, 42
National Opinion Research Center (NORC), 32, 33, 44, 51
Native Canadians: and family homicide, 162–63;
proneness to victimization, 273;
suicide rates for, 273;
and victimization surveys, 273
Natural victimization, 8
Neighbourhood Watch, 30
Nigeria, and armed robbery, 299
Noncriminal victimization, 11–12
Nonexchangeable victim, 223–25
Norway, Nazi occupation of, 188
Nurses, and occupational proneness, 280

O

Obscene phone calls, 17
Occupational proneness, 277–83, 344–45

Olson, Clifford, 188
Operation Identification: 30; effectiveness of, 247
Opportunity: 86, 341; and negligent victims, 105–6;
and the outdoors, 62
Opportunity model: 326; and attractiveness, 326;
and exposure, 326;
and guardianship, 326;
limitations of, 329–40;
and properties of crime, 326;
and proximity, 326
Other People's Money (Cressey, 1953), 135

P

Paternalism, in law: 104
Patriarchal societies, and victimization of women, 173, 272
Patricide (matricide): 157; and pre-victimization desensitization, 144
Pedophilia: role of parents in, 308;
and victim-temptation, 304–309.
See also Sexual abuse of children
Peer support, and aggressive behavior, 187
Pickpockets, and selection of victims, 239
Pimps, and violence toward prostitutes, 281, 282
Point Counter Point (Huxley) 96
Police: attitudes toward, 44;
and occupational proneness, 277, 278;
and violence toward prostitutes, 281
The Politics of Victimology (Elias, 1986), 19
Pollution, industrial, 9
Potential/latent victim, 176
POWER (Prostitutes and Other Women for Equal Rights), 281
Precipitation: defined, 290, 291–3;
as an explanatory concept, 290;
and "legitimate violence," 5;
vs. provocation, 291–93;
See also Victim-precipitation
Premeditation, 136
President's Commission on Law Enforcement and Administration of Justice (U.S.), 31
Pre-victimization process: 136–47;
and desensitization, 139–47 (table, 140);
and neutralization, 137;
and premeditation, 136;
and redefinition/auto-legitimation, 138–39;
table, 137.
See also Desensitization techniques
Primary victimization, 12
Prison guards, and occupational proneness, 277
The Professional Thief (Sutherland, 1937), 135, 146, 151, 230
Proneness: 259–85; and children, 265–68
deviance-related, 273–77;
and minority groups, 272–73;
and multiple victimization, 317–18;
occupational, 277–83;
and personality traits, 357 n.4;
and place of residence (spatial proneness), 264–65;
and relationship to accident proneness, 261, 356 n.2 (Ch. 10);
spatial, 264–65;
structural/cultural, 265–73, 346.
vs. vulnerability, 260–62;
and women, 268–72.
See also Vulnerability
Prone to Violence (Pizzey and Shapiro, 1982), 177
Property offenses: and denial of victim injury, 141;
and victim-facilitation, 299–301.

See also burglary; robbery
Prostitutes: as accessible targets, 240;
and occupational proneness, 280–83;
and police, 101;
violence against, 282;
as "worthless" victims, 101
Prostitution, as a victimless crime, 94
Provocation: in Canadian law, 290–1;
defined, 290–93;
as an exculpatory concept, 290;
vs. precipitation, 290, 291–3
Proximity: as a factor in victim/target selection, 235–7;
as an inhibiting factor in victimization, 258–9;
and risk of victimization, 326, 327
Public entertainment, places of: and alcohol consumption, 66, 76, 277, 285, 334;
as a scene of crime, 70, 76, 278, 280, 327, 334, 344
Public space, and risk of victimization, 128
Public transit: as a scene of crime, 70, 278, 344

R

Race: as a factor in determining injury, 194;
as a factor in victim response, 199–200, 205;
and victimization rates, 59, 120, 337;
and victim-precipitated homicide, 295–96
Random victimization, 16–17
Rape: as "aggravated sexual assault," 269;
and attitudes to victim, 140, 141, 146;
"avoidance" of, 215;
biological theories of, 269–70;
collective, 146, 204;
as a crime of power, 268–69;
and day of the week, 65–67;
and hitchhikers, 240;
homosexual, 180;
injury in, 195–96;
inside and outside the home, 75–76;
interpretation of behavior in, 190;
intersex patterns of, 180;
intraracial patterns of, 181–82;
and manageability of victim, 244–45;
and minors, 308;
pleas for sympathy in, 207;
problems of communication in, 189–91;
resistance to, 197, 198, 203, 205, 207-208, 208–210;
and selection of victim, 229;
social theories of, 269–70;
and time of day, 68–69;
and victim-offender relationships, 168–70.
See also Blitz rape; Confidence rape; Date rape; Felony rape; Hitchhike rape
Rapists: and attitudes to victim, 133–34;
stereotype of, 152;
types of, 207–8;
as victims of child abuse, 150
"Repulsiveness," as a personal characteristic of victim, 257–8
Residence, place of, and victimization, 265
Restaurant workers, and occupational proneness, 278
Retaliation, 189
Risk: absolute, 57;
as a factor in victim/target selection, 245–51;
relative, 57
victimization, 54–61;
Risk factors, and probability of victimization, 341–2
Robbery: and day of the week, 66–7;
injury and death in, 194–5;
intraracial patterns of, 182;

intrasex patterns of, 182;
killings, 141, 355 n.6;
in rural vs. urban areas, 71–2;
and manageability of victim, 244;
resistance to, 204, 210–11, 245;
and time of day, 69–70;
and victim characteristics, 239;
and victim-facilitation, 299–301.
See also Bank robbery; Burglary; Property offenses
Routine activity approach: 325–6;
and facilitating factors, 325;
limitations of, 329–40;
and opportunity factors, 325–6;
and proximity/exposure factors, 325;
Routine activity, defined, 325
Rural areas, and victimization rates, 71–72

S

Sadomasochistic relationship, 177–8
Sanctions, as a factor in victim/target selection, 250–51
Scapegoating behavior, 296
Secondary (second) victimization, 12–13
Security measures, and victim/target selection, 246–48
Seasonality, as a factor in victimization, 61–65, 352 n.2
"Series," defined, 358 n.1. See also multiple victimization
Sex. See Gender
Sexist attitudes, and rape, 191
Sexual abuse of children: 39, 150, 170–71, 356–7 n.3 (Ch. 10);
and institutional victimization, 16;
traumatic effects of, 171;
and victim-offender relationship, 170–71.
See also Children
Sexual assault: and "bad" girls, 151;
and reporting, 44–5.
See also Rape
Shoplifting, 105–6
Shops/service institutions, as scenes of crime, 278
60 Minutes (television program), 99
The Skyjacker: His Flights of Fantasy (Hubbard), 213
"Slave," defined, 354 n.1
Smoking, and noncriminal victimization, 11
Snow's Annotated Criminal Code, 291
Social Deviance (Wilkins, 1964), 222
Spousal violence, 167–68
Statistics Canada, 33, 34
The Sting (movie), 101
Stock fraud, 231
Stockholm Syndrome, 212
Structural victimization, 9–10
Suicide: and auto-victimization, 8;
extended, 134–35;
and native Canadians, 273;
as a victimless crime, 94
as victim-precipitated homicide, 298;
Surprise, and victim response, 203–4
Surveillability, and victim/target selection, 248–49
Surveying Crime (Panel for the Evaluation of Crime Surveys), 261–62
Sutcliffe, Peter. See Yorkshire Ripper

T

Taxi drivers: as accessible targets, 240;
and occupational proneness, 277, 278
Teachers, and occupational proneness, 280
Teenagers, and proneness to victimization, 268
Telescoping, and reporting of victimization, 40
Temperature, as a factor in victimization, 61–62, 352–3 n.2
Terrorism: as random victimization, 17;
and victim blame, 143

Tertiary victimization, 13
Thieves, and attitude to victim, 134
Time magazine, 213
Time of day, as a factor in victimization, 67–71, 324–25, 344
Traits/attributes approach, 188

U

Unemployment: as a factor in victimization, 319;
and victimization rates, 122
Urban areas, victimization rates in, 71–72

V

Vancouver Province , 281
Vancouver Sun, 281–2, 350 n.3
Vendetta, and victim blame, 143
Victim: animal as, 92;
behavioral types of, 103–106;
criminological definition of, 90–92;
criminological types of, 106–7;
cultural types of, 96–102;
data on, 86–88;
"juridical" person as, 92;
legal definition of, 89–90;
legally created, 104;
literary definition of, 89;
"natural" person as, 92;
nonspecific, 92–93;
potential, 93;
potential/latent, 176;
reasons for studying, 83–86;
sociodemographic characteristics of, 116–28;
structural types of, 102–103;
types of, 95–107;
types of (tables), 95, 102;
and victimizer's attitude to, 133–36;
willing, 297
Victim behavior: 289–310;
as an explanation of victimization, 289–90;
as a situational variable, 290–96
Victim careers, 107
Victim characteristics: 257–85; and attraction/repulsion, 257–58;
and proneness/vulnerability, 259–60;
and proximity/distance, 258–59.
See also Proneness; Vulnerability
Victim-facilitation (/participation/cooperation): 297–303;
and failure to take precautions, 298–301;
and fraud, 298;
and Good Samaritans, 299;
and hitchhiking, 301–303;
and mercy killing, 297–98;
and property offenses, 299–301;
and victim blame, 298;
and willing victims, 297
Victimization: concept of, 4–5;
and criminal law, 5;
defined, 4–5;
as a situated transaction, 188–89;
sources of, 5–12, table, 7;
types of, 8–18;
See also Criminal victimization
Victimization rates, regional variations in: 72–73
Victimization statistics: in Canada, 112–14, 116;
in the U.K., 115–16
in the U.S., 114–15, 116;
Victimization surveys: advantages of, 30–31, 44;
in Canada, 34;
control techniques in, 41;
costs of, 36–38;
history of, 31–33;
international, 33, 34–35;
interviewer effects in, 42;
and mail questionnaires, 36–37;
and native Canadians, 273;
problems and limitations of, 35–38, 42–43, 53, 150;